Miss Weeton's Journal of a Governess

Miss Weeton's
Journal of a Governess

a reprint of
Miss Weeton: Journal of a Governess

Volume 2   1811–1825

Revised Epilogue by Edward Hall

AUGUSTUS M. KELLEY, PUBLISHERS
NEW YORK 1969

This book was first published under the title of
MISS WEETON by the Oxford University Press in 1939
Revised epilogue © Edward Hall 1969

Published in the United States of America by
Augustus M. Kelley, Publishers, New York
Library of Congress No 68-27857
Printed in Great Britain by
Latimer Trend, Whitstable, Kent

FOREWORD

*T*HE *discovery of still another volume of Miss Weeton's Letters to Correspondents has complicated rather than simplified the editing of this, the second, and final, volume; instead of four years, as in the first volume, a period of fourteen years is presented, and as the two volumes of copied letters under consideration are not consecutive, it has been necessary to intrude rather more upon her than was the original intention; in order to do full justice to both continuity and the major phases of her life, in some cases a vital sentence only, in others the gist, of letters of minor importance, has been given. As a matter of fact, just prior to the discovery of volume 5 of the MSS., the Oxford University Press had accepted for publication the results of an effort to bridge the gap, 1811–22, the letters of volume 7 (1822–5) being given almost verbatim; but if some modification has left rather less of Miss Weeton in her later period, we have gained by the bridging of the gap indicated, in the only satisfactory manner, i.e. in the presentation of the period 1812–18 in a series of extracts from her own letters and Journal. To K. K. Marshall, Esq., now living retired in the Isle of Man, I am indebted for permission to use this fresh material. It appears that when Eustace A. Marshall, Esq., of Southport, made me the gift of volumes 2, 7, and the odd volume of the Occasional Reflexions for the year 1818, he was unaware that volume 5, containing matter of interest to Manxmen, was in his brother's possession. Certain extracts from this volume have already appeared in the* MANX TIMES, *I understand.*

I take this opportunity to acknowledge again my indebtedness to Mr. Eustace A. Marshall, for making possible this work by putting at my entire disposal the volume of Occasional Reflexions for 1818, and volume 7 of the Letters to Correspondents; and I repeat my thanks to the other two gentlemen mentioned in the foreword to volume 1.

For data prefacing the High Royd section, I have drawn largely upon Mrs. Mary A. Jagger's HISTORY OF HONLEY, *1914—a tangible instance of intense local pride which cannot be too widely imitated. For permission to use a happily much-handled copy of this work, from the shelves of the Public Library, Huddersfield, I am indebted to Mr. Horace Goulden, F.L.A., the Head Librarian. Mrs. Rachel M. Watson, of Meltham, a grand-daughter of Miss Weeton's pupil, Joseph, has kindly provided the portrait of the latter's father in his old age. A view of High Royd unfortunately proved unsuitable, owing to the all-absorbing presence in the foreground of a large sycamore (since removed), planted by Joseph to celebrate the victory of Waterloo.*

CONTENTS

ILLUSTRATIONS

SYNOPSIS OF CONTENTS OF VOLUME I

Chief events in the lives of MISS WEETON *and principal characters in her Letters and Journal*

1782. *Death of Captain Weeton in the course of an engagement with an American man-o'-war, specially sent out to end his depredations. Buried at Jamaica.*

1782-4. *Mrs. Weeton makes fruitless attempts to secure payment of her husband's 'prize-money', amounting to £12,000 or more. Her aged mother (late of Upholland) dying in the interim, she ceases taking in lodgers in Lancaster, and arrives in Upholland, near Wigan, in the month of May 1784, with her two surviving children, Ellen and Tom, hoping to find living cheaper in this locality.*

1788. *Her income proving insufficient for the support of the little family, she opens a village school, productive of never more than a weekly 10 or 12 shillings. The life of the daughter of the school-mistress from this time resolves itself into one of complete slavery and drudgery, Miss Weeton, from the age of 12, assisting her mother in teaching, and performing much of the household work in addition.*

1795. *Apprenticeship of Tom Weeton to a Preston attorney—the first severe blow to Miss Weeton's dream-life, resulting in much morbid introspection and frequent illness. Mrs. Weeton's ill health intensifies the hardships of her daughter's life; and her somewhat faulty notions upon education, allied to a too intense solicitude for her daughter's welfare, combine to warp the latter's character.*

1797. *Miss Weeton barely recovers from a long illness in time to assume full charge of the school, in place of her dying mother, whose death occurs on 5 December 1797. The responsibility for Tom's future devolves entirely upon his sister henceforth, and at incredible personal sacrifice and the contribution of her own income from her mother's estate, she renders possible the completion of her brother's period of clerkship.*

1797–1802. *Miss Weeton suffers shockingly in the comparative solitariness of her school, often being without a penny for food as a result of paying off her mother's debts, including one to Aunt Barton, whose avarice and absence of humanitarian attributes is aptly illustrated at this time.*

1802. *Termination of Tom's articles. After three months' sojourn in London, he is obliged to make an ignominious, and somewhat furtive, return to Upholland, where he proceeds to batten upon his sister.*

1803. *Marriage of Tom Weeton to a Miss Jane Scott, daughter of a factory proprietor in Wigan. Manifestly unfair proposals for the establishment of a joint household at Upholland, involving the entire sacrifice of Miss Weeton's income and liberty, provisionally agreed upon; but tardy recognition of the imprudent marriage on the part of the bride's parents proves the final blow to Miss Weeton's plans for a joint future devoted to her idol. Tom Weeton, disagreeably surprised upon learning of his mother's injunctions as to a fair and equal disposition of her property and money, has to be content with rather more than his own fair share (making no allowances for his sister's sacrifices on his behalf in the past), and proceeds to set up in business as Attorney in Leigh, Lancs., where, in process of time, he achieves the Clerkship to the Magistrates, and some local consequence (culminating in utter ruin, in or about the year 1833, following upon sharp practice). His wife consistently evidences a by no means kindly disposition towards the despised sister, whose position of village school-mistress galls her socially aspiring susceptibilities.*

1803–8. *Miss Weeton continues her school, and for a time supplements her meagre income (now reduced to 7 shillings per week) by the taking in of lodgers. Finally, she decides to abandon Upholland, in direct opposition to the desires of her dictatorial Aunt Barton. Meanwhile, her*

*brother grudgingly approves of her plan to secure a post
as governess or school-teacher elsewhere.   In the year
1804 she commences her life-work—7 volumes of closely
written* LETTERS TO CORRESPONDENTS, *interspersed
with* JOURNAL *entries, and including a* RETROSPECT *of
her early life.   Volume 2 (volume 1 of these copies of her
letters is missing) provides illuminating details of life in a
backward Lancashire village.*

1808 (Aug.). *Miss Weeton, thoroughly disillusioned and disheartened, finally quits Upholland, and, after a holiday
(of sorts) with her brother at Leigh, becomes the guest-
companion of a Liverpool friend, a Miss Chorley, residing
in Dale Street. Following upon most unpleasant experiences
and repeated snubs from this vinegarish spinster, she takes
lodgings at an isolated house upon the north bank of the
Mersey (where now stretch dock upon dock). Here, for a
time, she is really happy and contented, and invests her
savings in cottage property, thereby increasing considerably
her income.   The behaviour of the married couple with
whom she lodges eventually drives her into fresh lodgings,
this time in Liverpool itself, with the Winkley family; with
the eldest daughter, Miss Bessy Winkley, Miss Weeton
had struck up an intimacy which ripens into that of the
mutual confidantes of later letters from Dove's Nest. A
few months later, her attention being drawn by Mrs.
Winkley to an advertisement in a local paper for a Governess, Miss Weeton solicits the post, and is engaged to superintend the education of the daughter (by a first marriage), and
the ex-dairymaid wife of Edward Pedder, Esq., of Dove's
Nest, near Ambleside, wealthy son of a prominent Preston
banker.   The generous (for those times) salary of 30
guineas per annum is agreed upon, and Miss Weeton takes
up her duties in December of the year 1809. Her departure
by coach, ill-advisedly involving some secrecy, gives rise to
the rumour that she has 'gone off with a gentleman in a*

chaise'—an imputation upon her honour which subsequently causes her great distress, by no means alleviated by the culpable attitude of brother Tom in the matter.

1809 (Dec.)–1811 (Feb.). *Miss Weeton's letters to her brother during this period of governess-ship provide a wealth of intimate detail relative to the extraordinary happenings in the Pedder household, and the characters of its principals. With the girl-wife she quickly establishes a bond of genuine friendship and mutual sympathy; but Mr. Pedder, so agreeable upon first acquaintance, rapidly proves to be possessed of an ungovernable temper, and absurd notions of class-superiority, coupled, paradoxically enough, with a penchant for low company. To his drunken habits he adds wife-beating and governess-baiting. The accidental death, by burning, of his epileptic daughter provides the occasion for one of the most graphic and macabre of Miss Weeton's long letters. Miss Weeton's services after this event are retained on behalf of the illiterate young wife, who, however, commences to look upon Miss Weeton more in the nature of a pleasant companion than as a teacher, so that the governess's position becomes increasingly untenable. However, despite frequent 'scenes', her presence is tolerated by the master of the household until the early part of the year 1811, by which time she has completed the third volume of copies of her letters. At this point, volume 1 of the published correspondence terminated with an epilogue in the absence of a consecutive run of further volumes, the next volume, number 7, of the letters, dating from 1822. The discovery of volume 5 has comfortably bridged the gap.*

LAKE DISTRICT
AND
LIVERPOOL
(*including a trip to the* ISLE OF MAN)

FEBRUARY 1811–JULY 1812

B

LAKE DISTRICT
AND
LIVERPOOL
(including a trip to the ISLE OF MAN*)*

FEBRUARY 1811–JULY 1812

PERHAPS at this point it might be as well to detail the circumstances attaching to the possession, by the Marshall brothers, of three out of seven of Miss Weeton's volumes of Letters to Correspondents (as well as that containing the Occasional Reflections for 1818, and the abortive History of her life, penned in 1824). The Rev. William Marshall (1792–1861) was an intimate and highly respected friend of Miss Weeton (it is convenient to regard her throughout as Miss Weeton, though actually she married in 1814, and became Mrs. Stock) from the period of his institution as minister to the Hope Independent Chapel, Wigan, in the year 1822, to the end of her life. Not a word she penned about him was likely to jeopardize the future safety of any volume that might subsequently come into his possession. Far otherwise might have been the case should any of her former friends or relatives (if still living at the time her effects were dispersed) have dipped into them out of curiosity. As far back as the year 1810 she had written:

I have spoken too freely of most of them, or their near connexions, and to whom I can bequeath them at death, I know not.

However, an intervening thirty years can witness the burial of petty resentments with their owners, as well as the advent of a generation too little interested in the affairs of their elders to use even discretion in the disposal of a block of closely written volumes of copied letters. A perusal of the later letters only too pathetically indicates that the writer had outlived any generation

3

that might have cherished such mementos of its importance either in, or out of, the regard of Miss Weeton. Obviously there could be but few sufficiently concerned to bring about the destruction of the volumes from personal motives.

How came it, then, that the Rev. W. Marshall only secured these oddments, instead of at least a consecutive run? Might not a slight protest, or show of interest on his part, have secured the whole run, for possible future editing and publication? Maybe. But then, perhaps he considered himself lucky enough to secure what he did; for it is more than likely that all her books, being ignorantly bulked together into the usual indiscriminate 'lots' of the sale-room, became finally separated, never again to be wholly re-united. Let us be thankful that his oddments suffered a better fate than the companions to that single volume rescued from the bookseller-vandal in her home town, Wigan.

❊   ❊   ❊

The concluding letter in this particular volume was one addressed to Miss Bessy Winkley, and extracts from this terminated the selection in the volume recently published. The date of this letter is February 4th, 1811, and in it she comments upon 'the unhappy temper of the master of this house', and asserts her determination no longer to subject herself to his vagaries; and there is also 'his tyrannical treatment of me . . . if I have any value for my life, I must endure it no longer, and am quitting Mr. P.'s house about the middle of next month'. And at the end of this letter she refers the reader to the next volume of the series (No. 4) for a copy of a longer letter written just previously, which had proved too long for inclusion. Alas, this, and subsequent letters and journal entries for the next twelve months or so, are missing; but fortunately we are not entirely without information as to her movements and accidents of fortune during this period.

Miss Weeton's financial position about this time must have improved[1] (a considerable amount of back rent had accrued to

[1] Her last quarter's salary from Mr. Pedder took over a year to reach her; incidentally, she secured, at the same time, belated re-imbursement of mourning expenses incurred hopefully enough on the occasion of Miss Pedder's death.

her from her cottage property in Liverpool), and this must have influenced her in her decision to quit the Pedder household, and to proceed no farther with the project to commence schoolmistress in Ambleside. In a later letter to her brother she says:

Whilst I was at Mr. Pedder's, you rendered me essential service in procuring the greater part of the money from my agent in Liverpool, who would have defrauded me, for which I was very thankful. Why have you repeated that circumstance so ill-naturedly, as if you were angry with yourself for having done anything for me? You gave me your trouble, I suppose, but I paid all the expence.

However, at this time she was unaware that she was to be loser by £20 by his culpable slackness, and that this ingrate grudged his services. Dismissing another scheme over which she had pondered—that of settling down awhile in the Lake District to explore the possibilities of a small dairy-farm—she apparently became an inmate of the Lakes artist Green's home, spending seven happy months in and around Ambleside (including a stay at Harrowslack with a Mr. Roberts), until October. Writing later to Mrs. Green, she says:

Never during the whole course of my life did I spend so many happy months in succession as those I passed amongst you from the time I left Mr. Pedder, to the time I quitted your lovely country altogether; it was certainly a most romantic kind of life that I led there; but, as I knew that in all human probability, it could only last for the Summer, I determined to pursue the bent of my inclination whilst I was at liberty to do so.—Liberty! Oh, how sweet thou art! I never knew thee till I found thee on the banks of Winandermere; and in leaving that noble lake, I quitted thee likewise. I have lived almost altogether for others; whilst amongst you for the last 7 months, I ventured to live for myself alone, and do not now look back upon that period with regret, except that it is for ever fled!

5

Those familiar with Yorkshire moorland scenes as portrayed in Emily Brontë's *Wuthering Heights* will not find it difficult to account for the melancholy tone of these reminiscences in a 'foreigner' when it is taken into consideration that Miss Weeton wrote this letter a little over a year later—in November of 1812, to be precise—in the cold seclusion of her deserted schoolroom at Highroyd House, on top of a bleak hill overlooking the Pennines, in as lonely a situation as could well be imagined, four miles from Huddersfield; having exhausted her slender store of genuine correspondents, Highroyd House and its unfriendly atmosphere drove her to this work of supererogation— a stilted composition to a woman very unlikely, in the remembrance, to warm either her imagination or her gratitude. However, the letter is useful in that it supplies us with an itinerary for this period. Having kept a journal of her Lakes sojourn, references are scarce in later volumes; so the tardy recognition of her duty to the mother of her god-child was not entirely labour wasted from our point of view.

On leaving Harrowslack, I spent a fortnight at Mr. Edmondson's of Lancaster. I went next to Liverpool for another fortnight, to settle some pecuniary affairs that had long been in a very unpleasant situation, owing to the misconduct of the agent intrusted with them; however, with the assistance of my brother, I got them perfectly regulated, not losing more than £10 [in a later letter, she gives £20 as the figure], where I had been in danger of losing £120. I then spent six weeks with my brother, and as many more with my uncle and aunt Barton at Upholland. I then left them to go to reside with Miss Winkley of Liverpool, with whom I boarded for some months.

Apparently the visit to the Edmondsons passed with so little of incident as to justify the very brief notice accorded it. The Rev. T. Saul was to remain the unapproachable ideal, alas! Never again is he mentioned, not even allusively; and, significantly, there is one correspondent the less in Mrs. Edmondson. It was only at Upholland that she really began to pick up

the broken threads of her old connexions and associations in
that tattling, meddlesome district. What her letters had not
been able to effect, her presence should; and she as ardently
wished to trace a baseless and scandalous rumour to its source,
as to have the full opportunity to feast her longing eyes once
more upon her idolized brother, despite his evasive, not to say,
deplorable behaviour in the matter of the spicy tit-bit that had
been circulating of late anent her departure for the Lakes.
Time had, however, softened the blow, and suspicions of
brother Tom she had loyally repulsed; but exhaustive inquiries
in Upholland into the source, or sources, of the scandalous
imputation upon her honour served but to deepen her conviction that Tom, after all, was capable of such infamy, and
could thus unfeelingly grieve a sister endowed with a keen sense
of female propriety. That the ambitious Clerk to the Leigh
magistrates was capable of very despicable behaviour cannot
now be questioned in the light of corroborative proof of his
loose interpretation of the duties and opportunities of an
Attorney, details of which were later to become public property,
and to confirm Miss Weeton's later estimate of his real character. It seemed incredible that he could stoop so low, or that he
could be influenced, or frightened thus far, by the 'evil spirit
at his elbow,' Mrs. Weeton, jun.—no friend to Miss Weeton.

When I went to Mr. Pedder's in Westmorland, you
wrote me there that it was reported that I was gone off
with a gentleman! What possible motive could you have
for telling such a falsehood? I knew not then whose
fabrication it was; you, in a subsequent letter, told me it
was my cousin (Latham); but on my return to Lancashire,
I searched it out. My Aunt Barton, as well as my cousin
and others, told me that no such report had ever been in
Holland, only of your own publishing, and laid the invention of it to your charge. I went to Leigh, and asked
you who told you? Instead of clearing yourself, as I had
hoped, you flew into a violent passion, but wholly evaded
answering my question, and abruptly left me—this was

proof, aweful proof, that I had a brother undeserving of further notice.[1]

So she wrote, some years later. But neither subsequently (when she knew the real truth), nor at the time of her investigations, could she steel herself to be as good as her word where her brother was concerned; the incident of Tom's abrupt manner of concluding the cross-examination was only one of a series of unpleasantnesses, which were calculated to produce but a temporary breach. In a later letter to her friend Bessy Winkley she pillories Tom and his wife unmercifully for their behaviour to her on the occasion of this particular visit.

When I was last at Leigh, I was guilty of brushing my habit in the kitchen instead of taking it out-of-doors, on a most bitter cold day in December; and oh, what a commotion was raised! I was obliged to take refuge in my bedroom from the noise of Mrs. Weeton's tongue.

I was going to Church one Sunday morning. Mrs. W. asked me to take the children with me. I said I had no objection to take the 2 eldest, but would rather not take the youngest, she was so troublesome. When I went into the parlour to see if they were ready, how Mrs. W. had represented to my brother what I said, I know not, but my brother began upon me in the most violent language, for dictating to him whether or no he should send his children to Church, or which of them. I was, as usual, not allowed to speak; my brother insisted, nay *swore*, I should either take all, or none. For peace' sake, I submitted, and, almost heart-broken, took all three; even the children cried, and we all went crying together.

She had not precipitately plunged herself into this investigation—witness the long holiday in Westmorland; yet she suddenly found herself the centre of whole-hearted attempts to embitter her aunt and uncle against her, on the combined parts

[1] But it was not *proof* that he had *originated* the rumour, as she was subsequently to discover: his crime was rather one of difference in kind, than degree, as she too found out.

of her brother, his wife, and last—but not least—Cousin Latham. The mystery was to be unravelled later; but, meantime, she was little prepared to find herself buried once again in Liverpool, ignorant (or professedly so) of the reason why she was thus so cold-shouldered.

However, in the month of March 1812, she ran full-tilt into one of the principals of this precious conspiracy against her.

I met my cousin Latham one day in Liverpool, 6 or 7 weeks before I left it. She looked at me, with all the assumed indifference possible. At first, I did not appear to notice it; after asking how my aunt was, I inquired why she had never written? 'I don-n't know,' she drawled in answer. 'Don't know!' I said; 'you must have heard some reason for it; has she sent no message now?' 'N-o,' was all the answer, and she turned her head another way. 'And did you not intend to call upon me to-day?' 'I know not; happen I should.' 'Happen!' I repeated, in excessive anger, 'happen! there has been some strange mischief-making among you, and I should not wonder if you had been as busy as any of them.'

I waited to hear no more. I was so much affected by this little incident, that I could not forbear tears, even in the street—to think of my cousin's insolence! After this, I gave up any further idea of seeking a reconciliation, and Mrs. Price said she rejoiced at it; for that I had not had half spirit enough, and that if I did not wait till they sought me, I should deserve all she was sure they would make me suffer.

It is at this point that the newly discovered Volume 5 of copies of her letters takes up the tale.

✻   ✻   ✻

Miss Weeton's first letter in this volume is addressed to the cloistral, peevish, dying Aunt Barton. Conciliatory in tone, it elicited no response, and over a year was to elapse before her niece made another attempt. Meantime, Miss Weeton was

9

lodging, somewhat uncomfortably, with Bessy Winkley (very shortly to make Mr Price the happy man). In the departure of Ann Winkley, for Ireland, Miss Weeton had lost the sister whose friendship she most valued. Ann, young as she was (not 16) had secured the position of governess in the family of F. French, Esq., of the Navigation Board, Dublin, and of Sopwell Hall, Shinrone. To governess Ann (who, much to Miss Weeton's surprise, later made a success with her employers, and touchily resented the older governess's well-meant, but patronizing advice) Miss Weeton addressed a succession of extremely long letters, from the first of which the following extracts have been taken. After complaining bitterly of the (to her) incomprehensible attitude on the parts of both brother and aunt, and of her unbearable solitude in lodgings, she thus launches forthwith into her plan for escape.

I find, my dear Ann, that I cannot bear this inactive life; and though I have an income sufficient to keep me comfortably, I am on the point of engaging to instruct the children of a lady in Yorkshire. If I go, it will not be until the latter end of June. I shall there be too much engaged to have leisure to think with regret on those who seem so willing to forget me; and indeed I have always found myself to be most happy when most employed. I have so long lived a life of industry that I know not how to live in indolence; my conscience, too, reproaches me almost hourly for wasting my time so wickedly; and what a sad account should I give, if asked what good I had done for the last 5 years.

Mr. and *Mrs.* Price are gone to see Mrs. Higginson this evening; but neither Mrs. H. nor any one else knows (except such necessary kind of folks as the parson, &c.) that your sister has, as yet, a right to the name. They have managed to get over the ceremony very snugly, and no one seems to suspect anything of it. They were married three days ago. I was a good deal diverted the morning it took place. Your sister seemed to think that she was so perfectly calm and composed, and yet, oh, how she did post away to the church; like a person intoxicated, who runs because he cannot walk, she was much too agitated to walk slowly, and I, her only companion, could scarcely keep pace with her. We met several people we knew, and had they examined our countenances, they might have discovered what kind of errand we were *running*, there was so much more meaning and importance expressed in them than usual.

I could not prevail on Miss Winkley to speak civilly to those we met; not so much as to say 'how do you do?' I was quite in the humour for putting her composure a little more to the test, but she laughed, tittered, and trembled so, I could not get her to attend to us. Mr. Price, as was preconcerted, was in the church before us. In going up to the altar, your sister, with a good deal of mock modesty (so at least I tell her), hung back in such a manner, that the parson and clerk did not know which of us was to be the happy woman; my smirking face seemed to indicate that it was I; and besides, I had walked close up to the communion rail. 'Which is the lady?' several times the clerk, in a low tone, inquired. I looked at your sister; she advanced not! Now is the time, or never, thought I; if he asks again, I'll say I am.

It was with some difficulty that I refrained a fit of laughter, and while I held my handkerchief to my face, that I might compose my countenance, your sister seized the eventful moment, and stepped up between Mr. P. and me. They promised to love, and obey, and cherish, and to take for better and worse, in a sad, sad, faint tone of voice. Poor, poor souls! they had but a boding heart of it, I fear. There was a curious squinting kind of fellow stood close behind us, during the ceremony, with a leather brat on;[1] he was to personate the father, or guardian, and gave your sister away. He has given her to a husband; and the next

[1] brat = apron.

presentation may be to a grave, for he proved to be the sexton.

We were an odd group altogether, for parson Pugh is not overwhelmed with solemnity; the clerk looked very merry; the sexton, very significant and consequential; but what Price should look so pale for, I cannot imagine, unless he was afraid of the grave-digger. Miss W. was all modesty and propriety, and so obedient to the clergyman when he requested her to say as he did! And was it not very good of her? Neither did she show the slightest symptom of uneasiness whilst the ring was in putting on, though I am sure it hurt her, for it was rather too little.[1] As for myself, one comical idea, or other, was continually popping into my head, that I was obliged to hang it down in a very sheepish manner every now and then, that my grinning countenance might not be seen; then, again I looked up, and surveyed the different figures of the group, and thought what an excellent caricature we should have composed.

When the ceremony was over, I whispered to your sister to put her hands before her, and drop a curtsey to Mr. Pugh, and return him many thanks; but no, she had *lost her obedient spirit* the *moment* she was *married*, and would not mind what I said. Mr. Price and I are still obliged to call her Miss Winkley, to prevent discovery; but P. often smiles when he styles her so. They manage very snugly and quiet at present; but how long they mean to continue in secret, I cannot tell.

As I hope you will soon favour me with an answer, I may be able, when I write again, to tell you whether I really go into Yorkshire or not. One principal reason for my thinking of it is, that your sister and Mr. P. will most likely prefer a house to themselves; and I do not know

---

[1] Queen Victoria endured agonies as the result of a similar blunder on the occasion of her coronation.

where I could go, to board so comfortable, at so moderate a rate; and should Mrs. Armitage be a kind-hearted woman, she might be a friend and a protectress to me. I would at least try to make her so. I wish I could find her what you represent Mrs. French to be—one to whom I could look up with respect, admiration, and esteem. There is no greater happiness than to dwell with such beings.

I think I talked of visiting the Isle of Man when you were here; I still think of doing so in May, and to remain about a month; perhaps longer, if I don't go into Yorkshire.

To ANN WINKLEY   May 3rd. 1812.

Whatever you suffer in your present situation, bear it if possible; for, should you quit it, you *must* go to another perhaps no better. Situated as your sister now is, her house cannot be a home to you; at most, it can only be a temporary asylum. If you can save money enough, you may in a few years make yourself a home anywhere; I was 27 before I had a single farthing I did not earn.

We are all much surprised that Mrs. French should suffer her children to indulge such violence of temper; but since you cannot remedy the evil, become as indifferent to it as you can. In a few months, I hope you will have attained that command over yourself, that you will feel less hurt by the treatment you experience, and, finding many comforts, will become more and more reconciled to stay; perhaps even to be fond of your situation.

I rejoice to find from your letter to your sister, that your health is so much mended; change of air, diet, and want of exercise, have occasioned your indisposition. Whenever you have a few minutes leisure, by all means employ them in exercise if possible; the skipping rope, rocking horse, or anything; and avoid gravies and sauces; these little attentions to health may prevent many a day of sickness.

We have been at Mrs. Nelson's, Richmond Row; the party was rather an odd mixture, and I was a good deal amused; we had cards, dancing, and music. What a squalling singer, and key-thumper, is Bel Markland! Her sole excellence on the piano lies in the strength of her fingers; in judgment and taste she seems piteously deficient. I think she would have made an excellent drummer.

Goodbye, my dear Ann; may every comfort be yours.

The bustle attendant upon moving operations (the newly married couple moved from Prince's Street to the top of Copperas Hill 'to a pretty-looking, small new house'), illness, and the increasing melancholy of her thoughts, finally decided Miss Weeton upon the trip to the Isle of Man, from which place the next letter was sent.

To MRS. PRICE   Douglas: May 25th. 1812.

The day I left you (23d) was so calm, that after we were beyond the rock, we did not advance 2 miles an hour. I was amused with seeing a species of what I think were star-fish, swimming about, alternately closing and expanding like a bag. They are only seen in very smooth water. Porpoises, too, here and there made their appearance; a sign, sailors say, of approaching storm. We made so little progress till after midnight, that I had not the slightest inclination to sickness, and felt so hungry that I began to be alarmed at the deplorable decrease of my sea-store; for, at 4 o'clock on Saturday afternoon, we had the comfort of being told that we were farther off the Isle than when we set out, and there was such a dead calm, that the rising tide was drifting us far to the Eastward; therefore, to prevent our progress the wrong way, the captain cast anchor, where we remained for two or three hours.

Weary with doing nothing, I read over the *whole* of 2 newspapers, traversed the deck, and at last unpacked my box, and took out my flageolet; but I soon found that, like a street-fiddler, I got such a crowd about me, as made me feel quite uncomfortable. A rough-faced fellow, a journey-man saddler I suppose from what he said, produced a cracked flute; and, would you suppose it, he and I attempted several duetts. Oh, how you—No! not you, for you are not much given to laughing; but oh, how some people that I know would have laughed to have seen such a contrasted pair, piping and fluting duetts! I shall have many a *solo* laugh when I think of it. I hope I shall never be taken with a sudden fit of laughter in the streets here, should the recollection rush all at once upon me; for, if I am, the people will think I am crazy; or, if I hang down my head to hide my grinning face, the most charitable construction they can put upon it will be, that I am ill of the gripes. The man behaved as civilly as it was in his power to do; but his exterior bespoke him as a blackguard of no high degree.

The young man, whom you and I condemned for being rather conceited, and who proved to be a lieutenant in the navy, was so highly entertained with the distorted phiz of the flute-player, that he urged him on repeatedly to con-tinue his playing, till at length the quiz betrayed himself by every now and then slily holding the candle to the other's face, pretending to give more light to the notes. My playing had soon ceased on the lieutenant's descending into the cabin, and when the flute-player discovered that he, in turn, was played upon, he declined continuing his music, though he had too much good sense to shew himself offended. After this, the passengers, about a dozen in all, fell into a kind of general conversation; and the gentlemen, to induce the women to open their mouths, hit upon that *hackneyed, everlasting* theme, *love*; we were but 3 women in the front cabin, one of whom was a low kind of woman, with a child, so that I and another had the conversation principally addressed to us. Our fellow-travellers were all as civil as they could be; but there was a want of that delicacy and gentleness of manner which attends a cultivated and refined understanding.

I don't know that I ever was in such rough company before; towards ten at night, one or two of them frequently requested we women would go to bed, really intending to be considerate and kind. My companion looked at me and smiled; I knew what that meant; these men never thought of leaving the cabin whilst we got into bed, and as there was but one cabin, the men and women must all herd together. I gave a hint to the captain, who likewise gave a hint to the fellows (for they were not gentlemen). When we were got into bed, they came down into the cabin, and a sweet scene of riotous mirth ensued; their conversation and songs were rational enough, and void of any indelicacy, for which we were obliged, but too noisy to admit of any possibility of sleeping before two o'clock next morning. About 4, the vessel began to roll a little, and the wind rising, the ropes and sails rattling, made me feel apprehensive that we were going to have a storm. At 7, I could lie no longer, I became so deadly sick; and, for the next two hours, I heaved incessantly; the quantity of bile that came up, would have shocked any one to see. Ill as I was, I was thankful for it. I might well be ill whilst I was in Liverpool, with such a load upon my stomach, for I think I am not guilty of the slightest exaggeration when I say that there was above a pint of pure bile.

Between 9 & 10 on Sunday morning, we were moored in Douglas harbour; the custom-house officers were not very strict on their search, for which I was not sorry, merely because it saved me a little trouble, for I had nothing to fear. In going to bed, I had slackened my cloaths, but not taken them off, and in a totally unlaced, unpinned state, I was obliged to crawl through the streets, to the Inn, being perfectly unable to dress myself. I wrapped my coat round me, and threw my shawl over it; my hair uncombed, uncurled, my face wan, and eyes sunken, I presented no very beautiful picture. I remained at the inn that day, and till after breakfast the next, and recruited tolerably; but oh, such a filthy Inn throughout, I never saw! The house was good, and wanted nothing but cleanliness to make it respectable; I fancy it was one of the lower orders of houses. However, it must have served me, had it been worse. I dined with the family and a few of their friends, on a fine turkey, a fowl, asparagus, and potatoes, and paid only a shilling.

If I only enjoy my health, I shall not be sorry that I have taken this trip; but a contraction at my chest, which I have often felt, particularly for the last 4 or 5 months, gives me reason to apprehend an approaching asthma; however, if it does arrive, though I cannot welcome it with joy, I must endeavour patiently to endure it, as there will be no getting rid of it till my panting breath itself is stopped.[1]

We have pasteboard money here, instead of silver; and 14 Manks pennies for an English shilling: a 5s. piece of pasteboard, is an oval about 2½ inches long, and 1¾ broad: a 2s. 6d. a size smaller: a 1s. an octagonal piece a little bigger than an English crown. I must take care to bring none of them to Liverpool, for there they would be waste paper indeed. Their value is stamped in printed letters, and are issued by the Banks here.[2]

Everyone here, I am told, send for their letters to the Post-office; none are delivered. I can't see why the post-

---

[1] Her health, and her impossible relations, occupy far too many pages of this particular MS. volume; the reader will be spared many letters upon two subjects which were to depress (or enliven) her life for the next thirty years.

[2] From the year 1805 to 1817, owing to the lack of copper and silver coins circulating in the Isle of Man, many of the merchants issued their own money in the form of engraved or lithographed cards of various shapes and sizes. The lowest value was 3*d*. and the highest 10*s*. (For this note I am indebted to the Librarian of Douglas Public Library, Mr. H. C. Granville Clague.)

masters can't hire letter-carriers here, as easily as they do in England; nor why the inhabitants should not be as ready to contribute to the additional expence; for there would certainly be an adequate convenience. All letters regularly received or sent, come and go through White-haven, if I am rightly informed.[1]

I will not expect you to write to me unless you should have anything necessary to communicate; and probably I shall not write again whilst I stay. When a month has elapsed from the time I left you, you may daily expect me.

Miss Weeton duly returned on the 22nd of June (to learn of the sudden death of an old friend, the Rev. John Braithwaite, of the Priory, Upholland, upon the day previous). Dashing off a very short script to the bereaved Charlotte, she set about completing a letter of a little over 10,000 words in length to her correspondent, Ann, herewith.

To MISS ANN WINKLEY   Douglas. Isle of Man.
                    June 15—concluded July 5th. 1812.

It was my wish to have answered your last letter the moment I received it; for I found you had dwelt too strongly on one or two passages of mine.

Though I have *appeared* to neglect you, I have incessantly thought of you, and the unhappiness which I have caused you, my intention was, to prepare you for the evils which *might* happen; not to afflict you in reality. When I last wrote to you, it was certainly under a very unpleasant impression; my own suffering pressed heavily upon my spirits; and the gloom that overclouded me, gave a tinge to everything; I thought the excuses your sister made, when I urged her to write to you, were trivial, and I was much more hurt than I am sure I had any reason to be.

And now, my young friend, to present you with something more lively—to mingle sweets with bitters—the gay

[1] A regular daily mail was established as late as 1879.

with the grave—and narrative with precept, I will give you some account of my journey here; for I am at this moment in Douglas. The week after Mr. and Mrs. Price had removed to Copperas Hill, I prepared for my travels; and on Saturday morning, about 10 o'clock, May 23rd, I left Liverpool in the Brilliant. For three hours before I landed, I was extremely ill, and scarcely able to crawl out of the cabin when the vessel arrived at the pier. I went to a public house for that day; for, being Sunday, it was an awkward and improper day to inquire for lodgings; though, indeed, I did make an attempt in the afternoon, accompanied by a young married man who lodged at the house; notwithstanding I was unsuccessful, I was really rejoiced to find that the people had such a veneration for the day, as to think it improper to take in a lodger, or that I should apply.[1]

I contented myself as well as I could, in the dirty, uncomfortable house I was in, until next morning, when I set out alone. I rambled along the streets until I found the stationer's shop, from whence the Douglas newspaper was issued, which I had seen the day before. I inquired for the lodgings he had advertised; I was directed to them; those, and several others were engaged. One house was occupied by a barber, who told me that though his rooms were taken, such a one would perhaps be vacant. As I was a total stranger to every one, an old soldier, who was shaving, offered to go with me, and, escorted by him, I knocked at two doors, but they were not 'opened to me'. I did not knock at the 3d house in vain; the door was opened, the people civil and respectable, the house spacious and convenient, and my accommodation in every respect as

---

[1] The curious history of Sunday observance, covering this transitional period to, and including, the Victorian era, would make interesting reading. London, on a Sunday, Miss Weeton was subsequently to dismiss as pagan. Yet the German visitor, Moritz, in the year 1782, had to be careful not to offend the decencies on Sunday, despite the fact that the desperate expedient of Sunday Schools was then formulating against youthful depravity.

comfortable as I could wish. I agreed to lodge and dine with the family for 12s. a week, finding everything else myself. This was all settled by 10 o'clock in the morning, that same hour which for 3 days together had been propitious to me.

I was very anxious to see Mrs. Dodson, formerly Mrs. W. Singleton of Wigan, with whom, when she was Miss Prescott, I had spent so many agreeable hours in Upholland.[1] I was no sooner, therefore, settled, than faint and weakly as I still was from the violent sea-sickness I had undergone, I dressed and set out to call upon Mrs. Dodson. As I proceeded, I was a good deal surprized to find the streets so narrow and intricate; they are one continued zig-zag labyrinth; I never saw a town so ill-built, nor altogether so shabby and dirty. The best houses, with very few exceptions, are in an almost total want of whitewash, paper, and paint; and so mingled with little, dirty huts, as to present the most opposite ideas from those of cleanliness, comfort, or symmetry. The tradesmen's signs in any town, in my opinion, present the quickest and most just idea of the general taste and degree of opulence of the inhabitants; and here, they are strikingly mean; and the combination of trades in the same person, rather singular.

But I rather mean to give you an account of *my* peregrinations, than of the Island, which you may find in print. I will go on to tell you that I was received by Mrs. Dodson in as pleasing a manner as I could wish. It was a happy thing for her that Mr. Prescott settled her fortune upon her and her children, or otherwise she would at this moment have been a beggar; for Mr. W. Singleton's embarrassed circumstances drove him to this *Isle of refuge* for the *unfortunate* and

---

[1] It is indeed hard to reconcile this statement with the account given in the 'Retrospect' (see vol. i) of the slighting treatment she suffered at the hands of the Misses Prescott, under pressure of a mother's snobbish partiality for superior social contacts for her incurably shy daughter. Mrs. Dodson's flight from her husband's creditors was quite in keeping with her character: but one hesitates to accuse Miss Weeton of a conveniently short memory.

the *unprincipled*; for it literally swarms with English vagabonds. Mrs. W. S's income was near £400 a year; a very
comfortable support for the family; and better to be in a
sort of voluntary exile here, with her husband and children, than to live in England, and her husband perhaps
spending his days in a prison.

Mr. W. S. has been dead 2 or 3 years, leaving his widow
with 3 daughters and a son. About 12 months ago, she
married a Mr. Dodson, a Manchester gentleman, who had
seen richer days, but who now had absolutely nothing.
His manners were elegant, his conversation was intelligent;
but his habits had been dissipated. *He* wanted a home, and
in Mrs. Singleton's house he found one; *she* was pleased
with his manners, and, far removed from all her friends,
felt the want of an adviser and a companion. In hopes to
obtain both, she married him; exactly 3 weeks from the
day they were married—he died!!! His constitution had
been greatly injured by former dissipation, and 2 days
sickness carried him off.

Mrs. Dodson's friends, and those of her first husband,
were greatly displeased at so imprudent a marriage, and
rejoiced at Mr. D's death. It was an afflictive event for
her; but she did not meet with one to soothe or console
her. Her relations in England wish her to return, but she
says she is settled here, and can educate her children at
much less expence than elsewhere, and shall therefore remain for some years at least. She has a governess for her
girls, a Miss Maddocks, to whom she gives only £12 a year!
What do you think of this, my dear Ann? You have much
more; and yet this young lady has had an education much
superior to yours.[1] Mrs. Dodson keeps only 2 women servants, no carriages, and very little company.

There are many very pretty houses in the neighbour-

---

[1] And Charlotte Brontë's education was superior to both, yet she could only
command £20 (less £4 deducted for washing) a quarter of a century later.

hood of Douglas; and indeed, all over the Island. I have nearly walked round it, and think myself amply repaid for the fatigue I have undergone, by the pleasure I have experienced in viewing so romantic a country.

A promontory, called Douglas-Head, commands a fine view of the town, harbour, and some distant mountains; and when I am not inclined to take a long walk, I amuse myself with ascending here, where I can arrive in 20 minutes any time from my lodgings. For 2 or 3 days after my arrival, I took only short walks, to reconnoitre the country and the people. The want, the almost total want of wood, except a few ornamental plantations, gives the country a very bleak and naked appearance; for a day or two, I thought there had been nothing but broom hedges, which, being nearly in full flower, have a gaudy and flaring appearance. I have since observed many other kinds of fences; some are of earth and sods entirely; and it is no uncommon thing to see people walking upon the fences, which are quite broad enough, and path-worn. Walls prevail everywhere, particularly on the hills and mountains, and certainly as far from being ornamental, as a fence can be; 7d a yard is the price now usually paid to wall-builders; whether that is cheaper than making green fences, I do not know. The land is generally well cultivated; much better, I think, than in the North of England. Here, is very little waste land that can be made use of; and the commons are not so extensive as in many parts of England, where the ground is similar in extent and surface. The industry becoming prevalent here, is chiefly owing to the English farmers, who have settled in the Island; and the Manks, discovering the utility of the English method of agriculture, are by degrees universally adopting it; so much corn is grown in the Isle, that they are enabled to export a great deal, and can raise all the common necessaries of life without foreign aid.

Nothing is allowed to be imported, but for the consumption of the islanders; not for the purposes of trade, of which there is very little; of course, no merchants of any consequence. The imports, if consumed on the Island, are duty-free; which makes tea, wine, sugar, salt, and many other things extremely cheap.[1] Tea, which we procure in England for 8s., is here 5s. p. lb. Strangers are frequently charged 6s.; but it is invariably the rule here to impose upon the ignorant. Wine may be had at 2s. 4d. p. bottle; 3s. is, I think, the highest price; at the best hand it may be had at 24s. p. Doz^n. Brown sugar of the middle price, 6½d p. lb.; brown paper loaf 9d do. Rum 2s. 6d. a bottle; salt 5d for 14 lb. Bread is quite as dear as in England; wearing apparel of all kinds dearer, except coarse woollens. Butchers meat and vegetables no cheaper; and rents of land, or houses, extremely high. No land taxes, window-money, or poor's rates are levied; which are considerations of value.[2] The rents, on an average, may be nearly as they are in Wigan, and the country around it. To compensate for the want of poor rates, a collection is made in the churches every Sunday morning, between the sermon and concluding prayer.

Eggs are from 28 to 36 for a shilling; poultry is very cheap; fish is moderate, not so cheap as might be expected, herrings excepted; the season for which will commence in about a fortnight, and continue for several months.[3] This fishery is the principal support of the Manks; and the coasts of the Island during the time is as complete a scene of bustle as can be imagined. During this period, the interior is nearly deserted by the men, and as few of the women

---

[1] A blow at smuggling, long prevalent on the island.

[2] These 'considerations of value' have, of course, been modified, but the principal 'imports' (of which Miss Weeton and her dozen fellow voyagers were in the van) can still prove the strength of her observation *re* impositions upon the 'ignorant'.

[3] 'Life to man, and death to fish'—so ran a common Manx proverb.

left as can be helped. Douglas, and all the little sea-ports, are in one continued state of hurry and drunkenness. I should like to have seen a specimen of all this, and the fleet of little one-masted boats going out, and returning every day, but I cannot stay so long, for I must be in Yorkshire the 2d week in July, if possible; and I have only allowed myself a fortnight to prepare, after I return to Liverpool. . . . I am again wandering from my own little adventures, and telling you that, which I dare say you may meet with in many a publication.

The first long walk I took, was on the 28th, after my arrival. When I had been on Douglas-Head one day, I had seen some mountains at a distance, and this day I set out with the intention of ascending the highest, if it were not too far. By paying strict attention to a map which I purchased, I have had very little occasion to ask any questions respecting roads, distances, or places. I took my guide in my hand, and wanted no other. In this, and in all my walks, I have ever been without a companion; I prefer being alone; I can then stop, go on, sit down, proceed, turn to the right or to the left, as my fancy may prompt, without restraint; and, even were it probable I could find a *proper* companion who would with pleasure accompany me 12, 15, 20, or 30 miles a day, still, her taste would not perhaps assimilate in most respects with my own, and we should teaze each other—I, in listening to conversation which did not interest me, and she, in attending to observations to which she was indifferent. But, as it is extremely unlikely I should find one who would take such long walks, and give way to my taste, wishes, and curiosity in every thing, I choose to go alone, in places unfrequented by those of my own species, that my thoughts, as well as my feet, may ramble without restraint; when I enter towns, and crouds, I do then like to have a companion; but when the wonders of nature alone occupy me, when my soul is filled with admiration and rapture at scenes of rural beauty, or mountainous grandeur, I never wish for the company of one earthly being, save that of my brother, for whom it is in vain to sigh. . . . Oh, Ann, how the thought of him makes my heart ache! Once, so affectionate, so noble! now, so led by a malicious, envious, mischiefmaking wife! . . . but no matter.

On my way to Greeva (the name of the mountain), I passed by Kirk-Braddon, about 2 miles from Douglas; it stands at a distance from any house, and almost buried in trees. As I got a glimpse of it from the road, I thought it looked beautifully. This stands as a Church should do; retired from the haunts of business, or thoughtless levity; the remains of the departed here rest in peace, and a kind of sacred solitude reigns perpetually. I remained some time in the Church-yard after I went into it, and quitted it with sentiments of religious awe. Four miles farther, and I arrived at the foot of Greeva, which projects nearly into the Peel-road. I asked a girl, who stood at the door of a little hut, if I might be permitted to pass that way? She instantly complied, and showed me through the garden, from whence I began directly to ascend the rocks, which were very steep. I might have ascended a much less difficult way, but this was nearer; and walls, and rocks, are slight impediments to me. When arrived at the top, I could see nearly round the Island: east, west, and south, the view was clear, and fine. Snafield,[1] the highest mountain in the Island, impeded the view to the north. A number of sheep and a few goats (the only ones I have seen here), were feeding around me; and an old man and young woman were gathering furze for firing, and carrying it down the mountain on their backs;[2] the young woman was without shoes or stockings, and her feet bled very much;

---

[1] Snaefell.

[2] Coal, having to be imported, was an expensive commodity.

it grieved me to see it; often did she sit down to rest from her burthen, and the tears in her eyes evinced the pains she felt. The poor women in the Island seldom wear shoes or stockings, whilst the men seldom go without them; why there should be such apparent injustice or partiality, I know not; I see it every day. I sat some time on the top of the mountain, and saw distinctly the Scotch and Irish coasts.

When I descended the mountain, the same girl who had so civilly let me pass through her garden, even taking down some stones that I might the more easily get over the wall at the back, met me as I returned, and said she was glad to see me again, for she thought I was lost, and had climbed ever so high up the rocks to find me, but could see nothing of me; and expressed some surprise when I told her I had been to the summit of the hill. It is no very common thing, I suppose, to see strangers go up the mountains, particularly a decently dressed female, alone.

I returned home, highly pleased with my walk, which was about 13 miles; the few people I had met with, either took no notice of me, or spoke civilly; which gave me more confidence, as I confess my first walks were not without considerable apprehensions, lest I should meet with insult, as I was so totally unaccompanied; but to me, the country people, as well as others, have been altogether as civil as I could wish, sometimes entering into conversation, which I generally encouraged, that I might gain all the information I could. In return for my questions respecting the roads, gentlemen's houses, &c., I was sure to be questioned in turn. I never met with a more inquisitive, prying set of people in my life! Where did I come from? how long had I been in the Island? when did I mean to return? where was I then going? were questions asked by every one. Sometimes I answered, and sometimes civilly evaded their inquiries; for, though I thought their curiosity impertinent, I saw they meant not to be rude; and as they were ignorant that they were guilty of any impropriety, I should have been wrong to have answered them with ill-humour. Many of them spoke to me in Manks, and when they found that I did not understand them, would then address me in English; few of them, indeed, none, that do not understand English (which I think is principally, if not wholly spoken in the Manks towns; but in the hamlets, and scattered houses, the native language is most prevalent). The natives adhere with great tenacity to their original language, and will speak nothing else if they can help it, frequently refusing to answer strangers in any other. I have met with some instances of this, and felt somewhat chagrined at their rudeness and stupidity, when I have wished for a little information. The schools that are established all over the Island, teach only English; and that, only, is spoken in them, so that probably in 20 or 30 years, the Manks language will be almost obsolete. There is a school in Douglas on the Lancastrian plan, lately established; I was as much surprised, as pleased, to see so good a building erected for the purpose, for there is scarcely another instance of so much public spirit.[1]

My next long walk was on the 30th to Kirk-Santon, on the road to Castletown; it was rather an uninteresting road, and served only to give me a farther idea of the nature of that part of the country, which, as far as I went, is the least fertile of any. As I seldom go directly on with-

---

[1] Public spirit took some rousing, and it was not until 1833 that even a minor public school was established, though of course there are now high schools and a grammar school—with one regrettable consequence, for the Manx language is now almost extinct, consequent upon the spread of education. The mention of the school on the 'Lancastrian' plan indicates an interest in popular education which Miss Weeton was chary of showing. Joseph Lancaster (1778–1838) instituted a scheme of monitorial supervision in schools of his inspiring, which took some superseding by obviously better systems.

out swerving occasionally from the road, to ascend some eminence for a better view, my walks are often unnecessarily, though pleasingly, lengthened; and this, which was only in a direct road, going and returning, 12 miles, I stretched into 16.

Encouraged by the little fatigue I felt after these walks, I meditated others of greater length; and, on June 1st, going up to Douglas-Head to take a view of the country, I concluded upon going to Laxey, 8 miles distant, the road to which I could plainly see. I accordingly set out after dinner; some scenes along the road are very pretty for the first 4 miles. Kirk Conchan and the village near it have a rural romantic effect at this season of the year; some boys were tolling, or more correctly, ringing a bell for a funeral, when I passed; as few of the churches have any steeple, the bell is hung just above the roof, and the rope hangs outside the wall into the church-yard. When I first heard the odd manner in which this bell was jingled, and saw the children in the church yard from between the trees, I really thought they were making use of the church-bell, instead of a frying pan, to ring a swarm of bees into a hive; for it had exactly that kind of sound, and had I not asked a boy who sat on the road-side, should have thought so to this moment. How careful should travellers be of making conjectures, and of taking for reality, what only appears to be very probable.

I walked on, laughing heartily at the idea; the country for the remaining 4 miles, was very uninteresting, for want of wood; but as a compensation, I was overtaken by a *most agreeable fellow pedestrian* . . . an old Irishman, with a sack on his back! He made several attempts to converse with me, which I rather shyly answered at first, wishing to be rid of him; but when I perceived that there was not another human being anywhere in sight, I began to examine him with more attention. He was old, and rather

infirm, and I was confident I could overpower him, should
he attempt to rob me; at any rate, I can run five times
as fast, thought I. Thus *wisely* reflecting, I became *amazingly* courageous, and began to talk with him. He told
me he had walked that day from Ramsay to Douglas (16
miles) and was then returning! a long way, Ann, for an
old man between 60 and 70, was it not? He then asked
me what o'clock it was? I did not quite like this question,
as it appeared as if he wanted to know whether I had
a watch. I said I did not know; perhaps it was 4 o'clock.
Then the usual questions of, where did I come from, &c?
succeeded. If I would tell him, he said, where I lived in
Douglas, he would call and see me. I could have laughed
at this, for I saw the drift of it; he had, in a sly kind of
way, been wanting to beg of me. As there was no shaking
him off, let me stop, or walk at what pace I would, I gave
him to understand I had no money. Then, like a true
Irishman, he would call to see me, for the respect he had
for such a nice young woman. I *seemed* to be much pleased,
but said I was leaving Douglas soon . . . the cunning old
fellow. Accidentally, I recollected that I had 2½d, and
giving it to him for a glass of ale at Laxey, made a decided
stop, sitting down by the road side that I might get rid of
him. He had not the impudence to sit down too; but, as
he went, often stopped and turned. I watched him quite
out of sight before I proceeded.

Laxey is a beautiful little vale, and scattered village;
the houses are but poor, but in fine weather, they have
altogether a romantic, picturesque appearance. The vale
is long, and narrow; high hills rising steeply on each side,
and terminated at the upper extremity by Snafield, the
highest mountain in the Island. Cottages, huts, gardens,
orchards, and little patches of corn and meadow-land,
ornament the view for 2 or 3 miles in length, whilst in
front, the bay, surrounded with 30 or 40 fishermen's boats,

gives an animated finish to the picture. I walked near ½ a mile up the vale, and returned, highly gratified. I had scarcely quitted Laxey, when the old Irishman again made his appearance out of a hut by the road side, to repeat his thanks for the money I had given him. Certainly, I must never be quit of this old fellow! thought I; however, he did not follow me.

About half way home, I met a decent-looking woman, who, civilly bidding me 'good-even', encouraged me to ask a few questions respecting the different places within view. She was very communicative, and we had a long conversation. She was a pedestrian traveller, pedlar, and fortune-teller, and had a good deal of sly drollery. She offered to tell me my fortune. I laughed, and told her I dared not venture; for she could only tell me that I must die a miserable old maid. She would *fain* have persuaded me to the contrary, but could not succeed. We cordially bid each other good-bye, and parted. Had we both been walking the same way, I might have drawn from her many an entertaining anecdote. I have since wished I had suffered her to exert her talent in prediction; the future recollection of such an adventure would have entertained me so much—but alas! I cast the *silver* opportunity away, and—if I choose it, may live in sorrow that I did so all my days. Foolish creature that I was! when the *hope* of a husband, and a fine coach, might have cheered me even to my last moments, thus ridiculously to have lost all chance of the wretches' last resource! Goosecap! noodle! ninny hammer! no name is too bad for me!

I did not again take any long walk till the 5th of June, the intervening time being taken up in short rambles of 3, 4, or 5 miles around Douglas; and in dining and drinking tea with Mrs. Dodson, who has taken a great deal of notice of me indeed. I had seen little of her since her first marriage; previous to that time, we saw each other almost daily for several years. The sight of each other now, bring again to recollection 'the days that are gone', and we have many a long conversation. Mrs. D. is quite the gentle-woman; yet, there is something in her manner most strikingly peculiar; in my opinion, she will retain her life longer than her senses, although she is at present as per-fectly clear in idea as ever she was. She has vanity to a most astonishing degree, and it would scarcely be pos-sible to flatter her too grossly; but as I really am partial to her, and value her health of mind more than her favour, I am particularly cautious not to feed a vanity that strongly wants a check; she will sometime absolutely extort compli-ments and praises, and is almost as often guilty of praising herself, as is Mrs. Edwards.[1] It shewed an extreme weak-ness, which requires many a valuable trait besides to palliate. She has invited me to spend some weeks with her, next summer but one, if all be well; and urges me often to fix near her in Douglas; nay, has even offered me to live with her; and as she knows how tenacious I am in receiving obligations, has proposed such moderate terms for board as she knows I could easily comply with.

This last offer must be a profound secret, my dear Ann; for, as I am engaged to Mr. Armitage, I must fulfil it. Should it so happen that I cannot stay in Yorkshire, I am to inform Mrs. D., and then, if convenient to them both, come and stay with her. Such an offer has filled me with sentiments of the warmest gratitude; the more unkind my brother's family is, the greater friendship do I meet with from others. Mrs. D. one day said that I was a dangerous character to be near Mrs. Weeton; for that my virtues and my talents were so much superior, that my brother would continually be drawing comparisons to her

[1] The sister of Mr. Price, of whom Miss Weeton had little good to report. Her deistical opinions, for instance, Miss Weeton confused with rank atheism; but it is to be feared that Mr. Price's sister was in the habit of 'smoking' the governess.

disadvantage. . . . In transcribing this high compliment, my dear Ann, I am guilty of all the vanity of which I accuse others. I am weak as the weakest, and have not even the sense to hide it! Mrs. D. meant it kindly, and to reconcile me to the estrangement under which I now suffer.

You will scarcely credit me when I tell you that on the 5th of June, I walked 35 miles. I left home at half past nine, with an intention to go to Castletown, and as much farther as I found I could walk. So as to get well home, I put my map, memorandum book, 3 boiled eggs, and a crust of bread into a work-bag; and, thus prepared, sallied forth. I met with nothing worth observation until I arrived near Castletown, which I think is by much the prettiest town in the Island. I walked slowly through it, passing by the castle, an ancient-looking building; a few soldiers were scattered in groups here and there, and gave the place a rather martial appearance. The streets are wide, and more cleanly than either of the other three principal towns; and the good houses that are in it, are seen to more advantage than they are in Douglas, Ramsay, or Peel. I walked 2 or 3 miles beyond Castletown, to a rising ground that commanded an extensive view; and, springing upon a high copse by the road side, where I seated myself, I had the double pleasure of satisfying my appetite, and feasting my eyes. Then, retracing a part of the road, I turned towards Peel, thinking I would only go a little way, just to have a more extended view. I saw an old woman on the road behind me, knitting; I walked slowly, that she might overtake me, for I wanted to have a little chat with her, and to ask her a few questions respecting the country. She was very communicative, and we went sociably on till we arrived at some cottages, where she stopped and bid me a 'good day'. I have ever found women, when I, as a stranger addressed them, civil, humane, and hospitable, both here and in the north of England, (I have travelled no where else); but of men, I cannot say so; frequently, when I, or other females, have passed them, have I seen their sneers, or heard their rude remarks. Mungo Park makes the same observation in his travels, that, from men, he frequently met with unkindness, but from women, never; *they* protected, nursed, or fed him, whenever he wanted assistance; whilst from men, his life was frequently endangered.

'I will only go a little further, and a little further, just to that pretty house, or to the top of that high road,' I frequently repeated to myself, until I had got full 5 miles beyond Castletown. To return, or go through Peel, would be equally 15 or 16 miles. I stood hesitating for some time what to do. I looked at my watch, and found that it was half past 4 o'clock! I confess I was a little alarmed, but as there was no time for delay, I turned towards Peel, over a mountain road the old woman had shewn me; preferring that to the high-road, because it was in fact a much *lower* one; and I wanted scenery and prospect, not caring for the additional fatigue. Often and often, as I went on, did I turn to feast my eyes on the beauties spread out at my feet. The air was serenely clear; England, Ireland, Scotland, and Wales were all perfectly distinct; some Irish mountains appeared so near, I fancied I could row myself to them in an open boat; they were of a deep purple, tinged with the declining sun, and did look most beautifully! I could distinctly mark the mountains in Cumberland and Westmoreland; Skiddaw, Saddleback, Helvellyn, Coniston, and several others. I felt a pleasure in looking at them, for *there* had *my* feet trodden, and some of my happiest days been spent! To stand as I did, upon an island, and in one half hour see three kingdoms and a principality, is no common view.

Numbers of men were on the mountains as I passed,

cutting turf; many of them, when they saw me, ceased working, and stood to gaze; others sat down. I did not feel quite comfortable. Should they insult me, I thought, I have only my own temerity to blame. However, they did not utter a single word. A lonely female, dressed as I was, I dare say they never saw in such a place; for I had on a small slouch straw hat, a grey stuff jacket, and petti-coat; a white net bag in one hand, and a parasol in the other; and in their eyes, I dare say I made rather a singular figure. I got into Peel at 6 o'clock, having in my way down the mountains, and along the vales, seen many a lovely little cultivated patch of earth, and romantic lonely little hut on the sides of the hills, the streamlets running wildly at the bottom, over their rocky beds. There is a simple grandeur and beauty in such scenes, that infuses a greater portion of enthusiasm within me, than I can express. I admire! I wonder! I adore! Oh Ann! if you knew the pleasure I feel in running wild among such scenery, you would not wonder at my temerity, or at my undergoing so much fatigue to obtain the gratification.

The ruins of an ancient castle at Peel are worth seeing; and the view of them from the pier-head, and of the harbour, vessels, and town, are very fine. The town is, of itself, insignificant, and poor; it looks best at a distance. When I was on the pier-head at Peel, I had walked 25 miles, and had still 10 to go. The Tynwald mount, from whence all the Manks laws are promulgated, is about 4 miles from Peel, near to the road I had to go; it is only a small, circular mound of earth, with 3 rows of earthen steps, and derives all its consequence from the above circumstance.[1]

I now became rather footsore, and for the remaining

---

[1] The ceremony of Tynwald Court is still held annually. The laws decided upon by the House of Keys come into force only after promulgation from the hill, following Royal assent. An interesting survival is the reading in Manx of the headings of the laws.

6 miles, was more anxious to get home than to survey the beauties a setting sun displayed. I arrived there at half past 9, having been just 12 hours away. If you can get a map, you will see that I made quite a circuit of the southern part of the Island; a tolerable journey, even for a horse.

I was so tired, I could hardly undress myself for bed, where I immediately went on getting into the house. Mrs. Allen (my landlady) laughed heartily at me. 'Now really,' said she, 'if anybody had obliged you to go such a journey, you would have thought it the greatest hardship that ever was. Lord help you! I see you are almost killed; why, you'll never be able to get up tomorrow.' I joined her in the laugh, and begged she would send me up some tea, for I had not tasted since 2 o'clock. I took my tea in bed, but was so overpowered with fatigue, I was obliged to lie down between each cup, and almost between each mouthful of bread & butter.

Next day, I was well enough, only a little stiff and footsore. I rested that and the succeeding one, and on Monday, the 8th., set forward on another expedition. I had been told that the northern part of the Island was much more beautiful than the southern. I mentioned my wish of seeing it, and my intention of taking lodgings at Ramsay for a week, to Mrs. Dodson, who advised my going to Mrs. St. George's, of West-Kella, in preference. Miss Maddocks gave me a letter of introduction to her mother, and I went, and staid there till Friday the 12th. In going, I went a much longer way than was necessary, merely that I might see more of the country. From Douglas, I went by St. John's, Kirk Michael, Bishop's-Court, and Balaff, near 22 miles; the mountain road is only about 16. The second 8 miles of the way led along a deep vale, which was very pretty, though the view was confined. I have observed, that bare as the Island is of wood, wherever there is a cluster of huts, there is always a plantation of trees amongst them, so that they appear almost embosomed in trees. I several times sat down by the road side, to note in my memorandum book any observation or idea which I thought would be worth transcribing to you; for I had the road to myself nearly all the way.

Kirk Michael is a village near the sea, and there are many pretty country houses scattered around it. Bishop's-Court has an appearance of canonical antiquity and solemnity, as you approach, and pass it, that suits well for the habitation of a prelate. At Balaff, I became completely puzzled about the road; the place so marked in my map, and the road in which I was, I was convinced were not the same; and how to get right, I could not tell. West-Kella, not being down on the map, I knew not in what direction it lay, since Balaff was not in the right place. At length I met two men, who appeared for some time not to understand my question; they repeated the word West Kella? and, adding something in Manks, pointed up to the right. I turned that way for a quarter of a mile, but could see nothing of the house I was in quest of. I called at a farm house. The woman within could not speak English. I went on yet farther, till I saw 3 or 4 men lounging by a blacksmith's shop. I inquired of them; they knew nothing of it. I began to think I did not pronounce the word right. I said I had a letter, which perhaps they would understand better; and, untying my bundle, I took it out, and shewed it to them. A young man, who was chief spokesman, examined the direction, but could make nothing of it; there was no such place up that glen, he said; and I had better go back, and proceed 3 or 4 miles farther. I did so, and found the place, which is only a single house. Kirk Balaff only is marked on the map, which stands at some distance from the village, which was the cause of my mistake, naturally supposing the church

and the village would be together. I have always measured
the distances of places upon the map from each other; and
having a tolerable idea of the length of a mile by the eye,
and the time I take in walking it, I never made any mistake of the kind before, or since. If I travel north, or south,
east, or west, which I take care to ascertain on setting out,
the sun, and the hour of the day inform me which way to
go forward in an unknown country, where I meet with so
few people.

To give you any satisfactory account of Mr. & Mrs. St.
George, would be to write a little history. Mrs. St. George
is a most unfortunate, imprudent woman! She was educated in a convent in France; and, in England, married a
man highly respected, a Mr. Maddocks, a tanner at Elles-
mere in Shropshire, by whom she had 9 children. Her
friends were so displeased at her marrying a protestant,
that, until her husband's death, they would never notice
her; then, being in indigent circumstances, a wealthy
uncle again became a friend.

Some inconsistencies of conduct on her part, displeased
him a second time; and, becoming attached to a Mr. St.
George, he and she, with all or most of her children, came
over to this Island, where, after some time, they were
married. Mr. St. George boasted of himself as a man of
a great family, and allied to nobility; a gentleman really
of that family, happening to be in Douglas, and hearing
of this, investigated the matter, and he was proved to be
a complete impostor! It is said he has been a candle-
snuffer at the Dublin theatre, and afterwards enlisted as
a common soldier; that he deserted, and fled hither, not
daring to return any more. His real name is Rickey, but, as
he married under an assumed one, Mrs. St. George is living
with a man—not her husband—not worth a halfpenny
—not possessed of either virtue or talents—and, too idle
to earn a livelihood!!! Her eldest daughter is governess

to Mrs. Dodson's children; 3 or 4 boys are in England, and 4 girls are with her at West-Kella. She keeps a school, but everything wears the appearance of distress. What will become of her, I cannot tell. I fear she is wavering and unsteady; and her attachment to an idle fellow, will be the ruin of the whole family. Mr. St. George is younger than his wife; I dare say 10 years; and in my opinion, only stays with her so long as she can keep him. She has an annuity of £50, which she wants to dispose of for her life. I hope she may not succeed in selling it, for, if she should, I fear he will get hold of the money, and disappear. If she is but wise enough to keep her annuity, it will keep her and her children from starving.

West-Kella is a pretty-looking farm house, with a good garden and orchard. The day after I got there, I took a very short walk, being too stiff and foot-sore to take a long one. From Primrose Hill, I had a very pleasing view; the country behind, and to the right and left, was more mountainous; in front, spacious; the sea spreading far and wide. The mornings I spent, whilst I staid, in reading a manuscript translation from the French, by Mrs. St. G., and of which she wanted my opinion, as she had some thoughts of publishing it. It is an account of the suffering of the Princess Royale of France, whilst in prison, after the decapitation of her parents; and, entitled 'Irma', is represented as a Persian tale. Mrs. St. George is really a pleasing, well-informed woman; but as she has now placed herself, it is dangerous to speculate; and in publishing this work, it would be a great risk. The expense of printing an edition will cost £200, she says; for the London booksellers will not run the risk themselves, and it is very uncertain that it will sell; still, she seems bent on trying it. I dared not give her any encouragement; the risk is too great; yet the work has considerable merit. It is rather too literal a translation, which, in a work in the Persian style of writing, is a great fault; in Mrs. St. George's, there is great want of amplification and embellishment to make it sufficiently Eastern.

On the 10th., I walked, after dinner, to Ramsay, 4½ miles from W. Kella; and as I had a great wish to see where Mrs. Askins (Miss Chorley's[1] friend) lived, I inquired for her cottage, and found it; it was beyond Ramsay from W. Kella, near a mile. I went to within 50 yards of it, but did not call upon Mrs. A., though when I saw her in Liverpool last October, she desired I would, if ever I came to the Island; and even talked of introducing me to the Bishop's family. Still, I felt diffident; I had a great desire to see her, yet could not assume resolution to knock at her door. I lingered about the house some time; then, sitting down upon a high bank, just hid from view, I surveyed with delight the fine bay of Ramsay, still thinking of Mrs. A., and peeping over the bank every now and then, to catch another glimpse of her cottage. She is a most elegant woman, tall, handsome, dignified, affable. She is not now young, having children grown up. I got home at 8 o'clock in the evening, after walking 13 miles.

The next afternoon, I ascended a mountain not far distant; the view from it was new, and pleasing. After tea, Mr. & Mrs. St. George went with me again to the same mountain, to shew me a famous well on the top, which they had heard of, but had never seen. A countryman, of whom they were asking where to find it, offered to go with us; and, as we laboured up the mountain side, told us many a superstitious, wonderful tale. The well which we went to see, is shallow, and merely remarkable for curing violent diseases of the eyes;[2] it was first discovered, our

---

[1] No doubt the wretched, snobbish daughter of the retired tanner in Dale St., whose connexion with Miss Weeton (the 'pragmatical schoolmistress') is detailed at some length in volume I.

[2] Strangely enough, Miss Weeton's eyes became much inflamed shortly after marriage; but perhaps the waters lacked potency against such tears.

guide told us, by a blind man, many, many years ago; perhaps 2 or 300; who dreamed that on such a mountain in the Isle of Man, was a well, where, if he would wash, he should recover his sight. He left his dwelling place (I think in Ireland), came, and saw.

Everyone who washes, must leave a deposit near the place, or they will not be cured; and a neighbouring furze bush is literally stuck full of rags, ends of worsted, and bits of paper: money is sometimes left, and a little boy who stole some of it a few years ago, fell sick immediately afterwards, as our guide told us, and died. These deposits are, on a certain night in the year, all taken away by the fairies! The man (who was the *owner* of the mountain) really appeared to believe what he told us. I was surprized to see him tell it with so grave a face; but, as I could not expect to convince him of the absurdity, I looked as grave as he. There are three little springs; I washed my face, dipping my hand alternately in each as I was directed, and then put a piece of paper in the bush.[1]

The following afternoon, I left West Kella, for Douglas, accompanied by Mr. & Mrs. St. George. We walked over the mountains. Mrs. St. George entertained me with many an anecdote of what she had seen in France, in England, and knew of the families in this Island. As to Mr. St. George, he is a surly nonentity; handsome, but far from well-bred. I stopped, and took tea with them at a Mr. Woods, 3 miles from Douglas; after tea, Mrs. St. George came on and slept with me, as she had to breakfast at a friend's house in Douglas next morning, from whence she went back to Mr. Wood's to stay a few days.

[1] Agnes Herbert, in her charming book upon the Isle of Man, devotes a whole chapter to the folklore of the island, during the course of which she says: 'Tradition tells of myriad giants, *bugganes*, trolls, witches, elves and mysterious sprites of all varieties.' But alas!—'There is no connexion between seaside landladies and romance. She is quite the most realistic thing in nature.' Not so, however, a century or more ago; for Miss Weeton's landlady evinced a lively curiosity in her lodger, scenting a 'romance'.

The very long walk I had taken on the 5th. and the repeated ones just after, with so little intermission, caused blisters on my feet, and prevented them healing; and after I returned from W. Kella, I was obliged to rest a few days, amusing myself with short walks, writing, and visiting Mrs. Dodson, where, for the last 3 weeks I have spent almost half my time; she is extremely kind to me, and urges me to spend more time with her than is altogether convenient, as I wished to have seen a few places yet, that my frequent visits to her have prevented.

To find my society so much courted, is highly grateful to me; particularly after being treated at Leigh and at Holland as if I were a creature deserving every punishment that contempt and violence could inflict; and at best, better forgotten, than thought of. Were I to tell you, my dear Ann, how flatteringly I am treated, how highly complimented, by Mrs. D. and her acquaintances; how chearful, agreeable, intelligent, or humorous they profess to think me; you would justly condemn my excess of vanity. It was always my wish to please; but till I left Holland, I never so easily succeeded as I appear to have done since. Your sister sometimes says that never poor creature was so harassingly situated as I was, or a lot cast amongst such a strange-tempered set of mortals; for my aunt Barton, Mrs. Braithwaite, Mrs. Weeton, and Miss Chorley, are all notoriously ill-tempered, proud, and overbearing. Since I left Up-Holland, I have seen more of the world, care for it less, know better how to please, and am ten times more happy.

I set out on the 16th. with a design of walking to the top of Snafield, if the unusual coldness of the day, and lowering aspect of the sky, would permit. I often hesitated as I went—looked around me—meditated to return; yet still my feet carried me onward. A sort of irresistible impulse impelled me; perhaps, thought I, to my destruction, for mists are floating thickly round; but as the time of my departure is very near, I may not have another day to spare. When I had got about 6 miles from Douglas, I was in the midst of a dreary moor, terminated by mountains, over which the sun strongly gleamed every now and then. My heart ached at the sight of so barren a prospect, and with uncertainty whether to proceed; but curiosity surmounted caution, and I went on, apparently the only human being within view. The passing clouds flew swiftly, and light and darkness alternately covered the face of nature. There was a wildness in the scene and in the state of the air that impressed an idea of woe and desolation. The wind blew furiously, whistling sharply amongst the furze, sometimes moaning amongst the rocks like the voice of a human being in distress. It was a day to impress gloom, awe, and dread, and I felt as if *I* were the miserable creature doomed to experience it, with only now and then a bright ray of hope. I felt a sort of melancholy pleasure in the contemplation, as I walked on over a mountain road. Snafield, at length, reared his lofty head, and when I was about a mile from his summit, the road terminated, and I had to walk over peat-bog and swamp, wet and slippery to a degree. When I had passed over this, I was soon at the top; the wind was here a complete tempest, roaring most loudly; my slender figure could not bear up against it. I attempted to walk over a heap of stone piled on the highest point, but was blown down instantly. Determined that the wind should not entirely conquer me, I crept over on my hands and knees, though with great difficulty, and then added my mite to the heap, by placing a stone on the top. I ran to the opposite end of the mountain top, the wind urging me forward so impetuously, that I was nearly precipitated down the side, which was extremely steep; with difficulty I faced about, and returned to the heap of stones. I stood for a few minutes to view the prospect; the sea was in view all round, but no land beyond.

The surrounding country had a mistiness upon it, that obscured its beauty though it did not hide its features. I looked up and saw a large black cloud hang over me, one end of which I could almost touch! Terrified lest I should be enveloped in a fog, I ran down with the utmost speed, my senses and my breath almost battered out of me with the wind, and my fright not at all contributing to restore them. Nearly at the bottom, I saw the skeleton of a sheep. And I too, may die here, thought I, if I cannot get away before the cloud settles; for it is cold enough to starve me totally, and I am so far from any human habitation, that I shall soon be lost. And, thinking how *uncomfortable* it would be to lie dead in such a place, unburied, my cloaths battered off my body by the winds, my flesh pecked off by sea gulls, and my naked bones bleached by the weather till they were as white as those of the sheep, I heaved a sigh! . . . when, such is the mutability of my disposition, I burst out into a loud laugh at the charming picture my imagination had drawn. For some paces, I had been so busied with it, I had forgot the cloud, the mist, and my own danger; but now, looking up, I saw it had all passed away. Other clouds were fast approaching, and some of them might settle, so I walked homewards, and arrived safely, feeling as little fatigue after a walk of 20 miles, as if I had scarcely walked four.

On the 19th., I had sat at home all morning, and part of the afternoon, reading, and writing to you, when, at 4 o'clock, I heard the Friends would sail that evening at 7. The summons was sudden, as I did not expect it to sail till the 20th. However, I took a hasty leave of Mrs. Dodson and Mrs. Singleton's, and prepared as fast as I could for my exit. I sent to the washerwoman for cloaths she ought to have sent home the day before; and the stupid woman would not let me have them till she had finished ironing them! Four times did I send without effect, and the distance was almost half a mile. The vessel, I heard, was moving from the pier! You may suppose what a trepidation I was in; but, as expressions of anger or vexation could be of no service, I quietly sate myself down, and appeared at least to be patient. At last, the cloaths were brought, and, hastily locking them into my box, I hurried down to the pier. . . . The vessel was off!!

I wanted to hire a boat; the men said they would not go for less than 5s. 'Very well then,' I answered, 'I shall not go,' and was returning, when they said they would take me for 2s. I got into the boat; the sea rolled awfully, and the Friends alternately mounted, and then sunk, almost out of sight, sailing at a furious rate. I found it would be impossible to reach it; the boat I was in could never live in such a sea, so I ordered the men to turn about, and I again landed in Douglas. I was convinced the men must know they could not reach the vessel when they took me into their boat, and I would therefore only give them 1s., with which they were obliged to be contented. They made the attempt, merely by way of getting something for drink, but were almost as much disappointed as myself.

June 21st.

I am now, my dear Ann, closing my adventures here, as I have taken a place in the Dutchess, which sails tonight (Sunday), so I have only been detained 2 days.

I am much pleased with my visit to the Island; it will afford me a fund of entertaining reflection in many a lonely hour, and subject for conversation in society. The renewal of my acquaintance with Mrs. Dodson has proved highly gratifying, and in every point of view I rejoice that I came. I have received a great deal of pleasure, and have not bought it dearly. £7 will include every expence of my journey, travelling, lodging, eating, and servants.

I shall not soon again, perhaps, have an opportunity of rambling in a country rich and romantic; and I shall feel a degree of regret at taking a final leave of this beautiful Isle; for, most likely I shall not come again. I shall often think of the times when I sat on the rocks at Douglas-Head, the air calm and clear, the mountains, vales, scattered huts, farm houses, gentlemen's country seats, spread wide and far; on one hand the town encircling the bay; on the other, the sea spread out to a great distance beneath my feet, the waves dashing unceasingly against the rocks, and bounded far, almost as the eye could see, by English mountains—many a yawning chasm in the rocks, the sea-gulls hovering over them, and the fishing boats rocking on the water—altogether form a noble view. The hours I have spent here, have been hours of luxury indeed! Here, totally alone, my thoughts expanded with the prospect; and, free and unrestrained as the air I breathed, I was happy as mortal could be.

Were there any lakes here, this Island would be a paradise, but the streams descend so rapidly from the mountains, all the way to the sea, that they cannot form any, nor any rivers of consequence; many a noisy little rivulet runs down the glens; and many a little thatched hut is scattered along the banks, which, though they look beautifully romantic just now, must be wretched habitations in winter; for, being built with uncemented stone, the wind and rain must beat through a thousand crevices. The poor natives have one advantage here; the proximity of the sea air, whilst it renders the summers more cool, makes the winters less severe, the snow melting soon after it falls; and the frost is of shorter duration, and less intensity, than in most parts of England. They shelter themselves from the storms, by building most of their huts just under the

45

mountains; which are, many of them, cultivated to their summits. The people can have as much turf[1] as they please, for the labour of getting it; which is a great blessing where coals are so dear. An attempt is now making, for the first time, to procure coals near Peel, a seam having lately been discovered there; it is yet uncertain whether it is sufficient to afford the proprietors any hope of success.

The laws are very mild here, and seldom enforced in capital offences; even murder goes unpunished!! To the credit of the people, it is seldom committed; but 4 or 5 instances within 10 or 15 years, of which there were sufficient proof, were unnoticed by the laws. Yesterday, as a very uncommon thing, two women were publickly whipped in the market for theft;[2] petty thefts are very frequent; house-breaking seldom, or never heard of, or high-way robbery. Frauds and imposition of all kinds are practised to a great extent by the majority of the people; and litigious lawsuits are perpetually carrying on, in which the unwary stranger suffers most severely; for knavish indeed must that foreigner be, who can outwit a Manksman; yet the English, or Irish, have only to thank themselves for it; for, much to their discredit, the Manks have only been their pupils, and have paid dearly for their learning. A few, and but a few, 'retain their integrity to the last.' Happy are they, for they will meet with a joyful reward.

Liverpool: July 5th.

My rambles are now, my dear Ann, completed for the present; and my rambling account of them. If they afford you entertainment, I shall be pleased; if you feel a more animating sentiment, I shall be delighted; for, in propor-

---

[1] Presumably peat-turfs; the attempt to procure coal upon the island proved abortive.

[2] Whipping in public was abolished (at least, in England) five years later.

tion as I contribute to the innocent enjoyment of others, so do I feel happy.

My walks during my residence in the Island, have been many and long. I have set down in a concise journal the number of miles I walked whilst in it, rather setting down too little than too much; and I find they amount to at least 203.

You will have received your sister's letter before you receive this; we are afraid to give you the expence of postage, and therefore wait, to send our letters by a private hand to Dublin. I have been quite anxious that your sister should send her letter, even by post, rather than delay it any longer, as it is long since you heard from her; at last she has sent it, and my dear girl's heart will, in a day or two from the present moment, be relieved from a little load of anxiety, which I fear has possessed it some time.

I am leaving Liverpool on Friday next (July 10th), and have, ever since my return, been extremely busy. After I am settled in my new habitation, I shall give your sister my address; and as soon as she informs you, I hope you will write to me.

Mr. Gunrie was married on the 30th. of June, to a Miss Jones, whose parents are lately come from Wales to settle here; we are told she has a fortune of £8,000— Well done Gunrie, at last!

*   *   *

Five days later Miss Weeton had set off towards Yorkshire, there to commence upon two years' domestic servitude, Governess once again.

HIGH ROYD
NEAR
HUDDERSFIELD
JULY 1812–JUNE 1814

HIGH ROYD
NEAR
HUDDERSFIELD
JULY 1812–JUNE 1814

*O*N *April 11th, 1812, William Cartwright's mill at Rawfolds in Liversedge was attacked by the Luddites. Two or three years earlier, Cartwright had begun to introduce shearing frames, which displaced labour, thus creating much local distress and bad feeling. Courageous, resolute, but coldly unsympathetic, Cartwright slept nightly in his mill for six weeks prior to the expected attack. One hundred and fifty men, drawn from different localities, assembled in one of Sir George Armitage's fields, three miles distant from the mill, very variously armed. The attack was launched shortly after midnight, and met with a spirited defence on the part of the garrison—ten altogether. The story has often been told—the frightful sufferings of two wounded attackers, designedly left for hours to suffer where they fell; their subsequent dreadful agony under the alleged third-degree methods to extract information in the bedroom of the Inn, whilst soldiers rode up and down outside dragooning the menacing crowds; the militant parson, doctor, and justice, hovering expectantly over the dying Booth—' "Can you keep a secret?" gasped the dying man. "I can," eagerly replied the expectant clergyman. "So can I," replied poor Booth, and soon after calmly expired.'[1] All this is history—and fiction, too, of the highest order, in Charlotte Brontë's 'Shirley'.*

One week later Cartwright was shot at as he galloped home from the court martial of a soldier who had refused to do his duty in the mill, and fire on the attackers. On that same day Mr. Joseph Armitage, the future employer of Miss Weeton, and son

---

[1] *The Skilled Labourer, 1760–1832*, by J. L. and B. Hammond.

of a locally famous Justice of the Peace, Sir George Armitage (in whose field the rioters had assembled for the projected attack), found himself singled out for attentions of a particularly unpleasant character—for one of his type. Stones were thrown at windows of his Lockwood house, followed by shots as he and his wife lay abed. Charlotte Brontë mentions this incident in 'Shirley', though she falls into the trifling error of placing the incident before, instead of after, the Cartwright affair.

Mr. Armitage, jun., was no magistrate Radcliffe—or for that matter, no son of his father's mettle; he promptly packed up, and retired to a house a little farther removed from the scenes of trouble, giving Governess Weeton a rather specious reason for his reactions to that scare of the previous April. At High Royd, recently vacated by his worthy father, he was permitted to remain in peace, there to entrust the civilizing and educating of his children to the capable hands of one who was quickly to find how grossly mismanaged the parental discipline had been.

The better-circumstanced children of Honley were perforce governess-educated, or not at all. Apart from possible dame-school, and the primitive education sponsored by the newly established Sunday Schools, there seems to have been no organized local attempt to provide elementary education until 1816, in which year a National School was opened, 'agreeably to Bell's system of education, and on the principles and doctrine of the Church of England'.

So Miss Weeton entered upon her duties, with a clear field before her. She arrived at High Royd at the tail-end of the Luddite disturbances in the summer of 1812—a period in our history which almost beggars description; but as it concerned her little, so it shall be accorded but a brief note here. Suffice it to say that both North and South were seething with labour troubles; that Yorkshire in particular was giving occasion for much anxious thought (and prompt action) on the part of the authorities; and that the whole county was represented in Parliament by but two Members, notwithstanding the fact that the wool exports amounted to one half of all exports. All around High Royd silent tragedies were

*enacting (some not quite so silent), as power looms made redundant
the old domestic industry; and a Society for Purposes of Self-Pro-
tection, formed by the leading inhabitants, had been formed as far
back as the year 1805. High Royd overlooked the tiny village
of Honley, with its population of 2,529, almost equally divided
between the sexes—not forgetting the donkeys; for, so many of
these animals were employed for the transport of cloth by the
weavers that it was a common saying that there were more
donkeys than people. And now there was curfew at 10, with
Scots Greys, King's Bays, and 15th Hussars patrolling around,
and putting a stop to all courting under the moon, though not
interfering in another popular institution of nation-wide popularity,
and one which Miss Weeton was debarred from witnessing by
reason of her close confinement at High Royd; however, the son
of the local Postmaster (who was such a special favourite with the
elder Armitage and doubtless with the corresponding governess),
saw enough as a stripling boy to sicken him for life of Bull-
baiting—in England—c. 1812.*

*'My father [it is the author of the History of Honley who is
speaking] obtained a place nearer the stake to which an animal
was tethered that was reported to be of great courage. After
waving red flags before his eyes, blowing pepper up his nose,
twisting his tail, goading him with iron prongs, &c., the animal
refused to encounter the dogs. When pinned and brought to his
knees by a tenacious animal, my father always declared with
conviction that he saw tears as large as peas running down the
eyes of the bull, and that his bellowings were pitiful to hear.'*

*Inevitably these same villagers made vulgar sport of the senile
courting of which Miss Weeton was to be the object, and which
came under their direct notice—in church.*

*The Armitage family, as the oldest one in the district, dating from
the fourteenth century, holds pride of place in the chapter upon
Honley families in Mrs. Jagger's History of Honley. And little
bags of 'Heighroyd' earth attached to old documents (as the
custom was) attest the strong roots the family had in their mother*

earth. John Ermytage, that capable business man who exported cloth to Ireland in the sixteenth century, figures in Liverpool's annals, under the year 1574.

'*The good Marchant, Mr. John Armetage, of Farnley Tyas (High Royd) in the Countie of York, alais Clothier, with rich stocke from Liv'pole to Knockfergus after shipwreck came to hand and fell among the Rebell Kernes, and were then most villianouslie murthered, slayne, and cut in pieces as if the vilest kind of fleshe, contrarie to the will and pleasure of God.*'

To the trade of clothiers, the Armitages added coal-getting, and served the usual public offices, culminating in the famous 'Justice' Armitage, father of Miss Weeton's employer. Mr. George Armitage, 'Th' Justice', was born at High Royd in 1738, and dealt out justice during very difficult and dangerous times. Huddersfield and Holmfirth being without Police Courts, delinquents were brought to High Royd, in the entrance hall of which place Mr. (later Sir) George dispensed justice of a pretty rough and ready kind, attired in the flowered vest, silk stockings, knee breeches, and diamond buckles of a former generation, complete with powdered hair. Lawless to a degree were the Honleyites of those times, hardly one of whom but could boast a lost finger, ear, or nose severed in some local squabble, or inter-village vendetta. The local postman himself tipped the Justice into the mud, during a contest for precedence in the highway.

It will be seen that Sir George vacated High Royd in favour of his son in the year 1812, taking up his residence, along with his wife and daughter, at near-by Park-riding. He died in 1815, and was buried at Almondbury.

Joseph Armitage, J.P., Deputy Lieut. of the W. Riding, eldest son of 'Justice' Armitage, did not stay long at High Royd,[1] purchasing Milnsbridge House from Sir Joseph Radcliffe in the year 1820; these two justices had their mettle tested during the 'plug' riots[2]

---

[1] Whilst still at High Royd, during the years 1816–19, he served the office of Constable.

[2] So-called, because of bands of men who put mills out of commission by the simple process of removing boiler plugs.

of the '40's. Joseph Armitage erected the first woollen mill at Milns-bridge in 1822, to find employment for his sons. Another mill, of which the foundation stone was laid by Sir Francis Burdett, was erected by him in 1838. Part of the profits derived from tremendously long hours worked by his employees of both sexes, and of ages from 6 to 60, he set aside for the building of Milnsbridge Church, to the erection and furnishing of which his daughter largely contributed.

High Royd was in other hands from 1820 to 1884, when a grandson of his returned to the family seat, after having 'restored' the place—though we may be quite sure Mrs. Jagger meant no disrespect when she wrote:

> *'The present appearance of High Royd House, though belonging to one of the oldest families in the place, does not indicate any distinct period of architecture. It has been so altered during successive generations that I believe only the cellars remain of the original structure.'*

High Royd was sold out of the family in the year 1917, though descendants still reside in the district.

✲   ✲   ✲

With a minimum of self-advertisement (not even the Braithwaites were aware of her departure) Miss Weeton left Liverpool for High Royd, the residence of her future employers, on July 10th. The circumstances attending her engagement were a little peculiar, and not a little calculated to embarrass brother Tom and to exacerbate his wife.

It will be remembered that Miss Weeton once made some rather tactless inquiries *re* an old flame of Tom's—a Miss J. Lyon, of Preston.[1] From this source apparently came tentative inquiries for a governess, with a hint that the offer of Miss Weeton's services would be considered by the friend, a Mrs. Armitage, of Yorkshire, on whose behalf Miss Lyon made the inquiry direct to Tom. Tom, by no means anxious to oblige

---

[1] Letter 390—that convenient hold-all—discloses that in the year 1803 (that same year in which Tom married Jane Scott) Miss Weeton not only treated Tom to the Preston Guild jollification, but also Miss J. Lyon on his account—an outlay of £16 which had to be made up at the expense of many meagre meals later on.

his sister, but certainly anxious to oblige Miss Lyon, took the safe course of conveying the offer to his sister by a third party. Mrs. Armitage had relatives both in Manchester and Liverpool, and no doubt Miss Weeton came to the conclusion that there was nothing extraordinary in the coincidence of a friend of Tom acquainting her with this welcome opportunity; it was only after her arrival in Yorkshire that she learned of Tom's instrumentality, after he had had the impudence to solicitously make inquiries in Liverpool as to the whereabouts of his sister.

Her first letter following upon her arrival at High Royd, is addressed to the independent Bessy Price, who was still burdened with the presence in her new home of the outrageous Mrs. Edwards (a married sister of her husband), as also his unmarried sister, and who had consequently placed no obstacles in the way of Miss Weeton's departure. But the governess was sadly at a loss for correspondents these days, and Mrs. Price was promptly subjected to the test of real friendship —that of paying postage upon a double sheet.

I had a very pleasant ride to Manchester the day I left you, for I soon got the seat by the coachman, who was very civil and communicative, and described every object or place worth notice. After dinner at Manchester, I took a walk; *chance* led me to the old Church, and through the College-yard; from thence I walked down a road which led to a large building. I went up to it, and found it was the Lying-in Hospital. 'It won't do for me to be seen here', thought I, and I turned away. Presently I saw a road which I imagined would take me back another way into the town. I went up it, till I was stopped by a wall, which totally prevented any further progress; and, looking up at an inscription, I found I was at the back door of the aforesaid Hospital! I was both diverted and vexed at the accident. 'Chance! thou hast too much to do here', said I, 'thou needest not have brought me, for I have nothing to give thee.' If any person who had a slight acquaintance with me had been passing by just then, and seen me walk up to both doors, they would certainly have thought I intended to gain admittance, and might so have reported it to some persons elsewhere—at Leigh for instance, at Wigan, or at Holland.

The next morning was wet, and I was obliged to travel inside the coach, in consequence of which I was very sickly all the way, and for two or three days after I got here, was very unwell indeed, owing to the fatigue and sickness. Had I walked all the way in two days, I should not have been so ill; want of air affects me materially.

Highroyd is a country house, four miles from Huddersfield; it stands on very high ground, and will be much exposed to the storms and cold of Winter; but, as Mr. Armitage has plenty of coals on his own estate, only a few hundred yards off, we shall have fire enough; and I rejoice exceedingly thereat.

He and his wife are young people, not 30 yet, I dare say, either of them. Mr. A. is engaged in the woollen trade, has a handsome fortune of his own, and had another with his wife, though their parents are all living; at whose death, I suppose, they will have considerably more. They have no carriage, no in-door man-servant; there are four women servants. They kept a man till lately, but as Mr. Armitage's house at Lockwood was one of the first that was attacked by the Luddites a few months ago, he has not ventured since to keep a man in his house, as many gentlemen have been betrayed by their servants, who have been discovered to be of the Luddite party. Mr. A. has but lately come to this house; he had only just got well settled in it, when I arrived. His father had long wanted him to come to it, but his wife and he objected to so very retired a situation. However, the affair at Lockwood (3 miles distant), and the threats of his father to leave the estate out of the family if he did not come to it now, induced him to comply; the house and lands, all together, are a very pretty present from the old gentleman; but the situation is too retired for a young man who has any relish for society. There has been a good deal of company since I came; but, though I dine or drink tea with them, I am obliged to leave the room so immediately after I have swallowed it, that I may truly be said to see little of them.

My time is totally taken up with the children; from 7 o'clock in the morning, till half past 7, or 8 at night. I cannot lie any longer than 6 o'clock in a morning; and, if I have anything to do for myself, in sewing, writing, &c., I must rise sooner. At 7, I go into the nursery, to hear the children their prayers, and remain with them till after they have breakfasted, when I go out with them whilst they play; and am often so cold, that I join in their sports, to warm myself. About half past 8, I breakfast with Mr. & Mrs. Armitage, and then return again to the children till 9, when we go into the school-room till 12. We then bustle on our bonnets, &c., for play, or a short walk. At One, we bustle them off again, to dress for dinner, to which we sit down at a quarter past; the children always dine with their parents. By the time dinner is well over, it is 2 o'clock, when we go into school, and remain till 5. Whilst I am at tea in the parlour, the children eat their suppers in the nursery. I then go to them, and remain with them till 7, either walking out of doors, or playing within, as the weather may permit. I then hear their prayers, and see them washed; at half past 7, they are generally in bed.

Mrs. Armitage conducts her house in so excellent a manner, that we are as punctual as the clock. I never have to wait of any one; and I take care that no one shall have to wait of me. It is the same with all in the house; breakfast, dinner, tea, or supper, are always within five minutes of the appointed time. The only thing I feel inclined to grumble at, is the being obliged to attend the children at their play in a morning, as they are only in the yard. I should voluntarily choose to do it sometimes, but the nursery maid, I should think, would be sufficient in general; however, I get a little air, and it will render me less subject to take colds; it will do me good, though I don't like it.

The children, though well ordered by their parents, when out of their sight are as unruly, noisy, insolent, quarrelsome, and ill-tempered a set, as I ever met with. I am beginning to get them to pay some respect to my mandates, and perhaps by and bye, I may to my requests; but I assure you, I have had, and still have, a tough task to perform; and if Mr. & Mrs. Armitage had not given me every authority, in the most liberal manner, I must have despaired of doing any good. A few days ago, I felt a necessity of proceeding to some very severe methods; certain, almost, at the same time, I should meet the displeasure of Mr. & Mrs. A. in consequence, when they came to be informed; but how great was my satisfaction, when they expressed their approbation of the method and severity of punishment which I had inflicted. It has given me spirits to proceed with tenfold more confidence, and a greater desire to please them, than before. The little creatures are very affectionate to me already; and of the three younger ones, I think I can make something. Miss A., the eldest, is the bad sheep that infects the flock: punishment or reward make no lasting impression; I fear she is naturally depraved. Though 7 years of age,[1] she has no ideas of common modesty; it is a wrong thing in parents to inure children to be stript entirely in the nursery, whilst washing. I am endeavouring to correct this, by degrees, as no innovation must be made suddenly that affects the mistress of the house or the servants.

[1] Sarah Ann, born 29 July 1805.

I have begun to teach the children to dance; and a sweet boy of 5 years old,[1] to write; and he does both, admirably. Their instruction, and sewing for Mrs. A., keep me very busy the whole of school-time; I begin again to know the value of minutes, and to be very careful to waste none of them.[2]

Give my love to Ann when you write; and in your letter to me, let me have every information respecting her worth your trouble.

To MRS. DODSON. Douglas. Isle of Man.

Highroyd. Aug. 18. 1812

Feeling myself *comfortably* settled in my new abode, I shall attempt to give you some account of my proceedings since I quitted you. You will sometimes find that I relate little events in my letters, with extreme minuteness. I will tell you why I do so, as I know you like to have a reason for everything. Great events seldom occur in common life; and where an epistolary correspondence is frequent, trifles must compose the greater part of it; and if those trifles are not accurately delineated, they sink to nothing. To me, the everyday pleasures and anxieties in the domestic life of my friends, have an interest at all times; and I relate my own little affairs, in hopes to draw forth a similar communication from them.

I had not left your shores above an hour, when I grew very sickly, and for many hours, was extremely ill; so much so, that when I arrived in Liverpool, I could not walk home, and was obliged to get a coach. That voyage

[1] George, born Sept. 1806.

[2] It has been objected that Miss Weeton's somewhat limited experience in that capacity, hardly entitles her to be particularized as a Governess. That being so, another, and a far greater governess, has masqueraded too long under false colours, having even less claim upon the score of time served than her obscure prototype; for Charlotte Brontë, twice employed as Governess, yet spent little over a year in all in the service of others as such.

of only 24 hours, had reduced me almost to a skeleton; the difference in my size and strength, between the day I left you and that of my arrival in Liverpool, was really astonishing, and I was more than a week before I recovered either strength or spirits.

Be kind enough to tell Mrs. Singleton, that I forwarded the potted lobster by the canal as soon as I could get it out of the Custom-house, the day after I landed.

What troubles and turmoils people bring themselves into, by burthening themselves with children! Mr. and Mrs. A. might have kept their carriage, had they only the root and stem of the tree to have supported; but they have *foolishly* contrived to increase, and multiply, so many branches, that they must deny themselves many a gratification, in order to provide those branches with leaves. A fortnight ago, the eldest of six children completed her seventh year; and another will, I suppose, make its entrance into this comical bustling world by Christmas. I don't suppose the parents are either of them more than thirty, so they may have at least a dozen children yet, in addition to the present number. Heaven help them![1] . . . though indeed they don't seem to want it; I may rather crave it for myself, if I stay amongst them, for I am quite busy enough as it is; you don't know how much you are indebted for this scrawl; it has been almost the work of a week, my leisure moments are so very limited.

The children appear to have been allowed full liberty to a riotous degree; yet Mrs. A. seems to expect that I shall now, speedily, bring them into the exactest order . . . the task is a most arduous one! The eldest, a girl, is of that strange kind of temper, that she will purposely do the very thing that she thinks will excite most displeasure. I often

---

[1] Heaven help them, indeed—the poor wretch of a wife was to become the mother of fifteen children! Joseph Armitage spared no one, his wife least of all.

wish that I could exchange her for one of yours. Of this girl, I shall never reap any credit, I fear; but the 2d, a boy, not six yet, will evince to his friends whether or no I possess any talents in the education of children. He is a fine little fellow, and understands, with great quickness, every thing I attempt to teach him. I have begun to instruct him in writing, and the elements of grammar and arithmetic; and they all learn to dance. I have four under my care.

Mr. and Mrs. A. are pleasant and easy in their temper and manners, and make my situation as comfortable as such a one can be; for it is rather an awkward one for a female of any reflection or feeling. A *governess* is almost shut out of society; not choosing to associate with servants, and not being treated as an equal by the heads of the house or their visiters, she must possess some fortitude and strength of mind to render herself tranquil or happy; but indeed, the master or mistress of a house, if they have any goodness of heart, would take pains to prevent her feeling her inferiority. For my own part, I have no cause of just complaint; but I know some that are treated in a most mortifying manner.

When I was last in Liverpool, I had great reason to regret that I had never learned French; for, if I had only understood that in addition to my other attainments, I could have had a situation where I should have received a salary of a hundred a year, in a family of distinction. I could have obtained a situation in Westmoreland, in a wealthy family there, had I only been acquainted with that language. My Mother used to think it a very useless acquisition to the generality of Englishwomen.[1] She had

---

[1] An eighteenth-century author, Witenhall Wilkes, in his *Letter of Genteel and Moral Advice to a Young Lady*, echoes Mrs. Weeton's prejudices *re* the learning of French:

'Though I am not against a young Lady's amusing herself with French, Italian or Latin, yet since it is English that one educated in England must

no idea how great a loss my ignorance of it would one day be to me; for she never thought of my leaving Holland, but to live with my brother; upon this, she always calculated . . . how short and ill-judging is human fore-sight.

Huddersfield, from which I am only 4 miles distant, has been the principal scene of riot, depredation, and alarm. Mr. Armitage's house was the first, or one of the first, that was attacked a few months ago. He then resided at Lock-wood, still nearer Huddersfield, and he and Mrs. Armitage were shot at, and stones thrown in at the windows one night, as they lay in bed. They were obliged, in conse-quence of this, to be constantly guarded by a party of military, until they could quit the house to come to High-royd, where they have resided about 3 months, unmolested. Since I came here, an attack has been made upon one man of the name of Hinchcliffe, who resided only a mile or two from here; he was shot at, and blinded in consequence, but not killed.[1] I have heard of no other sanguinary or riotous event lately; and, for my own part, feel no alarm. I care little what becomes of me; all I wish is, that when I am tried at the great day, I may not be found wanting; and when my days on earth are terminated, it will make little difference whether my life has been long or short.

have constant use of, it is obvious to think that to be the Language she ought chiefly to cultivate and wherein most care should be taken to polish and perfect her Stile.'

[1] 'John Hinchcliffe of Upper Thong, parish clerk of Holmfirth, told the Rev. Mr. Keeling, whether correctly or not it does not appear, that John Schofield was implicated in Luddism. Schofield accordingly was arrested, but as there was no evidence against him he was released. Shortly after, Hinchcliffe was visited at night, according to his own story, by two men, who abused him for informing against Schofield and shot him in the left eye. Hinchcliffe was unable to identify either of them.' Hammond, *The Skilled Labourer, 1760-1832.*

Schofield rather foolishly absconded, but was recaptured; and Hinch cliffe himself was spirited over the border by the authorities, for safe keeping. Eventually Schofield produced a good alibi, and was acquitted.

To MISS C. BRAITHWAITE   Highroyd: Aug. 28th. 1812.

I am beginning to write to you in a very melancholy mood. I hope I shall not infect you, but that my own spirits may be exhilarated by the mental exertion; for I have often found writing to have that effect. Will you permit me to give vent a little to my present feelings? The mighty crime that has estranged me from an aunt and a brother, still remains unknown to me; and that I can so easily be forgotten by them, so strangely treated on such slight grounds (for slight they must be, or I should be conscious of the offence), is a matter of continual astonishment, and continual conjecture. The unfeeling may accuse me of folly in permitting the ill-treatment I cannot avoid, to make so deep an impression—it is easy for those to do so, who have some relatives to cling to, some one who can sympathise when they suffer; but let them be deprived of all, and then hear what they would say. Had I any domestic ties, the unkindness of those without doors would only mortify me for a short time; but having none in whom I can confide, none to whom I can speak my griefs, I dwell upon one depressing subject altogether, having nothing to divert my attention from it. Write to me before long, and tell me how my aunt's health is, and any Holland news you can collect; and particularly how you all are at the Abbey, for I have not yet learnt the agreeable qualification of forgetting old friends.

At this point, she informs Charlotte of her recent trip to the Isle of Man, and proceeds to divert her with the foibles of the daughter of the late Rev. Mr. Prescott.

With Mrs. Dodson, I was unusually talkative; the sight of each other brought in a torrent of ideas, and the days that were gone again flitted before us. You would have been diverted to have heard what a *gabble* we raised whenever we met; and lest one should have a greater share of the beforementioned elegantly termed *gabble* than the other, we occasionally repeated—'now it's my turn.' Mrs. D. is just the same kind of woman that Miss Prescott was; she does not even look older, *I* think. She fancies herself very thin!!! and very nimble!!! Oh dear, oh dear, I should be just as sorry to walk 10 miles with her, as she would with me. I would certainly prefer talking with her 10 hours, for she lets me give vent to all my odd whims and saucy speeches, and seems entertained with them; which is encouragement to go on. . . . Not so, Mrs. T. Weeton. She, on such occasions, would look wondrous wise!—or wondrous sour! not being capable of understanding me, and thinking what I said was either very silly or very insulting. When I have been at Leigh, poor Tom and I have suddenly become *chop-fallen* many a time in the midst of a hearty laugh, when we found, by Mrs. Weeton's dignified looks, that we were not better than a couple of fools. Heaven help us! When *I* keep a carriage, I will not have an owl for my crest, for there is no wisdom in mere gravity.

Mrs. D.'s 3 girls are fine children; her boy, in mind and manners, is quite an unlicked cub, though a great favourite with mamma. Mr. Singleton gave me a most satyrical account of many of the exiles in the Island; I was highly entertained with it, though it left an unpleasant impression. I would have taken down his anecdotes in my memorandum book, if I could have found any other title for them but that of 'The Scandalous chronicle'. There are a strange set of beings in that Island, particularly in, and about, Douglas; it is the *wicked* world, and nothing but the *wicked* world, in miniature. Mr. Allen, at whose house I lodged, called Douglas, Botany Bay, and the strangers, convicts.

Douglas is a nasty, dirty, filthy, scrubby, mean, pitiful (help me out with some more pretty epithets, for mine are exhausted), ill-built town.

I have begun a correspondence with Mrs. Dodson, a little reluctantly I confess, as thinking I should not now have much time for writing; but she would *insist* upon it.

I am going, next week, to commence head-house-keeper for 3 weeks, as Mrs. A. is going with a party to South-Port, near Ormskirk;[1] they have a house to themselves. Mr. A. will only go for a few days, as business must be attended to.

Let me again request you to write soon. I wish to know how you all are; I hope, better than when I last heard. And scold me heartily if you think proper, for the contrast between the beginning, and a paragraph near the conclusion of this letter; for indeed, I think myself reprehensible in giving vent to my thoughts and ideas on both subjects.[2]

To MISS WINKLEY, at F. French's, Esq. Sopwell-Hall. Roscrea. Ireland

Highroyd-House. Oct. 15 to Oct. 30th. 1812.

You can scarcely imagine, my dear Ann, how much I was rejoiced at the receipt of your letter; more particularly so, as it was the only one I had then received since I came into Yorkshire. I was beginning to be most seriously angry at your sister's neglect, when, the other day, I received her first letter; and such an one, that it banished almost all my displeasure.

It gives me great pleasure to find that you like your situation better than you did; and I hope that you will even like it better still; for I really am very desirous that you should remain in it. You will be so much benefitted and improved by it; the advantages you will obtain, will

[1] Surely this precise location of a place within easy distance from her correspondent's village was never inserted in the actual letter? It affords one more indication that the copy-books were written with another motive than merely her own gratification and future amusement.

[2] Referring to scatological passages deleted at the publisher's request as rather too objectionable for general reading.

far outbalance the mortifications you endure to gain them. You were in danger of becoming a vain, selfish, indolent character; you will now, I think, secure to yourself the opposite virtues—humility, benevolence, and industry. The pains which you say Mrs. French takes with you, is a great kindness in her, and I hope she will, in return, receive a part of the benefit as well as yourself; which she certainly will if you stay with her. But how do you manage, Ann, to go through a course of reading? For really, I find it almost as much as I can do, to keep my clothes in repair, and write to my correspondents, besides reading a newspaper now and then. I had pleased myself with the idea, that when I came here, I should have an opportunity to teach myself music and drawing; that airy castle, however, is vanished, as I am never a moment free from the children, from 7 o'clock in the morning, till half past 7 at night. I don't complain of this; it is no more than my duty; but certainly a governess is more a prisoner than any servant in the house.[1]

Last week, we were in danger of being deprived of a very good master, father, and husband, in Mr. Armitage, by a fall from a horse; but providentially he has recovered surprisingly. No limbs are broken, but he was in a senseless state for some hours, that his revival was scarcely expected.

The children have really made a very great progress since my arrival, in their books; but as Mr. A. leaves all

[1] Charlotte Brontë found that even in a 'kindly and friendly household', full measure was exacted of her, and her situation was similar to that of Miss Weeton's in regard to constant and wearying occupation. 'But as her definite requirements were few, she had to eke them out by employing her leisure time in needle-work; and altogether her position was that of "bonne" or nursery governess, liable to repeated and never-ending calls upon her time. This description of uncertain, yet perpetual employment, subject to the exercise of another person's will at all hours of the day, was peculiarly trying to one whose life at home had been full of abundant leisure.' Gaskell, *Life of C. Brontë*.

But in Miss Brontë's case, her employers were at least grateful; and she had not the task of civilizing four limbs of satan.

domestic management to his wife, and she never examines the children, I sometimes feel myself suspected of a neglect, of which I am certainly left at liberty to be guilty during school hours, but of which I never can, or will be guilty. There are some people with whom we cannot soon become acquainted; and others, who are like old friends at the first interview. The former seems to be the case with Mrs. Armitage and me; the idea of receiving wages, and being, in truth, a servant, keeps my spirit down, and throws a degree of reserve over me, which I sometimes think has a correspondant effect on Mrs. A.; and perhaps it is my own fault that she has hitherto treated me in a manner less open than I could wish. How should she know what is the cause of my reserve? For, that it should proceed from diffidence, would be the last thing she would suspect in a woman of 35.

To MRS. SUDLOW,[1] Thurlow Street. Liverpool.

Highroyd: (undated).

You will think I have been a very long time in writing to you; but if you were to see how fully I am occupied, you would scarcely wonder at it. I assure you, I often feel so jaded at night when the children are gone to bed, that I cannot exert resolution enough to take up a pen. When there is no company, I sit alone in an evening, in the school-room. This was part of my stipulation before I came, to have the evening to myself (imagining Mr. & Mrs. A. would not be sorry to be without a third person); and I wished to be at liberty to read, or write, and be at peace after the exercise of mind during the day. Yet really I should be very glad of some society in an evening, it would be such an enjoyment; but there is nobody in the

---

[1] Mrs. Sudlow was apparently a cousin, on the mother's side; probably one of the cheese-mongering Smiths of Dale Street.

house with whom I can be on equal terms, and I know nobody out of it, so I must make myself contented.

Present my best love to every one of your sisters; my second best to your brothers; and say everything that's civil and agreeable for me, to your own loving spousy.

To MISS C. BRAITHWAITE   Highroyd: Dec. 8. 1812.

Oh dear, Catharine! If it had not been to convince you that I am yet in this land of wool-packs, and likely to continue in it, I don't know when I should have written to you. Really, that was an unfortunate piece of news which you heard in the jangling village of Up-Holland— 'that I had returned to Liverpool.' 1st., because it was a f-i-b; and 2dly, because it obliges me to tell you so, after I had resolved, and determined, and concluded, upon letting my pen lie still and sleep for 3 or 4 months this winter.

That my uncle calls me unfeeling and undutiful, sur- prises me still more, when *he knew* my intention of engaging again as a governess; and both he and my aunt *approved* it. My uncle is, indeed, much to be pitied; for he has little comfort. My aunt is not able to attend to him in those little offices that compose enjoyment of domestic life; nor will she keep a decent servant to do the work of the house, or trust to her if she had one. She consequently does many things herself, totally unfit for a person suffering as she does, and increases her illness and my uncle's misery, along with her own. Often has he expressed a wish that I should live with them, and my heart has beat with fear lest my aunt should agree to it, and make the proposal, as I thought myself bound to do what my mother had said, and was apprehensive I should be obliged to tell them why I rejected it. The proposal was never made whilst I lived in Holland, and I therefore never told them, nor anyone else in that village, that my mother had desired I never would live with them.[1] My having promised my mother never to do so, would prevent my ever offering to go to them, if no other reasons withheld me.

Frequently when I have nursed my aunt, and been several hours with her, have I been suffered to go home to my tea, and requested to return again as soon as it was over. Once or twice I staid to make my uncle's tea, sat by whilst he drank it, and was not asked to taste, and went home to make my own. When my brother has been a guest at my house, he has often dined with my uncle, whilst I have dined alone. Feeling so much the want of friends and comforts in my own house, how I have enjoyed the sight of the happy family at yours! It was to me, certainly, as a picture only; but of a most delightful kind; and when I have spent an evening with you, and returned home, it was like quitting light for darkness. How has my heart ached to bid you good-night, and enter my own dismal, dreary dwelling, of which Darkness and Solitude seemed to have taken possession. This may account to you for my conduct once at Mr. Snape's. You know not how bitterly I felt the contrast between that gay party—surrounded by mothers, brothers, and sisters, enjoying health, affluence, and cheerfulness; and myself, who had not one of these. I could have refrained from so violent a fit of crying had it not been for the music and dancing; but my depressed spirits could not bear the sound of music and mirth. I shall never forget that day, and am sorry I ever went, or so conducted myself—I *could not* help it!

I am too comfortable here, my dear Catharine, to have any thoughts of leaving, and have no reason to suppose that my employers are dissatisfied. I love my little pupils,

---

[1] No proposal was made by the aunt, but a pretty broad hint given that she could board with them, on the same terms she was then paying Miss Winkley—which she indignantly spurned.

and receive many an affectionate embrace from them; it must be an advantageous offer indeed, that would now induce me to leave them.

Write soon. If I do not answer soon, be assured it proceeds from real business, and not from indolence or forgetfulness.

To MRS. PRICE   Highroyd. Dec. 22. 1812.

There has been a report in Holland that I had left Yorkshire, and returned to Liverpool; somebody makes themselves busy. I am not likely to leave, that I know of, for I am very comfortable and *contented*. I begin to like Mrs. A. much better than I did, and have no want, but —want of time, which is no great evil. Mrs. A. is really a nice, agreeable woman, and the genteelest woman I have seen since I came into Yorkshire. The manners and dress of the people here are much inferior to those of the same rank in Liverpool; appearances here are not so much attended to as there. I believe I have been thought quite dashing.

I am sometimes invited with Mr. & Mrs. A. to Mr. Armitage's senior, to tea and supper; excepting this, I am totally excluded all society out of the house; and have little but that of children within. The old gentleman's family consists of himself, his wife, and one daughter, a little younger than myself; two women servants, and a boy in livery. He is a justice of the Peace; his residence is about 200 yards hence.[1]

There is a something like selfishness in Mrs. A. that prevents her feeling warmly for anyone. She is a good wife, a good mother, and a good mistress, but she does not seem

[1] At Park-riding, the dower-house to the old seat of High Royd. Miss Marianne Armitage (Miss Weeton's junior by 9 years) proved a most liberal supporter of religious work in later years, and died possessed of the 'many virtues' typical of her age and class.

to carry her heart with her; or, if she does, it is devoid of melting pity; she is not one of whom I should like to make a confidential friend. Mrs. Armitage senior has presented me with a new scarlet stuff gown, in which you may suppose I look very glowing. She is a very generous, charitable, hospitable woman; and when I tell you that all that family are kind-hearted, you will suppose that I am very partial to them.

This part of Yorkshire seems to be principally inhabited by manufacturers and farmers; a plodding, money-getting, good kind of people; even everything in this house is conducted with tradesman-like regularity and bustle; no sitting after breakfast or dinner, as we used to do at Mr. Pedder's. I generally rise from table with some of the meal in my mouth. Yet I like the family far better than Mr. P's; no quarrelling, rioting, or drunkenness here, that used, when I was at Dove-Nest, to terrify me so. Here, I know what I have to do; there, I never did.

I could smile with contempt at my brother's accusations of my fretfulness and dictating spirit. He and Mrs. W. scold me by the hour; and when I attempt to justify myself, will not allow me to say *a word*. Mrs. W. seems to have conceived a most violent hatred against me, and has left no arts untried to bring about a lasting separation between my brother and me. She has been years in effecting it, but has succeeded at last; may Heaven forgive her!

To MISS C. BRAITHWAITE   Highroyd: Jany 14 1813.

I commissioned Mr. Leece, a clerk in Mr. Bird's office, Castle Ditch, to receive my rents for me, and it has been a very culpable neglect in him not to have applied for them long ago. I have written to him upon the subject since I received your letter.

The inhabitants of this part of Yorkshire have had very

anxious hearts lately, in consequence of the assizes at York; and their uneasiness will be some time yet before it be dissipated; for the numbers of turbulent people that must still remain, will have a burning spirit within them for some time. Though Mr. and Mrs. A. are extremely cautious in what they say on the subject, I can discover that they feel very serious uneasiness respecting the Luddites; and, they may well! having been fired at in their bed, and an intimate acquaintance (Mr. Horsfall) murdered, their terror will be some time ere it subsides. Even since the assizes commenced, Mr. Radcliffe's house has been fired into, I have just heard, by some unknown hand. He has been a most active magistrate, and by his means, principally, have the ringleaders been discovered and apprehended. He received, a short time ago, several anonymous letters, threatening his life if the men then in York were executed; these threats did not in the slightest degree intimidate him from proceeding with the utmost activity, and I hope he will not suffer in consequence of so dauntless a spirit. Mr. A's father is a magistrate, and between him and Mr. R., there is a great intimacy, owing to which I hear a great deal of him.[1]

To MISS ANN WINKLEY   Highroyd: Jan 26th 1813.

I could wish that my employers were more frequent observers of my exertions, as I have never, since I came

---

[1] It is a pity that Miss Weeton did not give us the substance of what she heard with regard to the prominent figures during the Luddite terror. Horsfall, a typical hard-headed, masterful, callous manufacturer, having voiced a wish to ride his horse to the girths in Luddite blood, and busied himself in the introduction of the hated frames, was shot at and murdered as he was returning from Huddersfield market, on 28 April. A reward of £2,000 failed to produce the four murderers, and terrorist gangs plundered the countryside, whilst the genuine Luddites secretly drilled by night. It was six months before Horsfall's murderers were apprehended.

With regard to the energetic Mr. Radcliffe, J.P. (afterwards Sir for his pains), he was the terror of the military as well as the Luddite gangs, and the despair of brother magistrates.

here, received the slightest acknowledgement of the improvement of my pupils. It appears like a tacit degree of
dissatisfaction with me; and when I do labour hard indeed,
till my spirits sink with the daily anxiety and exertion of
mind, and the excessive confinement I am kept in injures
my health, it is really mortifying to be left to suppose that
my services are considered as inadequate to the situation
I hold.

As Mr. and Mrs. A. never examine into the progress
their children make, except in a very trifling manner, they
are totally unacquainted with a great part of what their
children learn. A weekly account which I render every
Saturday, and which is totally my own doing, is listened
to with greater indifference than I could wish; and the
children's education has never, that I recollect, been a
subject of conversation since my arrival. For anything
the parents might know, I might teach the children to be
Deists, or Atheists; or, what is almost worse, might never
teach them anything like religion at all. 'Why does God
make lions?' said George one day, 'when they do nothing
but kill and eat us, or anything else they can catch?'
(George has often an idea of the superior excellence of
mankind in general, and of his own in particular). 'If flies
could speak, George,' I answered, 'they would say, why
does God make little children, who do nothing else but
kill us for sport?'

When I arrived, the two eldest could read but few words
of 3 or 4 letters; the 3rd,[1] words of only 2; and the fourth[2]
has his alphabet to learn; they did not appear to have
received the slightest verbal instruction! I never met with
children of such vacant minds, considering the natural
quickness of their capacities; and so indulged, that they

[1] Emma, born 22 November 1807.
[2] Joseph, born 24 April 1809. There was yet another child, Charlotte,
born 1812, who benefited by Miss Weeton's ministrations ere she left.

seemed not to know what obedience was. I have had, and have even yet, a hard task to bring them under any degree of subordination; but the worst, I think, is over, though I am still obliged to correct and punish much more frequently that I could wish. Now they begin to want more books, and I mentioned, the other week, a few such as I could wish them to have. Mr. A. made objections to all, without proposing any others in their stead. The expence seems to be an object, and I am surprised at it; for those who choose to keep a governess, should not be afraid of a few shillings in books, and I did not exceed in my proposal, ten or twelve shillings. I was so much hurt at the cavilling manner in which Mr. A's objections were made, that I really meditated leaving their house next Summer. I said nothing, but perhaps my countenance and manner expressed a part of my displeasure, for Mr. and Mrs. A. have been more conciliatory in their manner for the last few days, and I feel more comfortable; this evening he has been telling me he expected a few books from London for the children. I had mentally determined that I would myself purchase a few, and lend them to my pupils.

I really will begin to talk of everything I teach the children—of the trouble they give me—how often I repeat the same thing, before it is remembered—and boast of my continued exertions for their improvement; for it will, I believe, be necessary to my own consequence to do so.

My aunt and brother have begun to make a little stir about me, and have taken some pains to obtain my address from Miss C. Braithwaite. What they will do when they know where I am, I don't know; or what they will say for themselves, should they write. I assure you I dread hearing from them. Should I receive a letter with my aunt's or my brother's writing upon it, I shall be almost too nervous to open it.

There has been dreadful execution at York amongst the Luddites the last fortnight; no less than 17 have been hung! It was a necessary severity, and the threats of those who have been liberated, has spread considerable uneasiness in this neighbourhood; for I am in the centre of the mischief that has been committed by these mistaken people.[1]

✶   ✶   ✶

Vol. 5 of the MSS. is confined principally to letters; brief excursions in diary form occur here and there, and in one part of the book, several pages intended for that purpose still remain blank. It is only too apparent that utter fatigue ruled out all but her duty to her correspondents. What Diary (or, as at this point she terms it—Occasional Remarks) there is, is principally devoted to a recapitulation of her rather unexciting, though praiseworthy ideas upon child education; and under date January 20th we gain a further hint as to her employers' notions upon the scope of a governess's duties; for we hear of a discussion upon the consequences of the disobedience of Satan, carried out 'whilst Sarah Ann, and Emma lay in bed with me this morning'! It is comforting to note George (whose sex alone no doubt debarred his sharing a portion of the governess's bed) later in the day energetically declaring that he wished the Devil was dead. George was really a very good boy, and might have stepped out of, or into, the Fairchild family. At the tender age of 6, he charmed Miss Weeton with a summary bow upon every mention of the Deity; so it is somewhat disconcerting to come across the whole lot of children, George included, scathingly dismissed as utterly incorrigible, fifteen months later.

[1] The Special Commission at York had just completed its labours. As already related, Hinchcliffe's alleged assailant proved an alibi. One of the murderers of Mr. Horsfall turned King's evidence, and the other three were promptly and publicly executed; and the grim affair ended with the execution of fourteen men, hanged in two batches of seven—for Baron Wood had come to the conclusion that 'they would hang more comfortably' on two beams!

Well might the Armitages live in constant fear—but not so Miss Weeton, as is clearly apparent from her letters.

Meantime, Miss Weeton was continuing, in a very desultory fashion, her list of books read, with remarks interspersed, some of which illustrations of her taste make very curious reading to-day.[1]

A Satyrical view of London, by J. Corry. 1 vol.

The above vol. is a tolerable production; it treats principally of Fashion, Beaux, Belles, London Tradesmen, Quack Doctors, Lawyers, Parsons, &c. &c. &c.

Windermere: a novel in 2 Vols.

This is below mediocrity; the *title* induced me to read it; and with the title I am satisfied—and disappointed.

Letters on Mythology addressed to a Lady, by R. Morgan. 1 Vol.

A humourous and entertaining production, written in a light and easy style, to make it palatable to a lady's taste. [Whatever was Miss Weeton thinking of, to commit this observation?]

Lessons of a Governess to her pupils by Madame de Sillery-Brulart (formerly Countess de Genlis). 3 Vols.

For further remarks, see page 11th. [or, for that matter, almost every other page of Miss Weeton's letters, whilst superintending the education of the Armitage brats].

Lake of Killarney, by A. M. Porter. 3 Vols.

Rose de Blaguere, a foundling, is the heroine of the tale. Mr. Clermont the hero. Mr. O.Neil and his maiden sister bring up Rose, whom they found left at

---

[1] Mr. Armitage was a member of the Honley Book Club, founded in 1750, and which operated until 1823, in which year the books were divided up among the seven surviving members, of which Mr. A. was non-effective, he having removed to Milnsbridge. The Club met once a month at a local inn for discussion of both books and a dinner. Most likely it was from this source that Miss Weeton derived her store of reading matter. Incidentally, it would appear that Mr. Armitage was too niggardly to take in newspapers; at any rate, Miss Weeton arranged for a supply to be sent regularly from Liverpool during her stay.

their door and who eventually proves to be the daughter of the haughty Countess Dunallan by a first and private marriage . . . [really, Miss Weeton—even to 'the story ends happily'!]

Ellinor, or the World as it is, by M. A. Hanway. 4 Vols.

An Entertaining production, written in a light, easy style. [And three happy marriages to conclude, one following close upon the heroine's 'just going to precipitate herself into the sea'; but it is a story which 'cannot have the slightest tendency to injure the morals of any reader, whether they have common sense or not, when it is considered that there was a continued series of suffering for 20 years from first to last'.]

The Royal Sufferer, or Intrigues at the close of the 18th. Century. by J. Agg. 3 Vols.

[A profound silence upon this intriguing production.]

The Cottagers of Glenburnie. 1 Vol. by Miss Hamilton.

A little tale tending to shew the folly of adhering to old customs merely because they have been habitual for many generations, particularly the Scottish tenacity, indolence, and want of cleanliness in their houses and about their farms. The tale is told in such a manner as scarcely to offend even a Scotchman, and may very probably have some influence in effecting a reformation.

The Mysterious Gentleman Farmer. 3 Vols. by J. Cory.

There is nothing in this novel, or in the author's Satyrical View of London, that would induce me to waste my time again in a perusal of any other of his works. This may probably be worth five guineas at the Minerva Press; the author may earn a little money; fame is out of the question in such caterpillar productions. [From the Minerva Press poured out a long series of highly sentimental novels in the early part of the century.]

An Essay on Old Maids. 3 Vols.

> Has my approbation, although, or because, I am an Old Maid. What is the public opinion, I never heard —nor any opinion—but shall take the first opportunity to discover.[1]

And, lest such a feast of dangerously debilitating literature should make her forget for a moment her wrongs, real or imaginary, or induce in her a state of mind conducive to an easier settling-down into the scheme of things, she tackles, 'at various intervals' the whole of No. 1 of Vol. II of the *Edingburgh Encyclopaedia*, by D. Brewster—a volume obligingly lent by her hard-headed Yorkshire employer.

Meantime, she cannot for the life of her get any satisfaction out of Mr. Leece, the young man in whose hands she had placed the business of collecting her rents in Liverpool and Upholland. What money he does manage to collect, fails to entirely satisfy, too, as we learn from a letter to Mr. Price.

> I should not have troubled you so soon with another letter, had it not been for the circumstance of the £2 note which you mention. I am really sorry it has happened, because I feel myself under the necessity of saying that I cannot think I am liable to the loss.

> You must not think, in what I am going to say, that I mean to throw the slightest imputation on Mr. Price of anything intentionally wrong. I think him one of the worthiest men I know; but, as a similar circumstance

---

[1] She would have smiled rather wryly could she but have anticipated A. C. Benson's opinion, written within the century, and in a Diary (contained in a series of notebooks) which was to assume proportions which would have claimed her respect. 'I discussed marriage with Miss Browne. We decided that the old maid was much happier than the old bachelor, because she generally had a circle and home ties—no such selfish ineffective loneliness as the old bachelor. True, I think.' (*Diary of A. C. Benson* ed. Lubbock.)

happened between Mrs. Price and myself just before I left Liverpool (in which she accidentally paid me a £2 forged note, but which I discovered in time to return to her), it is possible Mr. P. may have made a mistake by mingling my notes with his.[1]

As I had every confidence in your agency, I gave no authority to Mr. P. to receive any money for me, and therefore he, I think, will be obliged to bear the loss.

Mr. Forster of Up-Holland will, I hope, have paid his rent by this, as I should be sorry to proceed to any extremity with him. The other tenant deserves no mercy; and yet he is so poor, that all he is worth would not pay half a year's rent. I have long tried to get him away, but cannot even buy him out, having offered to give him half a year's rent.[2]

To MRS. DODGSON. Douglas. I.o.Man.

Highroyd. Feb. 9th. 1813.

The grievous, afflictive, and heart-breaking information conveyed in your last letter, my dear Mrs. Dodgson, of the perfect recovering of Mrs. Wood after the birth of a little daughter, has affected me so much, and disappointed—so miserably disappointed—my high-raised hopes of becoming the spouse of Mr W., that I have never since been able to write to you. I now begin to feel my nerves a little stronger, and a cheering hope has just begun to dawn, that some other little accident may happen, so that Mr. W. may yet transplant a skinny wife into the place of a fat one; for, never flatter yourself that he will ever, if he has

[1] In case the reader should still suspect Mr. Price despite Miss Weeton's rather unconvincing exoneration, it is but fair to state in his favour that it was calculated that the false coinage was actually gaining upon the Mint at the beginning of the century; and, of course, forgery was rampant.

[2] Dick Jackson was a fair match for Miss Weeton, from the moment she purchased this cottage in May 1808, until she thrust him, cottage and all, on to Tom in part settlement of a sum due to him under their mother's Will.

the opportunity, choose one who has the most distant resemblance to his present well-fed rib! For what man of wit, elegance, and manly beauty (like Mr. W.) would ever take good-humoured, contented, sensible flesh and blood, that had the opportunity of receiving slim, pining, tall gentility.

Heigh ho! Oh dear! Lack a day!

At this point, this strange woman, thrice sought after in marriage, and once fallen hopelessly in love herself; and who was yet to excite amorous inclinations in a dotard of 70, and to marry a widower; this woman calmly takes the opportunity to confess in a footnote that she had been rallied by Mrs. Dodgson (Dodson heretofore) for admiring Mr. Wood, the husband of a woman 'whose manners were vulgar in the extreme, and person coarse and large'. 'Pray,' writes she to Mrs. Dodgson, 'have you got an evil eye? Oh then, shed its influence where 'tis wanted, and *I* may be the happy woman still.' Joking, possibly; but Miss Weeton in such matters was an incalculable quantity. And she was frightfully lonely.

I can give you nothing entertaining here in regard to myself; were I to tell you how I live, it would be the dullest account of the dullest life ever dragged on by mortal. I want for nothing, in the common acceptation of the word; but I go on in that monotonous tenor, in which there is no enjoyment; happily, however, for me, I can derive amusement from the oddity of my own thoughts, and have many a hearty solo laugh.

I am very sensible of that want of elegance so glaringly observable in some parts of my letter; but if you will only permit me to make fine speeches, you'll have wond'rous few of them! Besides, there's no drollery in them; and a little low humour, I should imagine, is better than blank paper. If you don't think so, what must be done? for, as to plain every-day chit-chat, I was never in the way of it, and am unacquainted even with the theory. I know nothing of my neighbours, good or bad—as to fashion, I might as well be blind and deaf for what I either see or hear; visits, balls, plays, concerts, card-parties, equipages, scandal, tempest, war, trade, and all the other epithets of busy, bustling life, are to me as words without meaning; my own ideas must either entertain me, or I must be in a most dismal predicament! whether they entertain my correspondents or not. I read very seldom indeed; having, in the first place, but very little time for it, my own sewing and letter-writing occupying most of my leisure hours; and in the 2d place, Mr. and Mrs. A. having never offered to lend me any books except an Encyclopaedia, which is not an every-day kind of reading. Highroyd is at such a great distance from any other house, that Mr. and Mrs. A. can have little or no company in Winter. Mrs. A. is now in immediate expectation of bringing an increase to her family. I never was in a house where there was a bustle of the kind; and whether or no I shall be expected to perform a part, I cannot tell; not a word has been said about it. Say what you will, ye wives discreet, you will never make me believe that labour, with all its terrors, can be anything very terrible, when ye incur the danger so often. I dare say I have suffered more from a fit of the toothache, the very remembrance of which would prevent my ever doing anything again that was likely to cause a return.

P.S. Don't forget to *cast an eye* upon Mrs. Wood when you *see* her.

To MRS. PRICE. Liverpool.   Highroyd: April 3d. 1813.

What is the matter, my dear Mrs. Price, that I hear nothing of or from you? Sometimes I say to myself, Oh, if I had her but at my elbow, how I would twig those idle fingers of hers!

I received a letter lately from Mr. Leece, to inform me of the repair of some chimnies. What sums of money have been laid out on those chimnies since the houses came into my possession! I hope, however, this is the last for some years to come. The regularity of the rent day has already, I find, been done away with.

Mrs. Armitage has introduced another daughter[1] into this troublesome world lately—six weeks ago; and although it may appear paradoxical until explained, my comfort has been considerably increased thereby. For some months after I came, Mrs. A. seemed to be determined to be displeased with whatever I did; cross looks were my daily portion, and unpleasant hints were frequently thrown out. Grating as it was to my feelings to be thus treated, I continued my assiduous endeavours to discharge my duty; God and my conscience were my guides. Mrs. A's manner to me determined me to keep at a distance, and threw a degree of cool reserve into my conduct that I could not divest myself of, however greatly I wished it. All at once, she has become pleasing and open (comparatively speaking), and treats me in a manner that has, as suddenly, banished my reserve. She began to alter in this respect 3 or 4 weeks ago; and but the other day, the nurse informed me that she is always very ill-tempered when pregnant, particularly at the beginning of the time. Now it so happened that *I* arrived here just at that unlucky period, and she has been increasing in size ever since, until about 6 weeks ago, when, being freed of her burden, she became as good humoured as she was wont to be; and I now venture to meet her with that ever ready smile which I bestow on everyone, whose own countenance is not too sour to return it.

Ann tells me you are likely to bring an increase of family; I wish you well over it, and comfort of the baby when it

---

[1] Eliza.

does arrive. For Heaven's sake, don't be like *my mistress* here, and make everybody miserable about you.

P.S. Of my brother or of my aunt, I have never heard a word—from them, at least. I think with you, that some of my relations don't wish to find me. They act most strangely! I suppose I may expect to hear by the next post from my uncle, or some one. I almost think I will write to *him* immediately, for *he* will hear reason. I am much grieved for the situation my aunt is in, and would long ago have visited and have nursed her, had she ever *asked* me.

And forthwith, to 'Dear and Honoured Uncle', the niece pours out her querulous, long-suffering love, tactless to the end. —'If my aunt does not wish to see me, let me beg of you to inform me, by return of post, how she is; I cannot forget her, though she has wished to forget me.' Unlamented, the dregs of her life were fast slipping away from the vindictive old woman, close-pent in her Upholland home; close-besieged by legacy hunters, too, whose rendering of the contents of Miss Weeton's letter would possibly have startled the authoress of that composition.

To MISS WINKLEY. Dublin.   Highroyd: April 8. 1813.

Although I begin my letter at Highroyd, it is with the idea that I may probably finish it elsewhere. If my aunt does send for me, what a nest of hornets am I likely to encounter! I assure you I dread going. However, I can soon satisfy them, if money is all they want; they shall have all the scrambling to themselves; I shall not stoop to do it. If I had been swayed by interested motives, I should never have resented my aunt's treatment of me, because that would, to a certainty, irritate her still more.

Should I be sent for to my aunt, it is most probable I shall not return here, which will occasion a vacancy that Mrs. A. must fill up with a younger person; for she will have no chance of getting a person of my years, experience, and attainments, to submit to the privations and humiliations I have done (though I could have staid contentedly, had not several considerations made it almost necessary that I should be nearer my Liverpool property). Mrs. Armitage's manner has been much improved towards me lately, and has made my situation much more agreeable. I rather suspect I am indebted for this improvement to Miss A., Mr. Armitage's sister, who has been a great deal here within the last two months, attending Mrs. Armitage during a confinement. Miss A. and her parents (who live near us) seem to think very highly of me, and treat me with great respect. I have frequently been to tea and supper there with Mr. & Mrs. A. Junior, and am going today, to dine with them; yet, such is the liberality of *my mistress*, that I am to stay with the children until dinner is quite ready, and to return to school as soon as I have eaten it, and go again to tea. It will be the first time I have dined out since I came here; and, if such again are to be the conditions, it shall be the last. To this day's arrangement, I shall submit in silence. I was served in the same way when invited to the old gentleman's to tea last summer. I had then to return home again at 7 o'clock to hear the children's prayers. After submitting to it once or twice, I objected, preferring staying at home entirely to visiting in such a way; after which, I was permitted to stay the evening, when I did go.

As long as a governess, or any other person, is admitted into the company of her superiors, she should be treated as an equal for the time, or else it is better not to invite her at all.

April 9th.

I could smile, my dear Ann, at a part of your letter, in which you imagine your method of instruction may improve mine. After being a teacher in a school upwards of 20 years, and for more than 10 of them having made education my more peculiar study, I should not now have to learn from a girl so young as you. I am not apt to boast *verbally* of my knowledge, and a person must be intimately acquainted with me, before they know my acquirements.[1] I know I appear more ignorant than I am; my brother has often told me so, for he thinks me *wondrous* clever, considering the opportunities I have had. When very young, I was disgusted with the pedantry of some girls, who pretended upon every occasion to a great deal more than they really knew. I saw how they were ridiculed, and secretly determined never to act like them. When a person is really possessed of knowledge, it will make its appearance without any pains being taken by the possessor. But it only discovers itself to the knowing; the ignorant cannot find it.

Having expressed myself thus, I am no longer offended, my dear Ann; but having often experienced the same kind of expressions from you when we were together in Liverpool, I think it my duty to caution you, for it has given greater offence to others than to me. *I* could excuse it, because I well know the vanity and inexperience of 16 is apt to think more highly of itself than it ought to do; and the addition of a few years will, alone, teach it more humility; for then, the equal, nay even superior knowledge of thousands of those around us, is discovered daily.

It is hardly surprising to record that 'my dear Ann's' answer was significantly prompt; in the meantime, mystified by the non-realization of the expected summons to her aunt's bedside,

---

[1] The Saturday 'reports', the 30-page treatise upon her methods of education (now in course of preparation), cannot, of course, be counted against Miss Weeton; but she was not in the habit, nevertheless, of hiding her light under a bushel; nor need she. All she lacked was that one valuable quality, especially in a governess—tact; as once again she was ruefully about to discover.

Miss Weeton addressed a letter to Dr. James Hawarden, of Standishgate, Wigan, the uncle of Mrs. Bessy Price. For once she read character aright, and the worthy doctor (just how worthy, Miss Weeton was at present mercifully spared the knowledge—a few short and bitter years, and to his home the present supplicant would fly, terror-stricken, in fear for her very life) busied himself on her behalf; but to little purpose, as the event will prove. Once more she turns to her Journal.

[JOURNAL] *May 1st.*

It is well that I have so little time for reflection, or otherwise I should almost weep myself into the grave; for my present situation is a most painful one! Forgotten, as it seems, by every relative, and almost every friend at a distance, and totally secluded from all rational society here, I must sink into melancholy if my days were not so completely occupied as almost to preclude thought. The little leisure, or rather the little time I have to myself, is a good deal employed in repairing my clothes, writing letters sometimes; and sometimes I sit with my face resting on my hands, indulging in melancholy, weeping bitterly; for no one interrupts me, no voice soothes, advises, or pities.

. . . Why am I thus treated? What have I done, Oh Father, to deserve to be thus deserted and neglected? What have I done to you, my aunt, to meet with such treatment at your hands? . . . What have I done to you, hard-hearted, selfish brother, to merit such strange cruelty of conduct? . . .

May 7th.

Since writing the above, I have received a letter from my aunt, in consequence of mine to Dr. Hawarden; and though it is such an one as would, at any other time, have plunged me into sorrow and have roused my indignation, it has *just now* affected me with the liveliest pleasure! It is *a letter from my aunt*, and I care not what it contains. Though I shall not even yet use the language of humility or submission (as I think I have been most unjustly, most cruelly treated), a chance, at least, of a reconciliation appears; and my heart bounds with joy at the idea. I will write to my aunt. Should my letter offend, I shall consider it as a proof that nothing but the most *abject* language can please, and spurn at the idea of calling one so to be conciliated—a relation.

The letter is written to her Aunt—couched in language singularly inappropriate (as may perhaps be taken for granted in the circumstances). 'I have answered it in a reasoning, complaining kind of tone'—she reports in a later letter to Mrs. Price. And she writes to that aunt—never much of a Christian, professing or otherwise, and sadly regretting her old comfortable rocking chair—'Oh aunt! . . . should you go to the arms of your God before I do, you will then perceive how much you have made me suffer by your neglect of me.' The dying woman, if she took the trouble to wade through the 2,500 odd words of this spirited defence and criminal charge combined, must have looked a trifle more ghastly than usual at the end of its perusal. And what a conclusion, too. 'Remember me with respectful affection to my uncle,

*Yours

E. Weeton.

*My aunt's affectionate manner of concluding her letter; and for once I follow so laudable an example.'

✻   ✻   ✻

Alas! what a strangely hard-to-please world it is; wearily the governess sits down once again, snatching opportunities as they offer, to palliate her offence with the touchy Ann.

To MISS WINKLEY   Highroyd. May 19th. 1813.

My dear, dear Ann! do you know, that on reading your letter, I have received both a very considerable degree of pleasure, and of pain,—of pain at finding you so much grieved with a passage in my last letter. When I wrote it, I really did it with a design of rendering you a service; but, on afterwards perusing it, my heart smote me for being guilty of severity. I hesitated whether or not to dash out the cruel words. I read again, in a milder tone, what appeared so angry, and I was more reconciled to them. If *I* don't reprove her, thought I, she has not another so much her friend as to do it. I will make the experiment. If she is offended, if she proudly resent, she is not the girl I could wish her to be. My heart again smites me painfully, at finding I have afflicted you so much (at the same time that I am delighted beyond measure at feeling more than ever assured of the goodness of your heart, and the increasing powers of your understanding). Oh! I was anxious that you should quit the dangers you were in, in Liverpool; for, as you say, so I thought, that 'your mind was poisoned by false ideas,' and that nothing would prove an effectual antidote, but the engaging in the situation which then happily offered. Mrs. Edwards, though the sister of a man I highly respect, is a most dangerous woman! She, Ann, has not wanted native goodness of heart, but, in her earlier days, has wanted better instruction, and I fear is now too far gone to learn. She is unprincipled to a degree! a scoffer at religion, a despiser of all moralities, and neglectful of common propriety. Her uncommon liveliness and gaiety of temper, render her entertaining and pleasant to those who can overlook all that is Christianlike in woman. And it is this which makes her so dangerous; she vents the most profligate opinions in a manner so irresistibly laughable, as to make the poison *dreadfully* sweet! She fascinates the imagination, whilst she destroys the soul. I do not think she does it from design; her sole aim is to be admired for the brilliance of her wit; and her incorrigible vanity will, I much fear, be her own destruction; (I hope, not that of others) . . . What a teacher at the head of a school! How careful should parents be, to investigate the principles of those with whom they intrust their children.

Mr. Pollard is a young man of irreligious principles; *professedly* so, a Deist, if not an Atheist; and one of Paine's disciples. His appearance is genteel, and his manners insinuating. I pity, whilst I blame him. I would pray for him, whilst at the same time I would avoid him.

The Jackson's of Mill-Street, too . . . too depraved for description! . . . These were, all together, a *sad* society for you; and I am rejoiced that you have escaped them in your youth, before the contagion of such examples had irrecoverably tainted you.

What a state for lower middle-class Liverpool to be in, indeed. Demurely must the 16-year-old governess have listened to the fulminations of T. French, Esq. (of the Navigation Board, Dublin, and of Sopwell Hall, Roscrea), against the writer of the *Rights of Man* and the *Age of Reason*. Perhaps, too, neither governess would willingly have bartered the society of the genteel and insinuating Deist for that of the lavender-gloved, lisping curate of Christ Church; and perhaps, too, Miss Weeton had her private doubts—could it be that all this fulminating against Deists was a protective measure against—herself?

Meantime, with summer drawing nearer, and with it the prospect of a whole month's holiday (as per preliminary articles drawn up between mistress and governess), there may yet be a visit to Dublin; almost certainly one to Aunt Barton, whether invited or not.

To MRS. PRICE   Highroyd: May 28th. 1813.

The time is fast approaching when I shall be permitted a month's cessation from my labours here, and as my affairs in Liverpool will oblige me to come there, I write

to request you will take me in as a boarder, if convenient;
if not, can I be with Miss Price? If neither of you can
accomodate me, be kind enough to procure me lodgings
as near to your house as you can, on as moderate terms as
possible. The 18th of June is the day I intend to arrive in
Liverpool; the coach goes through in a day, so it will be
9 or 10 at night before it gets there.

June 19th finds her duly in Liverpool, among friends, and
still writing to friends. Catharine Braithwaite is staying with
her married sister at Prescott, and Miss Weeton hastens to
acquaint her of her presence very near them.

I have just been contemplating Wm. Hindley's Holland
face, and received a Prescott letter from him, and mean to
do myself the pleasure of seeing the hand that wrote it, on
Monday afternoon. I prefer walking if the weather is fine,
and will set out a little before 3 o'clock; should it rain, I
will come by the caravan that evening.

What kind of shoulders they were on which the red cloak
hung that you saw on the top of the coach, I can't say;
they were not mine. I stared hard (as Miss Dannet says)
from the inside of the coach, as I passed Mr. Jackson's,
but the windows did not serve as a frame to one single face.

How straight I write, Catharine, don't I? Hold the
paper up to the light, and you will see the reason why.[1]
I never met with anything so convenient before, though I
know it's nothing new. When I begin to be purblind,
I'll use it constantly, writing on a glass table, with a lamp
underneath. What a reflection it will be to my eyes!

To MRS. JOS. ARMITAGE. Highroyd.
                                    Liverpool: undated.
Madam,
    In compliance with your request, I called at the shop
you directed me to, to make inquiries about the lamp you

[1] There were water-mark lines to write by [*orig. note*].

described. The proprietor informed me, that one with a large cut glass dish, encircled with a brass figured rim, six glass lights for candles, and a row of icicle drops, with a chain to hang it, could be furnished for £12; if additional drops were required, the price would be from £12 to £20 in proportion to the quantity of drops. The dish was very beautifully cut, but there was one valued at £15 that I admired much more; six candlesticks were placed upon a brass rim, from which was suspended glass drops, three in depth, and very thickly set; a painted glass cylinder, about 20 inches high, stood up in the middle of the candlesticks. It was ornamentally painted; I think, with a landscape; and intended to contain within it, either an oil lamp or a candle. The top of the chain by which it hung, was ornamented with glass drops suspended in the manner of either icicle drops, or the weeping willow—which you please; the cylinder was in the shape of a wine-pipe, widest in the middle.

I was very nearly losing all chance of obtaining either a place for myself or my little charges in the coaches from Huddersfield. Some young ladies, returning from school, were in the coach with us, and seemed much pleased with my little, chattering companions. They asked what school they went to. I said they had a governess at home. 'Thinks I to myself, I'll pass myself off for their Mamma.' So I kept my left-hand glove on, and talked very consequentially. Shaking my head, 'thinks I to myself, these children will betray me; I fear it won't do;' and just then, Emma exclaimed, 'Oh look, Miss Weeton, see what a deal of buttercups in that field.' It was too bad, now, wasn't it?

I was much amused the other evening at an exhibition of wax work; there were upwards of 70 figures, as large as life. I was remarking to Mrs. Price how very natural one figure was, that appeared to be looking at another; the figure *heard* me, turned round, and *looked* at me! It was a live man! Soon afterwards, as I was standing near some other piece of wax work, I felt something touch me, and move past me! Imagining it to be one of the inanimate figures suddenly inspired with motion, and going to seize me, I screamed out, and sprang away; it was only a little boy passing me. Mrs. Price, feeling rather fatigued, sat down near a canopy, under which was seated a Turkish sultan, and 3 female slaves. Three country fellows walked by. First one examined her, and then another; but when a third came up, she could contain no longer, and burst out with a hearty laugh, to the no small astonishment and amusement of *her admirers*.

I have inquired the price of shells such as you described. One, as large as yours, though not that kind, was 6s. 6d; smaller ones were 4s. 6d. and 2s. 6d. Yours are conch shells; these are called Queen's conches. Mr. Price says the large one is very cheap.

Whilst still in Liverpool, Miss Weeton was surprised to receive an offer of the post of Governess in the family of a Mrs. Wade of Port-Echee, near Douglas. As the position offered savoured little of other than an exchange of servitudes, she demanded a salary which she felt sure would settle the matter once and for all against her—£50; and gave very decided and minute directions as to how her next *mistress* should behave to *her*. The upshot of the matter was, that she eventually got the job for one of the cousin Smiths—though after a year or two of married life, she desperately cast out feelers for the chance to fill the post, at any salary mentioned (and no stipulations from herself); but Miss Smith was a fixture by that time. Meantime, if Mrs. Wade would care to see it, Miss Weeton would favour her with 'an exact journal of my method of teaching and proceeding with the little Armitages'—a *jeu d'esprit* of a mere 30 pages! This letter was written on 22nd July; an extension of leave had been graciously granted by Mrs. Armitage, and most gratefully acknowledged by the harassed holiday-maker, who duly returned in the course of this month.

To MISS ANN WINKLEY   Highroyd July 30th. 1813.

I received your letter my dear **Ann**, whilst I was with your sister; but so very unsettled did I feel all the time I was with her, that I scarce knew what time I had for writing, or what to say to you; one vexatious delay or other, defeated every little plan of pleasure, and my whole vacation dwindled away without my being able to leave Liverpool except a visit for a day and two nights to Prescot; and another, about the same length, to Holland.

My visit to Prescot was as agreeable as so short a stay would admit of. Mrs. T. Jackson, whom I went to see, and Miss C. Braithwaite, both urged me to go to see my aunt. Anxious enough I was to see her; but, so treated as I have been, it was a hard struggle to subdue my resentful feelings. I hesitated for some days, but at last summoned resolution enough to go, writing first to my aunt to pre-pare her for my reception, though not waiting to know whether I should be received. With an aching heart, I stepped into the canal packet; the company however soon became amusing to me, and for a time drove away all uneasy sensations. My cousin Latham's second son met me at Appley Bridge, and I walked from thence, dreading the coming hours, to which every step reluctantly hastened me.

My uncle opened me the door of his house, with a faint 'how do ye'. I trembled as I walked into the parlour, not knowing whether I was welcome. I asked various ques-tions respecting my aunt's health, which were very coolly answered. 'Are you for stopping here, or going to Mrs. Braithwaite's?' he inquired. Such a question set my lips a-quivering, and a coldness spread over my face. 'If I am not welcome here,' I said, 'as I cannot go back tonight, I must try if they will take me in.' Tea coming in just then, I was going to rise, as well as my trembling knees would permit. 'Your aunt will not see you,' said my uncle.

'Then I had better go,' I replied, as I endeavoured to stifle some convulsive sobs. . . .

My uncle looked at me, and in a softened tone, said 'But I will make you welcome, Nelly.'

Not all my intreaties could induce him to tell me the reason of the treatment I have, for so long a period, received from my aunt; the more I urged, the more angry he was at my speaking on the subject; he said he would have nothing at all to do with the business, and insisted on my dropping the subject.

I expressed astonishment at such cruel treatment, when I was totally ignorant of what I had done to offend; I was treated, I said, as an outcast, friendless and unprotected; and not so much as the *shadow* of an error laid to my charge! I was a condemned criminal, without being informed of the crime for which I suffered!

Not all I could say, availed me; and I am to this moment ignorant of what I have done, to offend my aunt so irreconcileably! In the course of the following day, my uncle repeatedly urged my aunt to see me (she was confined to her bed-room); but in vain. I did not desire my uncle to do this; I only twice asked whether my aunt intended, or wished, to see me; and being told not, submitted in silence. The whole of this day, my uncle was very kind to me, and we spent the greatest part of it by ourselves, in friendly conversation.

I called upon Mrs. Braithwaite; the altered appearance of that house, now the master of it is gone, and the boys who used to fill it being dispersed for want of their teacher, gave me such a shock, that I had no sooner sat down, than I burst into a violent fit of crying, in which I was in some degree accompanied by the widow and her daughters.

My stay at my uncle's was so extremely uncomfortable, that I determined not to stay a second night with them; so I concerted with the servant to get a sight of my aunt, unknown to her; she went upstairs rather noisily, that I might not be heard. I stood peeping at the door, whilst the girl talked to her. The irritated tone of voice in which my aunt *always* speaks now, I am told, and her ghastly countenance, were almost too much for me; I retreated, undiscovered, into the kitchen, and burst into tears. 'Oh! —I *never* shall see my aunt again,' I cried. The servant wept with me, and the tears stood in my uncle's eyes; indeed I wept bitterly. My uncle shook my hand affectionately, as he bid me farewell. I gave the servant a secret, but very earnest charge, to be kind to my aunt, for which I would reward her, and then departed.

I had not gone far, when my Aunt's servant came running after me, and said her mistress wished to bid me good-bye. In the first moment of resentment, I refused; it was too late now; however, I was prevailed upon to return. We shook hands, and, 'Good-bye' was all that was said. *I* could say no more, my heart was too full. I quitted her —*never more to see her*! for so I think.

I had only returned to your sister's a few days, when I was seized with a violent bowel complaint and vomiting, which reduced me to such a state of weakness that I was fit for nothing for ten days; indeed, I am not yet recovered; I am feeble and thin to a degree.

I was attacked again with sickness in the coach as I was coming here, and was very thankful that I was the only inside passenger from Manchester, as I had room to lie down.

Her intention had been to spend a further couple or three days at Prescot, as she passed through on her return to High Royd; but her agent, Mr. Leece, led her such an impossible dance—or rather, she found herself so obliged to hunt that very scarce gentleman back and forth from his house to his office— that her holiday resolved itself into a matter of business, of sorts. Back again at her duties, she pours out her plaints.

Indeed, Catharine, I was glad to get back again; the greater distance I am from Holland, and the more chearful and happy I am. I was glad to have 3 days of rest here, after the fatigue of travelling, previous to commencing my labours.

Highroyd is in a great bustle just now. Mrs. Armitage's mother (Mrs. Henshaw) came on the 31st. of July, bringing her two little grand-daughters, who had been spending the holidays with her—Miss Lacy, and little granddaughter; and a Miss Barker, a young lady about 16, just left school, who is under Mrs. H's care, and lives with her. Mrs. H., if I may judge from the short acquaintance I have with her, is quite the gentlewoman. She appears so good-tempered and so considerate, that I am at present a warm admirer of her; she treats me with such polite attention, speaks to me with so much ease and chearfulness, that if joined in by some *greater* folks here, would dissipate all the starch very soon, in which I generally feel enveloped when I am in *the presence*. I had many a laugh to myself when I first came here; for, really Catharine, I could plainly see that my *master* and my *mistress* did not know how to treat me, nor *what to do with me*; and their distant manner froze me so, that for the life of me, I could not tell what to do with myself when they were by. My arms and my legs were unusual incumbrances; my hands were quite in the way; and my bottom! . . . Lord help it! when I walked out of the room, it felt three times as big as it ever did before, and I thought it shaked most uncommonly! By degrees, however, I got rid of *this* ague. But the starchifying complaint frequently attacks me still, and my only remedy is a retreat into my own room, for which reason I frequently resort to it, that my limbs, and my . . . what? Catharine . . . I can't for shame say it again . . . may be *at ease*.

Miss Barker is a good-natured lump of a girl, with a very

pretty face, flaxen hair, and beautiful complexion of lilies and roses. She is peculiarly fortunate in having a home with Mrs. H. Her father is living, but she, being a natural daughter, cannot so comfortably live with him, as he is married; yet he intends to provide for her. Her mother was, I think, a relation of Mrs. H's. Miss Lacy is a sweet little creature, not 5 years old yet; her accent and manners, so elegant! her temper so endearing! that I feel already much attached to her. The contrast between her and her cousin Armitages, is very great; they are the rudest, most untractable set of children I ever had to manage; and I am afraid old daddy Time will not manage them much better, till he quietens them with his scythe. I am certain I could reduce them to order if I had them to myself; but spoiled, vulgar children, of boisterous tempers, can never be reformed *at home*, by any governess.

The roads about Highroyd are excessively rough, and in Winter, scarcely passable. Miss L. complains bitterly of them. 'We have no such roads in London,' said she one day; 'they are straight there! and so smooth! I can run upon them without falling and hurting myself.' The beauties of the country compensates, in my long-legged opinion, for the badness of the roads that lead you to survey them; though really, walking here is, *even to me*, almost as much of a labour as a pleasure.

To MRS. PRICE   Highroyd: Sept. 4th. 1813.

Returned again to solitude, and for the present restored to health, I commence an epistle to my dear Mrs. Price, that ought to have been written some weeks ago. Mrs. Henshaw, Mrs. Armitage's mother, has been spending above a month here, and only left Highroyd on the 30th. of Aug. During her stay, the house has been all animation and gaiety. I determined to indulge myself, and descended to supper every evening; not for the sake of what I could eat, but of what I could hear and see. Mrs. Henshaw is a sensible, good-tempered, benevolent, well-bred woman; she has won my esteem and admiration entirely. She always welcomed me, when I entered the parlour, with a smile and some little observation or other; so different to Mrs. A's gloomy, and I could almost say, sulky countenance, that acts like lead upon the spirits of one so easily affected by the expression of the features as I am.

I feel more at home here now than I have done any time since I came first into Yorkshire; and could be very comfortable if it were not for the perverse and violent tempers of the children. And they really are terrible; whether I can ever subdue them, is doubtful. For a few months before the holidays, I flattered myself that I had reduced my pupils to greater order than they had ever been before; but—the holidays have undone all, and again have I all to do. Such screaming and shouting and incessant loud talking I dare say you never heard in any family before; and such everlasting quarrelling. For a month since my return, the two boys *never* attempted to say a lesson without throwing themselves into violent fits of passion; screaming dreadfully, if I persisted in making them say it. I have at last resorted to the rod, notwithstanding it is so repugnant to the present mild system of education; and if you had heard their screams, you would have thought I was really killing them, when frequently I had only struck their clothes; but for the last week, I have made them feel it, and I have found the benefit of it, though my reward from the two Mrs. Armitages, is sour looks and cool treatment. A mother must indeed feel for her children, and so do I feel for them; my spirit droops under such a task; but my duty to God is to fulfil the duties of my present situation, which I cannot do by indulging the children in their own perverse ways, as their mother has done. The eldest girl, for some weeks, would not study a single lesson. She sat with the book or slate before her, doing nothing. What would you have done in such a case? I requested, persuaded, insisted; but she would only smile carelessly in my face, and toss her head. I then incessantly confined her at play hours, till she had finished not only her present lessons, but all which were in arrears. Cool looks from Mrs. A., were the consequence; Sarah Anne's health would suffer, she thought. So I thought; but something must be done, and as Mrs. A. did not propose any better way, I persevered, notwithstanding her unjust treatment, though a frequent fit of weeping was the consequence; and I think I have conquered. Miss A. is again become not only tractable, but affectionate.

And all this while, old daddy Time, having swept up a few odd Luddites, was sweeping towards the village of Upholland, where an old, cantankerous, vindictive aunt was seeing visions, none of the pleasantest; and on Saturday morning, September the 25th, 'my aunt died'. Grievously afflicted was the poor lorn niece; how could her aunt, nay, how dare she, in the face of God, make no sign despite the recent submission made to her? Nature had endowed Miss Weeton with pretty acute feelings where ties of relationship were concerned; and, having heard the news almost haphazardly from her cousin Latham's boy, she endured agonies whilst awaiting confirmation—confirmation which she did not doubt would arrive from a more authoritative source. Three weeks passed, plunged in miserable self-absorption; then despairing of that understanding, of that indulgent love for which she yearned in her own generation, she turned to her Journal—and our generation.

[JOURNAL] *Oct. 13.*

It is nearly two years since I received a letter from my brother, or wrote one to him; judge, then, you who read these pages and know what I have suffered from him, what must be my feelings this evening, on receiving a letter directed by his hand! What would it possibly contain? . . . I opened it, hesitatingly, but dared not read it; my heart beat quick; perhaps my Uncle, too, was dead!

For some days I have thought—have felt almost convinced it was so; my spirits have been very low since my aunt's death, and many a gloomy idea has possessed my thoughts; so much so, that my own dissolution has appeared momentary. Two evenings ago, I sat some hours alone by the parlour fire, Mr. and Mrs. A. being both from home. I felt extremely faint, as indeed I had done for some time. I trembled with weakness, and fancied that if I shut my eyes, I should faint away. I suffered the servants to go to bed without exerting myself to speak to them; I had not strength to rise from my chair . . . I felt *so* friendless—my aunt dead, in enmity with me; my brother, to all appearances the bitterest enemy of his sister, and the person who had set her against me—and from motives so mean! so base! For the sake of £100 or £150 which *perhaps* she might bequeath me . . . perhaps it might be more—it might be £200.

How weary a world this is! when such a brother as he once was, can take so much pains to bereave his only sister of every friend! I wept at the thought, and further reflected, that so unprotected as I was, where could I find a home when I wanted one? . . . I could not tell . . . God help me, protect me; and forgive my mistaken brother!

The melancholy state of my mind, and the feebleness of my body, made me alive to *any* impression of a gloomy nature; and the dismal howling of a dog, just as the clock was going to strike eleven, the sound of which seemed to be just outside of the kitchen door, terrified me so, that, finding the use of my feet, I ran precipitately up stairs, and hastened into bed. I now felt I should *die* if I shut my eyes—as if the whole of life were centred in my heart and head—as if I had no feeling, no sensation, but that of breathing and thought! At length, after some hours, I became more like a living mortal; my limbs grew warmer, and I fell asleep.

The next morning, I arose, still feeble and depressed—I felt as if I were certain that my uncle was dead—though I know not why I should think of *him*. . . . This evening, when my brother's letter was given to me, it was like a confirmation of my fears—for what else had induced *him* to write? Perhaps it was an explanation of his conduct . . . what a joyful idea! I read; my delight was somewhat damped on finding it a proposal to live with my uncle, in a style of the most studied indifference; but for the direction, I should scarce know for whom the letter was intended. The first words are, 'You have already been informed of the death of my aunt. I find my Uncle very dull, and it has occurred to me'—&c. &c.—and concluded with, 'Yours, T. R. Weeton.'

The abrupt beginning, without *any* address, and the cool conclusion, argue no returning affection. Oh! if I do see him again, I will endeavour to warm his heart with more Christian-like sentiments. I have begun my letter with, 'Dear Brother,' and ended with, 'Yours affectionately,' and I wrote what I felt, notwithstanding his cruelty towards me.

But what *was* her answer to this amazing piece of effrontery; this cool and confident supposition that she would throw over a comparatively well-paid post, in order to assume that of unpaid housekeeper to her bereaved uncle?—simply, that she would gladly undertake the duty, provided she was not expected *to pay for her board*. (The italics are not hers.) And what authority had Master Tom for the proposal? None whatever; but with an uncle surrounded by relatives upon the spot, and with an adopted son whose future must be considered, would it not be a master-stroke to have an agent upon the spot too;

malleable, sentimentally inclined towards relatives; above all, clearly unmercenary? Even Mrs. T. Weeton must persuade herself of the policy of allowing this trifling sop of a brother's written words to the long-neglected sister.

Meantime, ever on the watch to do a friend a good turn, the agitated governess writes to Ann Winkley, offering her the reversion of her job; and in case of a refusal, would she kindly get in touch with Miss Margaret Smith, as yet out of a job, and set her moving? Working herself all agog, she plans the purchase of mourning in Liverpool; how she will tackle Mr. Leece; and spiritedly inveighs against Mrs. Armitage for a recent 'little piece of unkindness. I had not received the intelligence of my aunt's death above an hour, when she called me to assist her in tying up some preserves—I complied, but secretly determined to quit her soon.' Nevertheless, Mrs. Armitage being soon afterwards upon a visit to her mother's at Blakely, next Manchester, the governess writes the expected duty letter, but cannot resist a little malicious jolt in conclusion.

Your little family under my care, are all very well, very happy, and highly delighted with their little letters; they have already been read 3 times. Joseph looks all gravity and consequence, whilst his is read; Emma all animation; Sarah-Anne much pleased; and George has had several fits of the capers during the *operation.*

My beau, J. Scholfield, Esq., paid me a visit one Sunday evening whilst Mr. A. *was out*, and made me a present of 3 mogul plums! He staid so long, that I was almost frightened out of my wits lest Mr. A. should come and catch him. John says he wishes he had another wife; and if he could find one such as the last, he would go 40 miles to fetch her. Do you know anybody near Blakely that would suit him? I must confess I had flattered myself a little, that I had been in John's good graces; but when he talked of 40 miles, 'thinks I to myself,'[1] I wish I was *far enough!*

---

[1] 'Thinks I to myself' was the catchy title of a contemporary novel.

Last week I received a letter from my brother, proposing my going to live with my uncle Barton; as my uncle was always friendly towards me, I immediately answered I should have no objection, if I knew the terms. As I look upon my departure as next to certain, I wish to inform you, as early as possible, that you may be preparing a successor; for, if my uncle wishes me to come at all, he will wish it to be as early as possible.

Mrs. Armitage having done the thing in style, and taken the nursery-maid with her into Lancashire, Miss Weeton finds herself with 'the sole care of four children, out of the school as well as in it; and the management of the house; so that I have been governess, nursery-maid, and housekeeper; and a complete Scrub, you may imagine—it has been rather too much for me; my spirits were not equal to the task'. But she finds herself not entirely deprived of society apart from the stale variety of that of her charges; for there is that comical old John Scholfield, so glad to find a willing, polite listener in her. To Tom she writes—

The principal amusement I have, is in going to or from Chapel on a Sunday, which is occasioned by the friendly attentions of an old, respectable, sociable farmer, named John Scholfield; as we walk together, he often regrets the death of his wife, and speaks so affectionately of her, that I cannot but admire the goodness of his heart. I tell Mrs. A. that he is my beau, and she often jokes me about him. I am afraid that you wont admire my taste, when I tell you that he is upwards of 70. He one day said, that old as he was, he would marry again if he could find such a one as his last wife. If he were but an *old gentleman*, instead of being *nothing* but an *old man*, I really think I would give him a hint to make an offer, for I like old John vastly; he tells me his grievances, and I try to console him.

Whilst the long days lasted, I was always *let out* with the children, morning, noon, and evening. Every morning, I was busy making them gardens, they assisting in bringing, or carrying away, manure, planks, stones, weeds, &c., and frequently going into the fields to collect wild-flower roots. At noon, I went into a little overgrown wood, where once had been a pretty walk, but Mrs. A. had suffered it to be neglected. Here, with a pair of great hedge-clippers, I worked for an hour before dinner, literally cutting my way; my little companions, with forks and rakes, assisting in carrying away heaps of slain. Should I remain here, this wood would become my hobby horse. Mr. A. has given me leave to have a few trees cut down, to open a view, and to plant an arbour in their place;[1] this will occupy my leisure hours next Spring, and my little ones please themselves with thinking what a delightful place the wood will be, for playing in at hide-and-seek. In the evening, we took a walk. But now that Winter has arrived, all these little amusements are put a stop to. I wish . . . I wish Winter was over!

I shall be obliged to you, when you write, to inform me whether you think my Uncle does, or does not, wish me to reside with him. I wrote to him immediately after I received your last letter, but have received no answer. What can be the reason?

A fortnight more of suspense, and the 'affectionate and respectful niece' again writes to Mr. Barton; once again she offers the sacrifice of her salary as governess, and expresses the 'hope, my dear uncle, you will not be displeased at anything I have said; I am sure I do not mean to offend any one'.

---

[1] That Miss Weeton was not indifferent to the inherent beauty of trees she evidenced in her later Welsh tour; but it is to be regretted that she should further the destruction which had been going on ever since Honley Moor had been enclosed in 1788. The roots of ancient oaks provided material for 5th of November bonfires for over fifty years!

To MISS WINKLEY, at Mrs. Price's.

Highroyd: Nov. 27 1813.

My dear Ann will, I suppose, have been expecting to see me for some days; and I must confess I feel considerably disappointed at the result of my uncle's determination —to go into lodgings with a tenant of his, who lived on an estate of my uncle's, near Holland. The proposal, coming from my brother, gave me reason to conclude that he was authorised by my uncle.

My uncle really writes very kindly. He says his house was in such confusion after my aunt's death, and his servants behaved so ill, that he intends to give up house-keeping, for a few months at least; he will keep the house and furniture as they now are, until he has tried how he likes his lodgings. I should have liked to have lived with him, merely because I could have enjoyed *some* society; here, I am totally shut out of it.

May I request the favour of Mr. Price to call upon all my tenants without delay, to inquire into the precise state of their accounts; for I much fear Mr. Leece is neglecting my affairs most sadly. Oh Ann! to have the prospect of *going home*, as it were, after not knowing what home was for near *seventeen* years, and then to be disappointed! . . . think how it must sink the spirit of a deserted, friendless female. How ardently I do long for *a home*! but I suppose there must be none for me until I arrive at the grave.

To MISS C. BRAITHWAITE. Holland Priory.

Highroyd: Dec. 2d 1813.

I wish my brother had not written, without knowing my uncle's sentiments, for it has placed me in a very awkward situation. For near two months I was in daily expectation of a summons, Mrs. A. was inquiring for a successor, and last week received intelligence of one, to whom she has since written backward. When Mrs. A. received intelligence of this young lady, I desired that if she felt the slightest disapprobation of my method of instruction, and thought this young lady (of whom she had heard a very high character) would suit her better, that she would not hesitate a moment in saying so; for the children's interest must be the first consideration. She said that she had not any wish to change, for she thought that the children had made wonderful improvement; and George, in particular, she could wish not to change his teacher until next Summer, when he must go to a public school.

My uncle says that my aunt has left a parcel for me, directed by her own hand. A few weeks ago, I had determined never to receive it, whatever it might contain; for my uncle does not seem to know; but Mrs. A. advises me to send for it, and in the hope that it may contain an explanation of her unaccountable conduct towards me, I have been induced to comply, and shall be obliged to you to request my uncle to send it by any conveyance he thinks the best, and to tell him that Rd. Jackson owes one year's rent, due Nov. 12th. last.

My health is restored again, and my spirits too. Mrs. A. treats me more and more pleasingly as the time passes on; we are almost like two familiar friends, and many a piece of would-be wit passes between us. The other day, I wrote a message on a slate, and sent it by one of my youngest pupils. She wrote underneath it, that she would comply with my request as soon as she returned from my Lady Kitty's (the necessary), but having received a very pressing invitation, she was under an immediate engagement, and could not then stay a moment!

What grand news we have, my dear Catharine! what English heart but must rejoice. You will surely have a ball in little Holland on the occasion; your bells have jingled, I dare say, till you are almost deafened with them; but really the bells ought not to be the only dancing materials you possess.

Yes, there was a war on—a long, weary war, which was having its repercussions in the immediate neighbourhood of Miss Weeton. Hardly a month passed but Miss Weeton had something to set down in her current volume of journal entries or copied letters—a volume covering six years of a period fraught with great danger to her country; yet this volume contains but two brief acknowledgements of the existence of the European conflict, the writer devoting the 110,000 words the volume contains to her own little world; nothing else mattered—which is perhaps as well for us.

There is going to be a ball at Huddersfield (they say). I almost wonder, for there is such a saving spirit throughout this country, that I feel a little surprised at the intelligence. Here, do nine of us sit in an evening, for near two hours, round *one* candle. To be sure, six of 'em are children; but I really think my neck is grown longer with trying to get near enough to the light to see to thread my needles. However, by way of drawback, what I gain by length of neck, I have the consolation to suspect I lose in a stoop of the shoulders; which is very well you know, for goodness knows I am quite tall enough.

Soon after I first came here, I was telling the little Armitages that I had formed but an unfavourable opinion of their manners on my arrival, but that I began to think they had good hearts. 'And do you love us better now?' said they. 'Indeed I do.' 'Well, and I'll tell you what,' said George, 'do you know, we called you ugly-face at first.' 'And do you like me any better now?' 'Oh yes, we do! you are so good to us, and tell us so many things.'

P.S. Since writing the above, a *most dreadful* accident has happened! 3 of Mr. Armitage's houses in Huddersfield were burnt down the other night, Nov. 30th. owing, it is supposed, to the carelessness of a servant boy, when going to bed. The boy, and a servant woman, were burnt to death. The tenants of the houses were severe sufferers; two of them were able to save nothing but themselves.

Neither letter nor parcel arriving from Uncle Barton, and unable any longer to concentrate upon or do justice to her work, the governess sought and obtained special leave of absence, in order to investigate upon the spot the mainsprings of the recent baffling conduct of her relations.

[JOURNAL]

I went, on the 13th. of December, to Liverpool, to settle my affairs there, and wrote a Note to my uncle to beg he would send the parcel by Wm. Hindley on the following Saturday, Dec. 18th. I called on Wm., but he had brought no parcel; he gave me a letter from my uncle, in which he said several things—viz: gowns, a muff, and a bonnet— were left me by my aunt, but that my cousin [Latham] had been so unwell the day before he wrote, that she could not come up to his house to take them out of the drawers. This, to me, appeared a strange kind of evasive language; there had been many days besides that one, in which my cousin might have packed up the parcel; and my stay in Liverpool being very limited, if I did not receive it *then* (on the 18th) I must return without it. I was much hurt and perplexed, and, not knowing what to do, at last I concluded on going to Holland the next morning, Sunday, Dec. 19th, in Wm. Hindley's cart, and went accordingly.

I first called at Mrs. Braithwaite's, not knowing where I should find my uncle, as he had talked of taking lodgings, and had not informed me in his previous day's letter whether he had left his house or no. Mrs. B. begged I would be her guest whilst I staid in Holland, and I very gladly consented. My uncle being at Church when I arrived in Holland, I waited till he got home. I then called upon him, and sat about half an hour; he requested me to take tea, and to sleep at his house. I declined it, as I had promised Mrs. B. to return to tea. I have since wished I had taken tea with him, as he appeared to be in a more communicative humour than usual, and he might have treated me with some confidence, and have told me many things which I was anxious to know; but afraid to keep Mrs. B. waiting, I soon left him, thinking I could make a longer visit the next morning. Whilst I staid, he said that it was indeed my aunt who reported that I had *gone off with a gentleman!!* and that she did it, because she knew not what was become of me, and was *afraid* it was so! My brother, out of *delicacy* to my *aunt*, had not confessed to me who it really was that told *him* so; but now that my aunt was dead, he did not doubt but that Thomas (meaning my brother) would tell me all about it. . . . I was astonished and filled with horror! that . . . my aunt could *so positively* tell me, in the presence of my cousin, that she had never said any such thing, nor had ever any such report been circulated, either by her or my cousin; and that *no one had ever told my brother so*. Gracious Father! and could my aunt so deliberately, so villainously, deny her own words? and be so depraved, so dreadfully wicked, as to charge my brother with inventing such a *lie*? . . . She *did* do it—and—Oh merciful Father! has died in the dreadful sin. . . . Heaven have mercy on her wicked, guilty soul!

My brother's *delicacy* to my aunt! roused my utmost indignation. *Delicacy* to the wanton defamer of his sister's character! and when he knew from the first, that his sister was perfectly innocent; even from the *appearance* of evil, was she free. Where was his delicacy to his sister! to suffer his aunt, or any other person, to speak ill of her in his presence, and never to resent it? . . . Contemptible, time-serving fellow! My aunt's money, or my uncle's, was of much more value to thee, than thy sister's character—than thy sister's esteem and affection. Take their money, if thou canst get it! and mayst thou never suffer for the meanness thou hast been guilty of to obtain it.

I was so overwhelmed with grief and wonder that my aunt should have suffered her last moments to arrive without ever confessing her injustice to me, and clearing my brother as much as she might have done, that I scarcely attended to the rest of my Uncle's communication. I did just recollect hearing him say, that 2 gowns, a black and a grey sarsenet;[1] a muff and tippet; and a marone velvet[2] bonnet, were left to me by my aunt. Until then, I had never heard what she had left me. That to my brother, she gave a purse containing 40 guineas in gold, and £10 in Bank notes; and the same to my cousin Latham. A purse for me she had left in his care, sealed; but, thinking of sending it by Wm. Hindley the Saturday before, he had broken the seal, and found a ring and five £1 notes.

The latter part of this information I caught but imperfectly, so absorbed was I in thought; and when it passed my ear, I thought that he must be alluding to something else. He said he would give me, in the morning, whatever was left me by my aunt; so, thinking I should then know whether I was mistaken, I took leave for the evening. As I proceeded to Mrs. B's, I felt more and more convinced that my Uncle really said he had broken the seal; but whilst there was a shadow of doubt, I would not condemn him for a breach of trust, of which perhaps he was not guilty.

Unwilling to speak ill of my aunt now she was dead, I did not mention any part of my uncle's communication respecting her to Mrs. B's family, except what I thought my Uncle said of the purse, which formed the whole

[1] A thin silk.   [2] Wine-coloured.

subject of our conversation for the evening; and the whole family seemed much hurt and astonished about it. 'If my Uncle really had been guilty of such a mean, scandalous trick,' Mrs. and Miss Braithwaite both said, 'they would believe him capable of any piece of villainy; they had heard it often said, that my aunt, notwithstanding the offence she had expressed towards me, had yet made no difference in the division of her property, but had left me equal with my brother and cousin.'

I called upon my uncle next morning, at 9 o'clock; he said but little; ordered the servant to fetch down the parcel of cloathes, and went himself to fetch the purse. He gave it to me, with the seal broken!!

He gave as his reason for it, that he did not choose to send it by Hindley, without knowing how much it contained, as the man might have been robbed. 'But then, you did not send it by Hindley, Sir?' To this, he gave no answer. 'And he is a man of such approved and long-tried honesty, that I could have trusted him with it.' '*He* should neither trust him, nor any one,' he replied, 'with uncounted money.' 'As to that, Sir, how should he know that it was uncounted money? or that the parcel contained any money, if you did not tell it? As I had requested you to send it by Hindley, all responsibility was taken from you; and *I* could have trusted him.' 'It was out of care for my interest,' he said, 'that he did it.' 'If you could not trust the parcel by Hindley,' I replied,' 'why did you open it? and why did you not inform me so, in your yesterday's letter? in that, you did not so much as mention it. Indeed, Sir, you should not have opened it.'

My uncle rose from his chair in a violent rage. 'Do you mean to insinuate,' he said, 'that I took any money out, or that the purse does not contain as much as your aunt sealed up in it?' 'I know nothing about it, Sir; I only wish you had not opened it.' 'It is just the same as accusing me of stealing money out of the purse,' said my uncle, as he paced the room. I was silent. 'Your aunt left £180 to be equally divided amongst you all, at my death; she could not legally make a Will, and it shall be as I please, whether you ever have it, or no; it shall be according as you behave; so you had all of you better take care!'

I could scarcely suppress a smile at this; for the mighty sum, for which we were to be so very circumspect in our behaviour, would only be £60 a-piece; and we might wait 20 years for it, for anything we knew. 'As to that, uncle,' I replied, 'I well know you solemnly promised my aunt, some years ago, to fulfil her wishes, and gave her your permission to make a Will; and your word ought to be as good as law.' He made no reply to this, but sitting down, began to write in an Account book. I rose, and saying good bye, left his house, never more, perhaps, to see it.

I had heard from several people, some months before her death, that my aunt had made no difference in the disposal of her property, leaving me equal with my brother and cousin; and so I believe she did; it was very unlikely that she would *seal* up £5 and a ring *not worth* 7s.

It appears quite as unlikely that my uncle should be guilty of defrauding me of so small a sum as £50, when he is placed so much above want; a man, too, so constant an attendant at Church; of such apparent, and boasted, integrity; of principles so rigid, that he never forgave any deceit practised against himself; but—my aunt herself placed no confidence in him, and many little mean actions speak against him, well known by different individuals.

My cousin Latham will submit to any meanness to forward her interest in the world. To supplant me in my aunt's favour, she invented many a mischievous tale to set my aunt against me; represented me as proud and high; that I was above my relations, and that I spoke with the greatest contempt of my aunt and uncle, and ridiculed them at every opportunity. By these mean arts, she obtained her purpose—*in part,* i.e., if my aunt really left me no more than this £5—but is, on the whole, dreadfully disappointed; she expected that my aunt would wholly exclude me, and that she had considerably more to bequeath. Finding a seven years labour in all the arts of hypocrisy and falsehood, have availed her so little, she has now cause to repent bitterly that she took so much pains to exclude me, who could now have been so great a friend to her. Had I gone to live with my aunt, my uncle would most probably have wished me to remain with him, and I should naturally have drawn him more closely to the interests of our family, merely because he would have seen more of us than of any other family; and because, having no relations of his own except a distant one, whom he has never noticed for years, he would have had no other family likely to have attached themselves to him. My absence having now totally estranged him from his late wife's family, he has adopted a little boy of that distant relation, and very likely will leave him all he has. My brother and cousin now perceive the consequence of their narrow-minded policy—and never were the guilty so deservedly punished!

My cousin, with the mean facility which she well knows how to practise, has already turned sides, and would endeavour to persuade me that she has a great respect for me! She complained much to me of my uncle's behaviour to her since my aunt's death; and indeed, he really has acted meanly. My aunt left my cousin all her cloaths, with the exception of the few things given to me; my uncle retains the cloaths in his own possession; is highly offended if anything is said about them; and does not say when he shall give them up. He has given several garments to his servants and others, which were indeed not his to give (if my aunt's dying wishes, and his solemn promises to her, were to be at all regarded). Whilst I was at Holland last, my cousin called upon me in the afternoon, over-abundantly civil. I, in return, was not uncivil, but cool. I felt disgusted at her effrontery in expressing so much affection for me, in the presence of the Braithwaites, whom she knew had been frequent hearers of her malicious insinuations against me. She took leave with expressions of concern at the shortness of my stay (only one whole day). She came again after tea, saying she could not bear the idea of my departure, without seeing me once more! I felt so displeased at her fawning conduct, that I could scarcely forbear expressing myself with some asperity—but—she was too contemptible, and I forbore. As I had occasion to see a tenant that evening, I rose to quit the room; she followed me. As we went throught the street, she thrust something into my hand. 'What is it, cousin?' said I; for the night was dark, and I could not imagine what it could be. I thought it felt like a small parcel of scrumpled paper. 'Never mind,' she said, 'at present; you'll see, when you get home.' Frank Braithwaite was escorting me, and supposing it was to be kept a secret, I put it in my pocket. On my return to Mrs. B's., I found a *pound* of *gingerbread*, which had just been sent to me as a present by my cousin! I took the little parcel out of my pocket, and found it to be a yard of handsome broad lace, not much worn, and recognized it to be some which my aunt once had on a cap. I shook my head, exclaiming to myself, Oh, cousin, cousin! do you think I am so weak as this? do you think that gingerbread and lace can make me atonement for the injuries you have done me? At the same moment, I resolved she should never be one shilling richer for anything I possessed. She seems to think she can make a mere feather of me, and blow me which way she pleases. Whilst there was anything to be had from my aunt, she took every pains to keep me at a distance; since her death, she thinks she can draw me back again, for she knows I have much more to leave than my aunt has left. She succeeded in the first, but she will find the second impracticable. In what consternation she appeared, when I told her of my uncle's determination—that it should be as he pleased, whether we ever received the money left by my aunt to us, at his death. She imagines we could claim it, perhaps, in right of my Grandfather Rawlinson's Will, as my aunt died without children. I had the Will in my possession, and promised to look at it when I got to Liverpool; and I confess I felt a malicious kind of pleasure in being enabled to inform her, by means of Miss C. Braithwaite, that she had nothing more to expect, for my Grandfather had left his daughters the full possession and disposal of their own fortunes.

Returned to High Royd, the picking up of the threads of her occupation seems to have left her little time for her correspondents; curiously enough; her first letter, towards the end of January of 1814, is addressed to that colourless woman, Mrs. Green, the wife of the Lakes artist, who was still living at Ambleside. She appears to have written but twice to this woman, and never at all to her godchild Green.

How does Mr. Green succeed in the prints he mentioned when he wrote? I was sorry I could do nothing for his interest here; the people in this part of Yorkshire appear to be *all* a money-getting, but not a money-spending people.[1] Taste and Science are words I never hear. Mr. A. himself is in the woollen trade, and works like a slave in his warehouse, and constantly attends the Huddersfield weekly market. He keeps neither carriage nor in-door man-servant, is extremely economical, and makes all his domestics work as hard as himself. I am most excessively

---

[1] This was Mrs. Gaskell's considered opinion of Yorkshiremen; and it is a trait not soon to be eradicated.

confined; so much so, that I think I shall not stay above 6 months longer; reading, music, or any other relaxation are almost out of the question. If I do leave Highroyd in the Summer, I should much like to spend a few months near Ambleside; do you think I could obtain lodgings, or board on moderate terms?

The country here is very pretty and romantic. Highroyd house stands alone, and very high; we have an extensive, and in some points, a fine view, from the front windows; but no view here equals those near you; and the confined life I lead, makes me almost hate the country in which I am so imprisoned.

We have a sad house at present. 4 of the children are afflicted with the hooping-cough, and have it violently. I am become quite a nurse, for Mrs. Armitage leaves the care of them almost entirely to me.

To MISS C. BRAITHWAITE   Highroyd: Feb. 4 1814.

I have been a long time, my dear Catharine, in finding time to write to you. It is not that the frost has had any effect upon my ink; although that might serve just as well for an apology in such intensely cold weather, as most apologies made by dilatory correspondents. On second thoughts, I almost wish I had given you that as a reason; it would have been something new; for, 'want of time', is such an old hack, everybody mounts upon the back of it when they are going to write a letter.

To tell you that I have been in want of a subject, would be so humiliating to my fancied variety and elevation of ideas, that I—I—I—do not like to confess it. Besides, I have felt myself very much out of humour lately, and if I write in ill-humour, perhaps I might make you as ill-tempered as myself; for I feel it is an infectious disorder, and I should be sorry to *spread* it—I was going to say, *propagate* it—but it is such a shocking word for a *delicate female* (say an Old Maid when you read it, Catharine) to use, that I forbore to insert it.

My good mistress is in the family way again, and—oh dear!—so odd-tempered, so Argus-eyed, so stingy, and so suspicious (as she always is at these times) that, reflecting her countenance and manner, we are, every soul of us at Highroyd, as cross as we can be—Mr. A. excepted. I wish some Don Quixote or other would come and drive the foul spirit away; he would be in little danger of being enchanted by any of us.

It is natural to think frequently on those objects which we are in the habit of seeing daily; and amongst others, Mr. Armitage is one who occasions me many a serious reflection, he appears so intent on the riches and honours of this world, and so totally forgetful of those of the next. He is a man of sense, talents, information, and industry, but every talent seems to be directed solely to the acquiring of riches and rank. He sets a great value on titles, and one day said that he thought a reigning monarch ought to confer titles on those who had, for two or three successive generations, been wealthy. Imagining that he was alluding to his own family at the time, I was silent; but often perceiving the value he placed on *such* honours, I have since taken occasion to remark, that no titles conferred dignity in my opinion, except such as were obtained by merit; and that Knighthood in particular was so frequently bestowed, that it had fallen into contempt, and become a frequent theme for ridicule; that even the King himself made a laugh of it; and several times, when Sir—this, or the other, was mentioned, I have asked, with a smile, if he were one of Peg Nicholson's knights,[1] or if he had

---

[1] 'Peg Nicholson's Knights' were the recipients of easy knighthoods conferred upon them for their loyal addresses of congratulation to George III following upon the attack upon his person by Margaret Nicholson, a poor demented creature, in the year 1786. The knife with which she struck at him, under cover of presenting a paper to him for his examination, penetrated

obtained his title by *nothing* but carrying an address? . . .
My mouth must not open again here on this subject; for,
only a few weeks ago, *Mr.* Walker, of Leicester (an own
uncle), carried an address to the Prince Regent at Belvoir
Castle, from his very loving and loyal subjects, &c., and
returned—*Sir* William. I dare not laugh here again on
this subject; but—thoughts are free, you know, and I
do think that Mr. A. himself will endeavour to obtain
some such Knighthood before he dies;[1] my pride would
rise too high for such a title. I would at least be a
Baronet, or remain as I am, were I similarly situated.
Mr. A. has several times expressed his surprise at those,
who, having carried addresses, declined the consequent
honour.

Mr. A's parents are strictly religious and charitable; the
latter virtue is as little known here as the former, and I am
surprised, that with such parents, Mr. A. should be so
worldly-minded. He seems to possess a much greater
portion of humanity than his wife; she really is not kind-
hearted. Were I to treat her children as she treats her
servants, I should not be long here; she is angry with them
if they are ill, poor souls!

We have a sad house just now; five of the children have
got the hooping cough; the two who are worst sleep in my
room, so that I have but little rest night or day. Mrs. A.
always takes the youngest at night, and has less rest for
the time than any of us; indeed, as a wife and a mother,
she is really an exemplary character.

To MISS C. BRAITHWAITE   Highroyd: April 19th. 1814.

I am answering your letter, my dear Catharine, a little
sooner than perhaps you expect; but I do it in the hope

the cloth of his coat only. After a confinement of 42 years, she died in her
99th year.
   [1] An honour, still much coveted in Yorkshire, in due course fell his way,
and he died a J.P.

of hearing from you again before I leave Highroyd, which will be about the middle of June. I wish I could conveniently leave now; my own affairs will hardly permit so great a sacrifice to Mrs. A., as that of staying two months longer. I would not have left Mrs. A., had she treated me like one of the family. Mr. and Mrs. A. are both very unpopular, I find, in this neighbourhood, from their pride and extreme illiberality; and change their servants so often, that they can scarcely get any to live with them. I have certainly been much better treated for the last twelvemonths, but am still a tenfold closer prisoner than any other governess in this neighbourhood, and am staying at home this afternoon (Sunday 17) for want of a decent bonnet to go to Church in. Mrs. A. knows this, but neither offers me a holiday, nor a conveyance to Huddersfield to buy one; and I'll stay at home these two months before I'll ask her.

The little wood I began of cutting some walks in last Autumn, has again become the scene of my daily labours this Spring, when I go out with the children. It has been a laborious, though agreeable employment. I have just finished cutting brambles, hollins, brackins, and broom, and planting flowers. Mrs. A. had an arbour of lattice work built in it last week, on a spot that commands a very beautiful view. I shall leave a memento behind me which I know the children will be grateful for. Mr. and Mrs. A. have not once thanked me, either directly or indirectly.

We have lately got a new curate at our village chapel, from, [or] at least a native of, Winstanley, near Holland. His name is Winstanley. He has prominent eyes and wears glasses; can you tell me anything of him? I *think* I have heard of his being at Mr. Banks's, and being a favourite there.[1] He seems to obtain considerable respect, but as he

[1] The Bankses of Winstanley Hall figure in a characteristic anecdote on p. 166 of vol. i. The Rev. T. R. Winstanley was one of a succession of curates who officiated during the suspension of the Rev. Robert Smith, M.A,

appears to be a literary kind of character, his conversation will be above—or—quite out of the way of the Yorkshire gentry here, for *trade* is their learning. His unassuming, easy manner, gains him friends. Mr. A. and all the respectables of the village (Honley), have called upon, and invited him. He has dined once here; I had no opportunity of speaking to him.

What glorious, blessed news we have had week after week, my dear Catharine, from abroad! It will restore health to the sick, gladden the sorrowful, and make the poor rich. I wish my aunt had lived to see this day! but —perhaps she is doing better.

It scarcely becomes me to say how warmly attached my little pupils are; it will give me many a pain to quit them; nor would I, if their mother were half so grateful as they. The eldest said today, that when she saw the gardens I had made for her brothers and sisters, and the flowers and trees which I had planted, the tears would come in her eyes, and she should almost weep. I can scarcely leave little Charlotte; I really think I shall kidnap *her*.

Give my love to everybody that cares for it.

Definite as the preceding may sound with regard to her plans ahead, yet an answer to another request for her services from Mrs. Wade displays many 'ifs and probabilities', despite the offer of the £50 a year salary stipulated (so unhopefully) by Miss Weeton. Her cousin Smith had for the time being been scared off, having heard that one of her future pupils was of her own age; and now Miss Weeton finds 'it would have been necessary for me to have known the style of life in which you lived, and the manner in which you wished your daughters to be educated'. Still, as she cannot possibly be at liberty for the next three or four months, possibly as late even as October, 'these inquiries are now unnecessary'. And so the wheel of fortune took its downward trend.

(for reasons tantalizingly withheld by Honley's historian), the holder of the living from 1802 to 1845.

To MRS. PRICE   Highroyd: May 24 1814

I have been in the daily expectation of hearing from you for a week of two, until at last my little stock of patience is exhausted; and, with scarcely time for writing, I am bustling at it as if business of the first moment depended on my present exertion and hurry. I hope to leave High-royd in 3 weeks from this time; I don't precisely know the day. As I hear nothing from you, I feel a little uncertain as to the place I must come to in Liverpool; will it be convenient to you to take me in? I shall be much obliged, if you can. Do not tell the tenants the time of my coming, lest they should remove in the meantime without paying arrears. If Mr. Leece would only see after the tenants up to the present, it would be much the best, and I shall soon release him from the trouble.

I am just now labouring under a considerable degree of vexation, from a circumstance ludicrous enough in itself, and which I have treated as such, until it has become too serious to laugh at. The country-people here have got it into their heads that I am going to be married to an old farmer of 74, with about £30 a year (on which alone he subsists); from no other foundation that I know of, than our chatting together as we go to Church on a Sunday— the only time I ever see him. The old fellow may have something in his head of the kind, and may have said as much to his neighbours; but such an idea never would have occurred to me, but for one of Mr. A's work-people, who mentioned it to me, and said it was reported that I was leaving Highroyd on that account. I now recollect many of the old man's speeches. I laughed at the compliments at the time, and joked again, imagining the difference of age, manners, and rank, were a sufficient licence and protection. He would sometimes wish himself 30 years younger, for my sake, and that he possessed a thousand a year, and he would bestow it all on me. I never returned this fine compliment, except by a laugh; but I have now reason to believe he is crazy enough to think seriously of it, from his conduct towards me. For several Sundays past, I have been obliged to go and return by different routs to avoid him, he waylays me so perpetually; if I am before him, I walk fast; if behind, slow, to avoid his company; and find some difficulty in doing it without publishing my reasons. Were I staying longer, I would complain to Mr. A.; as I go so soon, I am in hope to prevent the subject from spreading, by my apparent ignorance of it. I have thought more seriously of the affair, since last Sunday. I was stared at in a most unpleasant manner at Church, by several country-men, who then looked at old John, and laughed. If I were to make a stir about it, a greater noise would be made, which I hope to prevent by my speedy change of residence.

I used to respect the old man, because I thought him good-natured and friendly; and when he complained of, and lamented the loss of his wife (who died 4 or 5 years ago), I pitied him—little thinking I was gaining his affections!

Goodbye, old John—though not quite goodbye; for Mrs. Stock (Miss Weeton that was) will beg one of her late pupils to remember her kindly to you, in one of her letters to them later. And maybe £30 a year and old John might have proved a better bargain than Aaron Stock, with less than nothing.

And so, good-bye to Highroyd. Months later, the ex-governess penned the following.

I could weep now when I think of our parting the night before I left. I had seen them all put to bed, when, hearing some noise, I thought they were quarrelling, and went to see. I found them all weeping at the idea that that was the last night I should be with them; and the next morn-

ing they rose at five, and walked with me part of the way
(I had 4 miles to walk to the coach),[1] and when they left
me, went weeping home; the servants were very angry that
I was not sent in the Car.

The moral of which is, that prospective J.P.s do not like
being touched upon the raw; and significantly, Mrs. Armitage
was still pregnant.

To MISS ARMITAGE, Highroyd House.

Liverpool: July 27 1814.

My dear Sarah-anne,[2]

Your new governess will be with you soon, I suppose,
and I dare say you are very anxiously expecting her, and
wondering what kind of one she will be; she is sure to be
very fond of you, and very good to you if you are obedient,
respectful, and affectionate.

When I left Highroyd, I spent a fortnight in Liverpool.
One evening I went to see an exhibition of Androides;
your governess will tell you what that means;[3] I will only
tell you what I saw. There was a very pretty, baby house,
and a dog sat on the front step, so little that you might
have covered it with one of your baby sugar basins. The
man who shewed everything to the assembly, placed a
very little plate of artificial fruit, such as grapes, oranges,
pears, plums, cherries, &c., before the dog, and told it to
take care of it; and do you know, the little dog said 'bow
wow!', and every time the man spoke to it, it barked as if
it knew what he said; and when the man stole some of the

---

[1] Not until 1839 was there a coach-service through Honley—and then
only a bi-weekly one.

[2] The Sarah-Annes (and Mary-Annes) of those days, as even in these,
were given the full measure theirs by right of baptism.

[3] What a pleasant legacy to the new governess! However, the context
of the letter perhaps sufficed, with its illustration of automatons in the
resemblance of human beings, which put definitely into the shade anything
we have to show to-day.

fruit, it howled and barked and whined, in a most piteous manner! How ingenious the man must be, to make such a dog; for I suppose it was nothing but wood. A little doll, not so big as yours, stood at the door, and when the man told it to fetch any fruit, it went in, shut the door, and in two minutes, came out again, bringing whatever it was sent for; one time, an orange, another a bunch of grapes, &c. The man called for a chimney-sweeper, and bid him go sweep the chimney. A little figure, about two inches high, dressed like a chimney-sweeper, came creeping through a side-door, went in at the front-door, and in five or ten minutes, popped his head out at the top of the chimney, held up his brush, and shouted 'sweep!' Then he went down again, and bye and bye, he came out again with a bag of soot, and went away. There were many other things equally wonderful, but I have not room to describe them.

Almost, with the children, we echo the 'What a shame!'—for who wants to hear about that blessed brother at such a time, with all the wonders of that truly wonderful place, Liverpool, to display?

After I had been a fortnight in Liverpool, I went to Up-Holland, and staid a week with Mrs. Braithwaite; my brother called upon me, to pay some money owing to me, and shook hands very affectionately. I well remember, my dear Sarah-anne, how rejoiced you said you should be, when my brother and me were friends again; and the innocent, endearing warmth with which you, and George, and Emma, begged me to inform you of such an event taking place; and I now tell you of it, that I may afford your good little hearts a pleasure, so nobly disinterested in yourselves, and so gratifying to me.

Well, perhaps they too were gratified; for it is apparent that Miss Weeton had worked off a goodly proportion of their rusticity and applied at least a veneer of conventional politeness. But not to them did Miss Weeton pen the description of that poignant meeting; nor to any of her friends; her diary reveals it here for the first time.

[JOURNAL]

My brother called upon me at Mrs. Braithwaite's, and was shown into a front parlour. I was at work in a back parlour, when I was informed it was my *brother* who wished to see me. It threw me into such a state of agitation, I could with difficulty keep my seat. Miss C. B. urged me to compose myself, and go to him; I attempted, but could not rise. Catharine very kindly poured me out a glass of wine, and held it to my mouth—I could not drink it. 'Shall I shew him in here,' she inquired. 'Oh, stop a little—well—yes, do.' He was shewn in, and held out his hand in a very affectionate manner. I feebly presented mine, scarcely able to move it. He squeezed it, and sat down, and took out of his pocket, 5£ notes,[1] which he presented. I grew a little more composed, and faintly asked if I should not give a receipt. 'Perhaps it might be as well,' my brother answered, 'for Partington's satisfaction.' I wrote one, and a miserable scrawl it was. He observed that he was very late on his way home, and must go very quickly (he had been with his wife, spending the preceding day at Bispham, and had staid all night there; and coming through Holland on his way home had detained him). I answered, I knew that Saturday was a busy day with him; and then, his children recurring to my recollection, I was 'on the point of asking some questions respecting them, but . . . my heart filled, and I could not speak. A short silence ensued; my brother rose, and, taking my hand, affectionately squeezed it, and said 'good bye.' 'Good bye', I faintly answered. I tried to rise,

[1] Interest on a loan to a Mr. Partington, of Leigh, of which more later.

but my knees failed me, and I could not move. I was going to fall from my chair, but, resting my head on my hands, and leaning over the table, I supported myself; my brother left the room.

I burst into an agony of grief, for all hope of future intercourse seemed to be lost; why did my brother call, if he meant not to vindicate himself?

The above is the *whole* account of what passed in this interview, and yet . . . could it be imagined that my brother took advantage of these few circumstances again to traduce me!! He *has* done so. He has reported that I refused to shake hands with him, or to salute him. I can only imagine that he has told this *lie* to irritate my uncle still more against me, with the view of keeping us separate as long as my uncle shall live; it certainly being more to my brother's interest to be without a rival in my uncle's favour. Should my uncle die before me, I have no doubt but my brother would immediately seek a reconciliation with me; for, having obtained all he could from my uncle, his next object of attack would be myself; if he defer vindicating himself until my uncle's death, *he shall never* have the opportunity after.

WIGAN

K

WIGAN

SEPTEMBER 1814–APRIL 1822

*P*OOR, *deceived heart—for the very next letter is to 'My dear
Tom'. And what mystery underlies it! Within a fortnight
she was married—married to a blackguard; a widower about
whom unpleasant things had been said, and would continue to be
said; an undisclosed bankrupt, coveting that money which must
almost inevitably find its way into the calculating Tom Weeton's
pockets.*[1] *Where, and how, did she meet this scoundrel, Aaron
Stock (such was his unlovely name)? Could he be one of those
fellow-passengers, who, upon her return from that unlucky visit
to Liverpool, last December, had won her esteem by their superior,
not to say transcendent, behaviour in the coach, gently arguing upon
religion most of the way—with perhaps rather too much of cool,
subtle reasoning on the part of one (presumably Scotch), who was
opposed by (could this be her future husband?) 'a fat man, who
acknowledged himself to be a Calvinist; his religion appeared to
be in his heart. I took sides with the Calvinist.' It was a conversation which she felt she must long remember. Now, Aaron
Stock leased a factory in Chapel Lane, Wigan, owned by Tom
Weeton's mother-in-law. This at once establishes a possible connexion; and the fact, too, that she broke a two years' silence in
writing to her brother for a 'character' of her intended husband
(this letter, of course, she did not copy into her letter book), places
the matter in a clearer light, if it adduces no very considerable
evidence of wisdom on the part of Miss Weeton, in her selection
of brother Tom as casuist in this delicate matter (an interested
party, who stood to benefit to the tune of £100—a sum which,*

[1] It will be realized that the following account of Miss Weeton's marriage
affair, as also the preceding section upon High Royd, being drawn from the
information supplied by the recently discovered volume, cancels the largely
supposititious account given in the Epilogue to vol. i.

under the terms of her mother's Will, was to be delivered up to him upon his sister's marriage or death). As a cotton-spinner and factory manager, Stock would have to travel the countryside for orders, and perhaps he did indeed register himself in the good opinions of Miss Weeton upon this coach journey; but whether this might be assumed or not, the letter to Tom was a fact; and the astute Aaron, if he was aware of this unromantic procedure upon the part of the 'fair', would hardly be fool enough to fail to recognize the mutuality of benefit which must result therefrom for the male principals, and could confidently await the issue of her application. Tom, whether he was actually acquainted or not with Stock at this time, duly provided an excellent 'character', pocketed the £100,[1] and having thus exerted himself to the present satisfaction of his sister, gracefully yielded the stage to his wife, who proceeded forthwith to perform a pleasing little office; fated, however, not to meet with the desired response from either the staunch suitor or his bride-to-be.

'When I was on the point of marriage with Mr. Stock, he informed me that Mrs. Weeton desired him not to suffer me to be acquainted with the Braithwaites! This was a high piece of meddling. What had she to do with it? I was certainly old enough at 37, to choose my own acquaintance. Mr. Stock was as indignant at her presuming to give him advice and directions to behave unkindly to me, as I was. Mrs. W's dislike to them, was no rule to others. Who likes her? The Braithwaites were always more respectable than the Scotts—so much the more, that both names should never be mentioned in the same day.'

The foregoing is an extract from a tremendously long letter which the poor victim was to write some years later to her wretch of a brother.[2]

[1] In the matter of this sum, Miss Weeton proved to be a true Tom Weeton's sister; granting that, had she not reminded him of it, he would have remained completely forgetful of the arrangement, still, he must have pulled a wry face over the payment in *kind*, for she traded Richard Jackson's cottage, as representing one half, and a loan she had made, of £50, to a Mr. Partington of Leigh, as the balance of the £100!

[2] There will be many more extracts from this letter, indicated by an asterisk.

And now, to the letter that she had sent to Tom, with its adumbration of Mrs. Tom Weeton's machinations:

'I cannot easily express the pleasure and satisfaction which your last letter gave me; perhaps I can better do it when I see you. I thank you for it most sincerely; and the prospect which is now held out of an immediate reconciliation, is most gratifying.

'From some expressions in your letter, and from what Mr. Stocks [sic] says, it appears to me that you have been most singularly misled; and in my opinion, an explanation would tend to the satisfaction of both of us. There needs not, my dear fellow, to be the slightest irritation excited by it—but—we will defer any further discussion until some evening or other, when we can calmly sit by the fire-side and make an interesting, rather than a disagreeable subject of it.

'By way of elucidating a little, I will just inform you that the Billingtons, or any one belonging to them, I have never had any communication with; the Braithwaites have acted with peculiar prudence. I do not recollect hearing a sentence from them respecting you, which you might not have heard likewise. Let us be mutually cautious how we listen to any insinuations to each other's prejudice in future; judge of me with your own eyes and ears, and I will do the same; we shall still find each other deserving of all the esteem and affection we formerly felt, and possessed.'

Certainly, Miss Weeton allowed herself the luxury of rather too much altruism in her encouragement of the suit of Aaron (qualified, as we have seen, in respect of his 'character'); and all too hurriedly she secured what she had long pined for—a home of her own.

To MR. WEETON, *Leigh.*   *Liverpool: Aug. 31st. 1814.*
Dear Brother,
     In the midst of bustle and preparation, you must not expect that I can say much to you; it is enough for the present to inform you, that on the day you receive this, I shall most probably have

*resigned my prospects of future happiness or misery for this life,
into the hands of another.*

    My best love to your little ones.

                              Yours affectionately.

                                      E. Weeton.

*—so uniquely short a letter, that, considering its importance, it is
given in full.*

               ✻   ✻   ✻

Thus, in September of the year 1814, Miss Weeton became
Mrs. Aaron Stock,[1] with the privilege—nay, the legal obligation—of delivering up practically all her shrewd investments
and savings, to bolster up a tottering cotton-spinning concern
in a Wigan back-lane, and to minister to the grossness of an
unfeeling brute, who, having achieved his main object, proceeded forthwith to do his utmost to break the indomitable
spirit of his wife, and to drive the poor dupe out of his home
and life. Conjecture as to the reasons for Miss Weeton's allowing herself to be so egregiously deceived in her estimate of her
future husband's character must make ample allowance for
correlative, and to a large extent unknown, circumstance. As
has already been pointed out, the first mention of Aaron
Stock in her letters occurs but one fortnight before her marriage; and our principal source of information comes from a re-
shuffle of the allusions in that tremendous castigation, Letter
390 (12,000 words long, written and *twice* copied in the year
1822), which she was to administer to brother Thomas.

Aaron Stock was a widower, and he introduced his bride
to a home (situated at the back of his factory in Chapel Lane)
bristling with latent evil possibilities in the shape of a mischief-
making married daughter, Hannah Gilbert, and a younger
daughter, Jane (who, to a gallivanting propensity which inevitably indicated expedited marriage, was later to add theft).
In addition, there appears to have been a succession of easily
influenced servants, one of whom apparently never missed

---

[1] Incidentally, Dissenters were still compelled by law to marry in a church
of the established religion.

any opportunity to prejudice her master against the isolated would-be mistress of the household.

Mr. Stock was just 11 months the senior of Miss Weeton, having been born 24 January 1776—Tom's birthday, so a happy augury. In addition to the above-mentioned issue of his former marriage, there had been a son, thus alluded to by Miss Weeton, when making one of her subsequent, and futile, appeals for less hard measures where her own daughter was concerned:

> After suffering the loss of a fine boy by taking him from under a mother's care, let not the same kind of procedure deprive you of Mary too.

—indicating the existence of a constitutional unfitness on the part of Aaron to perform at all adequately in the dual role of husband and father.

It is perfectly obvious what must have proved the attraction to the man during the period of his wooing; and his astuteness in selecting Miss Weeton for his purpose is only equalled by her appalling blindness in the face of the known circumstances of his present struggling position, and the unfortunate issue of his former marriage. Her income at this period was derived from the fortunate speculation in cottage property, and the interest from £100 (apart from that £100 held in trust for her brother's future emolument). Roughly, it would be £75 from all sources. She had also inherited household goods from her mother, sufficiently substantial not to be cast out later, along with her, though apparently lacking in aesthetic appeal where the taste of a pre-Victorian generation of prospering mill-owners (of which Aaron Stock soon became one) was concerned. With the exception noted hereafter, Miss Weeton committed herself and her whole worldly possessions into the hands of her husband—an act of submission he could base legal claim to; but the shearing was apparently even then hardly close enough.

> Your benefit, and that of your family, was my sole study from the hour I married you; of which I gave you daily proofs—first, in giving you full possession of all the

property I had, £23 excepted, which was surely a mere trifle for pocket money, that should not have been grudged me, as it has been. £3 of this, I spent the week of our marriage, in presents to Hannah and Jane.

It is fortunate that we have Letter 390 to draw upon for this period; for Miss Weeton (it is convenient to call her by her maiden name throughout) wrote more letters than she either dared, or had the inclination to copy, for the next eighteen months; in a note to a letter written in the year 1816 (in which year she was becoming more herself, to the extent of resuming her old copying habits), she confesses that 'since I came to Wigan, I have copied very few letters'. A significant commentary upon her married life. During the remaining months of 1814 subsequent to her marriage she copied but one letter— to one of her late pupils, Emma Armitage; and in this we get her declared reason for not writing more letters, which no doubt sufficed in the case of a child just seven years old.

There is some danger, Emma, that you will find a difficulty in reading this bad writing. I have had such weak, inflamed eyes for some weeks, that I have been unable to read, sew, or write; this will, I know, be a very sufficient apology to my good-natured Emma for the trouble I give her.

Well, if the copy is anything to go by (and the copy must have been taken ere the letter was dispatched), tear-inflamed eyes had made hardly perceptible impression upon her invariably clearly legible hand.

She tells Emma but little of her home or family; but we are introduced to Jane—at present on her best behaviour, and no doubt glad of a step-mother's presence to escape further boarding school.

I have got one daughter. She was a big girl at first, do you know; 15 years old! She has a very pretty face, and she is of such a sweet, amiable disposition, that everybody loves her. She has been a long time at schools from home, and amongst other things, has learnt Music, and we have a very handsome Piano-forte for her. She will stay at home now, and I shall teach her.

Miss Weeton's views upon the sacredness of marriage, and the duties of the parties thereto, she had expressed sufficiently often enough in her letters to leave any room for doubt that she would endeavour to acquit herself other than nobly in her new situation; but, should she be in any doubt, there was Mr. Stock at hand to prompt her.

You required me to repair all your cloathing, excepting shoes, and I dare say you remember how readily and good-naturedly I submitted to your wishes. I disliked exceedingly patching breeches, coats, waistcoats, and even neck-kerchiefs, besides darning stockings up to the very knees; but to please you, I did it cheerfully.

Aaron's heart must have smote him about the cobbling omission; disillusion was quickly to follow for his victim.

The impression you made upon my mind, was that such extreme shabbiness must proceed from the continual danger you felt yourself in, of becoming a bankrupt, and for 6 or 7 years, I was in the constant expectation that we must all end our days in a workhouse; for neither you nor anyone else ever told me that you had realized any property. Consider how mild and patient I was, when I at length began to discover that you had been deceiving me, and that I had needlessly been kept in a state of penury and labour.

Mr. Stock was not wholly bad, though. It is an established fact that he was religious; witness his 'excellent Calvinistic Library', in more prosperous days ahead. In addition, he was to give liberally to Missions, Schools, &c. (and it was a thought malicious on the part of Miss Weeton to observe that his charities were limited to such good causes as issued lists of Subscribers for public edification and emulation). His library must indeed have made an excellent show; but Calvinism boded no good to those subject to the influence of its more fanatic exponents. The Rev. Alex. Steill, of St. Paul's Independent Chapel, made free use of its treasures, and accorded its possessor all the consolations of the religion they jointly professed—consolations which he never extended to the wretched partner of the marriage, though he appears to have blasted her life with his fulminations and desperate expedients to exclude her from active church membership, either in his own church, or within the sphere of his potent local influence.

Aaron Stock was a dyspeptic; and there were then no front-page advertisements to speed him to immediate relief. To her infant daughter Miss Weeton was to write (in the course of a letter penned during her subsequent exile and loneliness)

Your father, my love, had always better health when he had no supper; for when he had, he would be seized with vomiting, violent head-aches, could sleep but little, and no appetite for breakfast; yet became bloatedly fat, and was in danger of apoplexy.

The 'danger of apoplexy' was, alas, more apparent than real. He had 'nervous irritations, he wriggled and twitched', and he had a blind partiality for walnuts; with the best intentions in the world, Miss Weeton would send him a small peace-offering of these, from her lonely lodgings, some years hence.

This, then, was the man of her choice; this, the consummation of her dreams; after a period in Mersey-side lodgings enlivened with the 'goings-on' of a married couple who indulged in free fights on occasion, using chairs and whatever else came handy for the purpose; after experiencing the amenities of the would-be high-toned Chorley household in dismalest Liverpool; after a rather too intimate study of the Pedder *ménage*; and, above all, after suffering the long-drawn-out agony of the irruption of Mrs. Tom Weeton into her cherished dream-life—this man could so consummately fool her into such an anomalous position, and reduce her at once into a lower position than that of the meanest of his triumphant domestics! There must have been many to triumph that day, and to watch the course of events, only too certain, in their worldly wisdom and prescience, of the consequences of the folly of the 'pragmatical schoolmistress'.

＊　　　　　＊　　　　　＊

On 9 June 1815 a daughter, named Mary, was born to her.

I recovered [she writes in a letter to her cousin Smith, now comfortably installed in the Wade household in the Isle of Man] from my confinement very rapidly indeed, to the surprise of everyone who knew me, and quite unexpectedly to myself. My little one was healthy, and for above a month, we went on very well; we were then both taken very ill—the child appeared too weak to be weaned, and I was no longer able to nurse it. A wet-nurse was procured, and I then went to South-port for a few weeks; the child recovered rapidly. I laboured under so great a depression of spirits, that my recovery was very slow.

And what occasioned the depression of spirits? The motherhood had proved a bitter-sweet event. £100 had not bought off Tom; nor silenced his wife.

Even when I married, your wicked speeches did not cease. Mrs. S. Singleton told me that you and your wife then reported that I was pregnant before I was married, or I should not have married so hastily. Not crediting that you could say this, I told you what I heard, hoping you would vindicate yourself—you denied it not, but observed a total silence as my answer. Shame on your licentious tongue! Time soon proved the falsehood of your accusation; my little Mary was born 9 months and 9 days after we were married.*

There follows a sickening tale of consistent and calculated cruelty, with all the variations upon all the themes incidental to unhappy unions (and a few extra ones, incidental to the times); and ever there was the background of cavilling members of the family and servants, united only in their intense hatred of the interloper.

In the course of a later letter of condolence to a bereaved Wigan friend, she instances her own peculiar troubles from the time of her marriage.

Since then, cruelty from a *monster of a husband*; extreme want and houseless at one time; imprisonments and bruises at another; my life daily in danger, attended with constant terror for many months, supposing each hour might be my last, and not knowing in what shape death might come— expecting at one moment to be poisoned, and therefore afraid to eat or drink anything that my husband could possible have meddled with; obliged to be constantly on my guard against the deadly blows he would sometimes give me at the back of my ear, unprovokedly, and when I was least expecting it.[1]

But much of that she had as yet only every reason to fear; and the care of his child was her intense preoccupation. An uneasy armistice must have reigned between the two principals, though it is apparent that the servants by no means suspended hostilities. Continuing the letter to Miss Smith:

Since my convalescence, I have been much engaged with sewing, making short-clothes for Mary; my friends all flatter me in saying she is a beautiful child; she is very fat and lively, and I hope will prove a source of peculiar comfort. I think of having her weaned in a few weeks; and as we are to remove to a much larger house in a month or two, we shall of course be very busy, particularly

[1] That Mr. Stock could be free with his fists there is evidence of in the local Sessions Rolls of the period. 'On the 17th. July, 1815, Aaron Stock, cotton spinner, entered into recognizances (his sureties being Richard Eccles, surgeon, and Thomas Astcroft, a stone-mason) for an assault on Robert Balshaw, a cotton rover.' (S.R. 60/25.)

myself. I am sorry to wean the child so soon, but the nurse's conduct has been so very reprehensible, that I must part with her. She has behaved well to the child, and had she been commonly civil to me, and in any degree trusty, I would have kept her some months longer. If Mr. Stock would consent, I would go over to Liverpool soon, for two or three days; but he will not let me stir anywhere; no powers of rhetoric work upon him, so I must be contented at home. I should much like to see some of my friends there.

Surrounded all the time by inimical relatives of her husband, ever less inclined to be kindly disposed towards the mother of a prospective sharer of Mr. Stock's effects, and by no means so easily to be imposed upon by the master of the household with regard to his improving financial position, the state of affairs that had obtained in the Pedder home must have seemed almost a summer's idyll by comparison. Aaron Stock's relations with his two daughters could never have been of the best, especially after the loss of his only son. That he was a willing listener to their tale-bearing, can readily be imagined. Servants Miss Weeton tackled manfully; at least one enemy within the walls was to find that the worm could turn.

I had much to fear from that Kitty Barker—she was a fit instrument to help him in any foul deed, that made him so outrageous when I dismissed her. Providence was with me, and enabled me to discover their evil machinations most wonderfully, and yet I never betrayed that I suspected them.

But not so easily could she deal with her enemies outside the domestic circle. Fully qualified at a later date to shake a warning finger, she earnestly advised her daughter to take particular notice of the behaviour of a prospective suitor towards father and mother, sister and brother, and to be guided solely by the conclusions drawn therefrom. In her own case, love must have been blind indeed, or no extenuating circumstances could have befogged her so. Aaron's mother, apparently, was dead; but his father, poor fellow, was *not*—a brewer's journeyman, incapacitated by a crippling rheumatic complaint, and utterly dependent upon the only member of the Stock family, Margaret Stock, who would afford him the support he stood so much in need of. Margaret Stock was unmarried, and of Miss Weeton's age; and but for her the old man must have gone to the workhouse (popularly, and with some regard for truth, known as the 'bastille'), though his eldest son, Aaron, was to give him a notable funeral upon the occasion of his death in the year 1823, and to lay him to rest in the grave next but one to that of Miss Weeton's mother.

There were four other members of this precious family, either the tools or the despised of their rapidly rising brother. There were two married daughters—one, a Mrs. Woodward, with a husband in a poorish way, eager to ingratiate himself, by any low act, with his prosperous brother-in-law; the other, a Mrs. Perkins, at least showed abortive signs of a not un-sympathetic inclination towards her persecuted sister-in-law, but was loth to incur the wrath of her brother, one of whose cottages—late Miss Weeton's—she occupied in Roscoe Lane, Liverpool.

Of Matthew Stock nothing transpires save a notice in the letters of the death of his wife; but William, and his wife, those rather supine, lachrymose butts for the insensitive brother, engaged Miss Weeton's sympathetic regard, and tendered their futile support in her troubles.

As Mr. Stock's position improved, so did his social standing, thereby extending the complement of potential, as well as real enemies, as his wife pointed out, later.

One of these mean fawners you have at last found out, and I rejoice sincerely, for yours and your children's sake; for, had he had an opportunity to become an executor, as he *hoped*, your children might, and would, have been made beggars. He could not deceive me, and therefore, lest I should frustrate his designs upon you, he left no art un-tried to induce you to drive me; but he exposed himself once, and let the sheep's skin slip, and you discovered the wolf in time. But there have been other wolves; would that you may find them out.

Thomas Kearsley (not unknown to Tom Weeton, and a co-trustee with him in a local charity) with greater success endeared himself to the rising manufacturer. He it was who, years later, recognizing with unholy glee the unmistakable gaunt figure upon the deserted high-way, could amuse himself with an attempt to ride her down in his gig.

The sight of Thomas was like a dagger through me. He is a perjured wretch, and, for the present, he is suffered to triumph in his perjury.

Friends she had, though for the present untried; years of cruel usage must elapse before a woman of her temperament and native pride could advertise her private wrongs, and cast herself, terror-stricken, upon friend or stranger, for a crust of bread or the protection of a respected name. Meantime, things were not going too smoothly, despite the advent of Mary; greatly daring, the mother had defied the Liverpool ban.

To MRS. PRICE   Wigan: May 22d. 1816.

I have been very comfortable since I left you; Mr. S. never said a word on his return that could lead to the subject of his displeasure when we parted in Liverpool; and I was equally cautious.

I have been much diverted with Mary today. I took her by the hand, and she walked all the way from hence as far as our late house in Chapel-lane. She had so many things to look at, that I thought we should scarcely ever arrive. She stopped at every open door, to look into the houses. There were many groups of little children in the street, and she would walk up to them, and shout at them; she set her foot upon the step of a door where there happened to be a cake-shop, so I bought her a cake; and then she wanted to stand still in the street whilst she ate it. I thought her first walk should be to her who first nursed her, as she lives in Chapel-Lane. I knocked at the door; I had to wait a little, and Mary, too, would knock. After our visit was over, we walked to see a neighbour who lived opposite to our old house; many people were at their doors, and Mary stopped to look at them all, and if they had infants in their arms, she stood some time. Many laughed, and said she was a sharp little thing. She went up steps at one house to a child of 3 or 4 years old (with a little help), who gave her what he was playing with. The noise of looms in a cellar next attracted her attention; she struggled hard to go to the windows;[1] but she is so fond of kicking, that I expected nothing less than the breaking them, so I enticed her to go after some poultry, and there was a little race. It is the first walk she has had from home, but I mean often now to take her short distances.

And the proud mother adds a note to this letter, for the benefit of those curious—'just turned 11 months old'. Certainly Mary was a precocious child; but how would Mr. Stock react to his daughter's being paraded down such low quarters as Chapel Lane?—for, by this time, he was installed in stylish Standishgate (in a house very recently the head-quarters of the Wigan Education Committee, and since swallowed up into the building of a modern store. An illustration of the house as it appeared at this time is given. It is the large house at the extreme right of the picture). The only drawback was its too close proximity to Dr. and Mrs. Hawarden, uncle and aunt to Mrs. Bessy Price, and to whose house visits on the part of Miss Weeton were interdicted—a ban she inevitably broke,

---

[1] Whole streets of these old weavers' cottages still remain in various Lancashire towns; and George Eliot, in *Scenes of Clerical Life,* allows us a peep into one: 'and at that time—the time of the handloom weavers—every other cottage had a loom at its window, where you might see a pale, sickly-looking man or woman pressing a narrow chest against a board, and doing a sort of treadmill work with legs and arms.'

MARKET PLACE, WIGAN

From an old engraving

JOSEPH ARMITAGE IN HIS OLD AGE

just as she broke that put upon her visiting her Liverpool
friends.

In this early summer of 1816 there appears to have been a
sort of truce between husband and wife; and, 'our servant Alice
has behaved so extremely well since I came home, that I have
great hopes of her becoming valuable'. The spirit of carnival,
too, was in the air.

The town is going to be in a great bustle this week; for
the fair commences tomorrow,[1] on which occasion, it is
usual for everybody to clean their houses thoroughly, to
white-wash, paint, &c; the confectioners begin of baking
for the fair a week beforehand; and the shop-keepers to
polish, and set their wares, in the neatest order; large
caravans enter the town with wild beasts, monsters, and
Jugglers; likewise wooden horses, whirligigs, gambling
tables, barrel organs, fiddlers, and hordes of beggars; to
add to the *usual novelties*, a handsome new Cloth Hall will
be opened, built by Mr. Tennant, and *everybody*, I suppose,
will go to see it.

A visit to St. Helens had been attended with some un-
pleasantness in the item of Jane's impertinence; but on the
whole, she had reason to be more confident for the future, in
the triumph of her system of household management—with
Aaron Stock as the main focus. Thus, to Mrs. Bessy Price she
writes, on 23 June:

I could smile at the idea in your last letter but one—an
idea which you hold very tenaciously and which, indeed,
will *generally* hold good; that if *one* of a married couple
gives way to the wayward humours of the other, they are
sure to be tolerably comfortable. Your experience has
not shewn you, yet, the result of such a course of conduct.
I have often read the experience of others, and have seen
a few instances myself, where the accommodating spirit
began, and remained, on one side, without having any

[1] 23 May.

softening influence on the other, but on the contrary, *increased* its *malignity* by *indulgence*; and where, likewise, an occasional *firm*, *judicious* opposition, *increased* the comfort of *both parties*.

Again, I could smile at your thinking that I had been so long my own mistress, because I had remained so long unmarried. I never was uncontrolled more than 2 years of my life. No one, used to live in another person's house, can be said to have much of their own way. You don't know what it is, nor how great a trial and breaking of the temper it is, to keep a school, or to be a private teacher; married to one of so peculiar a temper as I am, it is scarcely worse.

I know how little success you would have, could you take my place for one year. Much as you think you could effect, you have not the most distant idea of such a situation, nor can words express it; yet I am indeed much happier of late than I was, entirely owing to being determined not to submit to a continuation of ill-treatment. Had I not acted with greater spirit, had I continued to take every means to please (which was taken for a principle of fear), I must have lost my senses or my life. The man who rules by tyranny, can never be obeyed by affection; he is submitted to from fear, and delights in abject submission; it gratifies the pride of his heart to see everyone trembling around him. But mark! the tyrant in power, is ever the abject slave when humbled; he knows no medium, and the only way of living peaceably with him, is ... not to be afraid of him; for ... tyrants are always cowards. By way of experiment, I have acted on this principle for the last 10 months; and with so much success, that we have all much more peace than we had. But don't suppose that I cease trying to please; it is my daily and hourly study; and you would think so, were you to live here. It is only where my own comfort is materially concerned, that I assume a resolute conduct. I love too much, to grieve my husband when I can make him comfortable.

I again repeat, that I am much happier than I was last Summer; I am better treated; and my little Mary is so sweet a tempered creature, that she is the delight of my heart. How blest I am in every way; my heart glows with gratitude to the Mighty Father, for he is drawing me nearer and nearer to him. I have been tried as it were in the fire, and am delivered.

As further evidence of the temporary success of her 'system', she sandwiches an account of a sea-side trip with Mr. Stock himself, in between the usual slabs of didactics addressed to her late pupils of High Royd.

I have been at Southport lately; the place where Joseph was with his Mamma once. Mr. Stock and I went in a gig; we went to the Inn, and staid only four days; the weather was very cold and rainy, and I was very glad to get home again. Mr. Stock says perhaps we may go again if the weather is warmer before the Season is over; if we do, we shall take Mary with us, I think, for Mr. S. likes to have her with him often. She cannot talk any, but she is a very funny little girl; she pulls such droll faces, and she clips and kisses pussy as if it were a little baby. She is not afraid of anything; she would play with dogs, or horses, or cows.

Fondly the ex-governess recalls her favourite, George.

George was the torment and the delight of my heart whilst I lived at Highroyd; for you know how very naughty he was often, he was so excessively impatient over all his lessons. I taught George a great deal more by talking to him, than I could any other way. George is naturally eloquent, and has a Genius for Poetry.

Perhaps the absence of that thorn in her side, Jane, really accounts for the fool's paradise in which she was living, destined to last until November of this year. Jane's movements are a bit mysterious at this period, but she appears to have been in Liverpool, either stopping with, or under the supervision of, her Aunt Perkins; and a thankless task must that lady have found it—though, as ever, Miss Weeton was quite ready to snatch the hot chestnuts out of the fire for anybody else. Meantime, so deceptive were the signs, that she felt she could interest herself in subjects ever dear to her heart.

To MRS. PRICE   Wigan: Oct. 23d. 1816.

At present, my dear friend, I have plenty of time, and abundance of inclination for writing to you; and, besides these, some degree of matter more than can at any time be collected in a town like this. I wish you would come and see me; the coach-fares are so very low, that now is the time for travelling. We are very comfortably fixed here, and I think you might spend a few weeks without being very unhappy.

We Wiganers have begun to raise our heads and commence a literary career, that perhaps may exalt us to the top of Parnassus. What think you of a Wiganer being able to compose, to write, to print, or to publish!!! Is it not most extraordinary! *We* have got no farther than a penny, and threehalfpenny pamphlets; *we* are only in our noviciate; but even these are most astonishing . . . for Wigan! And as I feel some pride at being an inhabitant of a place that is at length beginning to shew some slight signs of intellect, I feel some additional consequence in being able to join myself to this bright community, and, in speaking, to say *We*!

For some time, perhaps 3 or 4 years or more, there has been a debating society in Wigan, supported and conducted by some low fellows, principally journey-men; and they have gone on unnoticed, except now and then affording a good joke to their masters. One of them once got into the room; a servant of his got into the chair, but when he saw his master there, he was so confused, the debate could not go on, and the exclusion of strangers was very gravely voted.

And very gravely we note Miss Weeton's lack of sympathy with these pitiful, struggling journeymen politicians, who are increasingly going to suffer for their temerity; and Mr. Stock is not going to stand any confounded nonsense from his work-people, whether children too tired to wipe their noses, or old worn-out men in a similar plight, over their dancing looms.

Lately a shoemaker's son, of the name of Burdekin, a warehouseman, feeling some strong impulses, and mistaking them for the effects of Genius [not, we may suppose, of the quality of George Armitage's] and Patriotism, has opened his mouth in this society; and being looked upon as a great man among them, he begins to think himself very great indeed; and, from leading a few poor illiterate fellows, would all at once take upon him to conduct the house of Lords and Commons, the King, Queen, Prince-Regent, all the Royal Dukes, the Princes, the Princesses, and Nobility and Gentry of all descriptions; it is only the poor people whom he thinks capable of conducting themselves.[1]

To assist him in this arduous undertaking, some experienced-headed Reformers from Liverpool, such as Rushton and J. Smith, have of late frequently attended here, and have been honoured with the presence of hundreds of vagabonds. The richer inhabitants of Wigan begin to be seriously alarmed; and the Mayor, a short time ago,

---

[1] The Bishops, Vicars, Curates,
    Parliaments and Kings
  Not only evils are
    But worthless things.

(Quoted in Hammond's *The Skilled Labourer, 1760–1832*.)

remonstrated with the Reformers respecting their meetings; they were deaf, and ridiculed his interference. Then came out a little letter advising peace and patience, and perseverance in well-doing; a simple, well-meant thing, supposed to be written by Mr. Pigot, late curate here. A very hot answer was instantly returned by a Reformer, in which were a great deal of hard words, and no *little* vulgarity and scurrility, interspersed with a *little* Latin, and of course, a *little* learning; this, it was said, proceeded from the brains of *little* Dr. Holme, a young apothecary of *little* repute. Soon after, a third pamphlet was born, said to be produced by Dr. Cowley, a man of some talents; the bantling was very witty, and had more sense and argument than either of the other two; but should it not become any larger, will, like the other two, be soon forgotten. The Reformers treated this with great contempt; it was not worth answering; and indeed there were some questions which it may not be convenient to answer; however, they do not mean to stop here, and these new-fledged authors mean to have more feathers yet in their wings.

The bravadoes of the Reformists, and the fears of the Loyalists, are amusing to an indifferent Observer. The former imagine that they have quite frightened the latter, and laugh exultingly; the latter are not quite easy, but laugh contemptuously, and at the same time, prophecy riots the ensuing Winter by the meddling of these would-be Reformers. Should riots really ensue, perhaps I may laugh with neither side. Many people are seriously uneasy.

As well they might be, with rioting general throughout the country, mostly directed against the rise in the cost of food, the aftermath of the long Napoleonic war. About this time witnessed the practical birth of trade unions; small-town Reformers, such as those of Wigan which Miss Weeton sneers at, were to see their small squib develop into rocket-like proportions, only to come down as dead, for the time being, as the rocket's stick.[1] Surrounded as she was with evidences of appalling squalor and poverty due to the intensification of the industrialization of the north by the introduction of steam, difficult as it must have been to remain level-headed, one searches in vain for even common charity from one whose own sufferings should surely have given her clearer insight. One cannot escape the conclusion that Miss Weeton was intensely, amazingly self-centred (selfish she certainly was not), with little sympathy outside her own kith and kin. It was a limitation which decides the parting of the ways between governess Weeton and governess Brontë. But in her own sphere she was unrivalled, and a little bit of malicious tittle-tattle about Mrs. Tom Weeton's kith and kin never comes amiss from her quill.

Mrs. Bird, Mrs. Weeton's sister, has got to such a pitch of drunkenness, that she is the talk of the country. The other day, she was carried home almost senseless; and in her way up Holland streets, was followed by a mob, hooting and hissing. Mr. Bird has at last determined on

[1] The prosperity of the years 1812–14 had been succeeded by the year of 'soup and reform'—1816. Weaving, requiring comparatively little skill in the acquirement, attracted hordes of low-class Irish and discharged soldiers; the development of the power-cum-factory loom had not yet displaced the numerous units of the domestic system. Meantime wages, which had been as high as 14*s.* 7*d.* in 1815, dropped to as low as 5*s.* in 1816. The agitation for Reform dated principally from the rejection of the weavers' modest and moderate appeal for relief addressed to the Prince Regent and the House of Commons in 1811. The attitude of the Wigan weavers in particular caused considerable apprehension, and the Hammonds, in their admirable *The Skilled Worker, 1760–1832*, devote a paragraph to it: '. . . some declined to receive the local charitable subscription, "using very impious language and observing that they would have reform and not relief, and they went to the length of stoning a charitable committee sitting to consider the distresses of and to administer relief to the Poor" '.

The following year saw a revival of trade; but the convenience of parish relief was too apparent for the employers to take that burden off the rate-payers' shoulders, by improving the rate of pay in accordance.

Curiously enough, the cotton-spinners were never better off than in the crucial year of 1816, due to unrestricted export trade; and Aaron Stock undoubtedly benefited, along with others of a numerous class of small masters, in a trade requiring comparatively little capital outlay.

separating, and my brother is to meet him in Wigan next Tuesday, with deeds to that effect.

Another sister (-in-law) of Mrs. T. Weeton would yet weakly stagger in her way up the Holland streets; and her husband would come once again to Wigan on a similar errand on behalf of Aaron Stock's wife.

My little Mary improves, and is the delight of all; she is just 16 months old. She does not say a word yet, notwithstanding which, she has a thousand little engaging actions. Her hair is very light, and curls all over her head like a little mop; and she is all over so fat and so soft. I have many a kiss in the course of the day, and many a laugh at her little droll ways; her father would be quite lost without her, and I am sure, so should I. I wish I had another . . . but hush! don't tell.

Where is Mrs. Edwards; have you ever heard? How are Mr. and Mrs. Langdon, and Master—but come and tell me with your own mouth, and I will not now ask you any more questions. I often call at your uncle Hawarden's, for I am almost lost for want of society. I cannot ask them here, so I call there once or twice a week; they always receive me in a friendly manner. They have been painting and beautifying the outside of their house and that adjoining, which is let to a straw bonnet-maker, and fitted up stylishly.

You would hear of a coach being overset here lately, opposite to the Eagle Inn. Many were severely hurt; but their heads were proof, being *Wiganers*. One man's head was fractured, but he came from Bolton.

—which irresistibly reminds one of the Cambervell coachman.

About this time Jane returned from Liverpool; and following a good talking-to from her Aunt Perkins, her attitude towards Miss Weeton showed marked improvement; but Hannah Gilbert was clearly not to be depended upon.

My servant Margaret, notwithstanding what Hannah thinks of her temper, is the best by much that I have had since I came to Wigan; and I am really very comfortable with her. She is very steady indeed, and cleanly, and pays more respectful attention to me than any other person in the house. I found it necessary, soon after she came, to tell her how I was situated with regard to Jane; that she would take every means of setting her against me; and Margaret told me that she had already attempted it with her, but assured me she would always strive to conduct herself so as to deserve my approbation, and I have had no reason to repent the confidence I have placed in her. Her temper breaks out sometimes, but it is nothing compared with what I have suffered from all the rest; I can easily put up with it.

Unfortunately, Jane and Hannah had their suspicions of the antecedents of this almost perfect domestic, who had had a 'Committee' sit upon her, to decide her fate; it is nowhere positively stated, but there is reason to fear—that Margaret had seen the inside of a Penitentiary! Preposterous and refractory weavers might deserve a good talking-to from the Mayor of Wigan; but Margaret's case was one to engage her mistress's most sympathetic concern and her every effort 'to confirm her in the right way'. But how foolish to let Bessy Price into the secret! And apparently the 'system' demanded a more consistent and able exponent than its late enthusiastic defender.

To MRS. PRICE   Wigan. Nov. 4th. 1816.

Dear Friend,

Perhaps when I exclaim how enviable is your lot in possessing a husband so kind, that, where he is, your heart is treasured; his home, your paradise; I ought much rather to say, how much above you am I blessed! My heart is driven and buffeted about, seeking where it may find rest;

and, having none on earth, will, almost of necessity, be driven to heaven. Mighty Father, may this indeed be the result of my afflictions! Then shall I be blessed to the utmost of my wishes, and the misery I now endure will be an eternal cause of gratitude. My husband is my terror, my misery! and I have little doubt, will be my death. I earnestly wish I could obtain a situation at Mr. Wade's or elsewhere; I would not hesitate a moment. I shall never live to educate Mary, unless I quit this place.

A female friend lately, was confiding to me some of her plans for earning something towards making an addition to her income; her family is small, and one plan we thought of, was taking boarders in the Summer at Crosby, or at Bootle. A house of that description seems to answer very well at Southport; it is a *private* house, chiefly intended for ladies; very few gentlemen are admitted—only those whose conduct is strictly correct and sober. The question is, whether it would answer at all, and which place would be best.

I was gratified much by your letter, except the part that refuses me all hopes of seeing you here; it would have been such an enjoyment to me, for I have not many now. Mary is almost my only comfort; for her alone have I any wish to live. Oh, if I could but get away! perhaps I might live; if I cannot, she will soon know what it is to be motherless. If the plan of my friend here should answer, I could almost wish to try a school near her . . . but it is in vain to wish; these are mere words, the foolish effusions of a heart weakened by severe treatment, a severity so everlasting, that I am altogether miserable.

I wish I *could* come to Liverpool for a day or two; I wish I could come, never to return here again! But a day or two would be some alleviation to my misery. I have, for 4 or 5 weeks, been worse than usual; as low almost, nay quite, as I was at Southport. I have till lately kept up

my spirits pretty well. I see no prospect of comfort. Mr.
S. never will mend; he is worse and worse.

Master Joseph Armitage, of Horton House Academy, near
Leeds, is the only one of her correspondents favoured with a
line from her *for almost a year* from the date of the above letter
—and she must have been sadly off-colour when she wrote this
precious epistle, in April of 1817. 'I see you a tall, stout, rosy
boy of 8 years old; may you increase in goodness, as you increase in years, and then you will then be sure of enjoying
peace and comfort, although you should become poor.' Follows a string of warnings about the snare of desiring too many
holidays, a great deal of money, rides often on horseback or in
a carriage, plenty of sweetmeats; and the desirability, on the
other hand, of coveting the real happiness of the mind and
heart. . . .

But if Mr. Stock would not on any account tolerate his wife's
presence in the midst of her Liverpool friends, he found it,
apparently, convenient to get shut of her upon a holiday,
during summer, at Tranmere, accompanied, or chaperoned,
by step-daughters Jane and Hannah. From later letters we
gather that the holiday, though not quite a success in itself,
had a curious sequel in the gift of three months domestic peace
to follow. It was whilst upon this holiday that she noted a
laughable intruder into the Mersey's shipping. 'The steam
boats make rather a laughable appearance; they go puffing
and blowing, and beating their sides, and labouring along with
all their might.' The sight of them, and the gentlemen's
country seats dotting the banks, sets her off on a dissertation
about our duty to the Creator of these paradisiacal scenes, this
time for Emma Armitage's behalf. But in a letter to her
prosaic brother, apparently the first since she married, she
comes to earth again.

My circumstances seem to have amended with the
weather; for, since my return from Tranmere, I have
enjoyed a degree of domestic comfort superior to any I
have known for near three years. Mr. Stock spends all his

evening soberly and peaceably at home. Hannah has become cordial and friendly with me; the servant is respectful; and my little darling Mary becomes more and more engaging.

But it was too good to last; and she herself could not leave well alone where the absent Jane was concerned.

On our return [from Tranmere], Jane was left with her uncle and aunt at Liverpool, and has remained there ever since. I suffered a good deal at Tranmere on her account; a clandestine admirer followed her there, entirely unknown to me. Jane's uncle wrote for Mr. Stock, and his vengeance fell heaviest on me; he has since seen and confessed his error. The extremely unfavourable weather, and the distracted state of my mind, with the painful degree of solitude in which I was; not knowing how Jane spent her time, and not daring to inquire from her (as she would only have answered me with evasive insolence; neither durst I inform Mr. Stock, as all I should have got from him would have been, that I was trying to set him against his daughter); all together I spent a very dismal time there. I admire the place. I one day took a sail up to Runcorn, and admire it more than any watering-place I have seen. I had only Mary with me, who was very seasick. I was qualmish, but not sick. The vessel, a steam-packet, had a rough tide to work upon; for it is very unusual for passengers in a Steam-boat to be sick; but few escaped that day.

—or since. However, the upshot was, as already indicated, that Jane was left pretty much to her own foolish devices in and around Liverpool; and her step-mother was received at home 'with a most delightful welcome; and Mr. S. treated me with unabating kindness for 3 months, and I was so happy! I thought that Mr. S. was really an altered man.'—so she wrote to her friend Bessy Price in December of this year. But a sad, sad Christmas she might now look ahead to.

At the end of that time, he went to Liverpool on Jane's account, and came back in a dreadful humour; for two months past, I have had an unhappy time, 5 or 6 days excepted. He never speaks to me, except in anger; and keeps me so totally without money, that I am really pinched for want of many comforts. I accused Jane, or Mrs. Perkins's, of mischief-making; so I told him, and I felt convinced of it; he had been so kind during Jane's absence—so bitter immediately after seeing her. He denied, but I am not yet convinced.

Jane has been in Liverpool until now; tonight (Thursday) she arrived. Her protracted stay has given rise to an unhappy report, and on her account alone, I have earnestly desired that she had returned with her father. I have myself begged of him to send for her; I have got others to speak for me; but to no one would he give any satisfactory answer. Jane's character was suffering so materially, that at length, on Saturday last, I wrote to Jane to inform her how very necessary it was she should immediately return. On her arrival to-night, she informs us that her coming to-day was fixed some time ago!

What an unaccountable being he is!

And when his youngest daughter stole money from him, it was the simplest and most obvious thing in the world to accuse the step-mother of the crime. It would, therefore, have been little less than angelic had Miss Weeton forborne subsequently to draw certain obvious conclusions for her husband's benefit.

If Jane's conduct has hurt you in any way, consider [that] the snare she fell into in marrying Peck, was more Hannah Gilbert's doings than her own; and oh, what a serpent she has been in our family; the destroyer of all our peace, and the complete ruin of Jane.

But this is to anticipate; meantime, the reunion between father and daughter proves rather touching.

Tonight, I am much depressed; I anticipate much un-kindness from Jane. She has brought no civil message from her aunt or uncle. A small present of apples from them, are all given to her father; not one for me; and he has locked them up. These are but trifles, but they shew the intention.

Three weeks of this sort of life, and she felt she simply must solicit her brother's intervention. And fortunately we have the means of knowing, even more intimately than her letters would indicate, just in what manner she suffered in the beginning of this year 1818, and what led up to this decision. Religion may not have been an 'innate principle' in her, but the itch to scribble *was*. And perhaps the most singular fact of her chequered existence in the Stock home was that she managed to preserve, inviolate, the secrets contained in the mounting collection of manuscript copy-books of her Letters and Journal—books almost as bulky as this volume—no less than five of them to date. Mr. Stock was no Miss Chorley, and a tussle for the possession of an incriminating volume was not likely to be attended only with the politest of protests on the one part, and ineffectual, hysterical efforts to possess on the other.[1] Certainly we may be sure that it was behind locked doors that she obeyed her natural impulse, and commenced, in the confinement of her room (and prison) upon the tragically brief—

OCCASIONAL REFLECTIONS, A.D. 1818[2]

A.D. 1818. An intention of marking a few domestic events, but more particularly the religious state of my mind, induced me to attempt a kind of Diary. But so painful and heart-rending have been the occurrences of the few days which have yet passed in the New Year, that

[1] Refer to pp. 131–4, vol. i, for the tiff with that too curious friend, who, to her decided cost, penetrated some secrets of the Letter Book at that time in requisition.

[2] Contained in a volume independent of the Letters to Correspondents; this volume also contains the unfinished History of the Life of N. Stock, commenced in the year 1824.

agitation, anguish, and despair, have driven all thoughts of religion away. Have mercy! have pity upon me, Oh my Father! and enable me to sustain Thy chastening hand with more submission and humility. Forsake me not at this trying time, and help me to see which way I should act, so as to please Thee and save my own soul.

Is it Thy Will that I submit to the tyranny of him who so cruelly uses me, and abuses the power which he has over me? Oh, that I could say that it were any other than my own husband. He that should nourish, cherish, and pro-tect me; he that should protect me, so that even the winds should not blow too roughly on me—he is the man who makes it his sport to afflict me, to expose me to every hard-ship, to every insult. Or am I right in struggling to free myself from his griping hand?

Bitter have been the years of my marriage, and sorrowful my days. Surely the measure of them is full! My life, my strength, cannot sustain many more such.

Jan. 5th. Turned out of doors into the street! In the anguish of my mind, I broke out into complaints; this only was my fault. I took a chaise to Leigh; my brother not being at home, dismissed it and stopped two nights. He brought me home with an intention to effect either a reconciliation or a separation. He could do neither. Mr. Stock wants me either to remain at home pennyless, as an underling to his own daughter, or to be kept by anyone that will take me. I cannot agree to such a reconciliation, or such a separation, whilst he has plenty of money. I am obliged totally to withdraw myself from any domestic affairs, in obedience to my husband's orders; to live in an apartment alone; not to sit at table with the family, but to have my meat sent to me; and amuse or employ myself as I can.

When, and how will this end?

Jan. 10th. Still in my solitary confinement. Had a new cloak brought home, and the first thought on seeing it, was, Well! I have made sure of this, however (having long wished for a Winter garment of this description, and not had it in my power to obtain it). Alas! . . . how presumptuous! That very night might my soul have been required of me, disease have seized me, or fire have destroyed both it and me, and all else I possessed. But Thou, O Father, hast been very merciful. Yes! although my husband makes me, as it were, a prisoner in my own house, I have a Peace which he knows nothing of, a Joy which he cannot take away. Oh! that his heart would soften, and that he might repent.

Jan. 16th. My brother came with a view to assist, if in his power, to put an end to the unhappy state in which Mr. Stock and me were. It was done. My hopes are not very sanguine; but should this peace be of short continuance, or should it be more lasting than before, may I bear it meekly. Shouldest Thou again afflict me, let not despair, let not anguish of soul, drive me again to such a degree of madness as lately possessed me! I shewed little of it, but Oh, how I did feel it!

All things considered, Tom's position must have proved decidedly awkward at this juncture. Leigh is not many miles from Wigan, and the very promptness with which the Clerk to the Leigh magistrates came to his sister's aid is an indication of his conceit of himself and his fear of unpleasant gossip being connected with his name locally. There is an earlier record of his having paid a visit to the Stock home with his family, wife included; and presumably, if only from interested motives, he evinced an earnest desire to see the peace preserved in the home of the prospering cotton-spinner. The letter which secured his presence and led to the easing of the situation was dispatched on 14 January; it is a longish one, and one of the last in vol. 5 of her Letters to Correspondents; the obvious importance of it justifies inclusion in its entirety.

Jn Wright.

Standishgate. circa 1836.

STANDISHGATE, 1836, *with the residence of* MISS WEETON (1827–44) *at extreme right*

(*By permission of the* WIGAN BOROUGH LIBRARY COMMITTEE)

Photograph by JORDAN & METCALFE, St. Helens

To MR. WEETON, Leigh.   Wigan. Jany 14th. 1818.

Dear Brother,

I feel a strong reluctance to saying any more on a subject which now appears to me altogether hopeless; and after this week, be assured I will never more distress you or Mrs. Weeton by the sight of me, or of anything that can remind you of me. My late exertions have only been like the weak struggles of a drowning insect, and if I cannot now be rescued, I must inevitably sink! I would not, at this time, have applied to you, had it not been frequently said to me—'Why do you not apply to your brother? As your brother lives so near, it is his duty to protect an only sister from the ill-usage of an unkind, unfeeling husband.' I have often replied, 'What can my brother do? If he can do nothing effectual, it is cruel to distress him.'

It was not from mere momentary resentment that I came to your house. I have suffered bitterly by much the greater part of the time since I came to Wigan; and the time when I suffered most, was *when I endured most patiently.* I am at length most firmly convinced, that had I but strength and resolution to act with greater spirit, we should both live more peaceably. I am generally treated in such a browbeating, sulky, contemptuous manner, that I become abject and spiritless; if, like a worm, I shew a little impotent resentment, I am kicked and trampled on. Could I but assume more spirit, I should be treated with more respect; or, if a few individuals would interest themselves for me, the fear of what the world may say, would induce Mr. S. to treat me with more appearance of kindness. But he overawes all who come near him; even *you* feel it. Although many despise him, none dare shew any disrespect in his presence; and whilst they shew him so much outward attention, it is a tacit encouragement to his tyranny at home. I have long found that he grows worse by submission (I do not mean, to his reasonable wishes), and that resistance to his cruelty, although attended with terrible effects for a time, *ensures more peace afterwards.*

On every trifling occasion, he is ordering me out of the room, and threatening to turn me out of doors, until I am quite weary of hearing of it. Did you ever know what it was to be unwelcome? and did you feel happy in that place? If you had daily proofs that your wife wished to be quit of you, would your domestic lot be enviable?

Poor Tom—that was a tactless home thrust. Mrs. Tom Weeton had not the slightest intention of being quit of him; nevertheless, his domestic lot was far from enviable.

Mr. Stock is a man of that kind that would like a fresh wife every three or four months; his behaviour has been so unkind to me, that I wish it were in his power to change. It was supposed by many of his acquaintances that he was tired of his first wife long before she died, and that his unkindness hastened her end. Now it is my lot, and he will teaze me to death; I see no escape. Were he generally as kind as I this [last] Summer knew him to be for a few weeks, to live with him all my days would be most desirable, and to leave him, my greatest grief.

His saying I never was the first to be friendly, is false; I have numberless times made the attempt. I acknowledge that his repulsive manner intimidates me so, that my attempts are feeble; generally, by striving to enter into some conversation with him, or by some little delicate attention, which he has not delicacy enough to discover, but which *would win a heart like yours* directly. When I have attempted to put my arm around him, he has often pushed it away from him so rudely, that his hard gripe has hurt me exceedingly; the few times that I tried that way, I never recollect that it succeeded.

In his quarrelsome humours, which occur often, I can

do nothing right; and when perfectly placid, and he has nothing else to find fault with, my looks are ridiculed, my thin face, my haggard countenance, and skeleton figure. I seldom reply; I never make ill-natured reflections on him or his relations, let him say what he will of mine.

My principal ground of complaint is the being kept so totally without money, at times when he is angry with me; his frequently refusing it to me, and, at the *same time*, and for the *same purpose*, giving it to his daughter, to Hannah, or to the servant. With what patience I have generally borne this insulting usage, they can, any of them, testify, although continued for many weeks at once; and since I came to this house, at one time for a period of from 10 to 12 months; now lately, for 2 months or more. Frequently, when sitting with him in the parlour, and not daring to speak to him, I have recollected something that was wanted, and have gone into the kitchen to send the servant to him to ask for it; this is a *very common* occurrence; and as common to me to request the servant or Hannah to ask any question respecting dinner, &c. They know that he will tell them sooner than me; this is not just for a day or two, but a daily conduct for weeks or months at once. Any alteration or improvement about the house or garden, I hear of first from servants.

This invariable kind of treatment, naturally is the cause of my losing all authority and respect in the house; and at such times, it is a regular thing for Hannah or Jane to conduct the house, just as they please, without thinking it at all necessary to consult me. Further, the family know, that to please Mr. Stock, they must set themselves against me; and as I have neither money nor power, they can insult me as they please. I can neither punish, nor dismiss. If I complain, I am threatened to be turned out of doors, for there is no living with me. 'Why do you, then?' I reply. 'Let Jane and Hannah be mistresses, and let me go.'

In his ill humours, which I have told you continue for so long, it would be a crime of the first magnitude to sit down with him at supper; like a cat, I sit by and watch, but dare not touch. If it be shell-fish, sausages, &c., he eats all up, and however I may long, I can get none. I must either fare as the servant does, or go without. He frequently buys fruit, which he always locks up from me; if I am in high favour, I get a little; but that is so seldom, that it chiefly falls to Mary's lot, and he will sit eating, by the fire, without offering me a taste. But I have discovered that he treats himself, chiefly when out of the house, with fruit or anything very nice, eating it out of doors, or elsewhere. When he had quarrelled with me, he used to refuse helping me at dinner. I took it up warmly, and he has not done it lately; he only revenges himself, by not helping me to cheese.

I do not recollect that I ever was the first to begin a quarrel, until the last time, because he would give me no money.

As an argument, which I strongly insist upon in my own defence—if I were so bad to live with, do you think Mr. Stock would not think me cheaply bought off, for £70 a year?

It was no coincidence that £70 per year was just about the income she had enjoyed before marriage; and from this suggestion, merely tentative, she was eventually to make it a *condition* of her leaving him.

He well knows that I am such a check upon Hannah, Jane, and the servant, that much more of his property would be wasted, or spent extravagantly, than it now takes to keep me. If I were so bad to live with, Hannah and the servant would be glad to leave. I can easily prove that every servant I have parted with (through Jane's and Hannah's mischief-making), have been desirous to remain, or come again, except one; and I have had 6 or 7. Many of my acquaintance can tell you, that they do not like, or dare not visit me, owing to Mr. Stock; none of his acquaintance can say the same of me.

Some of his intimate friends can tell you of his stingy fits; and I can tell you, that in those fits, he is terrible at home.

If I remain here, my proposition is:

1st. That on no occasion of quarrel, I am ever again deprived of Money for house-keeping, and for my own and Mary's cloaths. I would prefer a regular weekly sum for the one, and an annual one for the other, half a year paid in advance.

2dly. Wholly to give up housekeeping to Jane or Hannah, and have only an allowance for cloaths, and pocket-money; and to live like a boarder in the house; I shall very willingly accede to this.

I will then give up my time to Mary's education, to reading, music, the cultivation of plants, or anything else that may make for peace, and prevent my interference in the family.

Peace I must insist upon; either in the house, or to be permitted to depart in Peace.

✶   ✶   ✶

And now, to return to the Occasional Reflections.

Jan. 18th. Having gone to Holland on the 17th., to stay 2 days at Mrs. Braithwaite's, I received a message from my uncle, requesting to see me. I called upon him, and he offered me an asylum at his house, should I ever want one. He had heard how I had been situated lately, and was then ready, he said, to take me in. I told him that a kind of reconciliation had taken place; that his offer, notwithstanding, had released my mind from an anxious burthen; for I did not know where to go when turned out before. At the same time, I would do all that was in my power to avoid being placed in such a situation again. I had ever striven to act as a wife ought to do; in the same way, I would endeavour to continue. I could not promise more.

Uncle Barton was to linger on for a couple more years, dying on 21 October 1820, at the age of 78. The niece had at least got £5 out of her aunt's legacy, after it had been tampered with; but Uncle Barton's legacy of £60 (less £6 Legacy Duty), was of course promptly forfeited in its entirety to Aaron Stock. There is no evidence that she ever saw her uncle again after this visit; he was dead when next she sought succour in Upholland.

Tuesday morning, Jany. 27th. Went with Mrs. Scott[1] to the Catholic Chapel, to see high Mass performed, and the consecration of the stone for the new Chapel. It was the first time that I had ever been in a Catholic place of worship. I have often heard their forms and ceremonies much ridiculed and highly censured, and have felt much pained at the want of charity in my Protestant friends. I have thought their bitterness equalled Roman Catholic bigotry, and felt much inclined to think they were not quite so ridiculous as they were represented. What I witnessed this day, filled me with the utmost astonishment, that so many millions of people, possessing as much natural sense and discernment as myself, could be so led by such boyish pageantry, or imagine for a moment that Christ, whose 'kingdom was not of this world', whose life in it was utterly void of grandeur or finery, should be pleased with that now, which he censured whilst he was amongst us in his human nature.

---

[1] Possibly Mrs. Tom Weeton's mother; if so, a distinctive evidence of Miss Weeton's being temporarily in favour in that quarter.

What insular prejudices are these governesses subject to! Nearly twenty-five years later, as one governess prepares to take leave of the world, another takes her first real taste of it, travelling along pretty much the same channel of thought as her predecessor. 'My advice to all Protestants who are tempted to do anything so besotted as turn Catholics is, to walk over the sea on to the Continent; to attend mass sedulously for a time; to note well the mummeries thereof; also the idiotic, mercenary aspect of all the priests; and *then*, if they are still disposed to consider Papistry in any other light than a most feeble, childish piece of humbug, let them turn Papists at once—that's all.'[1] In her subsequent sweeping condemnation, though, of Methodism, Quakerism, and the extremes of High and Low Church, the Yorkshire governess displayed not so much charity as Miss Weeton, who, during this breathing-time, was much exercised as to the state of her personal religion. And where the spirit failed, the flesh was willing enough to dash in a few details—fortunately less religious than personal.

Jan. 31st. Hard of faith as I know I am, and much as it grieves me that I remain so, I should be completely an Infidel if the Roman Catholic profession were the only Christian profession on earth.

The pomp observed in many of our Protestant Churches, and the frequent profligacy of the clergy, first shook my faith to the foundations; first discovered to me, that I was no Christian. Had I not been forced to reflection by these means, I should have gone on heedlessly to my last hour, imagining myself to be a very dutiful child of God all the time, trusting in my own works. Turning disgusted from the pompous folly of our Churches and Clergy, and knowing nothing of the Dissenters, the apparent simplicity of the Quakers had strong attractions for me. For years I went on thus unsettled, never being fortunate enough to become acquainted with one religious Protestant family or individual, yet seeking them wherever I went.

[1] Gaskell, *Life of Charlotte Brontë.*

And assuredly the poor wretch would have gone completely mad, had not 'God in his mercy thrown me among a set who follow what they profess, and, discarding all pomp and finery, give their heart to God'.

The Rev. Alex. Steill had at last indeed met his match, and brought about the setting up of the seceding Hope Chapel branch from his church (of which more later); and with these, Miss Weeton, the rebel, had cast her lot, for good or ill; not before time had she discovered a steadying influence. Those Liverpool Deists had left a pretty legacy. 'That Jesus Christ should be thy Son, is what my faith has not yet had strength to believe. If he were indeed God, thine *only* Son, help me to believe, and that soon; delay not the time, that these pages which have now recorded my doubts, may shortly record my comfort.' But it was not to be; one more entry—an analysis of a preacher's text—and thereupon, a break of several months before the next entry in this particular journal; in the interim, her accumulated troubles must have sorely mocked her heavenly aspirations, as Occasional Reflections for November of this year finds her, a fugitive, in Liverpool. Fortunately, we have still a letter or two left in vol. 5 of the copied Letters, and Letter 390 to draw upon to bridge the gap. Eager in her present state of mind to make converts all round, she had tackled her humoursome friend, Mrs. Bessy Price. In early February, she writes:

You do rejoice my heart; for, when I lived with you, it often ached for you; you seemed so fond of dissipation, of dress, and to have such a desire for the elegancies of high life, which were out of your reach. The kind admonition, the words of peace, now flow from you, instead of me. Speak on!

Intelligence is now forthcoming with respect to Ann, who for so long has been so strangely neglected; in fact, the last reference (and a none too friendly one) to that independent young lady, was over two years ago, in a letter to cousin Smith (for whom Miss Weeton had secured the post of governess in Mrs. Wade's family). It reads:

A situation such as yours is a very arduous one; you find its duties complicated and laborious, I dare say. Miss Winkley, when in Ireland, took care to have an easy time of it; what improvement her pupils would make, I cannot imagine; the lady she was with (Mrs. F. French), took a great deal of pains herself with the children. Miss Winkley married last Jany., to an officer of some fortune, who is, besides, an excellent husband. She expects to be confined soon.

Apparently confinement was to be a normal anticipation with Ann, for in Miss Weeton's letter of this February to Mrs. Price she writes—'I am certain you will feel much at parting with your sister and her little ones; it will be a painful weaning. I am not certain that the country is your sister's taste; but give my kindest regards to her.' And so, good-bye to the mature Ann.

Again to Margaret Smith she also writes in this same February; and has occasion to record her ephemeral experience of relative happiness.

I am at present chearful in mind, and well in health. My little Mary, now 2 years and 8 months old, is a most animated, interesting little girl; her father's whole soul seems wrapped up in her; she is a never-failing attendant on our tea-table, where she has perfect liberty—much against my approbation; but wives must submit, Margaret. She is all I have, and there is no prospect of more; I could have much wished for 2 or 3 more, I am so doatingly fond of children.

The bulk of this letter is devoted to the sounding of Margaret's religious sentiments; and, as a terrific example, she trots out the shocking Mrs. Edwards, who has 'quitted Liverpool in debt, about 2 years ago; and when next heard of, was in London, keeping a School; she has always been trying to live by her wits, having neither stability nor industry enough to settle steadily to any one pursuit; I fear she will both live and die wretchedly'. But Margaret must have been in no mood for homiletics, for she, too, disappears from the dwindling lists of correspondents. And with her we say farewell to vol. 5 of the manuscript.

Vol. 6 is missing, but that need concern us little, with Miss Weeton in her present mood; her later grasp of the situation must, and will, serve.

Miss Weeton had spent nearly three months in Liverpool before she made her next entry in her Occasional Reflections; those three months, apparently, had been spent in the hospitable home of her mother's cousin, Mrs. Smith, to whom she had fled from that of her husband on 16 September. Bessy Price's proselytizing zeal perhaps blanched at the contemplation of harbouring the homeless ex-governess; and it was only too apparent that the stay was not only premeditated, but to be one of some duration, for she brought with her her Letter Books (though it is to be doubted whether she ever stirred very far from her own doorstep without those justifications of life).

But three months after her arrival, financial pressure began to tell; that she should live upon pure charity would assuredly be highly repugnant to one of her susceptibilities. It is hardly possible, too, that she would be accompanied upon this, as upon other excursions, with her little child. With a yearning heart she once again takes up the quill.

November 29th. It is long since I recorded aught in these pages, which were intended to have been devoted to the spiritual state of my mind; to mark from time to time the progress I made in holiness; and to be a warning to me lest I, like Lot's wife, should look back again.

Although I have not, I hope, turned back, my progress is scarcely perceptible. I have been under the influence of such gracious words from the pulpit ever since I came to Liverpool (Sept. 16), that surely I am not hard-hearted and rebellious to the last degree; surely I shall grow in grace, for now I have no excuse. I have many hours each day full of leisure for devotion. I cannot grieve now, as formerly, that I have not time for reading the word of God; but, let me ask as each hour passes, as each day closes, have I improved those hours? and what is the sum at night?

Oh never, never let me rest, my God, when my heart wanders from Thee. Draw me perpetually as hitherto. Warn me, counsel me, afflict me, so Thou but secure me! And if ever I am again the mistress of a family, let nothing hinder my taking many opportunities each day to pray with them, to read to them in the Bible, and to teach them of Heaven as God shall give me utterance. Let not the dread of being scoffed at by my husband for pretending to sanctity, any more have influence with me.

Brave, fantastic resolve—but the woman of action is in process of being resuscitated.

Dec. 16. I am now on the eve of doing something which will materially affect my future situation. In the morning, I set off to Leigh, for I must either bestir myself, or starve. I have waited 3 full weeks for a remittance; my brother has kindly lent me £5, but I must not live on credit. If great exertions are necessary, I have great exertions in contemplation.

Oh, my Father, let me go forth in Thy strength. Work for me by what means soever Thou seest best. Desert me not in this hour of great trial. Be my Guide and my Counsellor. Give me the wisdom of the dove; and oh, have pity on me, and more particularly for the 3 ensuing days, in which I have much to do. Deal gently with Thy servant; let not the anguish of mind I must expect to endure, Oh! let it not quite overwhelm me. Give me much strength.

With this heartfelt utterance, the OCCASIONAL REFLECTIONS abruptly closes; but fortunately Letter 390 to her brother is by no means exhausted; and in addition, scattered references throughout later Letters and Journal help us to follow her fortunes—if the unrelieved tragedy of ensuing years deserves that term. So far as Tom was concerned, she could both bestir herself, *and* starve—alternations of which, during the next three years, were to reduce her to an emaciated, albeit still very animated, caricature of the plump governess of the Pedder household.

When you would do nothing, I was obliged to help myself as I could, and was literally forced home several times, to avoid starvation.

Forced home *several* times . . . the tragedy of it.

      *   *   *

The year 1819 is one of particular interest, as bringing Mary to the fore, both as companion to her mother during periodic exclusions from the Stock home,[1] and as a significant addition to Miss Weeton's list of dwindling correspondents. For a reason sufficiently plain, the only *actual* letter written by Miss Weeton to come down to us is available at about this juncture—a pathetic, folded sheet, found loosely inserted in the OCCASIONAL REFLECTIONS late in the possession of Mr. Marshall, and destined not to reach its intended recipient.

Mary was now old enough, apparently, to become an additional bone of contention, and either through perverseness, or in an honest desire to engage the affections and undivided duty of possibly the last of his legitimate children (for at this time, or certainly a little later, a 'kept mistress' was to grace

---

[1] There is later evidence to the effect that the coarse-grained, great-hearted Mrs. Braithwaite, of Upholland, harboured the two expelled ones for a fortnight or more in the spring of this year 1819, after which lucid interval, mother and child were obliged to return to Wigan—and to what reception that might await them there. Mary would be nearly 4 years old on this particular occasion; and a pleasant little companion she appears to have been—even to the point of exciting positive and active jealousy in the breast of another infantile visitor, then sojourning with the Braithwaites. A passionate attack on Mary, at her sweetest (if her mother's account may be accepted), resulted in the ignominious expulsion of the less pleasing child.

the board of Mr. Stock, whose Calvinism must have become somewhat modified as the child-slaves of his factory piled up his profits), Aaron Stock evinced a desire to wean the child away from her mother, and to give her the benefit of an education which must inevitably deprive her of her mother's influence for long periods. This was the more easy to effect, as Mr. Stock had now relegated his wife to the back quarters of the Chapel Lane factory. One consolation, however, the distracted mother could extract from the proposed arrangement —Mary, at least, would not now be exposed to the evil influences which surrounded her in her father's home; and so she submitted to her being transferred to the care of the Grundy partners, husband and wife, Principals of the Boarding Academy for Young Ladies, at Parr Hall, an ancient building which still exists, though adapted to even more humble requirements than in Mary's day.

Perhaps the events of the preceding spring and summer finally determined Mr. Stock; and it is not altogether fantastic to presume that, despite acts hardly suggestive of affection, Aaron Stock's defensive armour had proved easy of penetration by the daughter of the persecuted mother who had never sounded anything human as yet in his composition. The poor little thing, of course, was fated to be rescued from her shuttlecock existence, only to become the pitiful advertisement of the manifold errors and futilities, mis-labelled education, which the Principals of Parr Hall seriously offered as substitutes for the devoted care of a mother, in every way qualified to superintend the education, general, moral, religious, and physical, of her child.

Parr Hall Boarding School was a house divided against itself —the male Principal partaking somewhat of the amatory proclivities promiscuously indulged in by Mr. Stock, with a wife drinking herself to that impending death, so devotedly looked forward to by the employer of a staff of single, young lady teachers—an item we learn from Miss Weeton, who later descended to collecting the gossip of the locality when all other efforts failed in her attempt to secure the removal of Mary from such an improper atmosphere. The child does not appear to have suffered positive ill treatment at their hands, but she rapidly became painfully thin, and, under the blighting influence of this precious pair (perfectly well aware of the conditions attaching to Miss Mary's continued patronage of their establishment), she was to lose some of the engaging little ways which had so endeared her to her mother's suffering heart; here, her affectionate disposition was to be warped, and the weaning process intensified to such a degree as almost to alienate her from her mother. The strictest supervision, of course, was instituted from the start, and the mother's intercourse subjected to the chilling approval, or otherwise, of a couple whose manifest unsuitability to their charge cut the poor woman to the heart.

The existence of a deliberate system of interception of her letters (connived at by the Wigan post-master), and a difficulty in securing access by any other means to her daughter, accounts no doubt for the existence and preservation of the letter which follows. The obvious attempt to improve upon her usual, and always perfectly legible script; the generous spacing; the didactic style adapted to the infantile mind; above all, the tribute to the loathed Grundy partners, must have cost many, many bitter tears, quite apart from the subsequent fate of the letter, which is given in full. As for the doll, which apparently was to accompany the letter, it probably suffered the fate of a later one.

Wigan. Dec. 31st. 1819.

My dear Mary,

According to my promise, I have sent you a little servant to wait upon the young ladies that Mrs. Grundy was to bring with her from Liverpool. Her name is Ellen. I am afraid you will have a great deal to do to teach her, for she has never been in service before; but she is perfectly honest, no rambler nor a tell-tale; and as to her indolence, if you set her a good example, it may perhaps have a wonderful effect.

I have made her a few cloaths, and furnished your

cradle, and it has amused me very much; for indeed it is a pleasure to me to do anything for my little darling girl. Now you must be very contented, and not wish for anything more for a long time; for there are thousands of little children who cannot get any of those many comforts which you enjoy every hour of the day. Think often of this, my dear little Mary, and as often as you do think of it, thank that Heavenly Father who is continually taking so much care of you. You are no better than those poor little girls that go about selling sand or matches, or begging cold potatoes. God makes some poor, and some rich, to try which will serve him best: but let no one, my dear, love and serve God better than you. How you must do this, I have often told you; but if you forget, ask Mr. or Mrs. Grundy; they will tell you at any time, for they are very good, and very clean; and indeed they are very kind to you. Tell them your mother wishes to be very respectfully remembered to them.

I have written my letter in a large hand, in hopes you will try to learn to read it yourself. When Miss Knight comes to school again, I think I will write to you by her.

Give my love to your little companion, Miss Watt.

Your affectionate Mother,

N. Stock.

Poor woman; she must have been sadly at a loss for appropriate expression when she arrived at the Grundy partners. Fortunately, the opportune 'cleanliness is next to godliness' suggested itself.

With Mary safely disposed of—though in May of the year 1820 mother and daughter were once more driven out, taking shelter with a Mr. and Mrs. Allen, of Hale, in Cheshire—the course was now clear for the extirpation of the mother. The attempted doing-to-death process was, however, to be somewhat protracted by the attitude of the unreasonable subject. The spirit of the times actuated Aaron Stock—no quarter to either rebellious weaver or wife; the slashing yeomanry of St. Peter's field, the heroes of Peterloo, need as little fear the law as Mr. Stock need doubt the speedy arrival of the constable to jail his window-breaking wife. Let us turn again to Letter 390.

Repeatedly turned out destitute; twice imprisoned—the first time for a first offence of the kind; the 2d., *perfectly innocent*, having myself been beaten almost to death; several times obliged to flee for my life; the time when I broke the windows, if I had not by that means forced my way in, I must have been out all night, on the cold and wet pavement of a dark November night. I had then been turned out only for complaining, whilst enduring exceedingly unkind treatment. I was threatened with being sent to a Lunatic Asylum, only for asking for food. Cloaths I could not procure until I got them on credit; and that I did not attempt, only for the last year that I was with him. The second time I was in prison, was on a false oath; yet you said I acknowledged that I struck the man. I did not strike the man, and how you could construe the passage so, I know not. I should like to see that letter again, for I took no copy; for, owing to anguish of body from that dreadful beating, and distraction of mind at being at the point of being a 2nd. time sent to prison by my husband out of revenge for my procuring a warrant for him, I could not copy it.

With my bruises thick upon me—bruises such as the Doctor said would have mortified had I not been so extremely thin—was I imprisoned for two days, and you would not bail me out! Oh, oh, you unnatural being. I had no money, and no provisions were sent to me, and I was obliged to beg of the person in whose custody I was! I was just on the point of being sent to Kirkdale house of Correction for the want of bail (since you would not do it), when J. Latham and G. Oakes [for whom she had performed a kindly office as far back as the year 1809] of Holland, came over and bailed me out. Oh! this was a climax of misery! 'Tis strange I did not lose my senses, to think that I should have such a husband and such a brother!

At 8 o'clock that night, my bruises still undressed, and pitiably emaciated, I had to walk with these men to Holland, 4 miles. The night was dark, wet, and winterly; but I was now among friends, and I was nursed, and soothed, and comforted. Mrs. Braithwaite's door was open to me, if my brother's was not—and her door is often open to the friendless.

I soon returned to my miserable home, for I dared not stay long away, now expecting nightly or daily to be murdered—or worse, sent to a Lunatic Asylum in my right mind;[1] for so I was threatened; and I had no help to expect from you (for so you had assured Mr. Stock)! I had no earthly help, no help but of heaven, and I endeavoured to resign myself. I expected to be again turned out, although Mr. Stock lived in another house, and to be driven out destitute as I had often been, so that I kept myself locked up day and night in my bedroom, going out only by stealth in the evening, to fetch provisions, and let Dr. Hawarden's see that I was in Wigan, and alive. On returning one night, I found my room on fire, and my bed burnt! I most solemnly declare that I was not in the house when the fire commenced. In my opinion, it was done to procure my transportation, or perhaps even hanging; for I had no help to expect from you. I wish it had been investigated. I could easily have proved my innocence, and have brought home the charge to the guilty.

[1] What the threat of a Lunatic Asylum meant, even as late as Victoria's reign, can be gauged from a reading of that old classic, *Valentine Vox*. Miss Weeton may have come across the evidence of a contemporary chaplain, who could testify, in open court, in the case of a poor female lunatic, that her feet, tied above the ankles, rotted and dropped off!

I had now no bed! As I was reduced lower and lower in affliction, I often exclaimed—what next? After lying some nights on a Sofa, rolled in blankets, I again found shelter at the kind Mrs. Braithwaite's of Holland.*

   *   *   *

. . . deep laid plot . . . false charge . . . circumstantial evidence . . . hung or transported . . . Merciful Providence of a Good Father . . . Mr. Stock knows better than I do . . . violence of my temper was such . . . more like a mad woman than anything else . . .

—how often does one come across such snatches of sentences in letters to come. Mr. Stock was right—his wife *was* mad; but on the other hand, he was reputed to be sane.

   *   *   *

The following from the local Session Rolls are a sufficient corollary to the foregoing:

> In October, 1821, Aaron Stock, cotton spinner, entered into recognizances (his sureties being John Johnson, Book-keeper, and Joseph Crompton, cotton spinner) for an assault on Nelly Stock, his wife.

> On the 20th. October, 1821, Aaron Stock, cotton spinner, entered into recognizances (his surety being John Marsden, hatter) to appear at the next Quarter Sessions.

> On the 22nd. day of December, 1821, Nelly Stock, the wife of Aaron Stock, entered into recognizance to appear at the next Sessions concerning an assault she was alleged to have made on Thomas Sutton.[1]

—apropos of which, it is interesting to note that Mr. Stock's legal representative, Henry Gaskell, Esq., was the Mayor, before whom this recognizance was made. Piping times!

In April 1822 again appears the name of Nelly Stock,

---

[1] Who was accompanying Thomas Kearsley in the gig which attempted, some years later, to run down Miss Weeton.

charged with assault, her sureties being John Latham and George Oakes, of Upholland. There is a tick against her name, and the sheet is marked 'dis[charged]'.[1]

✴   ✴   ✴

DEED OF SEPARATION

Such a monstrous state of affairs now clearly called for out-side interposition. It was singularly unfortunate, but the good folk of Hope Chapel were not at liberty to intervene or mediate at this juncture, their time being fully occupied with internal dissensions consequent upon their newly established venture in faith. The spirited 'opposition' of St. Paul's were as little charmed with the ministrations of the Rev. Alex. Steill as was Miss Weeton; but all was not going well with the seceders; and only an ungenerous soul would have recalled the parable of the 99 and the one lost lamb. Besides, Chapel Lane was tucked away in a rather disreputable quarter of Wigan—much could, and did, happen there, the echoes of which would never reach Hope Chapel, or Standishgate, except by unfortunate mischance; and mischance had saddled Aaron Stock with most inconvenient neighbours in Dr. and Mrs. Hawarden, whose 'kindness to me at a time of extreme distress, was such as I hope I shall never forget'. Pertinacious Dr. Hawarden not only sheltered the unfortunate woman, but, matching purses with the manufacturer, demanded payment for expenses incurred on her behalf—and recovered them, too, by recourse to that law which had hitherto observed a decent reticence where Mr. Stock was concerned. Respectability—so must have thought Aaron—was to be dearly bought, if at all. There was, for instance, that Mrs. T. Marsden (sister-in-law of Mr. Stock's late surety) who was prepared to countenance and receive the friend of the Hawardens; and yet more humble folk were impertinently concerning themselves in the affairs of

---

[1] For these particulars from the Sessions Rolls I am indebted to the Head Librarian of Wigan Borough Library, Mr. A. J. Hawkes, F.S.A., and his assistant, who devoted to their discovery days of patient research among exceedingly dusty documents.

179

their betters, and voicing their unsolicited opinions under Mr. Stock's very nose. The very barber's shop under the old Market Hall was a prolific source of rumour and gossip; for here lodged one of Miss Weeton's 'late servants, who would speak of my domestic conduct and temper, and the cruel usage of my husband'.

The signs and omens were not lost on brother Tom. Despite the inconvenience,[1] in hot haste he posted over to Wigan, bringing along with him his respected friend, Mr. Marsh of Westleigh, Magistrate on the Leigh bench, under whom— not unhopeful of attaining equal status with his friend—Tom officiated as Clerk (with, no doubt, all the petty arrogance and pomposity common to one of his humble antecedents). In such august company, Tom's behaviour was undeniably handsome.

You did indeed strive to serve me, and paid all the expences at the Inn that day. Mr. Marsh was unsuccessful (to prevail with Mr. Stock to allow me a separate maintenance); but I was not the less obliged, and I repeat my thanks to you, as I shall to him if I have the opportunity. But it had long been too late for anything but the strong arm of the law, and that you would not assist me in (keeping true to your promise to Mr. Stock). Your cruel neglect was the astonishment of great numbers in Wigan, who said you would even be quiet if I were in murdering.*

[1] Tom's present successor to the Office of Clerk to the Magistrates of Leigh bench, T. R. Dootson, Esq., has obligingly traced one source of inconvenience to Tom at this time. The following is copied from *The British Volunteer and Manchester Weekly Express*, for Saturday, 4 August 1821:

'Leigh, 1st. August, 1821. TO BE LET: And may be entered upon on the 12th day of November next, ALL that newly-erected MESSUAGE or DWELLING HOUSE, situated in Bridge-street, within Leigh, in the county of Lancashire, opposite to the gates of Atherton Park. Together with the Stable, Shippon, Hay-bay, Wash-house, and Offices, detached, and situate behind the said Messuage, now in the occupation of Mr. Weeton, Attorney-at-Law. Apply to him on the Premises, or by letter, post paid.

'N.B. Mr. Weeton will remove his Office on the 13th. day of August instant, to a house on the opposite side of Bridge-street, late belonging to Mrs. Ashworth.'

Was ever man more sure of himself, even down to the 'post paid'?

If Mr. Stock could prove adamant with regard to separate maintenance, he was by no means averse to a Deed of Separation, and, having appointed his solicitor (Mr. Henry Gaskell, before whom, it will be remembered, both parties had entered into recognizances to appear at the Sessions), it remained only for Miss Weeton to name hers. Attorneys in that litigious district abounded; and a very decent, loyal crowd they appear to have been, all round; for not one would rob Tom of the privilege of appearing on behalf of his abused sister; and if *he* would not undertake the office—well, the inference was obvious.

Tom could be very nice in matters legal, and but for one fatal characteristic—an unsolicitor-like lack of reticence—he would no doubt have yet rubbed shoulders with his brother magistrates on the Leigh bench. But column-length 'Letters to the Editor', and the freer licence of the printed pamphlet, testify to a too earnest desire to explain his every action and motive to a public undeserving of such touching confidence. In the case of his sister, refusal was backed with excuses, the half of which would have carried greater conviction.

After I had seen the Draft, Jany 1822, I wrote to my brother to make some inquiries respecting the restrictions, &c., but said nothing as to the income. To this he never returned any answer to me, considering himself to the last as not my legal adviser, and persevering in his refusal to be so. The reason he frequently assigned to me for not assisting me, was Mr. Stock's renting a Factory in Wigan, belonging to his wife's mother, which, if he should give him any offence, he might throw upon their hands. Another reason was, that he dreaded the expence it might involve him in.

Well, perhaps in Miss Weeton's opinion, 'the Braithwaites were always more respectable than the Scotts', but domestic felicity, so far as Tom was concerned, was above the price of a doubtful legal fee. It was ungracious, though, on the part of the recipient of the £100 so readily forthcoming upon the

occasion of his sister's wedding, to advance yet another reason
—'you could tell Mr. Gaskell, as a reason for refusing to be
bound with me in a Deed of Separation, that I was not to be
trusted'.*

Deploring his many journeys to and fro (and still out of
pocket to the extent of the £5 lent to his sister three years
back, when she was in such desperate straits in Liverpool),
he was not to be deterred from a further magnanimous instance
of a disposition free from the vindictive.

3 guineas you paid for a Counsel's opinion. I know of
no more; for Mr. Battersby never commenced any proceedings at the time you promised to assist him—you
yourself soon after preventing him, as he told me, and
at the same time doing all you could to prejudice him
against me. . . . The Counsel's opinion I would have repaid you, if you would ever have proceeded upon it. You
never would.*

And even yet another reason—but Miss Weeton considered
this 'too silly to have any weight'. Simply it was—'that your
wife would not let you'.

Perhaps it was the only one the wretched fellow need have
advanced.

The great hopes entertained of Mr. Battersby (despite Tom's
vacillations and positive frustrations) were doomed, however,
to be dashed to the ground from quite another source.

Mr. Battersby would once have undertaken the cause
for me, and gave me great hopes to procure my child, and
a comfortable maintenance; but Mr. Banks, his partner,
put a stop to this. He would by no means consent; for
this reason (not avowedly)—he boarded at Mr. Alston's,
where Mr. Stock was intimate . . . the inference is easily
drawn.*

A time was to come when Deacon Alston would value the
co-operation of the wealthy and influential Miss Weeton,
member once again of the Hope Chapel flock; but at present

her influence was confined to the Sunday School scholars, and could be dispensed with.

But not so easily would the persistent client resign her hold upon the weak-willed Mr. Battersby. He was prevailed upon to try yet again, and:

The last time you consented to assist Mr. Battersby, you would only proceed on the plea of adultery against Mr. Stock. Yet you employed no one to discover it, and in a few weeks you took so much pains to prejudice Mr. Battersby's mind against me, that he treated me in a most insulting manner. Thus was I wholly abandoned to my fate, which had nearly ended in a Prison, Lunatic Asylum, or the Gallows! Yet I was perfectly innocent, in my right senses, and a dreadfully injured being.*

Meantime, Miss Weeton was in the most galling of situations, dependent for her very food upon the charity of apprehensive and hesitant friends. Sign or starve!

And the unkindest cut of all was imminent. Mr. Stock, not unobservant, astutely availed himself of additional legal advice; and Tom forthwith appears in the new guise of—opponent's attorney!

At last you came to Wigan, but instead of consulting with me, you chose to be employed by Mr. Stock against your own sister, and advised him to insist upon harder terms than he would have done, and had the impudence to shew me these in your own handwriting, which you wanted to force me to sign. And when I spurned at such treatment, you advised Mr. Stock to get the Deed drawn and signed on his part, and then presented to me to sign, so that I could not be allowed to read it—only to hear it read. I had no alternative but signing in ignorance—or starvation, a lunatic Asylum, or a prison. Dreadful alternative! I signed . . . and I find I have for ever signed my child away!*

Nor would her brother act as bondsman for her.

I was ready to befriend you on every occasion, yet you have since refused to be bound with me, the only time I required a bondsman. Oh! you ungrateful brother! And to do me all the injury possible on that occasion, you stated to my enemies' attorney (Mr. Gaskell, who himself told me—and he made the injurious use of it that might be expected), that you dared not be bound with me, for I was not to be trusted! Oh! shame on you. Yet, on the same day, you told *me* that the reason why you refused to be bound with me, was that Mr. Stock was such a villain, that you dared not be joined in any deed in which he had any concern; for he would be catching at some flaw, or procure some false evidence to bring you in to forfeit your money.*

The incident of the actual signing is thus recalled in a later letter to a sympathetic friend:

He came to me at Mrs. T. Marsden's, to persuade me to agree to the terms which Mr. Stock insisted on. His unbrotherlike conduct roused my greatest contempt, and I would not listen to him. I never saw him afterwards, or heard from him; and I hope never more to do so! . . . When, in two or three weeks after, the Deed itself was presented to me by Mr. Ackerly (Mr. Gaskell's clerk) to sign, I was obliged to sign it in great ignorance of its contents (not being allowed to read it, but only to hear it read by the clerk), for the sake of getting immediate subsistence, as people were unwilling to trust me on Mr. Stock's credit.

*   *   *

The Deed was signed either at the end of January or early in February of 1822 (attempts to trace copies of it locally have failed), and under its provisions Miss Weeton limited herself to three visits annually to her child, with an extra proviso (inserted on the instigation of Brother Tom, no doubt smarting under his dismissal) that the interview should take place only in the presence of Mrs. Grundy or her partner.

Would not your wife consider herself as grossly insulted by such a restriction? Certainly she would, and justly. And I am quite as fit to see mine as she is hers, and ought to have the same liberty; and you ought never to argue thus against me for an instant. I would never have signed such an infamous Deed as the last, but for your positive assurance that I could see Mary at any time. . . . Mr. Grundy has received positive orders not to let me see her, and is threatened, if he does, that she shall be removed where no one shall ever know where she is, except her father.*

The most amazing feature, perhaps, of the Deed is not merely the forbidding her residence within a two and a half mile radius of Wigan, but the interdicting of visits to that town upon any pretext whatsoever! That she openly defied this prohibition, and that the quarterly allowance continued to be paid (through an agent) to her, is hardly surprising; for surely the validity of such a priceless document could never have been upheld in open court, even in such anti-feminine times as those of the fourth George. The circumstances of its drawing up and presentation for signature would have charmed Simon Brass; assuredly it was high time for a Dickens to arise and smite.

UPHOLLAND

APRIL 1822–MAY 1824

UPHOLLAND

APRIL 1822–MAY 1824

*So, 7½ years after marrying, Miss Weeton found herself childless,
a wreck of her former physical self, and in receipt of practically
the same income (though now in the form of a dole) as when she
had married; to wit, £70—but the income only, the property and
investments which she had realized by exercise of a business acumen
rare enough in one of her sex at any time, remaining in the hands
of her husband. And, not to be denied any petty opportunity of
injuring his wife's credit locally, the quarterly allowance was
made payable 'in arrears', through a Mr. Stopford of Upholland
—fortunately, in the event, not unfriendly to Miss Weeton.*

*A wanderer once again, but her wanderings circumscribed, ever
to hover distractedly within reach of the greatest sufferer by this
precious production of the legal luminaries of that place of 'mental
barrenness'—Wigan—Miss Weeton retired to the loathed scenes
of her childhood and early womanhood—Upholland—shortly after
the signing of the Deed. She had been denied access to Mary
during the preceding Christmas holidays, but was now permitted
an interview, conditionally, as stated, at Parr Hall. Eighteen
months were to elapse ere she would see her daughter again, consequent upon her utterly refusing to be bound to visits upon specified
dates, not exceeding three per annum.*

✶   ✶   ✶

*In the year 1808 Miss Weeton had joyfully flung out of
Upholland, shaking (so she hoped) its dust from her feet for ever;
in the latter part of April 1822 she crept back—not humbly, we
may be sure, though the observed of all observers—an exile in a
free country, and took up lodgings near the summit of the hill-
side overlooking Wigan, within 7 miles of Parr Hall; for such*

must be her orientation now. Her scholars had grown up; marriage and death had reduced the number of possible acquaintances; and the emaciated scarecrow need be under no delusion as to the position she must be prepared to accept in the narrow village community. Good and tried friends she would be sure to find in the Braithwaite family; and, provided she would demean herself sufficiently humbly, there were other influential folk who would be quite prepared, in their vegetative existence, to listen and condole—up to a point. Mrs. Braithwaite was a dying woman, and the consumptive younger daughter, Elisabeth, was becoming less able to take an active part in the work of the household and garden attached to The Priory. Margaret, happily enough situated as the wife of the Master of the Assembly Rooms at Prescot, could afford a second home for Mrs. Braithwaite's youngest daughter, Mary. Upon the able shoulders of Catharine, therefore, had devolved the house-hold responsibilities; and, able and desperately willing as Miss Weeton must have been to become either substitute for the absent Mary or as another daughter to her old friend (the best she had on earth), she was suffered to immure herself in the darkest and pokiest of parlours up at Ball's farm (see illustration, p. 216). Mrs. Braithwaite was no doubt shrewd enough to foresee the endless complications which must result from any other arrange-ment, and worldly-wise enough to re-establish the intimacy upon a footing calculated to preserve the harmonies. Miss Weeton was to be undeniably welcome as a visitor; but gone, never to return, was the sociable atmosphere inspired by the presence of the late jovial, tippling master of the household; and gone also was the income from the school which he had so ably conducted, despite his manifest unfitness in certain respects.

Hard times had descended upon the tiny village, as upon the rest of the countryside, and Miss Weeton was never again to harp upon the old engaging subject of the possibilities of a small dairy farm, with herself as the ruling spirit thereof. Here she was to witness, at uncomfortably close quarters, the after-effects of a protracted war, which had never concerned her in its military aspect, but which had not been unwelcome to the farmers in its day. Here, intolerable tedium was to be her lot (varied at long intervals with a trip to Southport's sands in Mrs. Ball's company), whilst every available hand was employed in unremitting industry about the farm; here, she was to swallow solitary and comfortless meals, whilst the farmer and his wife fought off the spectre of Enclosure and rick-burning hands.

Obviously Miss Weeton's money was not to be despised by the Balls, if it would help even in a slight way to stave off either enclosure or foreclosure; but for Miss Weeton, too, there was a spectre, grisly enough—that of illness, amid strangers unable to spare a moment on her behalf; and there was the utter lack of even such amenities as the town of Wigan had afforded. Here was a Church that mocked her spiritual needs, where her active mind could not be droned into a semblance of pious reflection; and ever the cry to heaven ascended as she toiled up the hill, there to turn her prospect glass towards St. Helens.

But that way lay madness—madness which had been staved off before, and, please God, would continue so to be, whilst she lingered a little longer upon earth, whilst yet she could lock herself up in the seclusion of her den, and, with the six volumes of closely written manuscript copies of her Letters and Diaries lying on the shelf before her, devote the first page of the new, half-bound, blank copy-book to the initial flourish of:

LETTERS TO CORRESPONDENTS

Vol. 7.

But, alas for the list of Correspondents, now a sadly depleted one. What has happened to the correct Mrs. Whitehead, most faithful of correspondents, least easy to offend (however lengthy the epistle)? What of Mr. and Mrs. Chorley, of Dale Street, Liverpool?—dead; and the haughty, acrimonious spinster daughter has at last seen death even closer to face than the despised Governess. Mrs. Edmondson, too—as good as dead; and we shall never know *in what way she responded to that infinitely daring, infinitely guarded, request for information regarding the distracting, sadly disturbing Rev. T. Saul, occasional visitor at Dove's Nest. Aunt Barton?—but her tongue is at last silenced, the rocking-chair now motionless, for she lies beside her sister in the grave-yard below, the grave-stone plainly indicating 'two breadths', so literally does she lie beside her man; but never more to plague him—or his niece. And Tom!—but he is to receive one more letter, longer even than those in which he is in the habit of publicly defending his impugned honour. And what of Mrs. Dodgson, Mrs. Green, Ann Winkley?—but mere episodes of the past. And as for the young Armitages, the contact now is but perfunctory and will expire in the politest of epistolary atmospheres.*

There are, however, some new names to fill the regretted blanks. Mr. Grundy of Parr Hall is to be sadly snubbed in his own fortress; and the excursion to Georgian London will overflow from letters into an ever-expanding Journal—a Journal which tends more and more to absorb space between letters, until at last Letters to Correspondents becomes a misnomer, and, with but one correspondent (and that one, a pious recluse) so far interested as to desire a continuance of Miss Weeton's correspondence, for the first time in twenty years the proud head will bow wearily over the quill, and acknowledge the futility of its labours—a labour now continued only as one of love, dedicated, not to posterity, but to Mary. Volume 7 will accompany her to Wales, for her walking tour, necessarily lone; it will struggle on for a few more pages; then, with a Thy Will be done (and, most significant of all, a page and a half left blank at the end),[1] we shall take final leave of an amazing gesture for posthumous justice—and even, may it so happen, literary fame. Posterity—and it is worthy of record that America has called for a special edition—has endorsed her claim to consideration, and the concluding volume is confidently placed

---

[1] Miss Weeton was more than once taken to task for a stingy horror of leaving any part of a page blank. Unlike 'paper-sparing Pope', however, she did not, in addition, grudge the very paper upon which her letters were written.

before the public, timed, fortunately, too late to influence so original and forthright a stylist; one, fortunately for us, labouring life-long under the quickening spur of neglected genius, and an urge to sting her sex out of its deplorable, maddening complaisance.

✻ ✻ ✻

There now follows three years of a consecutive run of Letters and Journal, providing a staggering commentary upon life for the unprotected female of a century or more ago. Commencing in almost unrelieved gloom (as well it might), the story gradually brightens as mental tone reasserts itself upon this breezy hill-side, until we are spirited off by coach (romantic—or unromantic—just as the account may strike the reader) to London—'the great Metropolis, the mart of less fortunate nations, the—'but perhaps THE PICTURE OF LONDON, quoted later, will produce the desired, and desirable, impression. Off to London, in the year 1824, the Stockton and Darlington Railroad but in process of being laid down, and with no need on our part to have frequent recourse to the bottle of diluted brandy, the effects of which were so nearly to terminate, in quite undeserved ignominy, the career of the fatigued, though not unobservant, Miss Weeton.

✻ ✻ ✻

To MRS. PRICE   Up-Holland, July 19th. to 25th. 1822.

I cannot discover from your letter, that I am prohibited from going into the town of Wigan; for, if I could safely do it once, I might as safely do it again. Mr. Raincock seems to have confined his observations to the point of molestation. I did not want to consult him on that point, being well convinced of the tenor of the Deed on that head. The question was not whether I could go without endangering any forfeiture, on account of seeing or speaking to Mr. Stock; but does the Deed explicitly and directly prohibit my going into the town of Wigan, or to any place within 2½ miles of it—the seeing Mr. Stock, or speaking to him, being kept entirely out of the question; for I could venture to say that I could go to Wigan several times a week without any risk of seeing Mr. Stock, I know his times and his haunts so well.

That the Deed expressly prohibits my residing in Wigan or within 2½ miles of it, is very plain, but what I wished to know was, does the *Deed* state that I am to incur any forfeiture by *going* into the town, or within 2½ miles? It is what the *Deed* says, and not what anyone thinks advisable, that I wish to know.

I have powerful reasons for wishing to be satisfied on this head. My situation in regard to Mary calls strongly for it. If the Deed does extend its prohibitions so far, I shall, on Mary's account, be forced from a high sense of duty, *to go back*!

You see from this assertion, that a decisive and clear answer to that question is absolutely necessary. The idea of going back to such a husband is terrible indeed! yet, for Mary's sake, I must do it, if I cannot at any time go into the town or near it, neither see my child, as it has been so far. Does not your heart swell with indignation within you, when I tell you that Mary has been at home during the present vacation, with a *kept mistress in her mother's place*.

The cruel usage I have endured from *such beings*, makes me well aware what poor Mary's sufferings must be; and if I could only so much as go into the town at any time, it would at least perhaps prevent him having her at home at the holidays, if it were only to mortify me, as he would think; but rather than she should come to such a home, I would avoid the comfort of seeing her. What can, oh! what can that dreadful monster think of, to inure a little innocent child, his own child, to such scenes and to such sufferings as she must witness and undergo in his house;

first to vitiate her mind, and next perhaps to destroy her health, so that body and soul must perish together.

She has a mother of unblemished character, of the strictest principles and conduct; and oh! that any Law could be found to take the child from the care of such a father, and to give her to mine. But I am hopeless on this head. All I can do, is to go often into the town, by which means it will at least prevent him from having her at home at the vacations. If I cannot do this, I will myself go into the house at the next vacation, and if Mary must reside with a kept mistress, she shall have a mother with her.

Since my coming here, Miss Hawarden has been once to see me, and staid all night; she promised to come again shortly, to stay a week, but has not been yet. She has become my commissioner, so that I have often occasion to write to her, to make little purchases for me. When I see her, I will ask her, as from my own thought (observing your caution), whether she has written to your sister. I think with you on the subject.

I am sorry for the loss of my Hymn Book; my last hope was, that I had left it with you. I will search again at home.

I have been just reading a Tract by Dr. Hawker—'The Asylum for Female Penitents.' It is a beautiful and impressive piece. If paragraphs from that, and such other works, were often inserted in the Papers, I think they would do much good; and whilst so much is said in the Liverpool Mercury (and very properly) on cruelty to animals, surely Cruelty to Women is much more calling for public notice and public reproof.[1] Your information respecting the

[1] It is for us of the present generation to rub our eyes at the following, quoted recently in the *New Statesman*: 'The Mayor said he was a great animal lover, and he detested people who were cruel to animals. "It is bad enough with children, but when it comes to dumb animals, it is terrible," he said.' *Dorset County Chronicle*. With regard to The Female Penitentiary, Baines's *Lancashire Directory* for 1825 affords the usual classic mention. 'THE FEMALE PENITENTIARY, for reclaiming an unfortunate class of females, is one of those numerous charities to which the year of jubilee, on George III

ceremony of laying the foundation stone of the Liverpool Female Penitentiary induced me to make the foregoing remarks. Much remains to be done, to prevent the ruin of Females. Where it is too late, the Asylum is a most Christian-like Institution; may it prosper, until a time come when there are none who need to enter.

Tell Miss Price that the young ladies here from whom I expected a little assistance in preparing some ornamental works for E. Kenyon to draw, have been so much engaged with Hay and Fruit Harvest, and Corn and Potatoe harvest drawing on, that I shall be obliged to wait, as I have no talent for those things myself.

To her daughter, MARY   Up-Holland. Sept. 3rd. 1822.
(at Parr-Hall, nr. St. Helens).

I have expected to hear from you for some weeks past, and wonder why you have never written to me. Write to me soon, my love, if Mrs. Grundy will permit you, or I shall think you want to forget your mother. I have never received one letter from you, yet you wrote to your father almost a year ago, and I hope now you will write often to me. The sight of a letter written by your dear little hand, would be a great comfort to me, and I hope I shall see one in a few days after you receive this.

It is now many months since I heard anything of you. I earnestly hope you are well; but I never hear whether you are well, or ill.

I am still living at Up-Holland with Mr. and Mrs. Ball, and spend my time very agreeably, often going out to tea. Mrs. Braithwaite is exceedingly kind to me, and so are Miss Braithwaites. I sometimes go to dinner, and remain

attaining the 50th year of his reign, gave rise. Originally the establish-ment was at Edge-hill, but a building better suited to the purpose, and capable of accommodating from 40 to 50 penitents, has been erected in Crab-tree-Lane, and is now occupied by these "brands plucked from the burning".'

with them until bedtime; and if I am 3 or 4 days without calling, they express themselves quite concerned; and they are such intelligent people, that their conversation is always pleasing.

I was at Southport a few weeks ago. Mrs. Ball and I went together; we remained there 3 weeks. A very agreeable and genteel party were lodging in the house with me, and Miss Louisa Barge, a little girl of 7 years old, was quite a play-fellow for me. We got each a poney and rode on the sands once or twice for a long distance; and one day, we went to a sand hill, and made a sand oven, and sand pies in large cockle shells. I was the bakehouse woman, and Louisa, a servant, and made the pies.

I talked to Louisa about you, and we wished you were with us. I often laughed at her, for she scolded me for burning the pies and spilling the syrup, and sometimes I quite upset them, and then she had more to make; and just when we were tired of that play, and going to play at hide and seek, she said, 'Let us jump our oven in.' So we got on the top of it and jumped. It gave way rather suddenly, and down we both fell, laughing, and half buried. We soon got away, and played at hide and seek until we were tired.

I bathed frequently, and sailed several times, and now find my health much improved.

In the hope of hearing from you in a few days, I will conclude now with desiring you to present my respects to Mr. & Mrs. Grundy.

To MISS HAWARDEN, Wigan. Up-Holland. Oct. 19. 1822.

About 7 weeks ago, I wrote to Mary, and sent the letter, by Ed. Melling, to the Wigan Post Office, knowing him trusty, and not daring to send it by M. Forster. I requested an early answer from my little darling, hoping Mrs. Grundy would have the goodness to set her to the grateful employ.

More than a month passed, and I heard nothing. About a fortnight ago, I wrote to Mrs. Grundy to enquire if that letter had ever been received. To this I have yet had no answer. To make quite sure, I will try another plan. I will write again and beg of you to give it to Will. Kelly, the Coachman, that he may deliver it himself; for perhaps Mr. Stock may have intercepted the other at the Wigan P.O. Don't tell Kellys from whom it comes, although both he and his wife always interested themselves very kindly for me.

Perhaps you could get him to find out whether Mary is now at Parr-Hall, for I have strong suspicions that she is not there, and that Mr. Grundys' are commanded by Mr. Stock not to publish at present that she is removed.

If Mary is at Parr-Hall, I must consider some method of proceeding different to this which I have pursued for so many months, of being patient, and submissive. My spirits are exceedingly depressed. I think I shall quite sink unless I can see my child.

Inclosed is a latter to Mrs. Marsden (which I shall be obliged to you to deliver) on a very different subject, but which I shall request her to communicate to you.

Oct. 21st. Since writing the foregoing, I received a letter from Mrs. Grundy. I will send it you on account of one passage in it, a statement of Mary's, quite mysterious to me. She has not been at Holland, neither have I ever seen her since last March at Parr Hall. Shew it to Mrs. Marsden, and return it when convenient. Discover, if you can, whether some trick was played on the poor child whilst last in Wigan.

To MRS. GRUNDY, Parr-Hall.[1]

Up-Holland. Oct. 19th. 1822.

Having written to Mary nearly 7 weeks ago, and after waiting some weeks for an answer and receiving none, I

[1] 'St. HELENS: William Grundy. Boarding Academy. Parr Hall.' Baines's

next addressed a letter to you. I have still received none. If these letters never reached you, be kind enough to inform me by return of post. If they have been received by you, I intreat you to tell me why they were not answered, inclosing your letter in a cover directed to Dr. J. Hawarden, Wigan, who will safely forward it to me. My letters have been intercepted, and possibly may be again.

If my letters safely reached you, oh, how could you act so unchristian a part by me as not to notice them. Is it respecting the mother as much as the father? Is it doing as you would like to be done to? That my husband has ever treated me with the utmost contempt, is no excuse for such treatment from any other. Even if he has given you any such directions, it is not your duty to obey them. The fear of losing a pupil cannot surely be of such moment as that you should treat a mother unjustly to please the father. You did treat me with great kindness, and I was very grateful for it.

The calumnies which my husband has so industriously spread, should have no weight with you until you had heard both sides. I declare most solemnly that they are all false; and I should not be condemned unheard, not considered guilty, because I am accused. As I understand that you have listened to Mr. Stock, and as I find that you have acted in consequence, it is but an act of justice to hear me. Do not use me contemptuously before you know whether I am deserving.

Mr. Stock is afraid of anyone seeing me, or hearing me,

Lancs. Directory, 1825. As an educational establishment for young ladies, Parr Hall was advertised in successive Directories, as late as the year 1855, though by that time it had changed hands; it has not been possible to ascertain when Mr. Grundy's connexion with it ceased. For such meagre particulars as have transpired, I must acknowledge the collaboration of Mr. H. H. Edwards, Public Librarian for St. Helens, who was instrumental also in procuring the excellent photograph of what remains of the place.

in my own vindication. He knows he cannot stand that test, and for that reason he has ever endeavoured to shut me out of all society. Yet I never told anything but Truth, nor shall I ever depart from it.

I would now be silent, if he would but let me; but my continued sufferings justify me in speaking and acting in my defence, for even here his persecuting spirit follows me, and he is endeavouring to get me shut out from the comforts of Religion! Oh! that his heart might be changed before it is too late, for it is dreadfully hard and cruel.

So long as my child is with you, I shall consider it my duty to take every pains to clear myself from the falsehoods which have been heaped upon me. I do not want to accuse my husband, but I must defend myself. I can do it with Truth; and if I could but have the opportunity afforded, I could prove myself entirely innocent from even a thought of ill, and still more so of the deeds he talks of.

You will not refuse to give my love to my little Mary? Surely you are not forbidden to do that?

Oct. 21st. I had just written the foregoing, when I received your letter. I cannot comprehend what Mary means in saying she was lately at Holland, and saw her mother. I did not see her, nor ever heard of her being here. Has some trick been played upon the child, to deceive and bewilder her; was she taken to some other place and told it was Holland—which might be easily done, as she can know but little of the place—and shewn some other woman instead of her mother? Yet I think she cannot so far have forgotten me.

Surely, in resembling her father's family in features, she does not at the same time resemble them in falsehood.

You should not have told Mr. Stock of Mary's preparing to write to me. This is the first time I have ever requested any thing I did, respecting Mary, to be kept secret from

Mr. Stock, but now I think I am justified in it. If you will not let her write, let me beg that *you* will instead, about twice in each half year, that I may know the progress she makes in learning, and the state of her health; and say whether my letter to Mary can be received or not. Do not ask Mr. Stock respecting it.

To MRS. MARSDEN   Up-Holland. Oct. 19th. 1822.

I have been in hopes to have seen you here long ago; and all Summer I have thought you would be coming some day or other to see me, when the means of getting here were so easy by the Coaches from Wigan daily. They yet continue several days a week, I understand, but perhaps will not continue long. Let me have the pleasure of seeing you very soon, for a few days, if you will put up with half of my bed.

The congregation at Farr Moor Chapel, are about to form a regulated body for the first time since Mr. Holgate came amongst them; but, keeping it secret from me, innocently and unsuspectingly, a few weeks ago I expressed my desire to join them, whenever that happened; but so reserved were Mr. Holgate and one or two others, of their intentions, and so cool to me, that I thought something was wrong. Last week I became more urgent, for I began to find that they meant to get the formation of a Church completed without informing me. In consequence of my repeated inquiries, Mr. Holgate said he would call upon me, which he had never before done, and, on the 16th., he came.

Judge of my feelings when I found that Mr. Steill[1] had been calumniating me in the bitterest manner to him, so

[1] Rev. Alexander Steill, congregational (Independent) minister at St. Paul's, Standishgate, Wigan. Born 1786, died, apparently in Wigan, in 1832. A catalogue of his large collection of theological classics, works on philology, &c., was issued after his death.

as to make him believe that I should only bring disgrace on the Society; and that my name, if appearing in the list to be presented to Mr. Roby (who is expected on the occasion), would make him judge unfavourably of the whole, if such as I were admitted!

Mr. Holgate is a most worthy man, I do believe, but in this instance he has acted in a most unchristian-like manner. *First, he has condemned me unheard; secondly, because I was accused, he treated me as guilty*; and thirdly, treating me in this manner yet *keeping secret from me of what I was accused*, by which means *I was excluded all opportunity of speaking in my defence*, or *procuring any testimonials in my favour.*

I vindicated myself to Mr. Holgate as well as I could, but my spirit was so excessively cast down, I was almost unable to speak. I told him that he had heard but one side, and that, my bitterest enemy; that to prevent my representing the excessive cruelty with which Mr. Stock and his whole family had used me, I was nearly excluded all society. I earnestly desired he would call on you and Mrs. Hawarden, and he would find whether Mr. Stock or Mr. Steill were to be believed, and how dreadfully I was treated.

He seemed impressed with what I said, but still deferred receiving me into the Church, as it could be done at some other time, still expressing apprehensions of Mr. Roby.

The humblest Christian would almost spurn at thus being introduced into a Christian Church, as it were by stealth. Whether I shall consent to this or no, I shall consider.

You will see that my former doubts must have been much dissipated, and my mind confirmed, before I could so much as propose myself to join any Church . . . and to be thus rejected, is trying indeed!

You did not condemn me unheard. No! In the midst

of the deepest affliction, you came to comfort, and not to condemn. Your almost first introduction to me, was in tenderness and pity to my sorrows; and these brought you, when prosperity had never done it; you visited me at times when others fled far from me, in sorrow and in prison, and your own door was ever open to me for comfort.

Oct. 22. As I have kept this letter a few days, I will tell you what passed on Sunday, the 20th.

Ever since I came to reside in Up-Holland, I have attended as a teacher in the Sunday School at Farr Moor. I have gone regularly; no weather hindered me. Punctuality, perseverance, and patience, gentleness, and industry, were my undeviating rules of conduct (as they always were at home in my husband's house). On Sunday morning I went as usual, but feeling an intention to resign if I were still considered as unfit to be a member. This I would first ascertain.

I had a good deal of conversation with Joshua Tunstal, a young man very active in the school (Mr. Holgate was gone to Rainford for the day, and Mr. Toothill supplied his place). I found from Joshua that my character had been a subject in several meetings. I inquired what were the charges against me. I could not get to know. I then requested to meet my accusers, that they might give me an opportunity of defending myself; strenuously asserting that I was confident I could clear myself.

Accordingly, after evening service, they assembled in Mr. Holgate's parlour, who was then returned. Imagine what I felt on going in, and seeing ten or twelve illiterate, coarse-looking, poor men and women, before whom I had voluntarily brought myself, and who appeared to receive me as a poor criminal, come only that they might pronounce sentence; for I found that I had previously been tried and condemned, not in a Christian kind of way, but like the Inquisition in Spain, where the criminals were never confronted with their accusers, nor told what they were accused of. So it literally was here. I trembled as I sat down; but you know my ideas of strict Christian conduct, and these supported me.

For a long time, no one spoke. At length, the silence was broken by Mr. Holgate, (for my feelings overpowered me, so I could not begin first), who gave out a Hymn and Prayer. Next, Mr. Toothill. Then again a total silence. At last, I spoke to Mr. Holgate, requesting to know of what I was accused, that had been thought sufficient to prevent my being taken in amongst them at this time, and complaining of the great injustice done me in keeping the whole of their proceedings so totally secret from me in regard to their intentions of forming a church at this time, which I had only known a few days, and of what had been going on respecting me for several months; that they had heard only what my husband and Mr. Steill had reported —my bitterest enemies; and had, on the other side, never inquired from my friends; and this was not doing by me as they would any of them like to be done to.

Mr. Holgate spoke of the very favourable character he had heard of me by all the neighbouring people, but there were one or two present whose minds could not be easy to receive me, and he asked me if I could be content to be elected by a majority only, and not unanimously. I asked what these had to say. Not one person spoke. I rose, and bid them all good night.

My heavenly friend was with me, and I left them without any feelings of resentment. As a Christian society, they have made a poor beginning. May they become wiser.

If I hear no more of them, I go no more near them. There is only the Church, and the Methodist Chapel at Lamberhead Green. To one of these I must go.

On the 21st. (Monday night) Mr. Roby came to form them into a Church. Of course, I did not go.

The principals (if such they can be called) in this petty exhibition of religious intolerance, may at this point be accorded a note, whilst Miss Weeton awaits a final decision.

Mrs. Mary Marsden lived at the bottom of Millgate, and was the wife of a confectioner. She and her husband were prominent members of Hope Chapel and therefore hardly likely to be on the best of terms with the Rev. Alex. Steill (or his friend Aaron Stock). Miss Weeton could be sure of their ready sympathy in a matter which did not redound to the credit of the reverend gentleman. Incidentally, the Rev. Wm. Marshall, the pastor of Hope Chapel, was married to Miss Marsden.

The pastor of the newly forming Farr Moor Chapel was not to be envied in his election to the onerous office of casuist in this inquisition. Farr Moor is situated at a little over a mile distant from Upholland; and a more debased, vulgar, brutal district for his ministry could hardly have been his lot. Illiterate weavers and miners, just emerging from the barbarism of the eighteenth century, and their slightly worse womenfolk, would form his congregation. Our protagonists of all-in wrestling might do worse than study the history of the bloody encounters which were just beginning to attract the unsought attention of the authorities in this neighbourhood. The Rev. John Holgate closed his ministry with his death at the age of 63 in the year 1850. The Rev. Wm. Roby, Wigan born, was a popular minister in Manchester. As regards Miss Weeton's alternative choice, Lamberhead Green and its Methodism, this district was as sunk in besotted ignorance as Farr Moor; even to-day, a Lamberhead Greener bristles when reminded of the story of the Salvation Army band, members of which, on being requested not to disturb a sick women, took off their clogs, and marched by in full blast! For a closer study of the grosser appetites and behaviour of this district, the reader is referred to the *Wigan Times*, period 1850—sufficiently long after the period under review for civilization to have penetrated the Upholland district.

To MISS DALRYMPLE,[1] 44 Seymour St., Liverpool.

Holland: Dec. 12. 1822.

I have been in hopes of hearing of you for some time, and fear your health is little better yet, as you have never written. A few weeks ago I almost determined on coming to Liverpool for a week or fortnight, but as I have since concluded on deferring the journey, I cannot be comfortable any longer to delay writing to you, to inquire after your health; be kind enough to let me know by the bearer of this, who regularly goes from Holland every Friday to Liverpool, arrives that evening at Fairclough's (bottom of Dale Street), and returns next day, leaving Liverpool about noon.[2]

Since my temporal affairs have been more settled (my mind in consequence having gained more composure), I have come to that point which you have with so much zeal laboured to bring me: but what will you think when I inform you of the great discouragement I have met with at Farr Moor Chapel?

From the first of my coming to Up-Holland, I attended the Sunday School at Farr-Moor, with the utmost punctuality; it is a mile hence, yet no weather hindered.[3] The girls I taught were exceedingly attentive and attached to me; they increased in numbers, and I pleased myself with thinking that I was as a Missionary in a little obscure corner, where no one else scarcely would give themselves the trouble to labour. Here the talent which the Mighty One had given me, would not be hid in a napkin; and yet, if He blessed my labour, I might be of great and lasting

---

[1] A relative on the paternal side; semi-invalid, and much given to good works.

[2] Anthony Billington, the local carrier.

[3] The reiteration of the weather constituting no hindrance would have more weight with a generation unused to bus services, and under the necessity of stumbling along over execrable roads, wearing pattens to lift their feet out of the mud.

use amongst a race of beings almost lost in barbarism, in a way so quiet that my name would never appear in Annual Reports, or Missionary Chronicles.

Having a mile to walk, and my own apartments to attend to before leaving home (the people of the house I live in, do nothing for me), I rose early on Sabbath mornings, setting out soon after eight, and dining in the Chapel on currant bun, as I had to teach all afternoon; and often staying evening service, so that I did not return home till at night.[1]

All went on very peaceable. I attended to my own class, and interfered with no one else. I grew more and more attached to the place, and thought, now have I 'found rest for the sole of my foot' [here follows a recapitulation of the events leading up to her rejection of the minister's invitation to accept membership on terms]. Several weeks passed, and I heard nothing. Still patient and calm, though this was hint enough, I wrote to make sure. He answered he had not made any inquiry, and gave one false, and several flimsy reasons for not having done it. I have answered him at length, and sent for my books.

Is this the way that Jesus did when any offered to him? Do they, in the Churches at Liverpool, condemn any unheard? Oh Miss Dalrymple, I have suffered so much from this unmerited treatment, my spirit is sadly cast down; it has deprived me of many a night's sleep. I once thought I would come over to Dr. Raffles about it, but . . . I begin to feel almost reckless.

Mr. Holgate has not altogether rejected me. My past conduct was the ground of his rejection, therefore I will not come until that is cleared; for I cannot bear to come

[1] Sunday school hours were necessarily long, as a regular course of instruction in reading and writing had to run parallel with Bible instruction. As, in the majority of instances, the children's only chance of acquiring knowledge outside work hours was on a Sunday, the little factory slaves flocked to the Sunday schools.

to be looked upon with a suspicious eye by those members he has received, few of whose past conduct will bear looking into; thus to come before a set of people consisting entirely of colliers, weavers, and labourers! Here the business rests.

Many of the congregation are much hurt at the treatment I have met with; the parents of the children I taught, particularly. They say it is owing to Mr. Holgate's borrowing books of Mr. Stock, who has an excellent Calvinistic library, and that if he admitted me, Mr. Stock would lend him no more. Mr. Holgate I still believe to be a worthy man, but he has had improper advisers, and has been too ready to follow their counsels. Mr. Steill is a very worldly-minded kind of man, haughty, and over-bearing, and of a most bitter temper, and not a fit companion for any inexperienced minister.

It is but fair, before taking final leave of the Rev. John Holgate, to note that his was a most successful ministry: that he rebuilt the Chapel in 1824; erected, and taught in, the Holgate Day School; and that Farr Moor Chapel was so firmly established as to exist and flourish to-day.

To MR. STOCK, Wigan.   Holland: Jany 1st. 1823.

My dear Husband,

I have heard that my Mary is with you for the holidays: consider a mother's feelings, a mother's affection, and grant me the favour of seeing her at Holland, if it be only for a week, I earnestly entreat you.

It is very long since I saw her, and if you have any compassion for me, and any desire to afford Mary a real pleasure, you will at once liberally and generously afford us a gratification that will warm our hearts towards you with gratitude.

If you will but comply with this wish of mine, I will send for her in any way you may appoint, and return her punctually to the time you fix: only, only let be beg you will grant me as long a time as possible, considering that I never saw her last Summer, nor the Winter holidays previous.

Let me be favoured with as early an answer as possible, and it will still further oblige,

Your affectionate wife

E. Stock.

The result of this application was, of course, a foregone conclusion. The long-continued separation from her child was not being borne with a Christian resignation or submission of a type which would have won the approval of the Reverends J. Holgate and Alex. Steill.

Meantime, she had interested the wealthy Mr. Stopford (through whom she received her quarterly allowance) in her pitiful case, and he had made repeated efforts to achieve the setting-aside of the unjust Deed and its restrictions, especially with regard to the intercourse between child and mother; but to no purpose, except that brother Tom had taken upon himself to write to Mr. Stopford an insulting diatribe against his sister, the news of which stung her into the composition of the amazingly long Letter 390, her last to her brother. Much of this letter has already been utilized in the piecing together of the history of the period 1811–22; but a great deal remains which is of particular interest; for instance, the RETROSPECT (see vol. i) is supplemented with many particulars of her early life; and she is under no necessity to leave unrevealed any of the more absurd or ingrate characteristics of brother Tom. His wife, too, receives full measure from the indignant and caustic woman.

The letter, which is undated, must have been written in the month of February 1823, whilst Miss Weeton was paying a visit of five weeks' duration to a Mrs. Roxburgh, a Liverpool connexion of her mother's.

In consequence, Brother, of the many repetitions you have made of the great weight of obligation you have conferred upon me, both by speaking and in writing (some of the statements being wholly false, and all of them much exaggerated), I think it quite time to begin to act more openly in my defence than I have ever yet done.

Your accusations against me you have always taken care to bring forward at the very time I was most in want of a friend—when I was in the deepest distress. Was this the time for a brother to show his enmity and bitterness against a Sister who had devoted the best years of her life to serve him; who had, for many years together, literally deprived herself of the necessaries of life for his sake; who had made herself a slave that she might contribute towards his support; had been deprived of all the enjoyments of youth—and more than this—whose health was irreparably injured by the sacrifice which she made of all her little property and hard earnings to, and for, a Brother she dearly loved, and for whom she would have even sacrificed her life had it been necessary? Yet this is he who, not content with being the bitterest enemy of his sister, is indefatigably industrious to prevent her having any other friend. If any heart should melt towards me in pity for my excessive sufferings, and attempt to befriend me, then you come forward to prevent them. And in this way you have done me incalculable mischief.

If you will not befriend me yourself, why take such an unnatural pleasure in depriving me of the assistance of others? If what you said were true, you ought to be silent. But I repeat, your statements are either false, or exaggerated so as to injure me most cruelly.

When I served you with my property, my time, and my labours, I made you welcome. So far from twitting you with it perpetually, I did much I never told you of; for, up to the time you married, your affectionate gratitude amply repaid me. I received no other remuneration. I wanted no other. Up to the time you married, and for

some time after, I was your benefactor; not you mine.
I made no boast of what I did for you. It was a pleasure
to me to do you good, for I did much more than my duty;
but now I shall in my own defence take every opportunity
of stating what I did. What you have done for me, you
have so often twitted me with, have boasted of it and talked
so big about it, and exaggerated so ungenerously, that
you have cancelled the obligation entirely. If a regular
account were drawn up between us, you would be found
considerably in my debt, in money, time and trouble.

Poor Tom! she scarifies him through page after page, from
his birth onward, never omitting an opportunity to contrast
his behaviour as an unmarried man with that as husband of
Mrs. Tom Weeton.

For whose benefit, for instance, was this written?—

Once, since I married, when coming over to you in
great distress, the instant you saw me, you were taken ill
of the gripes, and at dinner you had the gripes very bad
indeed, and twisted and twined sadly. Notwithstanding
my own grief, I could scarcely forbear laughing, you
reminded me so strongly of Sancho Panza; fright had that
effect upon him. And you then told me it was of your
wife you were so frightened, she was so violent if you
attempted to do anything for me.

And the 'gripes' must have attacked him again at the
following:

The charge of ill-temper and obstinacy which Mr. Stock
lays so much stress upon, you know well is not true. It is
cruel indeed, and most ungrateful in you to join in it, so
good-tempered as I ever was to you. I never was called
ill-tempered by anyone until I married—except by your
wife, who should be the last person to charge anyone with
what she herself monopolizes. It is a pity but Mr. Stock
and her could make a match of it; for together, the very
sight of them would cure the whole county of ill-humours.

Thus, somewhat erratically, and with many apostrophes upon her brother's conduct, she eventually arrives at the period now under consideration. Animadverting upon Tom's consistent refusal to procure for her more humane terms from her husband, and upon his provoking interferences (so much to the detriment of her own efforts), she tackles him upon his recent letter to the Stopfords.

You told me I could see her [Mary] any time. Make good your assertion. I have never been allowed to see her since. If it be so easy to manage, why do you refuse to apply to Mr. Stock for me? Mr. and Mrs. Stopford have tried every means in their power to obtain Mr. Stock's permission to let me see the child, but he only insults them, and flatly refuses on any terms but 3 fixed days in a year.

Oh! if you had but firmly taken your Sister's part from the beginning of the cruel usage I received, it would never have come to this. And you might have done it, conscientiously, for my conduct as a wife was irreproachable.

As to the 3 days a year, I never will consent. Since you could so easily get 2 items in the Deed altered, why did you not try further . . . because you were Mr. Stock's attorney in an underhand way, and not mine in any way. Therefore, you were doing your best for your client. I found you out, notwithstanding your many pitiful disguises.

In your late letter to Mr. Stopford (obviously intended to injure me as much as possible in that kind and respectable man's opinion), you speak of the papers you last sent me, as remaining unacknowledged. Recollect, you directed them to Mr. Stopford, and not to me—unblushingly acknowledging that you did not know where your Sister was! If I had met with no kinder friends than you, I must have perished for want. You never inquired where your sister was, or you might have known; nor how she subsisted. For the first 3 months, I had nothing to live upon but charity and credit, owing to your not stipulating that each quarter should be paid in advance. Thus, for the first year, I have only had 20s. a week, and you have lost me £17. 10s. owing to the advice you gave Mr. Stock. I owe you great thanks! As to your son's labours, so pompously mentioned, what are they? I know of nothing but the copy of the Deed, which, had it come in time, I should have been obliged for; but as you had not said anything of letting me have one, Mr. Stopford himself took a copy for me previously, so yours came too late. Mr. Stopford did it pleasantly, and without seeming to think it any Herculean task. A favour handsomely conferred is doubled—grudgingly, cancelled.

You often say that I acted contrary to your advice. What in? Do state particulars when you make that assertion. What did I ever do to put it out of your power to command anything? Nothing, I positively assert. The fact is, you never would undertake any legal process for me; and as for any advice but legal advice, you are not capable of giving it. You wrote out some precedents, but you would not act on them, nor anyone else, so they remained useless.

As to you, in a more respectable family, you would have been as good and as kind-hearted a fellow as any in existence. I cannot but pity, while I blame you. You have said that my mother and my aunt reproached me with obstinacy. Dear me! if every angry word, hastily spoken, is to have such lasting weight, where do you stand? My mother often called you a little fool and a liar; and my aunt, featherbrain! My mother never did call me obstinate, but praised my temper highly. So did my aunt and uncle until I left Holland 15 years ago. Then only did they find it out, because I wished to improve my circumstances, and they wanted me to stay to nurse them without remuneration; and if I went, they must pay for a nurse, which they could well afford. They would not so much as give me my meat for nursing them; no, not even a cup of tea occasionally.

You say I quoted you as my Counsel—when? I never could get you to advise me, and often said so. In your letter to Mr. Stopford, you speak very highly of Mr. Stock! of the man who has used your Sister so shamefully; and say that I might obtain any reasonable wish, if I had less stubbornness and more discretion. These assertions are like the rest, false. If you are so well acquainted with the manner, the discreet manner, in which Mr. Stock may be prevailed with to allow me to see my child, for Heaven's sake point it out, for no one here knows how.

Various applications have been made, but all unsuccessful. He seems determined to force me to being bound to only 3 days a year, for that he proposes still. I repeat, I never will.

Some pictures which you had painted for me before I was married, and which you have since borrowed but never returned, I wish to have again. And as, since the portrait of a Sister so hateful to you and so persecuted by you, can be no agreeable sight, I should consider it as a favour if you would let me have it, although I gave it to you. I can find those who love the original better than ever you did.

Greatly daring, and with the scales of the law heavily weighted against her sex, she decided to pledge in advance a portion of her allowance, in order to secure some measure, if possible, of legal protection for herself and her child.

To MR. H. LATHAM,[1] Holland. Liverpool. Feb. 21. 1823.

I feel much pleased and obliged by your letter which I have just received, and shall be directed by your observa-

[1] Henry Latham, the eldest son of Miss Weeton's detractor, cousin Latham, and whose education she had provided for at her own expense, appears to have dabbled in law as a profession. He died 19 Nov. 1842, aged 44.

tions and suggestions. The information you give me of your journey to St. Helens, and Mr. Taylor's opinion of the present stage of the business, is very satisfactory.

Your delicate intreaty that I will not suffer myself to feel hurt at Mr. Gaskell's ungentlemanly and uncalled for sarcasms in his letter to Mr. Taylor, is timely, and your assurance that Mr. Taylor will not be influenced by them, gratifying. Mr. G's expressions have no truth in them, for, as to any personal Effects of which he says I have obtained possession (he does not know how), I know not what he means. I have nothing which does not most strictly belong to me, and I do not know that I have a single Article that Mr. Stock did not see me pack.

I acted quite openly, I took *nothing* in secret. I ought to have had much more; he drove me out as poor as I well could be. I rather apprehend it has been now as it was once before. Mrs. Peck (soon after I was turned out, about 3 or 4 years ago) robbed her father of all she well could, and then said I had got the articles away, thus artfully diverting his suspicions into a wrong channel. When I am absent from him, he is sadly robbed.

Meantime, Miss Weeton took the bold step of notifying her late tenants not to pay any further rent to Mr. Stock, or Mr. Perkins, his agent. And she further writes to her godchild and legal adviser:

I have considered your proposals and observations, and have come to this conclusion, that I will now spare 5£, which I can send you on Saturday next by Anthony Billington, as I have no other means of conveying it to Mr. Taylor; unless you think I had better go myself to St. Helens the latter end of this week—suppose Friday next, if you think I had. Write immediately on receiving this, and I will go. Five pounds more I could advance in a month hence, and for the remainder, I should be glad if your father could, and would, guarantee until I could release him from the engagement at the next two quarterly receipts, 5£ each time.

I could wish to know how long it would probably be before the business could probably be concluded, and whether, if I gained the cause at this time, Mr. Stock could remove it to some other court—which, if he could, he most probably would, were it only to harass me as much as possible, and then law expences would mount up so as perhaps to make me no gainer, although I should succeed.[1]

To MISS STOCK, Parr Hall. Up-Holland. April 16. 1823.

Will you not rejoice to see another letter from me, when I have been silent so long? I know you will, whilst at the same time you will wonder why I have been so long in writing. Indeed, my love, I had hoped to see you long ago, and for that reason I waited until I was certain whether I should be allowed to see you soon or not. I begin to think I must see you no more; but surely I may write and tell you how much I love you, and how glad I should be to see you. More than a year has passed since I saw my only darling child.

I continue to lodge at Mr. Ball's, in Up-Holland. I have a Bed-room, and a parlour to myself,[2] and, being

---

[1] But it was all to no purpose; the proceedings ultimately fell through, Mr. Taylor's attitude undergoing a suspicious change towards his client. In any case, as man and wife were at this period one under law, she would have had to be joined with him in any action against him!

[2] Ball's farm still exists, but is now known as Garnett Lees. Despite uninspired alterations and additions, it is still recognizable for the ancient building it was until recently, both in fact and repute. The doorway and sunken steps thereto (see illustration) are modern conveniences. Members of the Ball family represented the Newgate Division of the Parish of Upholland between the years 1802 and 1860.

Mr. Archie Hunt, of the Abbey, has kindly provided these particulars; and I am indebted to Mrs. Hunt for the trouble she has taken in securing several views of the 'poky parlour', from which this illustration has been selected, as giving the best (or worst) indication of its pokiness.

very much alone, I sometimes feel it very dull. Mr. and
Mrs. Ball are strict-principled, and tender-hearted people
indeed. I respect them highly. They treat me with great
respect, and so do all their servants; for, being farmers,
they have many. They are so busy every day with their
cows, their farm, that they have little time to sit in their
parlour, so that I have very little of their company. They
wish much to see you.

Mrs. Braithwaite often invites me to dine with her, or
to take tea and supper. Miss Dennett frequently invites
me to tea, and I go sometimes to Mr. George Gaskell's,
and to Mr. Stopford's, so that amongst them, I spend my
time as agreeably as I can. Sometimes I have a little tea-
party at my lodgings.

Mrs. Braithwaite is in a declining state of health. I fear
she will never be well again. Mr. Stopford's have left
Holland about 3 weeks ago, and have gone to live near
Roby Mill, about 2 miles hence. I am sorry they are gone
so far, they were so kind to me. During Summer I shall
often take a walk to see them.

You see, Mary, I introduce you as it were to all my
friends.

Miss Dalrymple is, I dare say, almost as old as I am,
and not at all pretty; but she is such a worthy, religious
woman, that I esteem her highly. She has been unable to
walk for more than a year, owing to exerting herself too
much, when she was well, in going about to collect money
for the Bible Society, the Missionary Society, to distribute
Tracts, and to visit the sick poor as a Member of the
Benevolent Society, by whom they were assisted and relieved. She is recovering, but very slowly, and is so chearful, it is quite pleasing to see her. Oh, Mary, if when you
grow up, you should be afflicted as she is, or as I have
been, may you know where to look for comfort, and to find
it as we have done.

To MASTER J. ARMITAGE, Free Grammar School, Manchester.

Holland: April 22d. 1823.

I felt most exceedingly pleased on receiving your last letter of April 12th., in addition to the usual well filled one at Christmas last; for I scarcely expected, that so young as you were when you last saw me at Highroyd, that you would recollect or care much about me. I was much attached to all of you, and took every pains to gain your affection, respect, and esteem, and it gratifies me much to reflect that I gained what I wished.

You will be 14 on the 24th. inst., an age, Joseph, when many boys are very thoughtless, and often very unfeeling to those unfortunate animals that fall into their power; let no example lead you to be so, and I feel a hope that you possess a mind of some compassion and refinement—a hope founded on the desire you express to learn to play the flute.

Music has a powerful tendency to humanize the disposition, and a fondness for it, I always think, speaks highly for the temper of any one.[1] I am glad your friends encourage your desire, and with a good instructor, I dare say you will improve quickly; and when you are at home, you may help to form a complete band of Musicians, with your brothers and sisters. If Sarah-Anne wont take any other instrument, she may assist with a marrow bone and cleaver.[2] Does George play any? As to Emma, she is, I suppose, quite an M.D.

You will be seeing all your brothers and sisters, I suppose, at the expiration of two months. Give my love to all who remember me. Probably, were they to see me now, they would scarcely remember my features again; they were

[1] And yet that gloomy contemporary of Miss Weeton and Master Joseph, philosopher Schopenhauer, was no mean flautist.

[2] Hogarth's 'The Marriage Morning' (in the Industrious and Idle Apprentice series) affords an excellent representation of a band of butchers with their marrow bones and cleavers serenading the newly weds.

all so young when they last saw me, and it is nearly 9 years ago; they would likewise be much altered, for Sarah -Anne was not quite 9 years old when I left.

I shall be glad to hear from you at any time, and I hope you will write me a longer letter, for I dare say you are never at a loss for a subject; any thing interesting to you, would be so to me, and you may write as familiarly as to any other *old* acquaintance.

To MRS. PRICE, 35, Seymour Street, Liverpool.

Up-Holland. May 8. 1823.

The time has, I think, arrived when I may begin to hope for the fulfilment of the promise you half made of coming to Holland when the weather should be warmer and the days of such a length as to make such an excursion agreeable. After you have received this remembrancer, I shall begin to expect you every week until you actually arrive; so let me beg you will not be long, and come with an intention to stay as long as possible.

I went to Wigan last Sunday (May 4) to Hope Chapel, where Mr. Ralph preached; since his death, Mr. Marshall from Macclesfield has succeeded to the Chapel. I was there by half past 9, and visited the school. I was most gratifyingly received (for I have not been at the place, since I ceased to reside in Wigan, until the 4th. inst.). Mr. Marshall and several others told me that when I left, the school diminished lamentably, and continued to do so until lately. It now revives again. My old pupils are all gone, except two or three who are become teachers. They received me most affectionately. I think I shall go often when the weather permits, taking my dinner in my pocket, as I did last Sunday, and eating it in the School, or at Mr. Marsden's, father-in-law to the minister.

When afternoon service was over, I called to see Dr. and Mrs. Hawarden, and took tea with them. The Dr. is no worse; his intellectual faculties appear as clear as ever. I found him standing by the window, reading the small print of some Magazine without glasses. He spoke with his usual chearfulness, and with that degree of wit and humour which you know is so strikingly peculiar to him —but his tongue falters—his deafness increases—and his limbs tremble under him! . . .

Two very fashionable-looking young men have become boarders with them; they conduct a shop lately opened in the Millgate by a Mr. Lee.

Readers of vol. i of the Letters will recognize, with pleasurable anticipations, healthy signs of the old Miss Weeton in the foregoing letter—the prolonged absence from the scene of her former distresses, the bracing upland air, old friendships and associations renewed, have produced a beneficial result which reacts increasingly favourably upon her correspondence. And once again the Journal appears, testifying to a revived interest in life and the concerns of those around her. The old buoyancy reasserts itself, and at the age of 47 the wander-lust finds temporary satisfaction in daring trips to the forbidden town, and a renewal of her associations with Hope Chapel—an association which was to continue almost without a break until the year 1844. Despite their lukewarm attitude towards Miss Weeton in the period of her greatest distress during the years 1818–22, this little religious community was to benefit (as years advanced and her position in Wigan was reversed from that of the social outcast to that of a wealthy resident) by the active, and no doubt material, support of the magnanimous foundation-member.

The history of Hope Chapel and its principal minister is worth a passing note, involving as it did that of Miss Weeton, as is apparent from a perusal of a manuscript record penned about this time by Deacon Edmund Alston (1777–1850). Incidentally, it will be remembered that the Deacon's friendship with Mr. Stock had indirectly occasioned the break-down of Miss Weeton's efforts with respect to the Deed of Separation.

The existing Hope Chapel, situated in Mesnes Lane, Wigan,

is capable of seating about 500 persons. It is a fairly modern structure, of no particular architectural pretensions, but is not insignificant in that it is a tangible reminder of the rebellion of a devoted few, Miss Weeton included, against the hide-bound religion which so mocked the spiritual needs of Wigan over a hundred years ago. It would certainly dwarf the original building, erected in Hope Lane, near by, and thus described:

'The Chapel was finished in its then form, being 5 yards high and without a Gallery in 1818, and opened 30th. of Aug^t, same year . . . the managers in 1820 took measures for raising the Chapel, and placing therein three galleries.'

The edifice thus improved, was looked at askance by another generation, which later erected a chapel—presumably in better taste, if one can judge from the contemptuous dismissal of the older one by a contemporary historian of Wigan. 'The chapel, in its style of architecture, bears the impress of the time when it was reared—plain brick, ill-lit, and high pews. In consequence of the building of the Market Hall close by, it is proposed that the Corporation should purchase the sanctuary in order to pull it down and give room to the thoroughfare.'

Its first minister was a Mr. Ralph, upon whose retirement in the year 1822 (cause unspecified, but probably due to a complete break-down in health, as he died in September of that year) a sum of £100 was subscribed by the tiny congregation, despite the fact of his sermons not having proved doctrinal enough. His position had been irregular, and the chapel had not been suffered to establish itself without energetic and subtle protest on the part of the Rev. Alex. Steill, whose attempt to cripple the effort at its inception is thus recorded by Mr. Alston:

'An answer was forthwith received from Mr. Fletcher, that no supplies would be sent from Blackburn Academy to Hope Chapel, except a reconciliation would be brought about between the People of Hope Chapel and Mr. Steill, the minister of St. Paul's.

'As there was not any probability that this could be accomplished, had it been attempted, and as there was not the *shadow* of an *inclination* to *try*, the scheme fell to the ground.'

The Rev. Wm. Marshall (1792–1861) had served the pulpit a number of times in the original chapel, and had delivered the inaugural service at the reopening of the enlarged chapel in 1820; but the replacement of Mr. Ralph was not to be devoid of petty squabbling. In *The Story of Presbyterianism in Wigan*, by Wm. B. Shaw, published in 1912, there is an echo of the bitter controversies and religious uncharitableness which marked his succession.

'Mr. Marshall was a Scotsman, was born in 1792, and received his education at Glasgow University. His settlement in Wigan was not so peaceable as his friends had expected, for it led to the secession of many members, as well as that of four members of its Committee of Management.'

And what was this mighty pother about? Miss Weeton is more explicit as to the reasons for the uneasiness of a few piously sensitive folk, the loss of whom to the congregation was amply balanced by the acquisition of a minister who was to establish the chapel on a firm basis, proof against the machinations of the 'Steillites' and the disgruntled seceding seceders.

'The minister of Hope Chapel, Mr. Marshall, is a young man I esteem very highly. Having married Mr. Marsden's daughter, my intimacy with Mrs. Marsden has occasioned me to see much of him. His talents are considerable; but what I think of greater importance, is the Christian softness, forbearance, and benevolent liberality of his temper.

'Whilst Mr. Ralph was at this Chapel, the ministers of the Union always refused to receive him amongst them; at his death, they were applied to, but they refused to nominate a minister, or suffer any belonging to them to supply the vacancy, saying they would not encourage divisions and separations, and Mr. Steill's Chapel was sufficient for the congregation. As Mr. Steill, from his exceedingly haughty, austere, and unbending manner, is greatly disliked, the people had no alternative but still to continue out of the Union, and invited Mr. Marshall from Macclesfield.

'About half of the congregation left on Mr. Marshall's coming in, but so determined were they not to have Mr.

Steill for their minister, and yet to be supplied by the
ministers of the County Union, that they have hired a large
room in the town, obtaining supplies as they can, by itinerant
and regular ministers, who visit them occasionally; so that
the Union, who would not encourage separations, assist a
second separation, which inconsistency has occasioned those
at Hope Chapel to rejoice that they do not belong to the
Union, nor are tied by its bonds, but that they are wholly
independent.'

Deacon Alston corroborates and supplements Miss Weeton's
statement.[1]

'The minister entered on his duties with zeal. He began
by preaching Seven times a week. Two of the weekly
lectures were delivered in Cottages, and many who attended
in these places appeared much interested. The stations for
these cottages were in separate parts of the Town, and surrounding neighbourhood.'

In this wise was the Reverend William Marshall launched
upon Wigan, and four of Miss Weeton's Manuscript Books
assured to a future generation.

✳   ✳   ✳

[JOURNAL]

May 4th. Sunday. Went to Wigan to Hope Chapel for
the first time since I ceased to reside in Wigan.

May 11th. Went again to Hope Chapel, returning that
morning to Holland. Was invited to dine at Mr. Alston's
and accepted the invitation.

(*18*) Spent this day again at Hope Chapel, having stayed
all night previously at Mr. Marsden's. On Monday the

---

[1] The direct references to Miss Weeton in this MS. record of Hope Chapel
activities are few, but important, affording the principal source of information with regard to her movements subsequent to the year 1825, and covering a period registering a vital change in her fortunes. The editor's thanks
are due to the Committee of the Hope Independent Chapel for permission
to reproduce such portions of the Alston MS. as have been used above,
and in the history of the later phase of Miss Weeton's life which terminates
this volume.

19th. (having likewise stayed at Mr. M's on Sunday night) I attempted to go to St. Helen's by Coach at 6 o'clock that morning, and got into the coach for that purpose; but not having taken a place, I was obliged to get out again, as all the places were engaged previously, so set off home, arriving there by half past 7 o'clock.

22ᵈ Thursday, after dinner walked to St. Helen's from Holland; saw Mr. Taylor, the solicitor; stayed all night at an Inn; saw Mr. T. again next morn^g,

23ᵈ and then proceeded to Parr Hall to see my little Mary, whom I had not seen for fourteen months before; dined with her and took leave at half past 2 o'clock.

24ᵗʰ Mrs. Braithwaite died in the evening, just after I had called to inquire how she was, on my way to Wigan, where I again went to be ready for Chapel.

June 2nd. Mrs. Braithwaite was interred in the morning; in the afternoon, saw my brother, his wife, and son, at my cousin Latham's.

It must not be supposed, from the bare relation of the death and interment of Mrs. Braithwaite, that Miss Weeton had become utterly callous as a result of her sufferings. There is later evidence that she reverenced the memory of this true-hearted woman. In addition, allowance must be made for the fact that the resuscitated Journal was only at this time in its trial stage.

18. Wednesday evening. Mary came home to her father for the holidays.

22. Having left Holland the evening before, spent this day at Mr. Marsden's, and at Chapel. Heard of Mary, but made no attempt to see her.

25. Mrs. Hawarden taken exceedingly ill.

28. Went in the evening to Wigan; found Mrs. Hawarden a little recovered, giving me hopes that I was not yet going to lose another mother; for one went when Mrs. Braithwaite died.

29. Went to Chapel; wrote a short note to Mr. Stock in the afternoon, requesting to see Mary, but he only insulted the boy who took it, threatening to kick him out of the house. This day I heard that Mr. Stock was thought by many to be almost insane; indeed, I had been hearing for some months before of many corroborative circumstances. A few days ago, he was seen going up Millgate without his hat. About a month ago, he was carrying a bundle of papers through Chapel-lane, flourishing them about like a ballad singer.

✳ ✳ ✳

To MISS DALRYMPLE, 44, Seymour St., Liverpool.
Holland. June 27th. 1823.

I ought to take blame to myself for not writing to you long ago. I was not expecting to hear first from you, and I have had no sufficient reason for deferring it so long. I was really anxious to hear of you, and hoped to have heard some tidings by Mrs. Price many weeks ago, and had desired that she would inform me. As she never answered my letter, I had concluded she had not received it; but yours of the 12 inst. informs me she has. I was rejoiced to hear from you, although concerned to find that you were still so weak; it appears that your recovery is not so rapid as could be wished, but yet you have hope.

I have been going on since I was at Liverpool, in a sort of every-day jog trot way. 6 or 7 weeks ago I began to go to Hope Chapel in Wigan, on a Sunday morning, taking my dinner in my pocket, and returning at night; since when, I have gone on a Saturday evening, taking a bed at Mr. Marsden's. Whether I can continue it long, I cannot say, for Mr. Stock will probably raise some obstacle. I have for some time past concluded on going into some kind of situation, the first that offers that may be eligible, or into some way of business, for I cannot get forward with the law suit I told you of, my brother preventing me. He is, on all occasions, my enemy. With a sincere, steady friend, and an able attorney, I firmly believe I could have gained it.

My stipend would keep me with moderate care, but I cannot have those domestic comforts here which a home of one's own affords. I seldom know what it is to have a comfortable dinner, and all my meals are solitary. If I am sick, I have no one to nurse or comfort me; if I am well, there is none to converse with, for which reason I often go out to Miss Braithwaite's, and to Miss Dannett's; but as it is not convenient to do this at all times, I am left much alone. I have lost a kind and long tried friend by the death of Mrs. Braithwaite, about a month ago; she had been gradually declining all winter, and I regret her loss much.

As I find Mary is come from school to her father for the holidays, I do not mean to be far from home until she returns to school, in hopes I may obtain his leave to see her. I then think of going to Southport for a time.

Should I get some situation in another neighbourhood, it may possibly be where there are more opportunities of enjoying religious society; for I often sigh to find, that when I have been for a time estranged from the society of pious people, and a place of Christian worship, I feel sadly weaned from them, and am almost inclined to look upon them, and it, as a piece of error and fanaticism, and wonder not at the many who speak or write under such impressions. But when again I mingle amongst them, the sky of Heaven opens upon me—but, placed where I am, what can I do? I must either seek lodgings elsewhere or draw a little circle around me here of untaught souls, and commence leader, for which I am not fit or able. I wish some one would plant, and then I would work as under gardener.

To MISS C. ARMITAGE, Milnes Bridge, near Huddersfield.

> Holland. [Dated October 12th 1823;
> but a note states that 'the above had
> been prepared in July last, but was
> not sent until the present date.]

The letter which I received from you all at Christmas last, was very welcome, and found me at Holland, in better health and spirits, and greater comfort and tranquillity, than any preceding one since I left you. I am much restored indeed in health; my situation is, as may be supposed, very comfortable in many respects, yet very comfortless in others. The enjoyment of rising and retiring to rest in peace, free from any fear, and spending the day free from any distressing anxiety, with no other employment than that of attending upon, and amusing, myself, is surely valuable; but then, on the other hand, the solitude necessarily attendant on residing in lodgings, eating every meal alone, no one to converse with me to enliven me in health, or soothe in sickness, is exceedingly sinking to the spirits; so much so, that I intend to engage in some situation or way of business as soon as I can meet with anything eligible. My income is too small to admit of my keeping house, and the support of a servant; and unless I can make a home of my own, I prefer employment.

Since I came to Holland, Mrs. Braithwaite's kindness has been unremitting; one or two days every week I spent there; but . . . this friend is gone! She died about 5 months ago; she had known me from a child, and was like a mother to me. Her daughters make up the loss to me as much as they can; but whenever I go to the house, there is one wanting.

Mr. Stock wants to insist upon my being bound not to see Mary more than 3 days a year, the days to be exactly specified, and a heavy penalty attached, if I were to see her at any other time. I reject such a proposal with indignation; but the consequence is, that he does all in his power to prevent my seeing her at all, and I have seen her only once for the last 19 months.

In May last I walked over to Parr-Hall, only 7 miles hence, for I am not rich enough to hire a conveyance. I saw Mary, and staid 3 hours with her. When I arrived at her residence, I expected to have been refused admittance, for such were the orders I understand Mr. Stock to have given; however, I was politely received. You may imagine how my heart ached at going thus to see my child; and when she was introduced to me, a 14 month's estrangement had caused us both to forget each other! Mary knew not her mother! and her mother hardly recognised her child, her only one!

Mary looked timidly and coolly at me; she was exceedingly pale and thin. By degrees, we became more and more affectionate, and she chatted with me quite familiarly. My heart ached to discover a very wrong system of education pursued for my child; but I must submit to it in silence. *No father is fit to educate a daughter*, and Mary is only preparing for a sickly life, filled with vanity, pride, and trifles—and a premature death. Poor, poor Mary, thy lot and mine is very sad!

To MR. STOCK, Wigan.   Up-Holland. July 1st. 1823.

Mr. Stock.

I again write to intreat that I may see my child. Why is it that I am thus debarred the natural right of a Mother? If no Christian feeling influences you, if no principle of duty to your God has any weight; nay, if only moral decency is disregarded by you—reflect a little—and consider that the very brutes act not thus inhumanly, except a few of those most horrible of all the animal creation, who deprive the mother of her young by devouring them![1] But even these know not that they are fathers. Oh, if you have any thing manly about you, shew that you have, by acting like one. Oh, if you have any soul-like feeling that there is a Mighty God, incur not His everlasting displeasure, by acting so contrary to His example and to His laws; for the power and the wealth which He bestows upon you are but lent to you to do good with, to make even the widow's heart to sing for joy. But I am as it were—a widow—yet is my husband living. I am childless—yet my child is not dead. I am likewise comparatively poor, yet is my husband rich.

Who has made me a widow?—You.

Who has deprived me of my child?—You.

Who has made me poor? Oh, that I could say 'twere any other but—You.

As regards my child, why deprive me of the comfort of her society, when you would in no way suffer yourself? You could see her just as much as you now do. It is in your power to make us all happier, for you would surely feel a pleasure in acting kindly towards me. There is a pleasure in doing good, and do you not know it? There must be a misery in inflicting evil, and have you not felt it?

Do you not love my Mary? Why then deprive her of the comfort of a mother? If you sincerely loved her, you would study *her* comfort and satisfaction. When in your house, what female society has she, capable of giving her proper instruction?—none. Too ignorant are they, and of language and manners not for her to copy; and when she leaves school, she must come home to be the companion of servants.

---

[1] The exclamation mark is Miss Weeton's own. Mr. Stock's is not available.

Do not educate her thus, I earnestly urge, but let her have the advantages of a mother's solicitude, which she may have, although we reside in separate houses, for I do not urge to live with you myself; but it might be managed so, if you had the desire to act with a liberality of feeling towards me, that we might both have the enjoyment of the society of a child that is dear to us, and which I surely deserve, if it be only for the exemplary patience I have shewn you since I left you.

✻ ✻ ✻

[JOURNAL]

July 1st. Packed up Mary's doll, to send it to her with all its cloathes, and took it to Edward Melling, to take to her at her father's in Wigan the following morning, along with the preceding letter.

2ᵈ Wednesday. When Edward returned, he brought the doll back with him, informing me that he called at a shop near Mr. Stock's (as I had directed him) to inquire first if Mary was still at home, and was there informed that Mary was, on Monday morning, 30th. inst. [? ult.] sent off by the Coach in a hasty and rather mysterious manner. For the remainder of the day, I was almost inconsolable, so bitter and inveterate a spirit is so perpetually manifested against me by my husband. However, I began to take comfort that my child was from under the care of such a father, for she is better anywhere than with him.

3ᵈ H. Latham told me he was going to St. Helens, and I instructed him to discover whether Mary was at Parr Hall or no; at night, he called on his return and told me she was there. I was now quite easy about her.

9th. My brother-in-law, Wm. Stock,[1] came with his wife and youngest daughter, who is dying of a consump-

---

[1] BAKERS: Stock, Wm. Wellington St. Scholes. Baines's *Lancs. Directory*, 1825.

tion. I requested them to let her come for a few days to try change of air and scene. They dined and drank tea with me, and then took leave, their little Margaret remaining with me.

12. Packed up Mary's doll again, and sent it her to Parr Hall by a Wigan Coach.

13. Sunday Morn^g. Took Margaret Stock to my cousin Latham's to spend the day, whilst I went to Wigan, where I arrived at half past ten in the morning, thoroughly drenched by a tremendous thunder shower. Remained drying myself by Mrs. Marsden's kitchen fire until noon. Went to Chapel in the afternoon.

16. Margaret Stock returned home by the Coach.

19. Spent the Sabbath at Wigan, paying Mrs. Marsden for my board for seven Sundays, reckoned as one week.

22. Set off in Mr. Ball's cart to Apply Bridge, at 12 o'clock, accompanied by Miss Dennett; sailed from thence in the packet to Scarisbrick Bridge. From thence we had a pleasant ride in a Landau to Southport,[1] where Miss Dennett's niece Catharine joined us in a day or two. Mrs. Walmsley, where Miss D's lodged, had not room for me; I therefore engaged lodgings at Mr. Lowe's for a week. Found two very agreeable female lodgers of the name of Heatley, from Manchester (sisters-in-law).

23d. Bathing, and walking, visiting Miss Dennett and conversation with the Mrs. H's agreeably occupied the whole of this day (Wednesday).

24th. Sailing and bathing, walking and visiting Miss D's, and riding with Miss C. D. and party, occupied the time most amusingly until the

---

[1] 'To such as are more disposed to economize money than time, the canal packets offer a cheap conveyance from Liverpool and Manchester as well as on the whole line of the intermediate country to Scarisbrick Bridge, where a number of handsome carriages are stationed to convey passengers to this place of fashionable resort, being a distance of about five miles.' Baines's *Lancs. Directory,* 1825.

26th. when Mrs. Heatley and I went with a party in a boat to Lytham; the day was beautiful, and although we were both very sick as we went, I yet greatly enjoyed the sail. We soon recovered on landing at Lytham, and, purchasing something to eat at a confectioner's, we went into the Church-yard, and sitting on a tomb-stone, ate a most hearty dinner, after which we rambled for a mile or so until it was time to return; we were not at all sick on our way home.

31st. As the Mrs. H's had left Southport, I paid Mrs. Lowe for my lodgings, not liking solitude, the expence, and my little stove of a bedroom; neither the continual drunkenness of Mrs. Lowe, nor the want of principle in the servants; and removed to Miss Lowe's, sisters of Mr. Lowe, where I could be at half the expence with honest, sober people.

August. Passed the time as before, very agreeably, until yᵉ 8th, when I hired Mr. Lowe's horse, and rode alone to Crossens by the shore, and returned through Church Town. When near Southport, I felt for my watch to see how long I had been away, as I paid by the hour, and to my astonishment, my watch was gone! The shock was such that I was not able to return to look for it, although I knew I had it after I had mounted. I proceeded home, and making known my loss, Mr. Lowe very good naturedly directly took his horse and rode precisely by the rout I had taken; in the meanwhile, I sent the Bellman, who had not finished his round ere Mr. Lowe returned with the watch. At Crossens, it was found lying on the road by a boy, who took it to his mother; from which, it seems it must have been thrown out of my pocket by the high trotting of the horse. The first person Mr. Lowe met with to make any inquiry of, was this very boy, who immediately said he had found it, and on restoring it, Mr. Lowe gave him 5s. I was much pleased on seeing my watch again; it was a valuable, old-fashioned gold one, given by my father to my mother immediately after they were married. The boy's honesty merited a better reward, and if ever I should be in that neighbourhood again, I will try to find him out.

14th. Set off to Liverpool, outside the coach from Southport,[1] on a tremendously wet morning. Had I not taken my place the day before, I would not have gone. I shall take care how I secure a place again, when there is no absolute necessity to go to a certain day, unless I could at the same time secure the weather. The wind blew so furiously, no umbrella could be opened or carried. The coachman was very attentive and kind to me; he gave me a stout horse rug to cover my shoulders, and another to cover my knees, and in this elegant costume, I rode through Ormskirk and Liverpool to the Inn there, as heedless and contented as possible, the rain soaking through all the way, driving in at a little crevice between my hood and my neck, and trickling in little streams down my back, so that I was literally wet to the skin; and when I descended from my elevated situation, my cloaths were so entirely wet, that I found I was a woman of much greater weight in Liverpool than I had been at Southport. However, my rugs had kept me very warm, so that when I took them off, I went smoking all the way to the coach stand, and procured one to convey myself and luggage from Red cross Street to Russel Street, to lodge a short time with Mrs. Roxburgh, where I got well dried after my smoking, and received no injury to my health.

18. Took Miss Roxburgh with me in a steam packet

[1] Coaches: *During the bathing season.* Eclipse to Liverpool every morning at 8, rets. at 7 in the evg. Baines's *Lancs. Directory*, 1825. 'As both these vehicles are set upon extraordinary rough springs, and the road nearly all the distance is paved with large stones, it is reasonable to hope that the grievous jolting inflicted on passengers during his journey thither may at least be conducive to his bodily health.' Head's *Tour of Manufacturing Districts*, 1835.

over the river to Birkenhead. For some time previous, I had had some thoughts of engaging in some business or other on Mrs. and Miss Hawarden's account, whom I desired if possible to assist, as they are likely to be destitute, I fear, before long;[1] and their kindness to me at a time of extreme distress, when turned out by my lunatic husband, and not knowing where to shelter, was such as I hope I shall never forget. With this view, I went this day to Birkenhead, thinking that taking in lodgers or boarders, and accommodating tea parties, might answer. I reconnoitred accordingly, looked at several new-built and unlet houses, and thought it probably would succeed, if they would like to come so far. On many succeeding days, I traversed many parts of Liverpool and its neighbourhood with this view, intending on my return home to inform them of the result. Had an exceedingly pleasant sail and walk back.

30. Sailed at 8 o'clock this morning with Mrs. Moneypenny and Miss Hawarden in the Steam Packet, to Bagilt in Wales.[2] Mrs. Moneypenny and Miss Hawarden rode in a Car to Holywell; I preferred walking there alone. The day was serene and lovely. I joined them at Holywell where we dined and went to see the well and a little of the surrounding country, and then proceeded all together in a Car. The same afternoon to St. Asaph, where we stopped at the Red Lion. Miss Hawarden and I took a short walk before bed time.

31st. Sunday Morn[g]. Miss Hawarden and I, rising early; took a walk towards Rhyddlan, and returned to Mrs. Moneypenny to breakfast. As these ladies were Catholics, I left them and went to the Cathedral. I was rather amused to see them enter soon after, thinking it would

---

[1] The good old doctor died 17 Sept. 1824.

[2] BAGILT—*Cambria*, sails with goods and passengers to Bagilt, near Holywell, Wales, every day, at eight morning. Baines's *Lancs. Directory*, 1825.

never be known by their friends in Wigan. Thinks I to myself, now if I should tell!

It appeared here as if 'praising and singing to the Lord' was a vast of trouble, very hard work, a great deal of pain, and much expence, there were so many people—men and boys—regularly employed and paid to do it; so hot, too, did it make them, and some of them pulled weary faces— so unlike the unaffected simplicity of primitive Christian worship. After service, as we walked round the Cathedral yard, the Bishop's housekeeper invited us to walk in the palace garden. We were pleased with the civility and entered; it was neat and retired. On coming out again into the Cathedral yard, we found the gates all locked! We were in a dilemma now, for there was no way out. We traversed round and round, and at last sat down in patient despair for half an hour or more, when luckily a boy passed by one of the gates. We sent him to the proper authorities, who came and let us out. After dinner, we all walked to Rhyddlan, viewed the ruined Castle, and re-turned to tea. Miss Hawarden and I again went out for a short walk after tea, and we all retired early to bed. Miss Hawarden took a great fright in the night on hearing a noise she could not account for; she made such a fuss getting up, and walking about and screaming out most shrilly and valiantly—Who's there? enough to have scared a whole host of thieves or hobgoblins; and because there was no answer, she was more terrified than before. She walked to the window, and catching sight of a man going to the necessary (being moved thereto in the dead of the night), she begged of him to call the landlady; he promised, but forgot—unfeeling man! She then dressed herself, determining to sit up the remainder of the night, to protect Mrs. Moneypenny and me. I wished her fast asleep many a time, and begged, if she could not sleep herself, to suffer me to rest, for I feared neither robbers nor spirits. She became more quiet, but sat up a long time. It was only a dog lying outside the room door.

Sept. 1st. Rose early, and set off from St. Asaph with Miss Hawarden, to walk to Bagilt, leaving Mrs. Moneypenny to follow in the Car. Miss Hawarden and I breakfasted at the Druid, a little public house by the road-side, where we had a hearty breakfast, and a good deal of hearty laughing at the shriekart of the previous night. Walked forward with renewed spirit to Holywell; took another peep at the well, and then continued to Bagilt, so little fatigued with a 13 miles walk, that for my part, I could have proceeded to Flint and back on foot; however, we joined Mrs. Moneypenny at a Car to Flint, returning to Bagilt to dinner. At 4 o'clock, we set off in a Steam Packet for Liverpool, and arrived there at 8 that evening.

4 & 5th. Spent these days in visiting Miss Dalrymple, Mrs. Price, and in walking. Saw a pretty, small house, in Toxteth Park, I should like much to reside in if I had but furniture; the situation is so beautiful, and the rent 18£.

7th. Sabbath. Spent this mornᵍ at home in solitude; went to dinner at Miss Braithwaite's where I had slept the last night, they very kindly meeting me at the late hour of my arrival, to invite me lest my own bed should be damp. Sat all afternoon and evening with Miss B's; returned home to sleep, my bed having been well aired by a good fire for some hours.

12. Took a walk to Wigan; found my little niece, Margaret Stock, declining fast.

14. Went to Hope Chapel in the morning; carried buns in my pocket, for dinner, which I ate in the vestry at noon. Took tea at Dr. Hawarden's, and after attending evening service, walked home.

To MISS DALRYMPLE, Liverpool.

Holland. Sep. 19th. 1823.

According to my promise of writing to you soon, I begin the performance. On the morning that I left Liverpool, as it was very fine, I preferred walking a part of the way, to riding the whole of 20 miles or more in a cart, so footed it very agreeably all the way to Prescot, carrying my dinner in my basket until noon, and then eating it by the way, about 2 miles from Prescot. I was downright hungry, and ate a large part of a twopenny loaf. I would rather have a repast in such a way, than sit down to a stately, luxuriant dinner table. At Prescot, I called on Mrs. T. Jackson,[1] and I sat 3 hours with her; at 4 o'clock, the cart arrived, and I was jolted in it for the next 5 hours, over as rough a road as any in the county, at the rate of $2\frac{1}{2}$ miles an hour. We Holland people out-do you in Liverpool in travelling, for I seldom hear of your travelling at this rate, except to the Church yard, where few are in a hurry to go.

I have felt very unsettled since I returned here, for I have been such a rambler for the last 2 months, that I cannot all at once relish sitting still.

I made some inquiry at Prescot respecting lodgings, but Mrs. J. could not inform me of any at present. I dare not attempt to think of Liverpool; rents are so high for such small incomes as mine. The place Miss Eden so kindly mentioned, I set out to inquire about, but my heart failed me before I got there, for I was certain, accommodations such as I wish will be 20£ a year or upwards; and if I pay so much for rent, I must be abridged of many other comforts and enjoyments.

I have inclosed a Copy of the Deed of Separation between me and Mr. Stock.

The Deed alone should be the guide, or what was a Deed

[1] Mrs. T. Jackson was a younger Braithwaite (Margaret), having married Thos. Tellaw Jackson in the year 1808.

made for? The very idea that Mr. Stock *can* get it altered if he will, because he now finds it as he does not like, is shocking, and, I should think, ridiculous. *I* may then do the same, for there is not one Article in it that I would not alter, if I could. I was forced to sign it as it is, or starve; the alternative was dreadful, so that I did not voluntarily consent to it in its present form; yet, having signed it, I am obliged to abide by it; and so should Mr. Stock.

I find that Mr. Wallace is Mr. Gaskell's Counsel, as well as Mr. Taylor's, so that after giving his first opinion, he had probably been consulted by Mr. Gaskell, Mr. Stock's attorney, and thus has been applied to on both sides.

In consequence of many falsehoods which my Brother has uttered, and other unbrotherly kind of treatment, I found it necessary about 6 months ago, to write in my own vindication, and if possible, to put a stop to his doing me more mischief. I send a Copy—it is rather long, but I leave you at liberty to peruse it or not.[1]

      ✻   ✻   ✻

[JOURNAL]

21st. Set off from home about 10 o'clock, to walk to Parr Hall, to see my little darling Mary, whom I had not seen since May 23ᵈ. I told no one where I was going. Not being well acquainted with the road beyond Billinge,[2] I walked near a mile in tracing and retracing. About half past 12, I arrived there. When Mr. Grundy entered the room, he looked so grave and solemn, not the least smile embellished his features, that I thought it was a prognostication of a refusal to see my child. However, I brought a cheerful countenance, and kept it, which seemed to im-

---

[1] This letter occupies 23 closely written pages of the Copy Book. So that, in addition to the original sent to Tom, at least two other copies were produced!

[2] Billinge is situated 5 miles south-west of Wigan—see map in vol. i.

part some of its influence to Mr. Grundy, for, by degrees the cloud on his brow disappeared, and he brightened his eyes and relaxed his mouth, and became very chatty and agreeable. He touched upon no topic relating to me or my child; a mother's anxiety touched my heart, for I began to fear they were conveying Mary away somewhere, she was so long in coming. In about a quarter of an hour, my little sweet one came into the parlour, looking very pale and very thin. She looked glad to see me. In a short time, dinner came in to me on a single plate. Mary was called away to dine with her schoolfellows. This was unusual; she had always before dined with me, in the little parlour in which I now was, except twice when I had gone with her to the large dining-room. I suppose it was some order of Mr. Stock's, to degrade me in the eyes of my child. However, I ate my dinner, asking no reasons, nor making any observations. I had come to enjoy for a short time, the company of my child, and strove to the utmost to drive away the approaches of dejection on being treated in so unmerited a manner. Mary came to me as soon as she had dined, but was soon called away again, to prepare for a walk. Mr. Grundy evidently wanted me to depart—unfeeling being! Knowing that I had walked 7 or 8 miles, and had to walk as many more, I surely wanted resting time. I appeared not to observe his manner, or take his hints, for I determined to stay as long as I thought proper. Mary coming in again with her bonnet, I desired she might remain with me, as my stay could not be so long, and she was suffered to do so, Mr. Grundy scarcely leaving us for five minutes; in obedience, I dare say, to Mr. Stock's instructions. It is a matter of indifference to me whether we are alone or all the world is present. I neither mean to run away with the child, nor to say any thing to her that I fear to have known; the greatest openness, and the strictest integrity, have ever marked my conduct, and ever shall. At half past three, I took leave, Mr. Grundy and Mary accompanying me a little way. Heaven bless her! a time may come when this distressing mode of seeing her may be done away with. If not—Thy will, Oh my Father, be done. With thy help, I can resign myself cheerfully, for, in a few years, death will silence us all, and then what matters it?

On leaving Mr. Grundy and Mary, I went with alacrity and speed, and arrived at home about half past 5, very little fatigued. Thanks be to Him who gives me spirit and strength.

22ᵈ. Went with Mrs. Ball to dine with Mr. and Mrs. Stopford. Miss Bird was there, and Mrs. Mylchrist from Southport unexpectedly arrived. She told me Mr. Stock was going to purchase a house at Southport, intending to reside much there.

26. Sunday. Spent the day at Wigan as usual.[1] My little niece, Margaret Stock, died, after a long illness, and on Wednesday the

29. was interred.

November 3ᵈ, 4ᵗʰ, 5ᵗʰ, and 6ᵗʰ. Spent greater part of these days at Miss Braithwaites, as well as many previous ones not noticed here. Catharine was at Dalton, at her cousin Prescott's, Miss P. being in very low spirits, a malady unhappily inherent in the family. Elisabeth, a constant invalid, wishes for society, for which her youngest sister, Mary, is unfit, being very subject to fits. As I am much at liberty, I can go at almost any time, and be, as they kindly tell me, a consolation to them; and it is a very agreeable change to me, from the solitude of my lodgings, to society at once intelligent, enlightened, and, what is best of all, strictly conscientious.

7ᵗʰ. Walked to Wigan, to inform Mrs. Marsden that I would, for the Winter, cease spending the Sabbath at

---

[1] Miss Weeton's many bare references to attendance at Hope Chapel may be taken for granted.

Wigan, as the days are too short to go in the morning and return after afternoon service; and my bed being only slept in by myself, would, I feared, be damp.

9th. This day, about 4 o'clock in the afternoon, Mr. Stock's father died. He was an old man   [1] years of age, and had lain in a helpless state for 5 or 6 years, from rheumatism which he contracted by being a brewer's journeyman. His only unmarried daughter, Margaret, attended on him, and supported him to the last, he having little or no property of his own, and receiving little, very little, assistance from his other five children. His eldest son, my husband, was best able to support him, but he suffered him to want the comforts, and almost the necessaries of life.

11th. The passing bell for the old man's death was this day tolled here (at Up-Holland).

13th. My father in law was buried here this day, about one o'clock, in rather a pompous manner, his previous circumstances considered. I expected this would be the case, Mr. Stock thinking probably he could blind the world to his undutiful neglect by a hearse, 3 chaises, and a dinner for 40 people at the interment of his father. The cost of two thirds of this would have made the old man very comfortable during some months of his life, and have been better spent. It is rather singular that my husband's father, and my mother, are interred within one grave's breadth of each other,[2] without any previous intention of any party.

As Mr. Stock did not cause any one to inform me of his father's death, or send me any mourning, I have therefore thought it advisable not to wear any. I can feel the same respect for the old man, without any ostentatious shew, and I can ill bear the expence.

I was in hopes this event might soften his heart a little, and that something like humanity would touch it; but— he could not finish the funeral dinner before he began to

---

[1] A blank in the MS.   [2] Aunt Barton occupies the intervening grave.

pick a quarrel with his brother William at the table, before all the company, by insulting his wife! 'William,' he said, in an abrupt, peevish, and sleering manner, 'whether are you or your wife president?' Mr. Stock has made many attempts to prejudice Wm. against his wife, and on this occasion, she was not invited; but as many other female relatives were even more distantly related than she, Wm. was hurt that she should be neglected, and brought her with him, and seated her by him at the dinner table; for she has ever conducted herself in a most respectable manner. This public insult wounded Wm. deeply; he was so confused, he scarcely knew what he replied, but said, 'My wife is president, because I choose to make her so; and I shall always take my wife's part as long as I live.' Saying this, he rose, greatly agitated, from the table before he had quite finished dinner, and taking his wife, quitted the room. She burst into a flood of tears; Mrs. Perkins, too, one of Mr. S's sisters, could not restrain herself, but left the room to give vent to her grief, but soon after returned. Wm. and his wife came to me at my lodgings, and returned no more to the funeral party; their minds were so deeply hurt, that they were some time before they could become composed. I could not help but weep with them, having myself so acutely suffered from the same malignant spirit. Wm., with all a Christian's meekness, prayed for his brother; his wife, in the true spirit of charity, joined him; and so most sincerely and earnestly did I, that the Almighty would turn him from the evil of his ways, ere his days were ended.

*   *   *

To MISS STOCK, Parr Hall, near St. Helens.

Up-Holland, Nov. 21st. 1823.

How often I wish to see you and hear you talk; your childish prattle would be very entertaining to me. But it is a pleasure that is denied me, and I most probably must never have the comfort of your society so long as I live. May the Almighty supply to you a mother's loss!

Although I have not the society of my little darling, yet my spirits are wonderfully cheerful. I work, and read, and sing, and walk, and write all day long; and in the evenings, go and converse at Miss Braithwaites, or Miss Dannett's; and on Sundays I go to Wigan, to the Chapel there.

Indeed, I never was so happy in all my life as I have been since I came to Holland; every body is so kind to me. The poor people, as I pass them, bid me good-morrow, or good-night, so cordially; and the little children call after me, quite pleased if I call them by name, or smile— every one has a pleasant word for me or a cheerful look — — God blesses me, Mary.

I spend a great deal of time at Miss Braithwaite's. Miss Elisabeth Braithwaite, the second sister, has very ill health indeed; she has an asthmatic complaint, which confines her to the house for at least 8 months every year, and since Mrs. Braithwaite's death, she has been more alone than ever she was in her life before; for her oldest sister, Catharine, is so busy, looking after the farm and attending to housekeeping, that she has little time to sit with her, and Elisabeth wishes me to be with her a great deal—poor Elisabeth! I fear we shall lose her before another year is over; she declines, evidently, and is worse this Winter than any preceding one.

She is fond of rug work, and has done a great deal in a superior and beautiful manner, but she seems to be less able to amuse herself with it now, than she was wont to be. She has a memory wonderfully strong and correct, and can converse upon most subjects with great ability; her manners are very ladylike, yet she has a diffidence and humility that render her very amiable. Catharine, the

eldest, is kind-heartedness personified; her manner is not
elegant, but she is full of animation, wit, and drollery;
she makes herself a slave to the whole family. You will
suppose, my dear Mary, that they are very agreeable
companions to me; and as I have known them from
infancy, they are like sisters to me.[1] Thus you will perceive, my love, that I am very comfortable. I could fancy
that I often hear that heart-piercing, anxious little
question of yours, whenever I see you—'Mother, are you
comfortable?' Yes, my dear, I am indeed. I should be
more so with you; but if I must not live with you, I make
myself as contented as I can. God gives me so many bless-
ings, that I should be a very disobedient child of his, if I
were to grieve because I had not every thing I wished.

I should be very glad if I could receive a letter from
you, if it were ever so short.

✼   ✼   ✼

[JOURNAL]

Novbr. 23. Sabbath. This day, Matthew Stock's (my
brother-in-law) wife died at her mother's house; thus
there has been a death in the family every 2d Sabbath for
3 times successively.

Went to Church to-day, and sat for the first time in Mr.
Morris's pew, having engaged with him for a sitting during
the Winter months.

Dec. 1st. Went early in the afternoon to Miss Braithwaite's, to tea. Elisabeth has been declining, I think, for
some months, much more rapidly than usual. She has
suffered many years from an asthmatic complaint. 3 or 4
days a violent bilious attack has confined her to her room,
and she looks most wretchedly reduced and deathly. In
the evening, received a Bill, drawn out to my brother,[2] by

---

[1] Catharine and Elisabeth were, at this date, aged respectively 41 and 32.

[2] As to whether Mr. Battersby received payment, and by whom, there is
no subsequent indication.

Mr. Battersby, for Legal advice &c. in the year 1821. My brother sent it by Peter Latham.

2d Went down in the evening to see Miss E. Braithwaite, and found her but little better; she had never left her bed the whole day.

Dec. 3d Went early in the afternoon to Mrs. Heyes's, of Holland-Moor, to tea. It was then fair; whilst I staid, rain commenced and the wind rose, and on my return it was very rough; however, I got snugly home at 8 o'clock. The wind increased, and blew a perfect hurricane through the night. No damage was done at Holland worth mentioning.

This day, Mrs. Grundy died at Parr Hall.

✳   ✳   ✳

To MR. STOCK, Wigan. Up-Holland. Dec. 9th. 1823.
Sir,

The time draws near when our little daughter, Mary, will leave school for a while, to enjoy the recreations so necessary to her age, and the comforts of a home where those nearest and dearest to her should assemble with her at the same fireside. Let her have two homes, and deprive her no longer of the affectionate caresses of a mother —that parent which is ever most necessary to a daughter's welfare, and who alone can pay that minute attention to her moral and religious principles, and her daily and hourly conduct, which is absolutely necessary. Let her time at the approaching vacation be equally divided between us. Your business will frequently call you away, and she must then be left to the care of a servant, an evil that has been the ruin of numbers, has been the ruin of poor Jane, and will be the ruin of Mary if it be suffered. Yet it will be exceedingly hard upon Mary, if to avoid this evil, she must be kept perpetually at school, and thus have *no recreation, no change of scene.*

It is the duty of both of us to do considerable violence to our own inclinations and feelings when the welfare and comfort of our child is at stake; and this might be without any inconvenience to you.

I hear you are about to give up housekeeping in Wigan, and intend to reside principally at Southport. If this be true, you will then, I dare say, have no particular objection to my residing altogether in Wigan, if I wish to do so? I should be glad if you would consent to this—but then, where is Mary to be at the holidays? What respectable, well educated female will take charge of her at these times, and supply a mother's place? None but a mother can, or will, act a mother's part. To spend the holidays at school, will be a comfortless, unhappy way for the poor child, and be in danger of depressing her spirits to such a degree, as eventually to undermine her health—indeed, *she is suffering now* from the great confinement she endures, and has endured, from $4\frac{1}{2}$ years old; it must be a stronger constitution than hers that can bear it. Growing girls up to twice her present age, require much more air and exercise than it is possible they can have at a boarding school.

If you still refuse me the comfort of my child's company, and her the advantages of a mother's care, let me intreat that you will make it up to me by allowing me those comforts which you can well afford me, and of which I stand in need, by increasing my income and giving me a little furniture, that I may have a home of my own, and the attendance of a servant. Should I be attacked with a long sickness, as numbers around me are, what must become of me? My present income will neither allow me a nurse or doctor; but even in health, I should have the comfort of a home of my own and a servant's assistance. My wishes are so reasonable, that you surely cannot deny me; for if you comply with all I have asked, it would, I should think, add a pleasure to your own hear to reflect that you were doing a husband's duty, by treating your wife as yourself. There should not be a single enjoyment on your part that is not equally allowed to me; yet I do not ask a tenth part, much less an equal share.

I have heard that you have reported that I have many things of which you do not know how I obtained possession, that belonged to you. *I assert in the most solemn manner*, that it is not so. You saw me pack up *every thing*. I left many things behind me in the hurry of packing up, which belonged to me; but I by no means conveyed anything away unknown to you. The strictest integrity ever marked my conduct, but a melancholy reward I met with!

The fire which took place in my bed-room, Mr. Bird and Mrs. Alston told me you laid to my charge. From this horrid accusation, I could easily have cleared myself, had you but told me that I was suspected; why say it behind my back, and not say it to me? I could at the time have easily proved my innocence. *I was not in the house when the fire begun.* How it happened, I know not. I gave the alarm instantly on discovering it. I had been above an hour and a half absent from the house. I gave the alarm in less than one minute after I entered, and which I could then have proved; and John Johnson himself said it had not been on fire above a quarter of an hour, so that it certainly took place whilst I was out. Besides, why should I do it? Everything I possessed in the world was in that room; it was but little, but it was all to me, and had it been destroyed, no Insurance Office would have remunerated me; neither would you, nor any one else.[1]

[1] It will be remembered that John Johnson was one of Aaron Stock's sureties in the assault case. See p. 178. Perhaps Miss Weeton's history might have been a very different one had this fire destroyed her Letter Books; perhaps, indeed, the shock would have killed her, or tilted the balance definitely in favour of complete insanity.

My perfect innocence on this occasion prevented my having an idea that any one could suspect me; but knowing that you had been accused unjustly on one such occasion, my anxiety that night (unkind and cruel as you had been to me), was to clear you. What a contrast between your conduct and mine! For this reason, I got several people in after the fire was extinguished, to shew them that all that belonged to the house, was still there. I unlocked every drawer, cupboard, and box of which I had any key, and shewed them the contents. I shewed them your bookcases, on which I knew you set so much value—and all *to vindicate you.*

Consider this, and let your heart soften towards me, and be a little more liberal. Let me have free access to my child, that I may do a mother's duty to her, and which she really stands in need of.

✻   ✻   ✻

[JOURNAL]

Dec. 9. From this period, I have been so greatly occupied in attending the wants of my dying Elisabeth, that I have neither had time nor inclination to write here until now (21st.). Poor Elisabeth! how she has suffered, and how gratefully she ever acknowledged the attentions she received. When shall I see her like again?

Her sister Catharine's assiduity in attending the dying beds of her Father; then her eldest sister Ann; a few years afterwards, her mother (24th. May last); and now, her dearest, and most loved sister Elisabeth, is beyond all praise. May she have her deserts!

Catharine and Elisabeth were nearest of an age, which naturally caused them to be more together. Their dispositions differed materially, but their excellencies were equal. They grew from infancy sweetly united together, like two roses on one stalk. Although Elisabeth was the younger, her judgment was more cool, and corrected Catharine's warm-hearted impetuosity. Elisabeth possessed a superior talent in delineating flowers on canvas; Catharine was content to assist the progress of her work, by filling up the subordinate and more laborious parts. Elisabeth from her youth was sickly; an asthmatic complaint prevented her taking much exercise; Catharine was ever ready to supply her every want. What one planned, the other could execute. In laying out their flower garden, or in any other amusement, their tastes were very similar. Catharine, with peculiar activity, would finish almost by the time Elisabeth suggested. Catharine's drollery, wit, and humour, enlivened Elisabeth's unavoidable retirement. Elisabeth's fine taste and peculiar delicacy of manner, were the delight of Catharine's heart. Together, they budded, bloomed, and expanded—but now!—one sweet rose has faded—withered—dropped—and how sad the other looks without its wonted companion. I fear it will wither soon. Poor Elisabeth! when I forget thee, my memory must have entirely lost its faculty. Elisabeth had the greatest rectitude of principle; her manners were very lady-like; delicacy of sentiment, with decision of judgment, were finely contrasted. Her memory was most extraordinary. In History, she would frequently allude to minute circumstances with a wonderful precision, as well as to events of greater importance. In Genealogy, she was quite a Court Calendar; she amused herself much with reading, and long remembered whatever she read; and when she alluded to anything in the course of conversation, which she had read at any time, she did it so unostentatiously and with so much simplicity, that it slipped by, as it were, at the time; after-recollection would bring it again in full force of surprise at a memory so unusual. In Geography, too, she was very clever, and in many other things which I cannot just now commemorate.

She excelled in whatever she attempted. When but a girl, and in better health, her superior cookery and domestic management were her mother's boast.

Poor Elisabeth! when shall I see thy like again.

For some years she had been confined to the house; for 7 or 8 months each year; but seldom missed joining the family at any period, before dinner, in the usual sitting-room. Reading and rug-work were her principal amusements. She did a great deal of sewing for her mother and sisters; she was their dress-maker and their milliner, and very clever at both. She was fond of the society of a few, but could never bear many; the one, she did not like to be without—the other, distressed her; and gratified am I to think that I was so frequently one of those few (not that I am vain enough to suppose I should have been so often selected, had the circle of Elisabeth's neighbours been more numerous; in a village like this, there are few to choose out of, who have liberty at any time to leave home; and I, alas! a wife and a mother, yet without a husband or a child, have that liberty—and then, she pitied me; and pity induced her mother, her sisters, and herself, to invite me often).

Since her mother's death, I had observed her decline very rapidly; yet, if any feeling of affliction on that account had injured her health, she concealed it. Still her rug-work and her books had charms to amuse—until lately; for, ill and spiritless indeed she was, when these failed. At last, she could no longer—she could no more—and about 3 weeks ago, she kept her room; in two or three days more, she took to her bed, from whence death only could remove her. Until within a day or two of her death, she suffered much; the fangs of death seemed most remorselessly to assail her in every part; she breathed with great difficulty, she burned with fever; pains in her head, her shoulders, her limbs, her bowels; and worst of all, the use of her legs were taken, yet excruciating pains remained; almost choked with phlegm—where had she ease?

Yet, under all these accumulated sufferings, she was so grateful to the Almighty for the many comforts she enjoyed! How delightful it was to hear her speak her gratitude, and thankfulness. She had a sweet spirit! She had no want, she said, but it was supplied; food, medicine, attendance, lofty and airy apartments; the best of sisters, and many kind friends.

On Thursday, Dec. 18th., she was seized with a kind of stupor; death had finished his work, and left her to expire in peace, after a few hours of something like ease. It was about half past 12 at noon, when she seemed more inclined to sleep than usual; about 4 o'clock, she roused a little, and conversed with intellects as clear as ever. Mrs. Gaskell, a favourite friend,[1] had come to see her that afternoon; about 7 o'clock, Mrs. Jackson and Miss Mary arrived (her two other sisters from Prescot), and although still sadly overcome with a deathlike drowsiness, she exerted herself to talk to them with great chearfulness all night, until 2 o'clock on Friday morning, when they retired. Catharine soon after adjusted her pillows, and then laid down on a bed, close by; poor Catharine was heavy with her previous watchfulness for many nights, and great bodily fatigue, and fell asleep; at half past 5 o'clock, she started up, finding she had lain too long; she wondered at Elisabeth's stillness, put her curtain aside, and found her—dead!

Just in the attitude of sleep in which she had 3 hours before left her, with her head resting on her hand, she found her, as if she had never moved—so peaceably she departed,

---

[1] This, of course, could not be the creator of Cranford and Miss Matty: somehow, one reads this dignified account of Miss Elisabeth's last hours with that emotion which never fails as one parts with the elder daughter of Captain Brown.

Friday, Dec. 19th. 1823, at the age of 32 years and 7 months.

Dec. 24th. Went down to the Abbey to see Catharine and Mary, and was shewn by Miss E. Leatham into the chamber of death, to take a last look at those features once so blooming and animated, but now pale, still, and lifeless. Death! thou art awful—but thou and I have long been acquainted; seldom an hour passes that I forget thee, or a day which brings not reflections of thy power. When the night comes, I resign my spirit to the Father whom I love most dearly, not certain that these mortal eyes may ever again see the light; and in the morning, I rise as one who has but another day lent to them; so loosely, as it were, does the garment of life hang upon me.

25. Christmas-day. On this, my Birthday anniversary, I have completed my 47th. year, and have enjoyed more earthly comfort for the last 12 months than I ever remember to have done for the same length of time.

Dec. 26. The interment of Miss E. Braithwaite took place this day, at 12 o'clock. My anxiety to hear something of my child, induced me to set off to Wigan. I called at various places, but could hear little—only that she was fetched from school on Monday, the 15th., in a gig.

27th. Saturday. Heard that Mary was seen the day previously, in the street, with her father.

(I have forgotten to say in the right place, that on my birth-day, I finished a Will, on which I had for some time before been employed, having a right to make one, by a clause in the Deed of Separation between me and Mr. Stock. Mr. James Ball, and his nephew, Henry Ball, witnessed it.)

29. Packed up a few toys for my little Mary, and wrote a note to Mrs. Alston, requesting her to give them to her; and to intreat Mr. Stock to let me see my child during this vacation.

30. As the Year is so near a close, I have this day made up all my money accounts, and find myself somewhat richer than I was a year ago; then, having only received from Mr. Stock, 3 quarter's annuity within the year— £52. 10s.—and my expenditure £64. 7s., I was £11. 17s involved. This year, having received the full income of £70, and my expenditure £64. 18. 7d., I have recovered a little—£5. 1. 5d.—which repays part of the last year's debt, and leaves yet behind £6. 15. 7d.

Drank tea with Miss Dannet in the evening, and passed it very agreeably with her and her intelligent, unassuming friend, Mr. J. Holcroft.

1824. January.

6th. Having heard nothing respecting my child, walked over to Wigan this morning, and heard that Mr. Stock was still inflexible, and was exceedingly angry with Mrs. Alston for sending the toys to Mary at his house; at which, she is so offended, that she considers me as extremely ill used.

12th. Went to Miss Dannett's to tea: the heat of the room was such, that on coming away and plunging into the cold night air, I received a violent cold, and was for several days in a burning fever; and at the same time an inflammation in my mouth, and gathered gums. By Saturday following, I was recovered.

22d. Took tea with Mrs. Ball, and met Mrs. Morris and Mrs. Walker. Mrs. Morris is a woman of peculiarly amiable disposition, and fascinating simplicity of manner, combined with good sense. How unfortunately she has married; the only child of her parents, and having a handsome fortune, it is all squandered away most unaccountably by a hog of a husband, and she now toils amidst a numerous flock of fine-looking boys and girls, like a galley slave. Mrs. Walker, a shop-keeper in Holland, is a woman of such strange manners, that I should never be surprised to hear she was become deranged. She is greatly to be pitied. The anxiety of business, and a family of 5 or 6 children to support, will be too much for her. I admired most of her sentiments, they appeared so correct; but the nervous, twitching manner she had, almost forced a smile even from pity's self.

February 2d. I have long contemplated writing a History of my life, and yet have deferred it from month to month, from what must appear a very strange reason by any one who sees the quantity of my writings—the reluctance I feel to attempt writing. Whether it proceeds from indolence, or some other undefinable motive, I cannot say; but whether I have a letter to write, a journal, or an account, it seems a task to me; and yet the activity of my mind perpetually urges me to it. It is a strange contradiction! but are we not all strange contradictory beings.

This day I arranged my books and writing materials on my table, determining to begin, when such a depression of spirits seized me at the melancholy retrospect, that I could not commence. I wept, I trembled, and my soul utterly refused comfort; like Rachel, I wept for my child. I tried to pray, to sing a hymn, but could do neither. I passed the whole of the day in melancholy inaction; the next day the same. I attempted to sew, I put it away again; I took my flageolet, but it pleased me not, my mind was not in tune; and, living by myself, I had not a human being to speak to. If I had, it would often make me more chearful, and would help greatly to restore my composure when my spirit is cast down.

4th. (*Wednesday*). This morning I was enabled to overcome my unwillingness to commence my history, and made a beginning, since when, I have proceeded by little and little; but if I get on no quicker hereafter, I shall be a long time finishing it. It is for my daughter's sake I am desirous to do it, and on her account I feel it absolutely necessary.[1]

12th. I think of my Mary from day to day, and mean immediately to make another attempt to see her, let Mr. Grundy treat me as he may. I think he means well upon the whole, but Mr. Stock has taken so much pains to prejudice his mind against me, that he is influenced to obey Mr. S's tyrannical directions much more decidedly than he ought to be if he were really a Christian; which I hope he is, almost.

18. (Wednesday). Left home a quarter before 10 o'clock this morning, to go to Parr Hall. I walked by the way of Winstanley, the Bear in the Ring, Senela Green [where a few years later her husband was to reside], & Black brook. I had just sat down in the parlour, when Mr. Grundy came in, looking exceedingly solemn. Whether he really grieves for the loss of his wife, or no, I cannot say. I am not inclined to give him credit for it. I fancy the jewel of joy is within, enclosed in a case of *black shagreen.* We had a good deal of conversation respecting my seeing Mary. Mr. Grundy informed me that he was awkwardly situated in regard to her, but he would endeavour to procure some precise instructions, and for the present, Mary should be immediately introduced to me. She came, little darling, as soon as she was summoned, and embraced me most affectionately. She is extremely tall for her age, and very thin and pale, but says she is well. I staid with her till a quarter past 3, and then left, perhaps never to see her more; for her father, in his mad passions, declares if I do not cease attempting to see her, he will place her where

---

[1] Miss Weeton used the blank pages left in the book devoted to the abortive OCCASIONAL REFLECTIONS of the year 1818. But the projected History of her life shared the same fate, terminating abruptly. However, it provides material not provided by THE RETROSPECT (written in the year 1809), and the two have been fused into the composite Retrospect which precedes vol. i of this publication.

no one but himself shall ever know. Poor Mary, what is to become of her?

I got home at ½ past 5, very little fatigued.

As I told Mr. Grundy that if I had not much more liberty of seeing my child, I should certainly return to Mr. Stock and run whatever risk I may of having my life sacrificed by his brutality, and requested him to inform Mr. Stock of my determination, perhaps ere another year has elapsed, I may have breathed my last. Oh, my Father! look with pity on thy oppressed servant; extend thy protecting arm over me, and put into my heart what Thou wouldest have me do. If I go to my husband, go with me; if I should not go, put such obstacles in the way as shall entirely prevent my attempting it; be with me at all times, for if Thou forsakest me, I am lost. Oh, be with me, and protect me.

22nd. Passed the Sabbath at home, and in going twice to Church. From this time, I intend going again to Wigan on Sabbath day; the weather and length of the days will now permit me to go in time for morning service, and return home after afternoon service. Sometimes, in an evening, I read a sermon.

26th. Took a walk to Wigan after dinner, and accidentally met with my nephew, William Stock, in Moyle's, the tea-dealer's, shop. Some months ago I had had some conversation with him about purchasing an organ; the subject was again resumed, and he now walked down with me to Atherton's, in Queen Street, who is an organ-builder. I was pleased with what I saw and heard there, and am strongly tempted to order one; but although he says he can make a good one for 15 to 20£, yet it is a serious sum to me, and I must deliberate a little.

29. Sabbath day, and the 5th. in this month, February. Went to Hope Chapel; met Mr. Stock in Hope Street. It is the first time I have passed him since we were separated.

We both passed without seeming to notice each other. He was coming from Standish, near which he last Wednesday went to reside, at the house that Mr. Ainslie, Mr. Standish's steward, lately lived in.[1] Mr. Stock, I am in-informed, gave 100£ for fixtures, has ordered 20 new chairs at 2 guineas each, a set of dining tables, an elegant new bed, and a new gig!!! and is to give 80£ a year for the house and ground.

Practically the whole of the month of March Miss Weeton spent with a friend at Southport, but the visit proved uneventful, and she has little to say about it.

April 10th (Saturday). Set out this morning at ¼ past 1 o'clock in Wm. Hindley's cart from Tower Hill to Liverpool. About 3 o'clock the wind rose and continued for some hours to blow furiously; at 5 it was a perfect hurricane, the horse was often in danger of being blown off the road, showers of snow and hail were very frequent. We were four passengers in the cart (a covered one), and notwithstanding the storm and the loneliness of the hour and the road, I was very warm, comfortable, and contented. The storm abated before 6, and at 7 we arrived at Liverpool.[2] I went to Mrs. Roxburgh's in Russell St, to breakfast, having brought the materials with me in my basket. The principal object of this journey was to ascertain the expences of a journey to London, and to obtain the necessary Maps and Tours, that I might become acquainted with the country I had for some time contemplated passing through. I dined at Mr. Price's, and afterwards called upon Miss Dalrymple, and at 5 o'clock, again entered Hindley's covered cart, and arrived at home between twelve and one at midnight, very little fatigued.

14th. Walked to Wigan to make further inquiries

---

[1] *STANDISH*: Stock, Aaron: Mfr. Prospect Hill. Baines's *Lancs. Directory,* 1825.

[2] A journey now accomplished in half an hour by rail.

respecting the London roads and coaches from Manchester, as Mrs. Stopford wishes her daughter and Master Barlow to go that way, and to go with me under my protection.

30. Friday. Having waited for 2 or 3 days for fair weather, that I might walk over to Parr Hall to see my little daughter once more before I went to London, I set out this day at 10 o'clock. The morning was fair and bright, but the wind blew quite a hard gale, and I had great difficulty in forcing my way through it, for it blew right in my face. I had for some weeks been rather weak and indisposed, and, on setting out to-day, almost despaired of accomplishing so long a journey on foot; but a mother's heart can do great things. The farther I proceeded, the more light and active I felt, and I arrived at Parr Hall at half-past 12. Miss Hammond, the teacher who was engaged on Mrs. Grundy's death, opened the door, and as I followed her through the writing room, my little Mary, who was there, advanced to me immediately, and we retired together to the little back-parlour where I always sit when at Parr Hall. Feeling apprehensive that Mr. Stock may remove my child some time when he thinks I am quite unprepared for such a blow, and she may be placed where I could not discover her, I had prepared a card with a direction for Miss Dannett of Up-Holland, and gave it to her now, telling her, that if ever she were removed to any other school, she must take an opportunity, in private, of writing to inform me where she was, and with whom, and to direct for Miss Dannett (for if my name was on the direction, it might be intercepted at the Post Office); and be very careful with whom she intrusted it, to put it there.

The child is so young that I fear she will hardly be able to manage such a business, should there be occasion. This is the beginning of my instruction to her to do any thing in secret; but after much hesitation and mature deliberation, I have come to the decision that if I had taken no such precaution, I should have been sadly wanting in duty as a mother. That it should be necessary, must lie at Mr. Stock's door; and on his head be the guilt. If he would act as a husband and a father ought to do, there would be no occasion to keep anything secret from him; it would be a crime to attempt it. I told Mary to put the card at the bottom of her box, and shew it no one; and if any one should see it, I think they would not know what it meant. I staid with her until 4 o'clock, and then returned home, less fatigued with a 12 or 14 miles walk than might have been expected.

May 4. Took tea with Miss Braithwaite; was seized whilst there with violent vomiting, and was very ill all the evening.

∗   ∗   ∗

To MISS STOCK, Parr Hall, near St. Helens.

Up-Holland. May 6 1824.

When I left you, my dear Mary, last Friday, I forgot to turn up the road through the wood, which Mr. Grundy once shewed me when he and you took me a part of the way, but walked down the road for almost a quarter of a mile, and found a way through some fields, near a good brick house on the left. Perhaps this way was as near, and I was in no danger of losing my way whilst I had Billinge beacon in view; for I had to pass near it, and through the village of Billinge, which appears to me to be about half-way between Holland and Parr Hall.

I met with few people on the way, and those passed me quietly and civilly; indeed, my dear love, wherever I go, no harm happens to me, nobody injures me, or puts me in fear.[1] You asked me if I was not afraid of robbers. No,

---

[1] Only a bold (or shameless) woman would have dared a lonely footpath walk at this time. London editors were in the habit of warning women and

my dear, because I never was robbed—by strangers. It seems to me as if, because I had no earthly protector, that God was with me wherever I went, and took care of me himself.

I had a pleasant walk, although rather tired. I took shelter from a shower of rain at Mr. Gaskell's, of Ox-House, where they very hospitably gave me some refreshment, and I then went home quite rejoiced that I had had the pleasure of seeing you that day; indeed, Mr. and Mrs. Gaskell both said they were very glad that I had been to see you.

I am afraid I shall not see you again for a long time; but you will feel some pleasure, I am sure, when you reflect that I am passing my time as agreeably as I can, and that all the addition I could wish for, would be the society of my dear Mary to chatter to.

I expect to set off for London on Wednesday next, May 12th. I shall meet the Liverpool coach at Prescot, along with Miss Stopford and Master Barlow (a youth from the neighbourhood of London, who is an apprentice to Mr. Stopford). Miss Stopford is going on a visit to Master B's friends, and I anticipate a very agreeable journey with them. As the journey is a long one, and I never travelled so far before, I feel somewhat anxious for you, my love; but if I should die, and you never see me more, may the God who has supported and protected me, take equal care of you, and—you will never be forsaken.

I hope your throat is better, and that you are now quite well again. When you are at liberty, go out into the garden as often as the weather permits; and always be out of doors when you can, that you may grow stronger, for you look very pale and delicate, and there is nothing better for your health than being much out in the open air. I

girls, at the approach of spring, that the season had arrived when it was unwise to venture unaccompanied into the fields around the metropolis.

believe I should be stronger if I were to go more out of doors, and I intend to be very little in-doors until winter returns.

I must remind you of the approach of your birthday. You will be 9 years old on the 9th. of June, which is about 5 weeks hence. You may be assured that I shall think of you when the day comes, and wish you every kind and good wish; but I suppose I shall be far distant at the time.

I have written to you now, because it may perhaps be several months before I could conveniently write again.

         *   *   *

[JOURNAL]

From the 4th. to the 12th. of May, nothing occurred but the usual routine of rising, eating, and going to sleep again. I made little other preparation for my journey to London than procuring my cloaths to be all washed, and taking care not to leave a single halfpenny owing. If I can but give in as clear an account at the day of judgment, as I keep with my fellow-creatures from day to day, with what confidence I shall appear before Thee, O my Father. But the debts Thy children owe Thee must be cancelled; they never can be paid.

I am now near 48 years of age, and since I left my husband, have increased in bodily health and strength, so much as to be better than I ever recollect being, for so long a time, at any period of my life; and have an apparent prospect of a constitution to last me perhaps 15 years longer—yet, ere another sun sets, these eyes may have been closed for ever; ere another day dawns, these limbs may have become stiff and cold; but Oh, if I am but with Thee, Thou Great and Mighty Un-nameable, what need I care.

In this state of mind, I set off for London; considering

it to be very probable I should never reach it; when such numbers are killed by the overturning of stage coaches,[1] what right have I to expect to escape? I prepared no finery, for I did not mean to wear it. The cloaths I had, were good enough to wear where I was wholly unknown.[2]

---

[1] 'Travelling was in a troubled state, and the minds of coachmen were unsettled. Let them look around and contemplate the scenes which were enacting around them. Stage coaches were upsetting in all directions, horses were bolting, boats were overturning, and boilers were bursting.' *Pickwick Papers*.

[2] Miss Weeton would never have fitted in at Cranford; but she anticipates here at least one Cranfordian sentiment: 'What does it signify how we dress here at Cranford, where everybody knows us?' And if they go from home, their reason is equally cogent, 'What does it signify how we dress here, where nobody knows us?'

LONDON

MAY 13TH–JULY 30TH, 1824

LONDON

MAY 13TH–JULY 30TH, 1824

*M*ISS WEETON *appears to have approached the proposed London trip in her usual methodical way, providing herself with maps and a guide-book. The particular guide she used was the authoritative* PICTURE OF LONDON, *albeit she had the misfortune to derive her initial information from an edition twenty years old; however, upon arrival, she remedied this error, and brought herself up-to-date with a current edition. By a perusal of this fat little volume, one can enter somewhat into her state of mind upon the subject, and share her pleasurable anticipations, from the farewell toot of the Guard's horn, as the coach, destined to deposit her at Islington, whisked away on its final stage.*

Ignoring the long preliminary history of London, and commencing forthwith upon the GENERAL DESCRIPTION (*from a study of which many contemporaries must have based their dreams of a gold-paved London*), *we learn that—*

'*The principal streets are wide and airy, and surpass all others in Europe in their convenience for trade, and the accommodation of passengers of all description; they are paved in the middle for carriages with large stones in a very compact manner, forming a small convexity to pass the water off by channels; and on each side is a broad level path, formed of flag stones, raised a little above the centre, for the convenience of foot-passengers. Most of the great streets, appropriated to shops for retail trade, have an unrivalled aspect of wealth and splendour; and perhaps, there is no town in which an inhabitant, who possesses the universal medium of exchange, can be so freely supplied as here, with the produce of nature or art from every quarter of the globe.*'

Miss Weeton was to find that her slender stock of the 'universal medium of exchange' was to be sadly frittered away upon the catchpenny 'produce of nature or art from every quarter of the globe'.

Much has been written about the perils of Georgian London's streets by night, but we are disabused, on the authority of Messrs. Longman, Hurst, Rees, Orme & Brown, the publishers, who assert on the contrary, that they are—

> *'most of them spacious, in excellent repair, and so well lighted by lamps, to a considerable distance, that foreigners arriving by night have imagined there was a universal illumination'— though, on the other hand, it is admitted that 'the entering streets are many of them mean, and calculated to inspire foreigners with very erroneous ideas concerning the real magnificence of this metropolis'.*

Passing over 1. The Lord Mayor; 2. The Sheriffs; 3. The Aldermen; 4. The Common Council, and all the Corporation; we arrive at the results of their combined efforts on behalf of the comfort and welfare of the fixed and floating population.

First, the provision against thieves, fire, &c.:

> *'It is calculated that 2,044 beadles, watchmen, and patrols, are nightly on duty in and around the Metropolis.' ['It has been estimated that London contains about 8,000 streets, lanes, alleys, and courts; 60 squares, and 160,000 houses, warehouses, and other buildings'—quoted from another section of the* PICTURE.] *'The City contains 25 wards, in which there are 765 watchmen, and 38 patrols. Watch-houses are placed at convenient distances in all parts, where a parochial constable attends in rotation, to see that order prevails, to receive offenders, and deliver them next morning to the sitting Magistrate.'*

The PICTURE *has an unfortunate knack of deflating its own bombast, however, and there follows a more particular description of London's 'watch and ward', hardly calculated to inspire Miss Weeton with confidence.*

> *'A few old men, called* watchmen, *mostly without arms, are the only guard through the night against depredations; and a few magistrates and police officers are the only persons whose employment it is to detect and punish depredators.'*

'*Ubique*', no doubt, was the watchword of the '*few old men,
called* watchmen' (*or more popularly* '*Charlies*', *by the nightly
prowling bucks of the Regency, whose especial sport they were*).

'*If a person is in any way attacked or assaulted by thieves or
o†hers, whilst walking the streets by night, he should instantly
call the watch. A cry of 'watch' three or four times repeated,
will instantly bring up the assistance of several of the watchmen,
and it is ten to one if the thief or assailant makes his escape.*'

In addition:

'*No city, in proportion to its population, is more free from
danger to those who pass the streets at all hours, or from depredation, open or concealed, on property. This is an actual
phenomenon in this metropolis; and is not to be explained on
systems of police, but belongs to that happy union of moral
causes, the chief of which* [*being*] *the ancient freedom of all ranks
in England, which have planted deep in the minds of the poorest
a love of social order, and a willingness to earn a subsistence by
industry.*'

Of course, the chances were '*ten to one*' *against any contact
being made with other than persons influenced by a* '*happy union
of moral causes*'*; but strangely enough, should you be under the
necessity of asking your way,* '*always apply at a shop or public-
house, and never rely upon the information which may be given by
persons in the streets.*' (*Thereupon follows a sufficiently alarming
catalogue of the various dodges resorted to by the incorrigibles of
the streets, whose ring-dropping, pick-pocketing activities must
have made the cry of* ' "Watch" *three or four times repeated*' *as
familiar to the ears as the Guard's noisy horn on the coach routes.*)
*Miss Weeton would doubtless be interested in the precautions
taken to preserve the health of a swarming population of over
1,000,000 (not counting visitors). An analysis of the returns of*
Diseases and Mortality *in those days was not half so depressing
as is the case of a corresponding one of to-day; exceedingly*

comforting must the return for 1816, the year given in the PICTURE *under review, have proved to Miss Weeton.*

Abscesses took off 106. Apoplexy would remind her of her husband, of which class of sufferer, 434 disappeared from the scene. Bile, no doubt modified by a course of Thames water and the astringent properties of well-water in close proximity to the numerous cess-pools, crept in with just 1. 'Bursten and Rupture' account for 35; and Cancer was gaining ground with 79. Chicken-pox, with 1 to its credit, contrasts with Small-pox at 653 (the year 1824 probably saw a significant increase upon this number; Miss Weeton alternating long walks in crowded thoroughfares, with attendance upon the small-pox consumed daughter of her landlady). Colds were a joke—19 only; Consumption, rather more alarming, with 4,272; and Convulsions, mostly no doubt infantile, took off 3,264. Cramp writhed away with 2, whilst 'Evil' (whether of the variety yclept King's, or merely personal, is not stated), reduced the population by 8. Gout had lost its eighteenth-century potency, merely accounting for 56, as against 408 who died either of Grief, Horse Shoe Head, or Water in the Chest. Two were Jaw-locked, and a solitary 1 succumbed to Lethargy. 'Purples', of course rare, secured 2, whilst 'Rising of the Lights' was limited to 1. Finally, Miss Weeton, abstemious as ever, could commiserate, whilst not apprehensive of a like fate, with the 26 who died of 'Stoppage in the Stomach'.

With regard to Casualties in a city not without traffic problems, no one was 'Fractured' or 'Frightened to Death', though 105 were Drowned. Fifty killed themselves, including 1 killed by 'Swallowing a Shilling'. Two were overlaid, 5 Scalded, and 3 Suffocated. A light list; and altogether a distinct improvement upon Wigan, where there were coal-mines, and factories, and child-labour galore.

The vagaries of the weather had been duly noted and reduced to an exact computation:

'There are about 209 days in the year without rain, and 156 in which it rains or snows; about 12 is the average of days in

which it snows or sleets; the number of cloudy days when the
sun scarcely ever appears, is about 50 or 60 out of the 209.'

(*Here is a strange silence upon the subject of 'London particulars',
but surely the longest fog on record, the '5 days continuous' of the
year 1814, might have earned mention, if only under the Historical
section.*)

'*The wind in London, blows from the south west half the
year, and from the opposite quarter, or north east, another five
months.*'

(*What happens during the odd month is not stated.*)

The drains are '*agitated twice in four and twenty hours by
tide*'; and '*immense quantities of water, conveyed into the houses,
even of the meanest, for domestic purposes, afford the means of
cleanliness, one of the surest companions of health*'.

That being so, '*the excellent condition of the bulk of the inhabitants*' would strike the most casual observer, and was to be
traced to '*the great quantity of animal food consumed*'. The more
exact—and vegetarian—Miss Weeton, would doubtless partly
ascribe this desirable condition to the close proximity to the metropolis
of 10,000 acres of ground, wholly devoted to the culture of
vegetables; and about 3,000 acres similarly devoted to the supply
of fruit for London consumption.
Should illness or accident overtake the visitor—

'*the medical assistance is the best the profession can supply; the
attendance is ample, and the persons employed as humane as its
nature admits,*'—

a qualifying afterthought, accompanying a decent reticence truly
admirable, upon a subject sufficiently full of horror and loathsome circumstance; as Miss Weeton would have quickly discovered
for herself had she made accidental acquaintance with some of
London's hospital wards.

However, indubitably with a light heart and a buoyant step, Miss
Weeton mounted to the top of the coach—to the cheaper seats; and,

delightfully agitated in mind and body, turned her straight back upon the unfeeling, unlovely (by contrast) north.

✴ ✴ ✴

To MISS DANNETT, Up-Holland.

London: May 22, 1824.

On leaving Holland, May 12th., Miss Braithwaite very kindly accompanied me a long way over the fields, and when we parted, I proceeded very comfortably, and arrived in Prescot at about 20 minutes past 4 o'clock. The following morning, we went to Mrs. Jackson's garden, and made several calls. After dinner, Mrs. T. Jackson, Miss R., and 2 or 3 more accompanied me to the coach, on which I set off exactly at 2 o'clock, outside all the way to London.[1] Miss Stopford and Master Barlow were snugly fixed with 2 middle-aged ladies, who travelled the whole way. At Rainhill, as the ostlers were fixing fresh horses, one of these got dreadfully frightened, and fell twice in the shafts; the 2d time, they had some difficulty to raise it, and then it backed and twisted so among the other horses, that although there were plenty of men, they had some difficulty to manage it. I expected an overturn. At last, we set safely off, at as great a speed as the coachman could drive; the poor horse got well whipped the whole of the stage. The inside passengers knew nothing of their danger until it was nearly over; outside, we were never more than half full, which was very agreeable to me.

At Warrington, I found my luggage at the Inn where the coach stops, quite ready at the instant. The air was so piercingly cold, that I immediately availed myself of some of my wrappings, and my wool-lined beaver gloves were a treasure to me. The air was so cold, and the sky so nearly without sunshine, as entirely to divest the surrounding

---

[1] The coach fare had been advanced by a Mr. Winstanley.

country of any picturesque beauty; and the whole road beyond Warrington seemed a continued flat, few passers-by to enliven the way; and not a gentleman's carriage, scarce a chaise, only three or four gigs, and as many horse-men, until within 40 or 50 miles of London. We passed through Litchfield at midnight, only stopping ten minutes. We had previously had our tea at 9 o'clock, but I was then so long detained with Miss Stopford upstairs, that I did not get half enough. At Litchfield, therefore, I was so starved with hunger as well as cold, that a 10 minutes warming was most gratifying at a roasting kitchen fire.

Mrs. Jackson had furnished me with a small bottle of brandy, and I here applied the hot kettle to some of it. I had not ventured to touch any before, for fear of being sleepy. I now found the cold air had power enough to keep me staring wide awake. I gave Miss Stopford some, and then set off again, famished but refreshed. Mrs. Jackson had given me some potted shrimps, and a good lump of cold tongue; but these, hungry as I was, I could not eat. Some bread which I had provided, vanished long before, and if I had but had some more, some biscuits, or some of Peggy Hodson's[1] buns, I could have feasted; for I am a graminovorous animal and not a carnivorous one, and in this, you and I perfectly agree. As I had no food on my stomach to warm me, I applied to my bottle *many was the time and oft*, although I was cautious to take no more at once than a table spoonful and a half, one third brandy! By this means, I got on through the night very well. My head and face were covered with a thick cotton handkerchief, tied under my bonnet.

A lunar rainbow was observable near 2 hours, but very faint, which showed there was heavy rain southward. We had none. This was the first lunar bow I ever saw. At 6 o'clock, we stopped at Lutterworth, to breakfast, to my

[1] A noted baker at Holland. [*Original footnote.*]

great comfort. I took care this time to accommodate nobody, but let everyone look after themselves; for I have not found, in this business, that spirit of accommodation from others which I had a right to expect, but a very great deal of selfishness. I took a hearty breakfast of coffee, and mounted the coach much the better for it.

This day was colder than the preceding one, and more cheerless as we came along the greater part of the day. The country might have been depopulated, we saw so few living beings; I think I did not see above $\frac{1}{2}$ a dozen in Buckinghamshire. We stopped to lunch at Northampton. Miss Stopford and Mr. J. Barlow would have nothing, and when I saw the table covered with cold meat, ham, etc., and not a potatoe or a tart, I set off to buy a loaf; but before I could find a bread shop, the coach was going, and I was obliged to go away empty, and without knowing how blessed are the hungry—when they are filled. In a very ill humour, I rode on; for, although keeping it to myself and troubling no one with my vexation, I inwardly grumbled bitterly at my own easiness of temper, which constantly makes me a sufferer to other people's humours; and, what is worse, I receive no thanks for it. Had I pleased myself, I would certainly not have travelled in such weather.

When within 40 miles of London, it began to rain, and continued the remainder of the way. It was now *quite delightful!* My frequent application to the bottle, whilst it prevented cold, at the same time added to my drowsiness. I had no difficulty to keep awake in the night, but now I was in continual danger of literally *falling* asleep. I have great reason to thank Mrs. Jackson for the brandy, for I believe it preserved me from taking cold. As greatly as I have puffed about my *frequent application* to the *bottle*, I have at least half of it left yet. Mr. John Barlow met us at Islington, and put me into a coach. Miss Stopford and

THE 'POKY PARLOUR' AT BALL'S FARM

Highgate Archway.

Bullocks Museum.

British Museum.

The New Church Strand.

Monument.

Burlington Arcade.

ILLUSTRATIONS TO *THE PICTURE OF LONDON*

Mr. James were quite well, and very little fatigued. We had many a bit of chatter through the coach window. I drove to Mr. O'Donoghue's; it was about ½ past 5 when I got there. He very kindly requested me to take tea, which I gladly did, and then walked to my lodgings with my landlady's daughter.

I got to bed as soon as I could, and never woke until near noon next day, quite well, and ready for breakfast, which I took in Mrs. Benson's[1] room, while she ate her dinner. I did nothing that day but buy in some provisions and coals, and went to bed again about 7.

Next morning, Saturday the 15th., I arose, completely refreshed. It rained incessantly this day and the day before, and I only went out with a rice pudding to the bakehouse.

On Monday morning, the 17th., after examining my map, I set out at ½ past 10, to deliver Mrs. Ducker's letter to Mrs. Johnson in Queen Street, Clerkenwell. In passing Whitechapel Church, about a ¼ of a mile hence, I saw a great crowd, and mingling amongst them, I was told the Bishop of London was going to hold a confirmation there; so I played truant, and went in, and witnessed the whole ceremony. When it was over, I was glad to go home and dine, for Dr. Littler's[2] medicine and my subsequent journey, have given me a keen appetite. Off I set again after dinner, and got to Mrs. Johnson's without further let or hindrance, easily finding my way. I staid tea with her, and we had a deal of chatter. Mrs. Johnson took me over the way to the lodgings. I have not yet agreed for them, for though I like the situation and vicinity to Mrs J., I

[1] Mrs. Benson's, 5 George Terrace, Commercial Road. Horwood's fine plan of London, 4th ed., 1819, as also Pigot's PLAN, circa 1824, illustrate the later observation of Miss Weeton as to its 'airy situation', the district being as yet largely unbuilt; and opposite her Terrace there stretched a Rope Walk. Commercial Road still smiled unsuspectingly enough to the heavens.

[2] The Upholland apothecary.

don't like the room, it is so small. I shall stay here one month, for I like my present lodgings with Mrs. Benson. It is a very light, airy situation, and I can see fifty times as much sky as I can in my parlour at Holland. It is a fine wide road, and very lively.

Tuesday, the 18th, I spent at Mr. Barlow's. I had received an invitation the day before to go, guided by two little gentlemen, old playfellows of Mr. James's. As it was so far distant, we were requested to leave home at 9 o'clock. We did so, and arrived at Hampstead a little after 11. I had been told, when at Mr. O'Donoghue's, that Mr. Barlow had had a severe attack of palsy, and I found that James and Miss Stopford had never seen him; nor had the family dared to tell him of their arrival. He is very nervous and ill, and but faint hopes of his recovery. It is very probable that I shall see Miss Stopford no more here. It is such a terrible distance, near 6 miles. The family were so stately and reserved (a mother, 3 daughters, and 2 sons), that I did not like my visit, and don't desire to repeat it. You will take care, I hope, to show this letter to no one but Mrs. Dannett, and Miss C. Braithwaite, for you will see there is much in confidence.

I have *accidentally* heard that it is quite a settled thing with the Barlows that James is to marry Miss Stopford. Whether this is as well understood at Roby Mill, I cannot say, but I think it will not be for Miss S's happiness. She is an artless, unambitious girl, and this family, I fear, are exceeding proud, over-bearing, and anything in temper but sweet.

Wednesday, 19th. I was confined at home all morning, cleaning, going errands, and cooking. After dinner, I took a long walk through the city by way of spying out the land, and walked round St. Paul's, but did not go in. I came home well tired.

20th. I set out in the morning to Mrs. Johnson's, to conclude about the lodgings, and found them engaged. It is of little consequence, for I did not like the room; it was so close and small. I rested all the afternoon, and after tea I walked along Shadwell and Ratcliffe Highway to see the Tower (only the outside), and London Bridge. It was the 1st. time I had seen the river, and I was much pleased with the walk. My morning's walk to Mrs. Johnson's, which is a very long distance, and this, fatigued me so, that to-day (the 21st) I must stay at home to recruit. My time has hitherto been so taken up with cooking, cleaning, and going errands, that I am half tired before I set out. The going up and down 2 or 3 pair of stairs so continually, adds to the labour as well as to the consumption of time. Next week, I intend to begin serious operations, and view the interior of some buildings of which at present I have only seen the outside.

I have now given you a long Journal of my Week in London. I am quite pleased with my visit, and enjoy myself much; but having everything to do wholly for myself, I can see but few objects in a week, and must therefore take a longer time to see all, than one who has everything provided for them.

Mr. T. Jackson lent me a Picture of London, but when I here begun to examine it, I found it of so old a date, 1803, it would not do; so I went to Lackington's, and bought one for the present year,[1] for there is no possibility of doing without one. I only got it yesterday. I can now go out with confidence, as I shall know constantly how to proceed.

From 70 to 80 caravans, each as large as those which usually convey wild beasts, are passing daily to the East

---

[1] The 22nd edition. The edition following, in the face of growing competition (actually one Guide had the impertinence to call itself 'The *New* Picture of London'), was re-written and enlarged. Both editions have been drawn upon for the purposes of editing the London section. Lackington, an eighteenth-century bookseller, wrote a famous autobiography.

India docks, and return filled with tea to the India House. What an amazing consumption there must be in England.

It will probably be next week but one before I can send a letter to Miss Braithwaite, for I must not spend much time in writing, I find.

To MISS BRAITHWAITE, Up-Holland.

Mrs. Benson's. No. 5 George Terrace. Commercial Road.
May 31st. to June 2nd. 1824.

You will before now have seen my letter to Miss Dennett, I dare say, so I shall not repeat what I have said there. You will neither expect nor desire that I shall give you an accurate description of what I see, for any printed book on the subject will, of course, be far better. In a correspondence like mine, where I feel as if writing to friends who are interested in what pleases, amuses, employs, or befals *me*, and who I suppose wish to know how *I* proceed, I think it better to relate such things concerning myself as may entertain those far away, who desire to be acquainted with them; and in this case, I think egotism (if it literally mean writing about my own affairs) necessary, and a compliance with your wishes, and not a reproach. On this plan, then, I will proceed until you request me to alter it.

I certainly was greatly pleased with my journey hither, although the weather was not the brightest and most pleasant. Many an object as I passed along, amused and interested, and no consideration could have induced me to travel inside the coach; the guard offered me an inside seat in the night, but I declined it, for the night was light, though not clear, and it was not near so cold as was the following day; many a drunkard's candle did I see, lighting him to bed past midnight, and a waiting family for the absent. Litchfield Cathedral looked solemn and grand, though passed hastily. I peeped in at many an

opened bedroom window, unclosed by early risers to purify
their rooms as the morning dawned and the day advanced;
and many a sickly invalid, I fear, would be startled from
their light slumbers by the guard's noisy horn; which was
of no use that I know of, for the coach made noise enough.
Riding on a coach is very easy; I never felt tired or be-
numbed with it.

About noon the second day, the scene grew more and
more animated; towns were more frequent, and villages
thickened; they increased in beauty too, the nearer we
approached to London. Mr. McAdam's[1] name was on
many a board as we approached; thanks, ten thousand
thanks to him, I say, for the easy ride I had had the whole
of the way. I should have been more shook if I had journeyed from Wigan to Southport; but on these roads, the
traveller has all the pleasure without any of the fatigue.

Whilst at Mr. O'Donoghue's, before I proceeded to my
lodgings the evening of my arrival, a Miss Steel and I
were for a short time alone. She told me that Mr. Barlow's
intended their son James for Miss Stopford. I thought it
was singular I should *come to London* to hear Holland news.
I think it is only conjecture at this end of the tail, though,
in my own opinion, they have got the right tail by the end.
(Don't tell how I came by this, or I may get my own tail
pinched for it; and Miss Steel's too)—for when, on the
following Tuesday (the 18th.), I was spending the day at
Mr. B's, the *most marked attention to Miss Stopford* was constantly paid, to the utter neglect of poor I. I had been

[1] John Loudon McAdam (not Macadam), 1756–1836, shares with Telford the distinction of having made possible efficient coach routes. Extensive travel over all the country had convinced him as to the necessity above
all for good drainage; a satisfactory top surface was secured by the use of
small angular broken stone, which the passage of traffic consolidated. The
consolidating process was attended with one serious drawback, however—
that of smothering clouds of dust. The advent of railways postponed further
experiments in road science until the motors once more trailed their dust
clouds about the countryside.

requested to leave home at 9 o'clock, that I might have
more time to rest there. I thought this kind, and did so.
The two boys, Master B's late school fellows, and myself,
arrived at 11. We found Miss Stopford and James preparing for a long walk to Regent Street, etc., and had we
been ½ an hour later, they would have been out. I thought
it very odd, as I knew no one else. I, out of over politeness, requested that our early arrival might not prevent
their walk, as we were too much fatigued to go with them.
They went, and I and the little boys, sat by ourselves
almost 2 hours before any of the family came near us. At
last, Miss Barlow came in, and her eldest brother. Some
time had elapsed before any refreshment was offered.
Ann and James returned, and they *all* sat down to a game
of teetotum,[1] Miss Barlow and all, leaving me quite in a
deserted seat.

Miss B. probably is 30 or more, and very like Miss
Broadhead. Young as Miss Stopford is, she should have
known better, and have devoted her time to me, if she
thought the game too childish for me to be invited to play
at. A 2nd. Miss Barlow came in a little before dinner, and
spoke to me 2 or 3 times, which the elder had scarcely
done. When dinner came, Mrs. Barlow arrived (Mr. B's
deplorable state justly excused her late appearance). On
sitting down, an elderly lady—the only other visitor—
Mrs. Barlow placed on her left, and called to Miss Stopford to take the right. I was going to sit down there,
but drew back to make room for her, when she was so
pointedly called to. She hesitated, for she was on the
other side. Mrs. Barlow, seeing this, said, 'Oh, very well
then,'—as much as to say, you may sit here if Miss Stopford won't.

[1] The Teetotum was a kind of top, of hexagon or octagon shape, with the
sides numbered (or in the older version, lettered T., H., N., and P.—Take all,
Take half, Nothing, and Put in again to the pool). *Put and Take* was a
modern variation of the child's Teetotum.

After dinner, the young folks all went into the garden.
I declined going; for one 6 mile walk, and another to
come, was almost more than I was able to accomplish.
Miss Stopford should have staid with me. A 12 miles
walk for her sake was no light sacrifice, and she has never
given herself that trouble for me, and probably never will;
and her treating me with so much slight was probably the
cause of the Barlow's doing so. I was very little spoken
to by any. Miss Stopford was more out of the room than
in it.

We were accommodated with early tea, and on taking
leave, Miss Stopford, Mr. John, and James Barlow brought
us a part of the way—truly speaking, Mr. John did not;
for a long way he chose to go along another line of streets
and roads, just getting a glimpse of us at the openings.
This was too pointed, for he did not need to have gone
with us. I now began for the first time that day, to feel
seriously offended. I still said nothing. Miss Stopford
had, much of the way, walked with me in her usual
affectionate manner. At last, the form of the streets pre-
cluded Mr. J. from keeping his chosen distance, but came
up to us, and offering his arm to Miss Stopford, drew her
so far back, that I had no more of her company, and
walked on alone. At last, James came up to me. At
length, I stopped, and saying, that as I found I could
not have Miss Stopford's company, it was a pity she
should follow me any further, and bid her good-night.
The 2 little boys and I had a very agreeable walk home
after this.

There are 3 sons and 3 daughters in this family. James
is the youngest. The house is handsomely furnished, the
rooms a good size for a single house. I saw 3 women servants. They are a very plain-featured family. James is
the handsomest. I really think, prejudice apart, that they
are not a good tempered family. James is very rude,

slovenly, and overbearing, and shewed no feeling for his father, but was most troublesomely noisy, although he knew his father was not to know that he had come home.

Poor Ann, I fear, will be made a sacrifice for her money, and will not know nor derive any advantage from it; and James Barlow has not the delicacy or feeling to appreciate the value of a girl like her. She is at present a sweet, innocent, affectionate girl, and I wish she might meet with a mind like her own; but an unfeeling son cannot make a good husband.

I am much pleased with my visit to London. The first view I had on coming, was in passing under the arch[1] at Highgate; and really, it was grand. The city appeared so immense, and St. Paul's, that emperor of buildings, towering amidst the whole. For some days, the confusion I naturally felt, prevented my distingushing objects individually. I now begin to feel almost naturalized.

I will now proceed with my journal from the day in which I broke off in my letter to Miss Dannett.

I wished to see the General Post Office, so on the morning of the 22[d] (Saturday), I took that letter all the way there, instead of putting it into one of the receiving Houses nearer at hand. It is a gloomy, dark place. A new Office is commenced building on another site, and much need there is of it. I find it necessary when going to some places in the city, to keep my attention quite awake, or I should pass by many a grand place, and not know it. So it was now; I was close by the P.O., and could not tell which was it.[2] I expected to have seen a crowd about the place of

[1] 'An excavation has lately been cut at an enormous expense, through the eastern side of the hill, with a view to diminish the draft of the horses in passing this way; and across this new road a grand archway has been thrown to connect Highgate with Muswell Hill.' *Picture of London.* The first archway was opened in the year 1813, freed from toll as late as 1876, and replaced by an iron bridge in 1897.

[2] The old Post Office was situated in Lombard Street, but the new site in

entrance, all bustle and business, but it was perhaps not a busy part of the morning, ½ past 10. I was obliged to inquire, and went up a gate way. When I had deposited my letter (and it requires some sagacity for a stranger to find the right hole), I turned inattentively to come out, and issued forth at a place totally different to the one where I had entered. 'If I could but mind what I am about,' thought I, 'I shall be finding all the fellows p-----g against the wall in this narrow place.' I opened my eyes and minded my way, and going cautiously round, got again into Lombard Street, to the spot where I had entered; for otherwise, I should not have known where I was.

I get off my Lesson from my Map at home, and drawing a rough sketch of the precise places I mean to walk to, if I deviate, I am bewildered—like a child saying off his task, who, if he be interrupted, must begin again. Having my little sketch in my hand, I knew now which way to turn. My plan was to spend the day in reconnoitering, which I find quite necessary, as I have no companion to go with me. I went to St. Paul's, intending to be there during morning service, and no more, at this time; but on entering, the doorkeeper informed me that there would be no service until the 10th. of June, as the workmen were now putting up scaffolding and benches for the annual assemblage of children at that time.[1] I paid the usual 2d.[2] and never did I see so grand a sight for so little money. I rambled an

St. Martin's-le-Grand was rapidly being cleared. 'The post-office is the most important spot on the surface of the globe . . . and hitherto it has been in a narrow valley, misshapen even to deformity, and scarcely accessible to the few mail-coaches which collect there for the nightly freights.' *Picture.*

[1] 'DIARY OF AMUSEMENTS: June: The Thursday before Whit-Sunday, the Charity Children of the metropolis unite and attend divine service at St. Paul's Church, to the number of about 8,000, and form the grandest and most interesting spectacle which is to be seen in the whole world.' *Picture of London.* Blake's 'Holy Thursday' exquisitely pictures such a scene.

[2] 'The body of the church may be viewed for two-pence . . . no person admitted, except during the hours of divine service, but such as are willing to pay for seeing the church and its curiosities.' *Picture of London.*

hour or more over the whole ground floor of the building. I wished for you to view what I saw. It far surpassed anything I had imagined amongst sacred buildings. It is in majesty what the lion is amongst beasts; in comparative size as the elephant; but in real beauty—to what shall I compare it? It is rich in ornament, but not loaded. Between 30 and 40 fine marble monuments adorn it. Such works were new to me, and my feelings were highly wrought upon. First impressions are often most exquisitely vivid. The shutting of a door now and then, the occasional knockings of a workman's hammer, resounding like thunder, had a fine effect as the sound wound up and reverberated within the dome, dying away by degrees as it ascended to the top. I left, with a determination to revisit it soon, and see the whole. I shall not be able to obtain admittance on the 10th. for want of a ticket, as they are not sold.

I next proceeded up Ludgate Hill, and part of the way along Fleet Street. The market here is the dirtiest heap of lumber I ever saw.[1] There had been several heavy showers of rain that morning, and the streets in some places were near ancle deep in mud. At the crossing places, there were such long strings of vehicles of every sort, that foot passengers had to wait a considerable time to catch an opening, and then it was run that run could. It was fine fun for me, for I like a good excuse for a run. There were famous long rows of us, and the longer we stood, the worse it was, for the line lengthened. It was market day too, and the carriages could only pass on at a foot's pace, like a funeral train. I could see neither beginning nor end of them. At last, I skipped across

---

[1] Fleet Market, which stood in the middle of the street, was opened for the sale of meat, fish, and vegetables in 1737. In 1829 Farringdon Market was built to house this offence to sight and smell, but the project long proved unremunerative.

like a Columbine—only I plunged one foot in a mud hole.[1]

I wanted to see Blackfriar's Bridge, and in the street leading to it, to procure Baldwin's Journal, for I was quite at want of a paper, having seen none since my arrival, and I chose to go to the fountain head.[2] I returned home, well tired, to dinner, rested till after tea, and then set out eastwardly, *reconnoitering* again, and found, accidentally, the road to Greenwich. I went on, thinking to gain a distant view of it only at that time, when, after an hour's walking, it rose to my sight like a piece of enchantment. The river was between us, for I had got to the extremity of the Isle of Dogs. The scene was truly beautiful. I was so completely fatigued on my return, that I was obliged to rest 2 days.

On Tuesday, the 25th., after an early dinner, I set off to go *quite* to Greenwich. I rambled all over the Park, the Town, and round about the Hospital. I was greatly delighted. The day was beautifully bright and clear, and made the whole scene look like a paradise. I got home a little before dusk.

On the 26th., I went to St. Paul's, and saw the whole, from the vaults below, to the Ball above.[3] I purchased on my way there, a quire of large paper, the benefit of which you are now receiving.

Next day, 27, I set out at 7 o'clock in the morning to go from the Tower stairs in a Steam packet to Gravesend, and got home a little before 9 that night. It was near 30 miles each way. I was much pleased; the day was lovely

---

[1] 'The principal streets are wide and airy, and surpass all others in Europe. . . . All mud or other rubbish that accumulates on the surface of the streets, is taken away by persons employed by the public for the purpose.' *Picture of London.*

[2] *Baldwin's Journal.* Union Street, Blackfriars. (Pigott's *Commercial Directory*, 1823-4.) This London paper was published every Saturday.

[3] Greatly daring, Miss Weeton must have laid out the sum of 2s. 8d.; an analysis of the various levies upon the sight-seeing public produces that total.

and the scenery interesting. I now required rest again. Friday I staid at home, cleaning, cooking, sewing, reading, and writing; as likewise Saturday, until evening, when I took a walk to Hackney.

Monday, 31st., I took a long walk to see Temple Bar,[1] the Strand, and Waterloo Bridge. I had previously visited all the other bridges on this side. I went in to see the Wax Work in Fleet Street[2]—poor stuff: and the Invisible girl.[3] Next, a Panorama in the Strand, of the ruins of Pompeii, and surrounding country. It was very beautiful.[4]

June 1st. I went to see Westminster Bridge. On my way, I visited the Menagerie in the Tower,[5] intending to

[1] Temple Bar, the Strand, &c., are too well known to justify notes; as applies, of course, thoughout the visit with reference to the more familiar and extant London sights.

[2] Originally and popularly known as Mrs. Salmon's Waxwork; the Exhibition, after many vicissitudes, was now situated at the Water Lane corner of Fleet Street, miserably deteriorated, and within a few years of ignominious dispersal under distraint for rent. Timbs, in his *Romance of London*, gives an amusing account of the freakish and destructive humours of burglar visitants a year or two after Miss Weeton's visit.

[3] *The Invisible Girl*: 'The philosopher will here experience an uncommon result of the union of catoptric and acoustic principles. A globe is suspended by a ribbon, under which four tubes are adapted, but they do not communicate therewith, *and are likewise insulated*; by these, conversation is carried on with an invisible lady, who answers every question, breathes on you, and tells every visitor whatever they hold in their hands, in an instant. Price of admission two shillings and sixpence.' (*Picture*, 1803.)

Miss Weeton's reaction to 'the union of catoptric and acoustic principles' is sufficiently indicated.

[4] Barker and Co.'s Panorama, opposite the New Church in the Strand (St. Mary-le-Strand).

'This exhibition constantly challenges the curiosity of the Geographer, Topographer, Antiquarian, and Politician, by a succession of views of scenes in nature or art, or subjects of history. Admission 1s. to each picture.' *Picture of London.*

There were frequent changes in the programme, and the 21st ed. of the *Picture* records 'beautiful representations of the city of Athens, and the town of Dover'. The building became the Strand Theatre (the 'Band box') in 1831.

[5] From which exhibition can be traced the expression 'seeing the lions in the Tower'; though in 1822, according to Walford's *Old and New London*, 'the Tower Menagerie had sunk to a grizzly bear, an elephant, and a few birds', subsequently increased by the labours of a new keeper. In 1834 the collection was removed to the Zoological Gardens, Regent's Park.

pay another visit to see the other curiosities; not having time now, for I had a tremendous long walk before me. I next went to Billingsgate; the noise, confusion, and dirt there, is diverting, stunning, and disgusting. From thence I proceeded to the Monument, as the day was clear. I mounted 310 steps and it was not labour lost.[1] At last I got to Westminster Bridge, and finding it a much more convenient, as well as agreeable situation, I set about seeking for lodgings, for I am such a dreadful distance from the West End, and I have seen most of the places at this end.

I shall have finished the month I engaged for here, on Thursday, the 10th., and have taken lodgings from that time, for a month, at Mr. Hudson's, Carlisle Place, Lambeth.

June 2nd. I have a commission from Mrs. R. Jackson of Prescot, which I find I have no chance of discharging whilst I continue here. It is to find a certain Female Agent's Office; or, if that is not carried on, any other of a similar description. I have hitherto made what inquiry I could, but unsuccessfully. After I remove, I will take all the pains I can; I have never forgotten it. I shall be obliged if, when you write to your sister Jackson, you will request her to inform Mrs. R. J. of this, and to assure her that I will not neglect it. This is to be a total secret from all but to those whom it is unavoidably imparted.[2]

I have never seen nor heard a word from Miss Stopford since the day I was there. She might have written, at least, as I do not know her address precisely, (and she

---

[1] Miss Weeton miscounted, the actual number of steps being 345. Wren's design to give the illusion of actual flames (in brass) issuing forth from the loop-holes, was given novel effect to by 'portable gas' illumination, a year subsequent to Miss Weeton's visit, to commemorate the laying of the first stone of the new London Bridge.

[2] It speaks volumes for Miss Weeton's notions upon the claims even of a slight friendship, that she should sacrifice days of her holiday in this search for a domestic post for Mrs. Jackson.

does mine), nor Mr. Platt's. I shall be obliged if you will request Mr. Stopford to remit my Quarter's Annuity on the 21st. of June, as he proposed, through Mr. Platt (all except what was paid for my Coach fare by Mr. Winstanley). And when you write, you can give me Mr. Platt's address, and I will call upon him. It will save postage.[1]

I shall be glad to hear from you as soon as convenient.

To MISS DALRYMPLE, Liverpool.

London: No. 5, George Terrace. Commercial Road.

June 8th 1824.

Since I arrived here, I have often thought of my promise to write to you, but other and prior promises at Up-Holland have prevented my fulfilling it before this, and my time has hitherto been so fully occupied, that I find I must let little writing serve. I have no attendance at my lodgings, and having all my own cleaning, cooking, errands-going, and waiting to do my self, much of my time each day is taken up with it.

I arrived here on the 13th. of May.

In a few days after my arrival, the weather brightened, and I have enjoyed the novelty of the scene much, and think of remaining here until the middle or the end of July. I am about ½ a mile from Stepney, in a pleasant, healthy situation; but it is too remote from the west end of the town, to admit of my having seen any thing as yet of the gay scenery there. For that reason, I have taken lodgings in Lambeth, at No. 16, Carlisle Place, and go there on the 10th. inst.

I have taken all the advantages of my present situation that it would admit of. On a Sabbath, I have gone to such Chapels as were not too distant. The Church and Chapel at Stepney are only about 150 yards distant, and

---

[1] Postage on a single letter to Wigan would be 11*d.* at the rates then obtaining.

a Tavern with tea gardens stands between them, the visitors of which may literally be said to be within the *sound* of the gospel. All the way, as I go to any place of Worship, fruit stalls are in the road, and confectioners shops open, as on any other day.[1] I wonder much at it; I never saw it so glaringly elsewhere.

As a contrast to all this, on Whit Monday afternoon (7th.), I went to Greenwich fair, a high wrought scene of fun, frolic, and folly. I was highly diverted with the nonsense and mirth of which I was a spectator, and could laugh now when I think of it. A grand fair is held there in Whitsuntide, for 3 days. I had to walk a mile and half, and then, taking boat, was ferried another mile.

The boats here are of a much narrower and lighter construction than any I ever remembered at Liverpool. We were 10 passengers—6 of them lads, to my joy—though in other boats no larger, I saw 14 grown-up people.[2] The weather was so hot, that the waterman stripped his jacket soon; by and bye he swelled so with heat and exertion, that—first modestly apologizing—he unbuttoned the waistband of his breeches — — We all sat as still and as grave as judges.

Hundreds of boats and thousands of passengers, all for the same destination, together with the extreme beauty of the day, made the scene most animated. As soon as I landed, I saw people as old as myself, mingled amongst the young, swinging away merrily in the large boat Swings, shouting, laughing, and screaming, as they mounted aloft in the air, like hey-go-mad. 'This is the finest fun we have had to-day,' shouted some — — Need

[1] In deference to veering public opinion, tobacconists in the early years of Victoria's reign kept one shutter up on Sundays.
[2] The apparent frailty of Thames craft had in the last century attracted the attention of another Northerner, Tobias Smollett. Mr. Matthew Bramble's party (*he* went by coach) took the water route to Vauxhall 'in a wherry, so light and slender' that, according to Miss Lydia Melford, 'it gave them the appearance of fairies sailing in a nutshell'.

I tell you that I did not get in? I walked on to the Park, which is always open to the public; it is a most lovely place. Here were innumerable groups walking about, and innumerable groups amused themselves by getting to the tops of various hills in the Park, and, taking hold of hands, 2, 3, or 4 together, they run down with the utmost speed; often some unlucky wight places himself just before them as they are in full speed; down they tumble over him, and over one another, men and *women*, boys and *girls*. I sat on the grass, watching this sport until I was tired of laughing at it. I was surprised to see such a number of genteel people there, spectators like myself; but still more, so many well dressed ones actually joining in it. As to servant girls, apprentices, and others of a worse description, the wonder is not so great. The shows, too, were in great numbers—and the grotesque figures!!¹

Many of these fellows make as clever speeches for their purpose, as Mr. Canning or Mr. Brougham;² and Mr. B.

¹ Greenwich Fair has been too often described to need further introduction. There are many old prints depicting the 'fun of the fair' in all its aspects, particularly dwelling upon the indelicate exhibitions incidental to the famous hill-side sport. Dickens, in his *Sketches by Boz*, has given a colourful account of the fair just anterior to its decline; and, who knows, one of the lads in Miss Weeton's boat might have been the great Boz himself!

Besant, in his *South London*, thus describes the scene: 'I rejoice in being able to remember one of these delightful shows. There was a great booth with a platform in front, and canvas pictures hung up behind the platform. The orchestra occupied one end of the platform, playing with zeal, between the performances. The company in their lovely dresses, stood on the platform, and danced a kind of quadrille from time to time.'

² George Canning, 1770–1827, the great orator, and disciple of Pitt; Prime Minister in 1827. Lord Brougham, 1770–1868, basking in the fame he acquired as a result of his defence of Queen Caroline against George IV, was at this period on his way to political eminence. Less truly of Queen Caroline than of this obscure governess, he said: 'Her courage was of the highest order of female bravery, scorning all perils in the pursuit of worthy objects, leading her certainly into adventures that were chiefly recommended by their risks, but, like the active courage of a woman, suffering occasionally intervals of suspension according to the state of the animal spirits, possibly influenced by the physical constitution of the female frame, although the passive virtue of fortitude never knew abatement or eclipse.'

STAGE-COACH OF THE PERIOD
(*Note hand-rail*)

PENMAENMAWR

and Mr. C. might just as soon have been show men. How
can any boast of the superior understanding of the *human
race*, when they see so many, naturally as wise as themselves, making themselves more ridiculous than any other
creature living? If they would but reflect justly, they
would see how full of folly the wisest of them are, and
what a slight shade of difference between them and an
idiot.

To MISS CATHARINE BRAITHWAITE, Up-Holland.

London: July 6th. 1824.

I wish I could do by this letter as you have done by
yours, and save you the expence of postage. I was beginning to be anxious to hear from you, when your letter
arrived. The bearer had paid immediate attention to it.
I got it by the twopenny Post.[1]

Balloons are going up here almost weekly. On the day
I last dated my Journal to you, the 2nd. of June, one went
up from some where not far from Pentonville (one of
the villages adjoining London on the North).[2] I knew
nothing of it until I got into the Aldgate, on my way to
put my letter to you into the P.O. It was then 3 o'clock,
the very hour advertised for the ascent, so I hastened to
Blackfriars Bridge, as I knew the wind would bring it that
way, and I could not possibly have got to the place of its
ascension had it risen punctually to the time. After waiting an hour and a half, I saw it come, and rise out of sight
over my head, in fine style. It descended very safely, I
afterwards heard. Not so the one which had gone up a
few days before. You will have heard of poor Harris's
awful fate. His balloon I did not see, not having heard

[1] Probably the coachman from Prescot had earned himself a copper or
two. The twopenny post operated only within the London area, country
postage continuing to be based upon mileage until 1835.

[2] Most likely from the grounds adjoining that popular resort, White
Conduit House, the scene of many balloon ascents.

of its intended ascent until after the Catastrophe had taken place. When I heard of it, I was glad I had not seen it.[1]

Whilst I was at Mrs. Benson's, I was sadly out of the way of hearing of anything going forward in or near the metropolis; and if I had heard, I was too far off to benefit by the news. Harris's funeral was going along the road, as Graham's Balloon was ascending—how unfeeling!

Thursday, June 3rd. I went after dinner to the Tower, to see the Jewel Office. I was rather disappointed here, for all the grand baubles (worth, I suppose near a million of money; perhaps two or three) are contained in a place no bigger than a recess for a sideboard. The place is perfectly divested of daylight, and shewn by lamplight. It is well enough to see for once, but had I the choice, I would prefer seeing the emerald isles of Winandermere, the ruby coloured setting sun, its golden rising, the silvery clouds, the azure sky, or even the simple yellow butter cup. The admission for one person is 3s; the armoury 3s. I thought both sights too costly, so declined the latter.[2] A Warder conducted me from the Tower Gate to the office and back, a very kindly, goodnatured old fellow. The costume of a Warder is very antiquated—scarlet coats, with skirts full all round like petticoats, flat crowned broad-rimmed hats, etc.

---

[1] 'May 25, 1824, Lieut. Harris, R.N., ascended from the Eagle Tavern, City Road, with Miss Stocks; the former killed by the too rapid descent of the balloon.' Timb's *Curiosities of London*, 1855.

Harris allowed too much gas to escape through the valve. His female companion was only slightly injured.

[2] 'The Jewel Office . . . is a dark and strong store room. A single person pays one shilling and sixpence.' *Picture of London*. This statement is at variance with that of Miss Weeton as to the charge made, though perhaps the *Picture of London* was not quite up-to-date in this matter. As recently as 1815 a 'female maniac' had forced her hands through the bars (subsequently strengthened), and 'literally tore the crown in pieces'. Gas had apparently not as yet penetrated the fastnesses of the Tower.

4th. Set off after breakfast to see a few streets with comical names to them—*Cloth* fair, *Petticoat* Lane, *Curtain* Road, *Threadneedle* Street, and passed through the Court of Bartholomew Hospital, Charter House Sq., but could not get the least glimpse of the school and gardens, they were so enclosed by high walls. I next walked all round West Smithfield, quite full of cattle. I could fancy I heard their roarings and bleatings now; it is a very large square —it smelled wofully. I then went to Paternoster Row, near St. Paul's—a narrow, dark, dirty street—and called at Longman, Hurst, Rees, Brown, and Orme's, to ask on what scale my map was drawn, as they are the publishers of the Edition of the Picture of London which I have; and lo and behold! L.H.R.B. and O. could not tell! Pretty fellows!—No thanks to them, however, I have since found it out by my own self, after *persevering* efforts and *intense* study. A pack of Lazy, Hoggish, Rascally, Blockish, ganderlike Oafs!!!

Seriously, I was rather plagued for want of a scale to my Map, and as the Book requests, as a great favour, that it may be told of its faults,[1] I thought I might as well shew my desire to be civil, and perhaps I might have obtained the desired information—I did but see a shopman, who, as the representative of this many headed Lord Lghbro, very respectfully told me, that—he could not tell me—but —mark the next reprint if you should ever see it. I got home to a late dinner, and after tea, had a very pleasant walk to Bow.

5th. The next day, I was so weary with the many miles walk I had had the day before, that I could not go out till after tea, when, going past Shoreditch Church, I went a

---

[1] '. . . the multiplicity of the objects which this Work embraces, rendering it impossible to avoid some errors or omissions, the Editor respectfully solicits the communication of corrections, addressed to him, at No. 39, Paternoster Row.' *Picture of London*—and trust Miss Weeton to oblige!

long way up the Kingsland Road. I found I could not get into the country; truly, if once you get into London, you can get none out; my feet are not able to take me out, however.

6th. Sunday. I rested myself by going 3 times to Chapel.

7th. I rested at home, all morning, that I might be able to go to Greenwich Fair in the afternoon, it being Whit Monday. After I landed, I saw 4 shows and gave a gratuity for 3½d; bought a penny worth of gingerbread and got cheated; laughed at myself, and walked on. (It is unnecessary to repeat here what is sufficiently detailed to Miss Dannett in the preceding copy).

8th. Rested till after tea, then took a walk to the farther end of Holborn, a part of the town I had not seen before, and saw many new and interesting objects in the streets and shop windows.

9th. After dinner, walked to Pentonville; a long, but very pleasant walk.

10th. Packed up in the morning and *flitted* in the afternoon to my new lodgings, 4 m. Westward.[1]

11th. I had now got, as it were, into another world, and a flood of interesting scenes flowed in upon me. Another Balloon was to ascend this afternoon from Pentonville. I directed my steps that way; when I got there (4 miles), I found the ascent was postponed, as the day was threatening. I was vexed, yet I could not but laugh as I returned,

[1] Carlisle Place is situated at the lower end of Carlisle Street, Lambeth, just behind the old Canterbury. Only a few houses remain of those indicated (and numbered) in Horwood's *Plan*, 1819 edition. Number 16 has vanished, but there still remains a plaque over one of the remaining cottages— CARLISLE PLACE. At the period of Miss Weeton's visit fields stretched from here to Lambeth Palace; the houses now to be seen higher up Carlisle Place, and on the left-hand side of Royal Road leading to the Bishop's Walk, were not yet built. Squalid slum property was near at hand on the site of the present St. Thomas's Hospital, but Lambeth could still establish a claim to the picturesque and almost rural. Walking down Carlisle Street now, one can only envy Miss Weeton her well-timed visit.

I met such thousands on the same fool's errand. However, I consoled myself as well as I could, by walking after tea round Westminster Abbey, and viewing the exteriors likewise of both houses of Parliament,[1] all which I had never seen before.

12th. Next morning, I walked upon a bank along the river side to Chelsea and Battersea, saw the Hospital, and went into it and all round about it. I returned home quite delighted with my excursion of 10 miles.

13th. Sunday. Went to Rowland Hill's Chapel in the morning;[2] and to St. Margaret's Church, close by the Abbey, in the afternoon.

14th. After dinner, visited the Monuments in W. Abbey for the 1st. time. Admission is 2s. now; it used to be free.[3] I am rather sorry at this change, as it must exclude me from visiting it as often as I could wish. I admire it greatly, but in my estimation, it is second to St. Paul's.

15th. I went to the opening of a new Independent Chapel (Brunswick) in Mile end Road, in the morning and evening, which, as it is 5 miles off, caused me a walk of 20 m. I was much gratified indeed, but so weary when I got home, that the next day I never stirred till after tea, and then went by Carlton Palace;[4] found as it were by accident St. James' Palace, Burlington Arcade,[5] and the Haymarket Theatre. Passing a Jew's shop window, I saw

[1] The old Houses of Parliament, destroyed by fire in 1834.

[2] The Surrey Chapel, in Blackfriars Road, an ugly, octagonal building, of the Calvinist Methodist denomination, built by the famous preacher, Rowland Hill, in 1783. It was closed in 1881, and after serving as a boxing hall, was demolished.

[3] 'Formerly the great western door stood open the whole day, and strangers could see the greater part of the church gratis; lately, on account of the monuments having been broken and much destroyed, they are excluded from all but the *Poets' Corner*, which they may still visit without a fee'. *Picture of London*, 23rd ed.

[4] Carlton Palace, the town residence of His Gracious Majesty, George IV; no one, from its squat exterior, would have deemed it a palace.

[5] Burlington Arcade, a great novelty, was built in the year 1819.

abundance of labels pinned to various articles, very humorously, e.g. 'Guineas taken with delight,' 'Sovereigns received with joy,' 'Double sovereigns with transport,' 'Half sovereigns taken with avidity,' 'Crowns hailed with pleasure,' 'Half crowns received gladly,' 'Shillings quite welcome,' 'Sixpences, as many as you please,' 'Pence will be looked on with smiles,' 'Halfpence will not be refused,' 'Farthings rather than nothing.' I have never been able to find this shop again, not noticing at the time what street it was in. I see many a droll sight as I go along the streets, and many a hearty laugh I enjoy by myself at home. I would prefer having some one with me to enjoy and join in the laugh, but that cannot be. Whilst I was at Mrs. Benson's, I bought my coals and potatoes of Mr. J. Thurtell, own coz to the noted J. Thurtell.[1]

We are not half sharp at Holland; why, one person here makes his bull to draw a cart; and dogs are quite commonly put to that use here.[2] Catharine, do *you* keep a bull, and make Mary drive. Oh! as I pass the shop windows, and see many a tempting thing billeted—'Only this,' and Only that—', I find to my cost, they are sad money traps, and I Only have my money melted out of my pocket, I hardly know how.

Some of Miss Weeton's itinerary has been omitted; it is apparent that she was now out to achieve a startling pedestrian record, and though there is not the slightest reason to doubt her veracity as to the estimated mileage, the recital of street names becomes tedious, except to those familiar with Georgian London. As Miss Weeton commenced upon her Journal at

---

[1] J. Thurtell was the principal in a notorious murder case. He was tried and executed for the murder of Wm. Weare in the early part of this year. His accomplice, John Hunt, was sentenced to be transported.

[2] The cruel practice of the use of dogs for draught purposes was abolished —so far as concerned London—as late as 1840. In the early years of the century it had been still quite a novelty, but the butchers, notoriously cruel, did not fail to abuse this convenience. As late as 1834, large, ferocious dogs were used in Manchester for goods transport.

this date (17 June), and as both Letter and Journal are complementary, the following itinerary is a composite of both.

> Number of miles I walked in one month, not including many short walks of ½ a mile or a mile in quest of provisions or other business
>
> $$213\tfrac{3}{4}$$

Well might my feet become so swelled and painful, when the heat of the weather is considered (for the Summer was a peculiarly hot one), and the little previous exercise I had been in the habit of taking. I am astonished at my own strength, but—I have a kind Friend above, who permits me to have some enjoyments, in pity to me for those He thinks proper to bereave me of for a time.

June 17th. (*Thursday*). Expecting a long walk in the afternoon, I did not go out in the morning, but staid at home amusing myself with writing and reading. Immediately after dinner, I set out to see the Balloon ascend; I walked round by Fitzroy Square, to discover if possible where Mrs. Burne lived, who keeps a Female-agents Office, as I was very anxious to discover her now, without any further delay, that if possible I might render Mrs. R. Jackson of Prescot a service by making an application for her. I could not succeed, so proceeded onward through Islington, to White Conduit House, Pentonville. Arrived there at 3 o'clock, and waited in a field 3 hours before the Balloon ascended, which it did at 6.[1] I did not see it filled, as admission was 3*s*. 6*d*. I saw as much as I wished.

18. I was busied at home all morning, cleaning; after

---

[1] White Conduit House was a famous old tavern dating back to the times of Charles I. The building then existing was erected in 1753, and was rebuilt shortly after Miss Weeton's visit, when an attempt to ape Vauxhall drew all the depraved characters of the town, to the great disgust of those who could recall its past glories. Graham used to make balloon ascents from the gardens, and he it was whom Miss Weeton probably saw. George Cruickshank passed some not unobservant evenings here.

dinner, I set out, determined to find where Mrs. Burne resided, or persevere daily until I did. I recollected, that on my way the day before, I had passed a Register Office, and as one thief is said to be the likeliest to catch another, so it occurred to me it would be in this case—and I was right, for the mistress of it directly informed me where to find Mrs. Burne, viz, 24 Howland Street, Fitzroy Sq. I went and returned home quite pleased, and spent the evening in writing to her [Miss Weeton kept no record of this letter]. The two following days very wet.

21. Walked in the morning to Blackfriar's Bridge, to inquire particulars of the steam Packet to Richmond; then proceeded in a line up through Fleet market, left along Holborn, and Oxford St., which I had not seen before, purchased some lace, ribbon, and gloves, walked round Soho Sq., went to an Exhibition there of models of scenery in Switzerland, &c. I visited Hyde Park and Kensington Gardens for the first time, and St. James's and Green Park—a very long walk indeed, but the various scenes drew me on from one place to another.

22nd. Had a beautiful sail to Richmond.[1] Walked on to Twickenham; returned, and dined in Richmond Park in the hollow of an old oak tree, and walked through, and all round about the village and Hill, walking near 6 hours incessantly. The sail home from 6 o'clock until near 9 was glorious; the sun set just in such a manner as betokens approaching wet or storm, beautifying, whilst it threatens;

---

[1] 'Steam Packets . . . being provided with low-pressure engines and regulated by proper valves, nothing can be more secure or more pleasant, than such a day's voyage. The vessels are elegantly fitted, the fare is moderate, and every kind of refreshment is provided on board, on moderate terms. There is also a band of music, and the voyage is enlivened by dances on the deck. . . . In due time, all navigation will be performed or assisted by steam.' *Picture of London.* This gem fittingly closes the *Picture*, being added as an afterthought, on the verso of FINIS. An amusing description of the river trip to Richmond is given in Hone's *Every-day Book*, 1825, accompanied with a view of the long-funneled vessel leaving Richmond.

thousands of windows appeared in full blaze, and all the country a rose colour.

Rain and fatigue kept me in 2 days.

On the 25th. I set out to try to find Mr. Platt, as you had not procured me his address, which after some trouble, I managed. Do you know, Miss Stopford has never made the least inquiry after me. I was above 3 weeks at Mrs. Benson's after I had given myself the trouble of a 12 miles walk to go to see her; and during that time, she never wrote, came, nor sent. When I changed my lodgings, she of course could not know where to find me. I was completely thunderstruck when Mr. Platt informed me that Mr. Stopford had not made the slightest mention of my money to him—it's all of a piece! With little enough of money left, I have to wait 10 or 11 days till Mr. Platt hears of a remittance. I was made to appear like some swindler, asking for money not belonging to me. Mr. Platt told me Miss Stopford was now at his house. I neither offered to call, nor left my address, as it was not asked for, but said I would call again at the warehouse on the 5th. of July. I next went forward to Mrs. Benson's; she said J. Barlow had called 3 days after I left, and when he heard I had changed my lodgings, he walked off before Mrs. Benson could tell him where I was gone to; for I had told her.

26th. I walked to the Regent's Park, and upon Primrose Hill. The Buildings erected, and erecting, round the skirts of the Park, are grand and noble,[1] surpassing anything in housebuilding I ever saw. I visited the Diorama at one of the entrances into the Park; 2 Paintings shewn in a peculiar manner. The floor of a very elegant and spacious room, turns round like a snap table with all the

[1] 'A grand circus of houses, with painted and handsomely railed areas in front, will overlook the park from the opposite sides of the New Road; and another, of uniform magnificence, is proposed to be built near the centre of the park itself.' *Picture of London.*

spectators, slowly and almost imperceptibly, from one view to the other. The paintings are stationary, and admirably executed. The change takes place 4 times an hour. I had an hour and a half's riding; for every one may stay as long as they please. One view was of Trinity Chapel, Canterbury; the other, a lake and mountains in Switzerland, with real changes of shade as of passing clouds, and day and night, moonshine and sunshine. I was too much gratified to think I was moon-shined out of my money.[1]

27th. Sunday. After dinner, Mrs. Hudson, with whom I lodge, proposed that her husband and son John, should take me through the Parks and Kensington Gardens; she is so lame, she goes little anywhere. I was desirous to see the Parks, with their Sunday company, and really it was amusing. It is just like what I have read Ranelagh was, only this is out of doors.[2] I saw one person there from Wigan—Mr. Swift, who was an apprentice with Dr.

[1] This ambitious venture was situated at the east side of Park Square. It was built by Morgan and Pugin (the famous architect of his day) and opened in 1823. Daguerre, of early photographic fame, and another Frenchman, had been responsible for its exhibition in Paris. The pictures were changed two or three times a year, and measured 80 feet by 40 feet. They were suspended in separate rooms; ground glass in the roof tempered the light from above and made possible the semi-darkness requisite to the skilful effects of light and shade achieved. The takings on Easter Monday of this same year exceeded £200. In 1848 the building was sold, and was converted into a Baptist chapel.

[2] 'One of the most delightful scenes belonging to this great metropolis, and that which displays its opulence and splendour, is formed by the company in Hyde Park and Kensington Gardens in fine weather, chiefly on Sundays, from March till July.

'The spacious gravel roads, within the park, are, on a fine Sunday, covered with horsemen and carriages, from two till five o'clock in the afternoon. A broad footpath, that runs from Hyde Park corner to Kensington Gardens, is frequently so crowded during the same hours, with well-dressed people passing to, or returning from the gardens, that it is difficult to proceed.' The *Picture of London* ventures to insinuate a prohibition—'With regard to Kensington Gardens, no servant in livery, nor women with pattens, nor persons carrying bundles, are admitted into the gardens. Dogs are also excluded.' Ranelagh had been the fashionable counterblast to Vauxhall in the eighteenth century, but now it was only a memory.

Cowley, but as I never had any acquaintance with him, I did not speak to him now. I suppose we traversed this day not less than 15 miles; my feet, in consequence, suffer from these many and long walks. In other respects, I never was in better health.

28th. The next day, after dinner, I went to see some streets I had not walked into before, but not very far. In the evening, I went to Vauxhall. I had long wished to go, but the idea of going alone to an *evening* amusement, had kept me back. At length, I run all hazards, and, though feeling exceedingly timid, I ventured to brave the difficulties, and was more comfortable than I might have expected. This was a new scene of enchantment; many thousands were there.[1] I got quite safe home at one o'clock in the morning; although I had not less than a mile to walk, the watchmen very civilly directed me when ever I asked anyone the way, for my fears made me blunder.

29th. On this day I was obliged to rest.

The 30th., I went for the first time to the British Museum,[2] and staid near 7 hours. My poor feet were sadly swelled, and yet I could have no mercy on them, nor on my dinnerless stomach. Got home at $\frac{1}{2}$ past 4, and never

---

[1] Vauxhall was on the wane, but persisted still a household word; numerous accounts have been given of it, both contemporaneous and subsequent to the last flicker of its myriad coloured lamps, late in the 50's. Pigot's *Commercial Directory for 1823* affords it a note, and good-naturedly allows 'there is occasionally some good singing,' along with 'extraordinary performances on the rope'—but 'This delightful place of evening amusement was lately advertised for sale by auction, and it was supposed would have been sold for building ground'. The calculating genius of 'two spirited gentlemen' who interposed and gave the gardens a new lease of life, happily coincided with the period of Miss Weeton's visit. Miss Weeton's fears of Vauxhall by night were justified by the evil reputation of its covered walks; she had the misfortune to arrive too early to avail herself of the innovation of Vauxhall open by day; the reader is referred to Dickens's account of that in his *Sketches by Boz.*

[2] British Museum, then Montagu House, in Great Russell Street. The present building, designed by Smirke, had been commenced upon in the

sat down the whole time. The distance, going and returning, 5 miles.

July 1st. I set out on the next day after dinner, with the
intention of seeing many streets, and particularly squares,
which I had not before introduced myself to. At last, I
got to Tavistock Sq., and seeing crowds of people all going
upwards, and finding poor Harris's Balloon was their
object, I slid in amongst them, and had a very near view
of its ascent; for I am so thin and so tall, that where I see
a little crevice in a crowd, I can easily get possession of
it, threading in and out where short people dare not go,
and fat ones cannot. I think there could not be less than
100,000 people there. When the Balloon was got out of
sight, I walked for 2 miles homeward, and yet saw no end
of the crowd; shoved, shuffling, and squeezed along, all
that way. It was often laughable. I arrived home after
a walk of 12 m., most sadly tired. I never chose to
inquire my way, as I was no way concerned at going a
little round about. I saw so much more of the city by that
means, and I knew the metropolis too well to be lost in
it now.

2nd. Went little out; the rain had pity on me.

3rd. Went to see a number of Squares which I had
missed by going a Balloon hunting. Took a second walk
to Regent's Park, and returning through Leicester Square
home. I went in to see Miss Linwood's exhibition of
Needlework. I think every candid, unprejudiced person,
must say that they are superior to any paintings. One
picture of grapes, a bunch of purple and another of white,
struck me, and reminded me of one who would have
looked at them with an earnest eye, could she have been

year 1823, and was completed by 1847. Miss Weeton's fatigue reflects itself
in an inaccuracy about the time she spent at the Museum. In any case, it
was only open between the hours of 10 and 4—incidentally, the Museum
was closed to the public three days of the week.

present.[1] A year ago she said, if you go to London, you will be sure to visit Miss Linwood's works.[2]

4th. I went in the morning to Surrey Chapel and heard Mr. Elliot, of Devizes, preach. In the evening, I went to the Magdalen. The place was full, but I was not particularly pleased; it was very formal and insipid. I shan't go again.[3]

5th. This morning, I went to Mr. Platt's Warehouse, No. 38 Cateaton Street—apparently a very fatherly, tender hearted kind of man. I sat chatting with him about half-an-hour, while my money concern was going on. He said he was going with Miss Stopford into Lancashire in about 3 weeks, and asked me what time I should be returning. I said, in about 3 weeks or perhaps a month (we got no nearer the point). He did not say that Miss

---

[1] Poor Elisabeth Braithwaite [*orig. note*].

[2] Miss Linwood's Exhibition was a stock feature of all editions of the *Picture*, and mention of visits to this famous London show-place occurs in many diaries and letters of the period. She has earned herself a respectable notice in the *D.N.B.* 'Linwood, Mary (1755–1845). Opened an exhibition of Pictures in Worsted, in Hanover Square, 1798. Removed to Leicester Square and toured chief provincial towns. Her exhibition contained one hundred copies of pictures by old and modern masters, and a portrait of herself, after Russell, taken in her ninth year. The Countess of Wilton, writing in 1841, speaks of the exhibition as still open in London, and in terms of great admiration. "Miss Linwood's Exhibition", she writes, "used to be one of the lions of London, and deserves to be so now." . . . She was also a musical composer of some note.' *D.N.B.* Timbs thus describes her art: 'The designs were executed with five crewels, dyed expressly for her, on a thick tammy, and were entirely drawn and embroidered by her own hand.'

The Empire Cinema, Leicester Square, occupies the site of her Exhibition; the building itself was burnt down in 1869. It is still possible for the 'candid, unprejudiced person' to adjust his preconceived notions on painting, for there is an example of her work in the South Kensington Museum.

[3] Magdalen Hospital, St. George's Fields, was opened in 1758, 'for the relief and reformation of wretched young women. . . . The hours of divine service are a quarter after eleven in the forenoon, and a quarter after six in the evening; and on account of the fascinating pathos of the singing, which is performed by the females (screened by a curtain from the general eye), no place of worship in the metropolis is more worthy the attendance of a stranger.' *Picture of London.*

The attention of the stranger was discreetly drawn to the fact of a little formality at the door, where a collection was made previously to admission.

Stopford ever mentioned me, or wished to see me, and I
was equally silent. I should be glad to know whether she
has been thus instructed from her parents. I shall certainly inquire into it when I return. I have not fixed
exactly when I shall return; but present my respects to
Mr. and Mrs. Ball, and tell them I shall be preparing in
about 3 weeks, and then they may expect me by Anthony
Billington some Saturday. night from Liverpool (I'll
come none with Miss S.).

I never heard of the King's going in state to prorogue
Parliament until all was over; was it not mortifying? I
have never seen any of their Royal faces yet; I have likewise missed two reviews in the Parks, and have not seen any.

Write to me as soon as you can. Perhaps you will hear
more from me until you see my phiz.

Would you take an early opportunity of requesting Miss
Hawarden to do me the favour to desire Miss Bullocks
(Mr. Henry's daughters) to call on my Mary? Or, if they
can get to see her at Chapel, to ask her if she has any doll
but the one I dressed for her? If not, I will bring her a
tall, jointed one. If her father or any one else has given
her one, I will bring her something else. I would rather
her father knew nothing of it until I return, and then I
will manage the rest. Your early attention to this would
oblige me greatly. Miss Bullocks had better not tell Mary
I want to know, for the poor child cannot keep a secret;
but inquire as a mere matter of curiosity of their own.

6 and 7th. Heavy and incessant rain prevented me from
walking for these two days. It rendered me a service, as I
had plenty of employment in writing letters and memoran-
dums, and repairing stockings, &c., as well as setting my
apartment in order; besides, I obtained a necessary rest
and a recruit of strength for further long walks. I always
considered a rainy day as a very kind friend with a
homely face and a dark garb. Had the weather been

altogether fair, I should probably have exerted myself in walking until I had brought on a fever, for the heat was intense.

9. Walked after breakfast to Clapham; met a gentleman on a dark grey horse, with white tail, most strikingly like my brother; returned at 12. In the afternoon, I took a walk into Piccadilly to Bullock's Museum, in the Egyptian Hall,[1] and saw the room where specimens of *modern* Mexico are exhibited. I did not enter his exhibition of ancient Mexico; not from want of curiosity, but money; it dwindled very fast.

10. *(Saturday).* Went immediately after breakfast to a Review in Hyde Park; saw the Duke of York[2] for the first and last time; likewise the Duke of Wellington and Lord Hill; I could not learn the names of the rest of the officers. The heat was such as to endanger the lives of both men and horses. The fat Duke of York looked, as we say in Lancashire, 'as if he wur aw of a swat, an welly meltit, and smoort,' with his high fur cap and wrappings round the neck. The spectators had plenty of scampering to keep out of the way, and yet get a good view. It was a high treat to me; for, amongst so great a crowd, I passed unnoticed, although wholly unaccompanied by any one I knew; and as I have said before, I like a good excuse for a run, as old as I am. Sometimes a few of us chose to stand

[1] It is curious that Miss Weeton does not seem to recall that she had already made acquaintance with this museum, as originally established in Liverpool, prior to its removal to its quarters in the Egyptian Hall. The *Picture* devotes several pages to a categorical description of its departments, not forgetting the Natural History department with 'the cameleopardalis, seventeen feet three inches high'. Admission was 1*s.*, and the extent of the collection may be judged from the fact that catalogues cost 2*s.* 6*d.* Subsequently the building was used for popular entertainments, lectures, exhibitions; and, last but not least, the feats of legerdemain associated with the names of Maskelyne and Cook.

[2] The Duke of York, so irreverently treated by this obscure unit of the huge crowd, died in 1827. He was the second son of George III, and was the best of a bad bunch; certainly the most popular.

our ground, close to the muzzles of the muskets as they were firing, but hanging down our heads, and setting up our two shoulders to protect them; the noise was completely stunning, and the clouds of smoke blackened our faces and half smothered us; when it was all over, we were bold enough to laugh.

12. Went over Westmr. Bridge to George St., to see Lord Byron's funeral. Waited amongst the crowd opposite his house for more than 2 hours. At length, the procession set forward; I followed it to the top of the Haymarket, and then returned home.[1] Afternoon, walked with Mrs. Spearman to Doctors Commons.[2] Mrs. Spearman was a neighbour of Mr. Hudson's, where I was now residing, and had been a lodger of theirs. She was going to consult a Proctor, wishing to be separated from her husband, and I had a desire to see the place. The heat was at this period so intense, I could go very little out.

July 14. The heat was still excessive, and about noon, distant, yet loud and aweful thunderings began. I would not have ventured out this day, but in the hope of rendering a service to Mrs. Jackson of Prescot, I had for several weeks attentively noticed the advertisements in the newspapers, which I saw almost daily; last evening I saw one in the Morning Herald, for a Housekeeper and companion to an elderly gentleman. This I thought would exactly suit Mrs. J. I set out amidst increasing thunder, to Mr.

---

[1] Lord Byron died, 19 April 1824, at Missolonghi, in Greece. His body was brought to London, and the putrefying remains there lay in state for seven days, in the front parlour of Sir Ed. Knatchbull's house in Great George Street. The funeral procession, speeded on its way by Miss Weeton, went up Highgate Hill, where another woman, as famous as Miss Weeton was obscure, paid her last tribute from a window as it passed by—Mary Shelley.

[2] Doctors' Commons, the ancient seat of Doctors of Law. Readers of Dickens will be familiar with the atmosphere of the place. The Court of Probate Act of 1857 abolished the ecclesiastical functions of the Court; the College property was auctioned off in one lot in 1862, and the place was subsequently demolished.

Rennie's, 59 Charlotte St., Rathbone Place.[1] I was shown up-stairs to a small, but elegantly furnished drawing room, in which was an elderly gentleman of very pleasing appearance. He told me he had already engaged one; he said not less than near 30 had applied the day before. I felt very sorry I had not seen the paper sooner, and made an earlier application. Got home to tea. The thunder now increased, and the lightning the *most aweful and incessant I ever saw*! Long as I live, I shall recollect it; it continued till 9 or 10 o'clock. The rain was very refreshing.

15. After dinner, walked to see Dulwich College—the outside only, as was generally the case with most places I went to see, for, being alone, I felt too timid to venture inside. The walk was a very pleasant one, 10 miles. After tea, went to have a prospect from Southwark Bridge, and saw a man there with a cage, in which were a Cat, 2 Kittens, near 20 mice (many of them white ones), an owl, a Hawk, 5 or 6 small birds, and a Guinea Pig, *all together*.[2] I never went out that I did not see some curious exhibition in the streets, and as my dress was plain and no one knew me, I often stood looking at them and remained unnoticed, except by the exhibitor, for whose *kind condescension*, I generally presented him with some half pence.

Number of Miles I walked from the morning of June 17 to the evening of July 16. 133½.

July 17. As I was fond of seeing Westminster Abbey, I often went round it if my plan for the day allowed me

---

[1] Not the great bridge builder, who died in 1821.

[2] 'Most of our London readers have doubtless witnessed John Austin's exhibition, on the Waterloo Bridge Road, where "the cat, the rat, the mouse, the hawk, the rabbit, the guinea-pig, the owl, the pigeon, the starling, and the sparrow, each enjoys, as far as can be enjoyed in confinement, its respective mode of life in the company of others; the weak without fear, and the strong without the desire to injure". Yet we have seen one of John Austin's rats bite his finger viciously, merely because it was asked to stir itself and be exhibited along with its brethren.' *Penny Magazine*, 1838.

time. To-day I walked past the front of it, and then turned into St. James's Park to Spring Gardens, to see the Panorama of the Battle of Waterloo. I liked it very well, but I am not very fond of anything relating to Battles, and that was the reason why I had deferred this visit so long; I had once intended not to see it at all.[1] Walked next up Regent St. to the new Church at the top, which I admire exceedingly; it is a beautiful finish to a noble but imperfect street.[2] Returned, and visited the Cosmorama in this St.[3] on my way home. I had now seen many of the —ramas in London, Ignoramus' and all. In the evening, went with Mrs. Spearman into Westminster, to order a pair of stays.

19. In the morning, going through St. James's Park, I saw a great number of soldiers collected, and following with the crowd, was led on down into St. James's Palace Yard, and was gratified with the music of the band; when they had finished, I went forward alone to Mr. Bleacall's, Dentist, Newman St. Returned home through Soho Sq.

20. Remained at home all morning, cleaning; walked out after dinner to discover where the Oedephone was to be heard; my Picture of London says No. 9; I could find nothing of it, nor any such number in the Haymarket. The Street appears to have been recently improved, and

[1] Spring Gardens dated as a pleasure resort from Elizabethan times. Marshall's 'Peristrophic' Panorama of the Battle of Waterloo was an exhibition operated upon similar principles to that visited by Miss Weeton near Regents Park.

[2] All Souls Church, built by Nash 1822–4, crowned his Regent Street achievement. It would be interesting to know just in what consisted the imperfection of Nash's newly designed Regent Street, according to Miss Weeton's notions of what constituted the perfect. The principal contemporary objection was to the stucco.

[3] The Regent Street Panorama was designed to meet the taste of those desiring to improve the mind. As a social function, the Diorama achieved the distinction of the modern 'private view' before general release. And even Ruskin himself waxed almost lyrical over Burford's Panorama in Leicester Square, deprecating the indifference of the Government to its ultimate fate.

the new buildings not yet regularly numbered. I returned into the Strand, and went next up St. Martin's Lane, to hunt out the Apollonicon; was more fortunate here. I found its situation easily, went in, saw, and heard it. It is a grand instrument of the Organ species; it had no case; its powers were great. Only 4 or 5 people were there besides myself, as it was not one of the chief days of performance.[1] I proceeded next up Tottenham Court Road, to Howland St. to make an inquiry of Mrs. Burne for Mrs. R. Jackson; returned to the bottom of T. C. Road, and espying some of Gaskell's Eye Snuff in a Druggist's shop window, went in and purchased a box, 1s. 1½d.,[2] purposely that I might have an opportunity of inquiring where Mr. Irving preached, of whom so much has been said, and such immense crowds of the Gentry, Nobility, and even Royalty.[3] I obtained the requisite information, and lost no time in going to reconnoiter the place. I had wished to hear him from the first of my coming to London,

[1] 'APOLLONICON: It is well known to the least scientific of the public, that there are two distinctions of organs, the finger and the barrel. A most superb instrument combining these two distinctions has been built at an immense expense for Lord Kirkwall. It performs any full piece of music with the finest effect. This instrument is now exhibiting to crowded audiences at Messrs. Flight and Robson's manufactory in St. Martin's Lane, whose merit in the invention and construction is very great.

'THE OEDEPHONE is another curious instrument of this kind, exhibited at No. 9, Haymarket—Admittance, 1s.' *Picture of London.*

[2] Miss Weeton had perfect sight by day, but found writing by candlelight very trying to her eyes.

[3] Edward Irving (1792–1834), a Scottish preacher and founder of the Catholic Apostolic Church, which still has its devotees spread among over 80 churches, and its Cathedral at Albury; he first preached in Cross St., Hatton Garden, in the year 1822, and from 1824 at the Scottish Presbyterian Church in Regent Sq. Following a charge of heresy, he opened his own church at a private house in Newman St. in 1830. Charles Lamb, Coleridge, and Carlyle and his wife were among his admirers. Ruskin, in his inimitable allusive style, thus epitomizes the Irvingites as a sect: 'My father's second clerk, Mr. Ritchie, wrote unfeelingly to his colleague, bachelor Henry, who would not marry for his mother's and sister's sakes, "If you want to know what happiness is, get a wife, and half a dozen children, and come to Margate". But Mr. Ritchie remained all his life nothing more than a portly gentleman with gooseberry eyes, of the Irvingite persuasion.'

but could not tell where in all the wide Metropolis he was to be heard of, since Mrs. Benson, Mr. Hudson's, my Picture of London, nor my Evangelical Magazine could give me no information. I examined, many a time and oft, the numerous Portraits of him in the Print shop windows, but they never told me where he preached, or where he lived; and I was too shame-faced and too poor to enter and purchase, by way of paying for the information. Now, hearing from the Druggist's shopman that he preached at the Caledonian Church, Cross St., Hatton garden, and that tickets were requisite, I proceeded direct, and passing the Church, went to an open door of a Milk house, where I saw a woman cleaning a cream mug. She very readily told me how I was to manage to procure a ticket; I was to write a letter, stating my request, and giving my name and address. I returned down Fetter lane home.

21. (*Wednesday*). Left home in the morning at ½ past 9, crossed St. James's Park, stood above an hour listening to the military Band; then went up the Haymarket, and the first shop I saw on turning into Piccadilly, was the droll Jew's shop window, mentioned in p. 145., which I could never find from that time to this, never during the time turning that precise corner. I now accurately copied the labels in his window; the others were from memory in p. 145; I cannot be quite sure of their accuracy. I think the Jew alters them occasionally, as these appeared very different to what I saw before. They were as follows. 'Guineas taken with sang froid, Aye! and seven shilling pieces, or Demi Guineas.' 'Guineas taken with glee.' 'Napoleons sold and bought.' 'Light guineas taken at full value.' 'Old silver taken with rapture.' 'French silver taken with alacrity, quite Novel.' 'Napoleons, Louis d'ors and Gold of every sort and denomination taken with peculiar adroitness.' These were each written on a card, about twice the size of a common playing card, in a large Roman hand, and disposed amongst the drapery in the window.[1]

I next walked along Piccadilly, inquiring at several Coach Offices the Liverpool fares; they were all 4£ inside, and 2£ out. I next went to see the apparatus for hatching by steam (chickens);[2] walked on to Hyde Park corner, and getting a pot of curds, walked up to Cumberland Gate, and turned to the right along Oxford St., inquiring at various Offices the fares of Liverpool coaches; they were all as in Piccadilly. Proceeded to Hatton Garden, and put my Letter to the Caledonian Elders into their Office, Hatton Court, behind the Church; home at ½ past 5 o'clock, having had no dinner nor any food since I left home, but some curds and one or two penny buns; in any of these long walks, I had no more refreshment, for I could never bring myself to that degree of confidence to enter a Cook's shop to dine.

22. (July). After dinner, walked past the Elephant and Castle, and along the Greenwich Road to Blackheath; the day was very clear and beautiful, and I greatly enjoyed my walk. I entered Greenwich Park by a door in the wall next the Heath, traversed the Park and through part of the walks amongst the buildings of the Hospital; thence, took a boat to the Custom House stairs, and walked home over London Br.; in all, about 14 m. (without the sail).

23. Remained at home all morning to rest. After dinner, I went to see some parts of the Borough which I

[1] The Jew's device to attract attention throws a significant light upon the effect of international wars and complications upon our coinage, not without close parallel in our day. 'Light' guineas, of course, were clipped or otherwise mutilated coins. The following year was one of financial crises.

[2] The age-old novelty was attracting considerable attention at this time, one book published in 1824 being entitled the *Daily Progress of the Chick in the Egg during Hatching in Steam Apparatus*, by J. H. Barlow.

had not seen before; I turned along Horseleydown, interpreted by some Painter of Signs, more ignorant of Etymology than of his art, into Horse-ly-down; accordingly, he has painted for a publican's Sign, a fine horse in the act of lying down, with a crowned rider on his back.[1]

24. Did not go out until after dinner. At $\frac{1}{2}$ past 12, went to hear the Apollonicon in St. Martin's Lane; before I went in, being too early, I strolled towards Leicester Sq., purchased 2 small shawls and an embossed Silver thimble. I then went to hear the Apollonicon, and was greatly pleased with it; there are 6 sets of keys, admitting of as many performers at one time, who sit fronting the audience, with their backs to the Instrument. There are two immense barrels which go by a kind of clock work when wound up, and perform very finely. There were a considerable number of people there to-day. First we had the Music which was performed by mechanism; afterwards, a blind gentleman performed very admirably on two sets of keys; the other sets were never touched to-day.

Mr. Hudson, with whom I had lodged ever since I left Mrs. Benson's, had been a master carrier, but was reduced in the world, and now worked as a journeyman. By his first wife, he had 4 children living; the 2 eldest were boys of 14 and 16, remarkably fine looking youths, who worked at their father's business; the two younger were girls, Ann and Keziah, of 10 and 8 years. The youngest was a most diseased child, yet fat and rosy; one eye had run quite away, and the other seemed to be wasting fast, and gave her great pain; one elbow, too, was diseased, and the arm gradually wasting; added to this, her temper was very bad, and all together, she gave her father great un-

---

[1] 'Popular legends derive its name from a belief that the horse of King John lay down with that monarch upon his back, and hence horse-lye-down, but as the entire tract so called was, according to Stow, a grazing gound, called Horse-down, it is more probably a corruption of that title.' *Old and New London*, by Thornbury.

easiness. To add to the calamities of this afflicted child, she had now been near a fortnight ill of the small pox, and was completely loathsome. Poor, poor Keziah! how thou didst suffer; yet we thought she appeared very likely to recover; and if she did, she would be one of the most deplorable objects ever seen; but her constitution seemed naturally strong.

Mr. Hudson's second wife was sister to his first, and consequently, aunt to her first step children. I felt greatly concerned when I heard of this, but made no observations to them about it. Mr. Hudson was an uncommonly fine-looking man in every respect, his figure tall, athletic, and portly; his countenance, voice, and manner, most benignant and impressive. He laboured hard for his family, working over hours on his own account at home when his other work was done. I felt high respect for him, and had become quite attached to the family; and in all appearance, so had they to me. The present Mrs. Hudson was a little weakly woman, with one leg shorter than the other. Mr. Hudson had married her for the sake of his children. I spent many an agreeable hour with her, for she never left the house, and no acquaintance called but Mrs. Spearman.

July 25th. Went to the Caledonian Ch., Cross St., Hatton Garden, in the morning, to hear Mr. Irving. My letter for an admission ticket, which I had put into their letter box the previous Wednesday, had not been noticed; but this, I was informed by the mistress of the milk-house, was scarcely to be expected, as applications were so exceedingly numerous, that the Elders, who could only give as many tickets as there would be seats in the Church, were obliged, in justice, to send them in rotation according to the earliness of the application, and numbers had to wait 2 or 3 Sabbaths. I however could not wait, for, ere another Sabbath had passed, I expected to be far away at Liverpool. I ventured without a ticket. When I arrived at the door, the carriages of gentry and nobility continued in a line the whole of Cross St. and Kirby St., and a crowd at the door of elegantly dressed people. I had taken care as regarded my own dress this day; for, however contrary to Scripture, there is scarcely any obtaining decent treatment in plain cloathing. I often attribute the civilities I receive, to my dress. On speaking to one of the Elders at the door, who was receiving tickets, to ask if I might be allowed to enter without one, he with very great civility replied, that it was against their rules, but however, we will say nothing of it—giving me a nod to pass on. I got very agreeably situated in the gallery.

Mr. Irving's appearance struck me as peculiar; he appeared to me in physiognomy, dress, and manner, like the wild genius of the mountains. I was exceedingly impressed; his eccentric gestures frequently excited the smile of the congregation; yet it was the smile of approbation, for his manner and language appeared quite natural, and peculiarly his own. I should much like to know the opinions of others respecting this preacher, for I have not yet heard a single one.[1]

July 26th. I felt as if I now was constantly bidding adieu to every object in or near London; it was an uncomfortable

---

[1] Charles Lamb wrote: 'I have got acquainted with Mr. Irving, the Scotch preacher, whose fame must have reached you. Judge how his own sectarists must stare when I tell you he has dedicated a book to S. T. C., acknowledging to have learnt more from him than from all the men he ever conversed with. He is a most amiable, sincere, modest man, this Boanerges in the temple. . . . Judge whether this man be a quack.' Mrs. Oliphant, in her life of Irving, attests his popularity, in the permanent Sunday feature of queues to see and hear this phenomenon of the pulpit. 'It is wonderful how a man of so great a frame, and of out-of-door tendencies, strong and long cherished, should have been able to bear, as Irving did, confinement in one of the most town-like and closely-inhabited regions of London.' No doubt on this particular Sunday he excelled himself, as he had just become a father.

feeling, and with sensations of regret. I spent my time in London very happily; the people, both in Carlisle Place and in Commercial Road, had behaved in a very friendly manner to me, and the Hudsons I had become much attached to. Ann Hudson was a fine, open hearted girl, and as to poor Keziah, I pitied her greatly, and prayed for her much. I could not but weep to witness such excess of bodily suffering. I think Job's disease must have been the small pox—and yet, had it been so, as it is an infectious complaint, someone would have had it immediately previous, or directly after he had.

On setting out this afternoon, I inquired at Charing Cross respecting the rout of their Coaches, for the fares everywhere were the same. As these did not travel the way I wanted to go, I went into Piccadilly, and from the Spread Eagle Office,[1] corner of Regent St., a coach was driven through Oxford to Liverpool. I particularly wished to see Oxford, so resolved on going by this coach. I returned down to Charing Cross, along the Strand, Cheapside, to the end of Aldgate, as before stated, and on arriving at home, found poor Keziah had died whilst I was out! I was thunderstruck, for I had all along thought she would eventually recover—It was a providential release, for, had she recovered, she would have been a heap of disease. Poor, suffering child, thou knewest no comfort in life.

27th. After dinner, went into the Haymarket, Piccadilly, Burlington Arcade, and crossing the Haymarket, walked along the Strand, as far nearly as St. Paul's. I had no precise object in view now in my walks, except to see again places that had afforded me much amusement.

One favourite walk, and a short one, was up Carlisle Place, turning left along Royalty Road,[2] and left again

---

[1] The Spread Eagle was one of the minor Coaching offices.
[2] Royal Road, one side of which was flanked with fields.

into Bishop's Walk, under the wall of Lambeth Palace; here there was a view of the River, and often I walked this way when the heat or fatigue prevented a longer walk. The view was very fine—Westmr. Abbey, the Bridge, St. John's Church, Vauxhall Bridge, and the many vessels on the River, were altogether highly picturesque, interesting, and animated. A walk of this kind I have seldom set down in my calculations of distances; I think, only some of my Sabbath days journeys, a few of which were not like the Sabbath days journeys of old; that I was in London, and only for a short time, probably never to see it again, is the only excuse I have to offer for my Kensington Gardens and Hyde Park walks.

Ann Hudson was now taken ill of the small pox, although she had been vaccined a few years ago; she had them very mildly during my stay.

28 July. Took a place outside the Coach to Liverpool, to go on the following morning at ½ past 5 o'clock. In the evening I packed up.

Number of miles I walked since July 16th. 104 miles.

The whole distance, then, will be as follows for the 11 weeks which I resided in London.

From May 17th. to June 16 213¾ miles.

From June 17 to July 16 221 miles, which added, will be 538¾ miles.

29 July. Set off outside the Coach from the Spread Eagle Office, Piccadilly, at ¼ before 6 o'clock. Very agreeably to me, the passengers throughout this day were few and well behaved, the morning as lovely as it could be, and the whole day's ride most delightful. Windsor Castle was a grand object, adorned as it was with the early morning's sun. Oxford was a grander object than I had expected; but previously to this, Henley-upon-Thames delighted me most; it appeared to be in a lovely, romantic country.

I was quite gratified with the sight of Oxford, although upon a Coach and never descending, yet I made good use of my eyes the short time we stopped.[1] I had provided basket store sufficient in buns and biscuits, and for a drink, a bottle of cold tea; for I had learned to be wiser now than to touch any strong drink during the journey. My life was in imminent danger on my journey to London on account of the drowsiness occasioned by the brandy and water I took. It was but little, at the most a half pint bottle, more than half filled with water, but not in general being accustomed to any strong liquid, it took the deeper effect, and the more so as I was exposed to the air so many hours. Even as it was, I should not have taken any with me, while ignorant of its injurious effects, had not Mrs. T. Jackson in a manner forced it upon me, from the kindest of motives, thinking it quite necessary for me. My own experience teaches me quite the contrary; and I believe, that if there were no strong drink in the world, and little other than vegetable diet, there would be less disease, and greater length of life, and greater rectitude of conduct; for stimulating food and inflaming liquors cause most of the vices and wretchedness of society.

So little have I heard of what is going on in the world for great part of my life, or even in England, that I was quite astonished when we arrived at Leamington, never having heard any thing of the place but its name; it appeared to be a very beautifully built and fashionable watering place. It was about 6 o'clock in the evening when we got there. The coach stopped near half an hour, during which time I got a good warming at the kitchen fire; for, hot as the weather still was for walking, I found

---

[1] Oxford, through the medium of its Press, has made its bow to Miss Weeton, and her eyes would have opened even wider could she but have been aware of the honour in store for her.

it rather cold riding, towards evening. I think we had passed Warwick just before; having no maps or any other means of reference, I cannot just now recollect on which side of Leamington Warwick was situated. The sun was setting low as we passed through, and its fine rays upon the Cathedral and Castle added much to the grandeur of their appearance. When I think of the beauties my Heavenly Friend has this Summer permitted me to witness, my soul swells with feelings indescribable, and is ready to burst the bands of the body, and fly upwards instantly to worship at his throne.

When we got to Birmingham, it was just dark, and I could see little else than a vast number of fires and lighted windows. At the Inn, we changed coaches, and took up 6 Irishmen of the lowest description, which wholly destroyed the comfort of the remaining part of the way, by their selfish rudeness. One of them had usurped my seat. I was quietly submitting to it, rather than contend with him, but the guard took up my cause, and a long scuffle ensued, in which I thought, between them, they would have overturned the coach. I then begged the guard to say no more, and I rode the rest of the night on a very dangerous outside seat behind, backwards. We were four upon it, and it was too short by much for the number; but every seat was equally crowded. It was very necessary to keep my eyes open, for the least drowsiness, and I should have dropped headlong. The man on my left kept a constant motion with his head upon my shoulder, up and down, the night through, being heavy to sleep, the brim of his hat endangering my eyes. The guard and he quarrelled again, but neither good words nor bad had any effect. I expressed my obligations to the guard, and begged him to trouble himself no more with the man, and so made peace, for the Irishman seemed determined to have the last word and the last blow, had they quarrelled for a week. The iron rail bruised me sadly,[1] I was so jammed against it. About 6 in the morning, one of the Irishmen in front left the coach; when I saw that, down I dropped, and up into his seat like a cat, and was much more comfortable, although I had one on my left as filthy as possible, and his head likewise jolting against me perpetually. It was intolerable! I very quietly requested he would let his head nod on the other (the out-) side. I thought the man would have beaten me; the coachman then interfered, and they had a long quarrel, and at last a scuffle, as the driver was determined to hurl him off the coach unless he behaved better. I was really frightened, and could not but weep; the women in Ireland must have a dreadful time with such fellows. A young woman on my right, the only female companion I had had, said she had passed a dreadful night, an Irish pig driver on each side of her, and another in front, snoring and resting their heads against her, to prevent themselves falling.

I extracted sweets from bitters, and enjoyed the ride and the prospects, arriving in Liverpool at 11 o'clock, the morning of the 30th. July. (Friday).

I am so far from indulging in that general prejudice which the majority of the English have against the Irish, that I ever feel a great deal of pity for them, as an oppressed and neglected people; and the viciousness and violence of their tempers and conduct is a great deal owing to want of education, and the residence and example of their land-owners. If it were possible to hold the seat of Government 4 months in the year in some central part of Ireland, it would effect a wonderful change in that country for the better, and be no injury to our own.[2]

[1] Note the iron guard-rail on the illustration.
[2] The question of the Irish immigrants and cattle drovers at this time was a vexed one, particularly in Lancashire, where they would gladly have banished the Irish back to their own country.

On leaving the coach at the Blue Bell, in London road, I proceeded directly to Mrs. Roxburgh's, 4 Russel St. Her lodgings were all let. She recommended me to a Mrs. Cash, 4, Bridport St., where, as soon as I had dined, I went to bed at two o'clock in the afternoon, and slept soundly till 8 the following morning, Saturday, July 31st.

PRESCOT

AUGUST 1824–MAY 1825

Saturday July 31st. After dinner I called on Mrs. Price in Seymour St. and spent the remainder of the day and evening with her and Mr. P. most agreeably.

August 3ᵈ. I had long been dissatisfied with the gloom, loneliness, and seclusion of my abode at Up-Holland, and had determined to leave it as soon as possible. I wished to be in a market town, as the difficulty of providing food comfortably for one person, with a delicate appetite, was very great in a retired situation. I likewise wished to be nearer to Parr Hall on my Mary's account, as I had no chance whatever of hearing anything of her at Up-Holland, except in a very casual way sometimes at Wigan, when I walked over there, or in walking to Parr Hall, which I dared not often attempt on more accounts than one. Mr. Stock's threats of removing her to some distance, where no one but himself should know, had some effect, although but little, for her removal from that school where she now is, is very desirable, as Mrs. Grundy is dead. The loneliness of the road was my greatest fear, and no stated conveyance to go by; and to hire one expressly was too expensive, so that I was forced to walk, and as it was 7 miles each way, it was not at any time of the year or in any kind of weather that I could go. And besides, after Mr. Holgate's unchristianlike treatment of me at Orrel, I had so far to go to Chapel (to Wigan 4 m.). All these objections would be obviated in a considerable degree by a removal to Prescot, which was the only place near enough to Parr Hall where I had any acquaintance, and that combined all the advantages I sought—cheap lodgings included. This day, therefore, directly after breakfast, I walked to Prescot and called on Mrs. R. Jackson to inform her of the result of my inquiries at Mrs. Burne's, Howland St., and to request her assistance to procure me lodgings, which she promised in the most friendly manner to do in the course of a week or 10 days, when, as I should be coming through Prescot on my way to Holland, I could select a lodging from such as she found to be vacant. I spent the remainder of the day in Prescot most agreeably with Mrs. T. Jackson, with whom I dined, and walked back again to Liverpool, where I arrived at ½ past 5 o'clock to tea (16 miles), intending to stay, in the whole, a fortnight at Liverpool.

The remainder of the week was passed in the common routine of cooking, marketing, sewing, walking, visiting my 2 friends Mrs. Price and Miss Dalrymple, and going to Chapel, until Wednesday, the

11th. when I went with Miss Dagnall (a highly respectable lady, lodging at Mrs. Cash's where I was) at 8 o'clock, to the Lyceum to hear a little girl of 4 years old, play upon the Pedal Harp. Her performance was so astonishing, that I wept with rapture. Yes! and as often as I think of it, I shall weep with extacy. Her manner was peculiarly angelic; she had to climb upon her chair when she was about to commence playing; she looked upward as she touched the strings, as if invoking the inspiring Muse, in a manner so sweet and natural, and so totally unlike *acting* as if from any private instruction, that the tears at once gushed into the eyes of many. One gentleman there (I think, a Mr. Yates), with his wife and 3 little daughters, was quite as much affected as I was. I could not but venerate him for the feeling he evinced; that man cannot but be a kind husband, and a good father—oh that mine were so!

The child's whole performance was delightful. Her parents were with her; her mother sat close by her. For the sake of present gain, those parents are sacrificing their child; it is impossible she can live long while her talents are so cultivated to the utmost; her tender years cannot sustain it, and she does not appear to be more than her parents say she is—4 years old.

Poor Lyra! as thy talents are premature, so will thy end be!

12th. Journeyed this evening to Prescot by the Coach, as I had all my luggage to convey. Mrs. T. Jackson had very kindly invited me to stay a night or two at her house, that I might fix upon my lodgings, which I did the next day at R. Tyrer's in Hillock St., until I could find others more convenient—Mrs. R. Jackson going with me, and pointing out various places that she had heard of.

14 (Saturday). Went on foot to Up-Holland in the afternoon, the 2 Mrs. Jacksons accompanying me the part of the way; my luggage I sent by Anthony Billington's cart. I arrived at Mrs. Ball's after a 13 weeks absence, and was received as usual with a kind and friendly welcome. 10 miles.

16. I had little to do now but prepare for removing to Prescot, by informing my acquaintances, and taking leave of them. Mrs. Ball was in Liverpool; I had seen and left her there, and now intended informing her of my plan as soon as she came home; for I had not the heart to do it when I met her in Liverpool. I knew she would be hurt, and Mr. Ball too. In a few days she returned, and with some difficulty to my own feelings, I told her of my intentions. She was so grieved that I almost repented of having thought of leaving them; yet it was for my own comfort. I value the two old people greatly, for they are very deserving of esteem.

27th. Walked to Wigan to take leave of the Hawarden's

—of the poor old Doctor for ever! unless we are permitted to meet and know one another in a future state—and of Mrs. Marsden.

28th. Walked to Parr Hall to see Mary, my dear, dear, child Mary, and spent some hours with her most delightfully, walking in the garden together a long time. Whether I must ever see her again, is doubtful, for Mr. Grundy told me that Mr. Stock had again enjoined him not to let me see her without his previous permission. I fear I shall be forced back again to my husband's house, for I will not very long be so treated; Mary's welfare demands that she either never goes home, or that her mother should be there. I walked back with great ease, and little or no fatigue, and perfectly safe. 14 miles.

Sept. 1st. Saw my furniture loaded early in the morning, and then, taking an affectionate leave of Mr. Ball's family, walked to Prescot, 10 miles. The heat of the weather still continued intense; I several times sat down by the wayside to cool and rest. In the course of a few days after my arrival at Prescot, I got very snugly fixed, and Mrs. T. Jackson's kindness renders my abode here very agreeable; for I often call.

✶   ✶   ✶

To MISS STOCK, Parr Hall.   Prescot, Sep. 9th. 1824.

On opening the parcel, you will find I have recollected your requests. As I found, when I saw you, that although you might know how many inches or feet were in a yard, you had not a distinct idea of the real length of an inch, foot, or yard, I have sent you a small ivory case with a ribbon marked for a yard, with 36 inches. I bought it in London, and gave 8d. for it; at some shops in the country, they ask a shilling for such a one. I expect you will keep it very neat, and not spoil it by childishly amusing your-

self with repeatedly unrolling and rolling it. I have inclosed 4 different kinds of Gimp,[1] of 4 and 2 yds length,
as you may perceive when you measure it, (my mother
once had Gowns trimmed with it—perhaps 60 years ago);
a little narrow green ribbon, which is of little value; it
may serve you to draw your doll's work-bags. Of these I
have still many yards left, and I shall think them well
used, if they afford you, my love, any gratification. The
green ribbon is part of a large box-full my mother (your
grand-mother Weeton) once had; they were taken in a
prize which my father captured during the American war,
between the years 1775 and 1782. The vessel was Spanish.
The surgeon in my father's ship had the box of ribbons,
amongst other things, to his share, and made a present of
them to my mother. I am thus minute, my Mary, that
you may know something of the history of your mother's
family; not for the sake of the ribbon, for it has all been
used by degrees, except a piece of the narrow green, which
was so poor as to be almost useless.

Print for patchwork is sold by weight, in small bits such
as I have sent you. I purchased it in Prescot market, 4th.
inst. The man asked 2s. 8d. p. pound. I thought it dear,
so I only bought 2 oz., for which I gave 4d. I thought it
would be sufficient for you for the present. The piece of
patchwork is out of an old Quilt I made above 20 years
ago; it may serve as a pattern. The Hexagon in the middle
was a shred of our best bed hangings; they were Chintz,
from the East Indies, which my father brought home with
him from one of his voyages. He was never in the East
Indies himself, but probably purchased the Chintz in
some foreign market. My mother bequeathed the bed to
my brother, and I therefore sent it to him when he married, and I suppose it is now worn out. I suppose your
patchwork is only for the amusement of leisure hours, and

[1] A kind of silk twist or lace. *Walker's Dict.*, 1824.

that you will manage it entirely yourself; your ribbon measure may be useful to help you to cut your paper pattern exactly.

I have no white muslin, but may perhaps buy you some in the Spring. The old cambric muslin I know will be useful to you to cut into patterns for sleeves, bodies, caps, tippets,[1] &c., preparatory to cutting out real ones. It is so old, you need not be afraid of wasting it. I have thus, I think, provided you with materials for amusing leisure hours for a few months, in rainy or cold weather; for I particularly wish you never in fine weather to stay in doors, or spend your play hours in, or out, in sedentary amusements. Your health, strength, and spirits, absolutely require that you should have as much exercise as possible in the open air; you have enough of sitting still during your unavoidable studies.

I hope you learn the Theory of Music, along with the Practice; and that you understand the composition of many of the pieces you have learned to play; at least, in a great measure. I have understood that many modern teachers begin with uniting theory with practice, in teaching little children, so I hope you will be as clever as others; don't be afraid to ask your teachers frequent questions respecting the meaning of any thing in your lessons you do not understand.

You told me you did not much practice speaking French; do not let diffidence prevent you, for if you do not learn to speak it now, you never will speak it well, and all your time and your father's money will be quite thrown away, as is the case with a young lady I know, who has been learning the language 7 or 8 years, and would be as unfit to travel in France as any person who never attempted to learn.

      *   *   *

[1] Tippet=a neck covering.

[JOURNAL]

Sep. 15. Had an exceedingly pleasant walk to Liverpool and back. 16 miles. The practice I have had in London this summer, makes me think little of such a walk.

Sep. 29. (*Wednesday*). The death of Dr. Hawarden[1] made me feel anxious to see his widow and daughter, and I set off this evening by the coach, to see them. I found them, as I expected, grieved but resigned. I staid all night, and walked over to Holland next day.

Oct. 2ᵈ. Returned from Holland on foot.

Oct. 13ᵗʰ Walked to Liverpool and back; the weather is become more mild now.

20th. Wrote a letter to Mary, and took it myself, along with a little print for patchwork, to the cottage at Parr Hall gate; had I been an hour earlier, I should have seen Mary, walking amongst the rest of the young ladies—so the old woman at the cottage told me. I can take care to go sometimes at this hour on a Thursday, when Spring returns, if not before; but now, the rain, and storms of wind are almost incessant. I will be tolerably quiet for the Winter.

*　*　　　*　*　　　*　*

To MISS STOCK, Parr Hall.   Prescot, Oct 20th. 1824.

You would feel a little surprised perhaps, on receiving a pound of raisins with so short a note inclosed. I will tell you how it was. My old and very great friend, Dr. Hawarden, died Sep. 17; when I heard of the event, I determined to go and see Mrs and Miss Hawarden, and to go by way of Holland; and to procure some cake or fruit for you at Wigan, and leave it at the cottage at Parr Hall gate as I returned past it by the coach. When I changed my plan, it was at too late a time to allow me to write you a longer letter. The raisins were not the best, but

---

[1] 17 Sept. 1824.

I really thought they were the wholesomest; for the best raisins have so thick a skin as to be almost as indigestible as leather; it should never be swallowed, nor indeed should the skins of any fruit. Do not think you are guilty of any extravagance in not eating the skins of fruit; it is a sin to eat them, because they injure the stomach, and eventually destroy the health.

I walked from Holland on the Saturday morning, and got home, not at all tired, about 11 o'clock; and it is 10 miles. I am very snugly fixed here for the present. I intend to take a small house if I can obtain furniture; a year ago nearly, I did petition for some, but was not successful. I will try again; I should much wish to have a home of my own.

Last week I took a walk to Liverpool, which is 8 miles. I dined at Mr. Price's, and called to see Miss Dalrymple, who continues to recover; she was seized near 3 years ago with a spinal complaint, which is of tedious cure; 2 issues in her back, and frequent sea-bathing are her best remedies. She is such a pious, religious woman, that I respect her highly. She invited me to stay all night, but I declined it, for I was so little fatigued, that I could walk back again very well; and if not, I could ride by a coach for 1s. or 1s. 6d; however, I managed to walk.

The weather is now becoming very stormy and winterly, and I shall be obliged to be much in doors; but I am seldom at a loss for amusement; my Flageolet, and Harmonicon, my books and my needle, are an ever-varying source of pleasure; and thinking of you, my dear, dear little girl, and praying for you and your father, occupies many a portion of each day.

I was much pleased with your very correct sentiments on several subjects, the last time I conversed with you, as regards your companions and your daring to set your face against actions that were certainly wrong. When you reprove another, do it in an affectionate manner, not angrily, and then you will deserve to be so treated yourself.

Good bye, my dear girl.

           *   *   *

[JOURNAL]

From the above date (October 20th.) up to the present time, Thursday November 18, I have scarcely gone out, owing to the heavy rains, and almost perpetual hurricanes. My time has passed most agreeably in sewing, music, copying music, reading, and bringing up the arrears of this journal.

About a fortnight ago, I received a Letter from my cousin Latham of Holland, with a Bolton newspaper, in which Mr. Guest of Leigh has exposed my brother's inconsistency of conduct and bitterness of spirit, at great length; it corroborates what I have said of him, for I have suffered greatly from him; he has done me irremediable mischief by his calumnies.[1]

           *   *   *

[1] Richard Guest, master manufacturer, was not to rest until the carefully reared edifice of Master Tom's local consequence was tumbled into the mire of intense party politics and local prejudice against a parvenu attorney. Radicalism, objected against Mr. Guest, was countered by cruel gibes against the man who could object to the warbling of sacred music by opera singers, and who nearly sliced off his own nose in an absurd midnight sally against non-existent riotous weavers. Mr. Guest might indeed be 'a scamp . . . married into a respectable family', but he was happily to live to note Tom Weeton (late Esq. and magistrate's Clerk) wryly complain that, during the course of a semi-official interrogation of his friend and himself (implicated in some shady business over a forged will in the year 1833), they had been addressed as '*these men*, alluding to Mr. Newton and myself, and not deigning to consider either as a gentleman!'

His sister's concerns having prior claim, it is still to be regretted that extracts from his various pamphlet defences cannot be given. The style is the man, and very much so in Tom's case. Pedantically apt as he was at thrusting Latin quotations at Richard Guest (just as he had tantalized his staunch sister years before at their mother's humble fireside), Dr. Johnson's observation that—'he did not care to speak ill of any man behind his back, but he believed the gentleman was an attorney', is apposite in this case.

Upon p. 48 of vol. i will be found a brief note upon the career of this man

To MISS STOCK, Parr Hall, near St. Helens.

Prescot. Dec. 14 1824.

The basket, my dear Mary, which accompanies this, is stored with the Doll's dinner Service I mentioned to you when I wrote about 3 weeks ago—2 small Dutch dolls, that may serve as little daughters to your larger one; they wont require much dressing, for they are born, as you may see, with stockings, shoes, and gloves on, and their hair ready curled; a frock, and one petticoat, are quite enough to wear at once; they need no further underclothing. You will have some old cloaths of your own which you may cut up for the use of all your dolls; perhaps a coloured tabinet frock, and a few other things that are too little for you. If you have not sufficient, I am sure your Father will let you buy, at Wigan, any thing you want. One of the little ladies cost 10*d.* and the other 6*d.*

A Cocoa Nut, and a hundred Walnuts (that is, 120, or 6 score[1] to the hundred) I have likewise inclosed; offer

and his ultimate ruin; and copies of the following pamphlets may be seen at the Central Library, Manchester. Apart from their Weeton interest, they breathe the spirit of the stirring days of Peterloo, and provide local colour in the history of the period.

A LETTER signed Richd. Guest, addressed to Thomas Richard Weeton, Attorney, of Leigh, Lancs., which appeared in the *Manchester Guardian* October 16th. 1824.

AN ANSWER to a certain Scurrilous Publication signed Richard Guest, inserted in the *Bolton Express,* and *Manchester Guardian* Newspapers, of the 16th. October instant. By T. R. Weeton. *Bolton.* Printed by J. Yates. Express Office. 1824.

A REPLY to a Late Pamphlet published by Mr. Weeton. An Attorney at Leigh. *London.* Printed by J. H. Cox. Lambeth Road. South-wark. n.d.

MRS. BEVAN'S WILL: MR. WEETON's Statement of Facts as to the preparation by him of MRS. BEVAN's various WILLS and CODICILS. *Leigh:* Executed at F. William's General Printing-Office, Market-Street. 1833.

MRS. BEVAN'S LETTER to MR. WEETON, in Reply to his Pamphlet Sent to Her, Entitled [as above.] *Wigan:* Printed at the Office of D. Critchley, Market-Place. n.d.

[1] It is still the custom in Wigan to order by the 'score'—a score of apples or a score of potatoes.

your father a part, my love; I know he is fond of them; but
do not on any account eat more yourself than 6 or 8 in a
day of the Walnuts; a larger number would make you ill,
and take away your appetite. The Cocoa Nut was 6*d*, the
Walnuts 1*s*. the hundred. I tell you the prices, that you
may understand the general value of such things, and to
give you as much knowledge as I am able of the prices of
many of the common articles of sale; for you will never be fit
to be a housekeeper until you know the value of most things
in daily use. Do not open the basket until you get home.

I have written this letter by candle light, which is rather
distressing to me, for I can see but imperfectly, even with
two candles, and I cannot do with less; yet I can see
almost anything with bright day-light; but I think you will
read it easily.

Your holidays are very near; I hope they will be spent
very agreeably.

Christmas-day, Dec. 25th. is my birthday; don't forget
me on that day.

To MISS HAWARDEN, Wigan.   Prescot Feb. 3. 1825.

I have been expecting to hear from you, my dear Miss
Hawarden, for this fortnight past, as Mrs. Bent said she
would inquire if Mary was returning again to Parr Hall,
and inform you that you might let me know. May I ask
the favour of you to write immediately, to inform me
where she is?

I have been passing my time in almost total solitude
since I was with you; but it was much the same at Holland
—and much the same at Wigan, and—all my life time;
still, I can never be so used as to be reconciled to it. So it
is with all females of small incomes who have no families
and few or no relations; if forced to live in lodgings, they
are shut out from domestic comforts and a social fireside—
the very kind of life that the most valuable part of either

sex would prefer. A single woman so situated, is a poor lost creature, and those who ought to be the protectors of such, are often the insulters! the ruiners! and the persecutors! Oh, what a heavy judgment will those fathers, those brothers, and those husbands have to undergo, who are the cause of so much female suffering.

I have certainly passed this Winter more comfortably and cheerfully than the 3 preceding ones, for my present *cage* is light, which the other was not.

I have not been in Liverpool since I was with you in Wigan, until Monday last, when I left home a little before 9 and had a very agreeable walk, the road was so dry.[1] On my way, hearing a gig following me where there was no footpath, and the middle of the road overspread with logs of wood, I turned round to see on which side the gig was overtaking me, that I might give way. I was on the right side, and I found the gig was coming on the same side. Immediately I crossed through the mud to the left side, and had scarcely done so, when the gig was driven across likewise, and I was in danger of being run over. I looked at the driver, and was surprised to find the gentleman who had so little politeness to an unprotected and accommodating woman, was Mr. Kearsley of Wigan, who was driving, and Thomas Sutton with him. The sight of Thomas was like a dagger through me; he is a perjured wretch, and for the present, he is suffered to triumph in his perjury. The natural buoyancy of my temper enabled me to soon surmount the effects of this little mean insult, and, finding a decent young woman on the road, we continued the remainder of the way together, for mutual protection. How very common it is for men to insult unprotected women, for whom there should be a universal feeling of pity; their very helplessness should be their safe-

---

[1] The mildness of the preceding month, January, had excited general comment, rendering walking not only a possibility, but a pleasure.

guard, and it should be a common principle of honour and feeling in all men, ever to afford protection to, and at the least, to avoid insulting an unprotected woman.

I walked half way back again, and then got into the caravan[1] just before dusk, for I dared not walk alone by moonlight; one of the male passengers observed that all four on our side (for we were 7 in all) were none of us very heavy. I replied, that whenever I travelled, I always found it very convenient to myself and my companions, to be thin; for I required little more than sky room, and of that there was always plenty. When about a mile from Prescot, the same man said, he thought we should get home by moonlight. 'We surely shall,' said I, dryly, 'or else we must ride all night,' for the moon was then shining finely, and likely to do so till 5 o'clock in the morning—at which speed, had we not arrived by moonlight, we must have been 11 hours in going a mile, as it was then 6 o'clock in the evening. I set the whole company a-laughing; for I durst have wagered all England, to travel in a one horse carriage at that rate, and have been sure of being beaten, by which I should have been the winner.

Give my kind respects to your mother.

To MISS STOCK, Parr Hall, St. Helens.

Prescot March 8 1825.

It is near 3 months, my dear, dear Mary, since I last wrote to you. Have you been thinking, my love, that I had quite forgotten you? If you have thought so, I do not wonder; yet indeed, my dear child, I never do forget you. I do not certainly know where you are, and that uncer-

[1] This 'caravan' would be that of Sothern's, which plied daily (with the exception of Tuesdays) between Liverpool and Prescot. The term caravan was usually applied to Pickford's vans, for the transport only of goods. Readers of *Tom Brown's Schooldays* will remember the 'two-oss wan, more like a hearse nor a coach', as contemptuously dismissed by Tom's guard. They were (not unaptly, as the moonlight journey of Miss Weeton and her companions illustrates) popularly termed 'sociables'.

tainty has prevented my writing before now; but in the supposition that you are at Parr Hall, I at last make the attempt. Do you often think of me? Do you often talk of me? I hope you do, for you have not a better, or a more sincere friend in the world. I cannot give you money, nor that which money has bought; but, Mary, I can bestow that which millions of pounds can never purchase—a mother's love.

I dare say that it will give you pleasure to know that I am well. I am blessed indeed with excellent health, and have been for 3 years, growing stronger as I grow older; but that can only be for a time. I expect the usual approaches of infirmity which age brings, but I am at present as lively, cheerful, and healthy, as I was at 25 years old; and yet I am 48—very near 50, Mary, is it not? Your father is 49; he is just 11 months older than I am; your father's birth-day is on the 24th. of January, and so is my brother's, your uncle Weeton af Leigh; which is rather remarkable, only he is 5 years younger. I suppose you never see him—he is no friend of yours.

I have been very comfortable at Prescot since I came to live in it; the people I live with, treat me kindly and respectfully, and wait upon me in almost every thing I want; but I always, wherever I am, take care to give as little trouble as possible. When I first came to R. Tyrer's, I did not think I should have staid a month with them, as I do not like the situation of the house; I thought only to have staid with them until I could suit myself better, but their great civility has made me so comfortable, that I have remained for the Winter.

To MISS HAWARDEN, Wigan.　Prescot March 11 1825.

Your information, my dear Miss Hawarden, that Mr. Stock had purchased an estate in West Derby,[1] was quite

[1] West Derby is a suburb of Liverpool. Mr. Stock did not apparently

new to me; neither have I been able to hear any thing
further; whether he is going to live at it, who lived there
last, what he has given for it, or the exact situation. I
should like to know some additional particulars.

I am writing to you upon paper which I bought in
London at 5d. p. Quire, so don't be saucy and call it
shabby. I shall inclose yours in one to Miss Braithwaite
on a sister-sheet; and sure it was bought in Lunnon too,
for did I not buy it there my own sel; and if I could but
have known how long I should live, I would have bought
as much as would have lasted my life; and, alack a day, I
did but buy one Quire, and sorrow to me, I may happen
outlive it, and then what will I do?

You do not know my direction, you say—Humph! and
do ye think I'm sic a tiny body, that Mrs. Jackson's must
be added to mine, afore they can discover me.

Have the Literati of Wigan commenced a Newspaper
yet? I apprehend they have not, as I have seen no an-
nouncement. Perhaps if they knew—the learned ones of
Wigan—that so able a pen as mine might be engaged in
their service, they would proceed; tell 'em, will you?[1]

Why did you not remind me, when I was at Wigan at
Christmas, to mend or make you some pens? I am sure I
was as willing, as able; don't neglect the next feathery
opportunity. Bring some Quills with you, or old Pens to
renovate,[2] as soon as Lent is over, and stay a while with
me at Prescot, and we can see Liverpool some day; for next

take up residence there. There were grounds for the rumour, as shortly
afterwards he went to reside at Seneley Green, Ashton-in-Mackerfield, no
doubt to superintend his new interests in coal-mining.

[1] Two ambitious, but short-lived, attempts to establish local newspapers
occurred during her subsequent residence in Wigan, but neither contain
any contribution attributable to her pen.

[2] Steel pens had been introduced as far back as the year 1803, but Miss
Weeton was true to her quill, and her writing continues as firm and bold as
ever at this period. Her office as quill-mender must have been greatly
appreciated by her friends, as, owing to rapid wear, they had to be purchased by the score, by the unskilled in the art of 'fining'.

month, I have no doubt but we shall have some fine weather.

Give my kind respects to your Mother.

To MISS BRAITHWAITE, Up-Holland.

Prescot March 11 1825.

How are you all going on at Holland? as like vegetables as ever? or do you approximate to locomotive steam engines?[1] are you torpid in the Winter at your *foreign* country? or do you burrow in holes in some seasons; or are you like piss-i'th-mires,[2] minding nobody's business but your own, and always swarming on your own hillock? I am fond of natural history, and should be glad to know, having heard little of your *distant* land lately, or of what kind of creatures grow there.

Give my respects to Mary, and tell her I am looking forward to the period when the light of her countenance will shine upon Prescot, as I am led to expect it will be next month.

Remember me to Mrs. Ducker and Miss Dannett; and say to Mrs. Dannett, that I have never called upon Mrs. Green about the lodgings, as the situation is not open enough. I think I shall not move until I can find apartments in Fall Lane or the Market-place, at a rent not exceeding what I give here. The worst of it here, is, my bed is too small for more than one person, so that I cannot offer half a bed to a friend for a night or two, neither could I cook in the day, so that I must look out for better accommodation before very long.

I have to thank Mrs. Ducker for my introduction to 2 or 3 families here. Soon after Mrs. Ducker left Prescot at

---

[1] This was the year of the opening of the Stockton and Darlington line for passenger traffic. The Bill for the Liverpool and Manchester Railway went into Committee of the House of Commons in this month, and all Lancashire was agog.   [2] Ants.

Christmas, Mrs. Johnson invited me to tea; last week, Mrs. Pickford invited me to tea & supper. Mr. Brown's were there, and they all seem quite friendly disposed towards me.[1]

✳   ✳   ✳

[JOURNAL]

March 4. I paid my first visit to Mrs. Pickford.

Sunday March 20. I had, from the first of my coming to Prescot, intended that as soon as the Winter was over, and the weather fine enough, I would make a practice of going to St. Helen's on a Sunday, or any other day that was likely for Mary to be met with: this day, therefore, I set out immediately after dinner, and walked through St. Helen's, and about a mile beyond I saw Mr. Grundy's young ladies approaching over the bridge, a little on this side of Parr Hall; and for fear they should see me and perhaps take Mary back again into the house, and so prevent my meeting with her, I slipped into a cottage close by, until they all arrived opposite to it. I then issued forth and joined my little darling, who, with two others, was walking close after two of the teachers. I fell into the rank and walked to St. Helen's. Miss Hammond seemed agitated, but what cared I? She appeared inclined to be insolent when I apologized for coming in such a manner; but I avoided altercation—what an unfeeling world this is! none but married women seem to have any tenderness.

I chatted to my dear girl as well as I could, but our peculiar situation threw a great deal of restraint upon us. Mr. Grundy and Miss Jackson were no where to be seen— courting perhaps. I left Mary near Tontine Street, thinking it was as prudent for the present not to go to Chapel

---

[1] [*Orig. note to above, not included in letter.*] Mem. I have not been to Mrs. Johnson's any more, nor has she yet been prevailed with to come and see me, so that I have derived little advantage as yet from the introduction.

with her. I can meet her there, perhaps, some day if Mr. Grumblety does not make a fuss and write to Mr. Stock about it—which I hope he will be simple enough to do, for I much wish Mary to be taken away from the school; so that I shall effect the latter purpose by going on Sundays, if I miss the other; and either is better than as it has been. Poor Mary may be kept up for a while, but that cannot last for ever.

22nd. Set off to Liverpool on foot at $\frac{1}{2}$ past 8 o'clock, and prevailed with Mrs. Price to accompany me from Seymour St. to Mr. Perkins, 14 Roscoe Lane, brother-in-law to Mr. Stock, to request his mediation, and that of Mrs. Perkins, to prevail with Mr. Stock to let me have more liberty in seeing Mary, and to increase my income. Mrs. Perkins was not at home. Mr. Perkins was so kind and friendly, that I was quite rejoiced and grateful; he promised me to make the attempt.[1] I returned home, feeling as if God had prospered my going out this day, as well as on Sunday.

*　　　　　*　　　　　*

To MR. STOCK, Standish, near Wigan.

Prescot March 25 1825.

Mr. Stock

Let me request your considerate and calm attention to what in this letter I am about to urge. A strong sense of duty alone is my motive, and a friendship for you as sincere as ever was in the bosom of any human being, notwithstanding all the afflictions you have caused me.

It would be very consoling, could I be permitted to use a term warmer than that of friendship; let me at least ask for yours in return; be my friend, and be no longer my

[1] Later, Miss Weeton followed up this visit with an impassioned plea by letter to Mr. Perkins, soliciting his direct intervention on her behalf, on the lines suggested in her letter to her husband, which follows.

enemy; and in the present instance, let me beg that a candid and benevolent construction may be put upon what I say, and upon my intentions; and indeed, upon all occasions, for I never had any sinister motives, I never was selfish, I never was malicious. Your benefit, and that of your family, was my sole study from the hour I married you, of which I give you daily proofs.

Allow me those comforts you can so well afford me. If you gave me 200£ a year, it will only be what you ought to do, when your own circumstances are considered; and you would never miss it. It would be far from half your income; yet you swore to endow me with *all your* worldly goods, which surely means one half of every thing. I swore the same oath, and *gave you all*; and never, whilst I lived with you, asked for any thing in return but your affection and tenderness, friendship and protection, your confidence, and as much money from week to week as would merely keep the family in comfort. Was I unreasonable? Oh no, and if you had not been made the dupe of mischief makers, we might still be as happy a couple as most in our own rank. Those evil counsellors, who were constantly endeavouring to poison your mind against me, were your enemies; under the insidious cloak of friendship, they were only studying to obtain money from you, or some advancement by your means, unfeelingly working your misery as well as mine. I saw plainly into their views; then, what was the intense anguish of my mind, when I saw you fall into their snares, entrapped by their fine, fawning, flowery speeches.

Be assured that my enemies are yours; and they are only mine, hoping to get something out of you; for were you poor, and I rich tomorrow, they would the same day turn from you, and endeavour to attach themselves to me. There are some who endeavour to keep up your prejudices against me, by ridiculing and speaking contemptuously of me—they are but bloodsuckers! If they were Christians, they would strive daily to make peace between us. But let your own sense of a Christian husband's conduct, induce you to treat me more liberally.

I only wish for what you can well spare, without depriving yourself of a single comfort—a better income, and the same liberty of seeing my child that you have. My income is much too small, considering your circumstances; you would raise yourself much in the estimation of all respectable people if you would not act so penuriously towards me. I can but just procure myself the common comforts of life, but my narrow income shuts me out of either genteel lodgings or society. There are many families of great respectability, who have known me from a child, and with whom I could now be on terms of intimacy, could I afford it.

It is certainly a hardship that I must be obliged to live in other people's houses, or in a little mean house by myself. A comfortable, small house, respectably furnished, and one servant, with the means of dressing respectably, and of enjoying intelligent society at a moderate expence, is not an unreasonable desire. I ask no more than 200£ a year *for life only*, and your means are so ample that you would not even feel the poorer for it. And reflect how meek and patient I have been ever since I left you, although you have made me suffer daily; yet my conduct in every respect has been most exemplary.

I have heard a report that you have settled 600£ a year upon Mary, and only 200£ upon Jane. If this be true, let me intreat that you will alter it. Is not Jane equally a child with Mary? and why make a difference. Had you left Mary only 200£ a year, I would not have said a word.

You and I are verging upon 50; when Mary is grown up, we may be both dead, and if Mary has not Jane for an affectionate sister, she will be but a lost creature, with all her money; for, as to my brother's family, his unnatural conduct in never calling to see her, is proof enough what she has to expect in that quarter. I earnestly hope that you will consider this, and be not offended with me in touching on a subject that I have long had at heart.

Oh, that you would, with the feelings of a Christian husband, as well as a father, yet listen to my wishes, in allowing me to see my child without restraint. She would be better under my care than that of any other person; she has not been placed under the care of any one equally able to instil firmer principles into her mind, or more decided piety. You are not aware, perhaps, that when you took her from me, you placed her with a drunken woman; and that she is permitted to visit occasionally at a house where the mistress of it is a drunkard. She has never looked so well since she was taken from under my care, as she did before; and if she must have a chance for health and strength, a mother's care is necessary.

I have written at great length; excuse me, for I have but seldom troubled you. Look with an eye of candour on what I have said, and attribute none but the kindliest motives to me.

Yours respectfully
N. Stock.

*　　　*　　　*

[JOURNAL]

March 29th. Tuesday. As Mary had requested me last Sunday but one to buy a few Prunes and some Spanish Juice for her, I had no way of conveying them to her but by taking them myself to the old woman at the cottage, near Parr Hall gate; so this morning I purchased, and took them. It was a lovely morning, and I had a very pleasant walk. I sat about ¼ of an hour with the old woman, who promised to take up the parcel to the Hall, and give it to the cook, which she said was the only way, for otherwise Mary would not get it. When I had arrived within a quarter of a mile of St. Helen's on my return, I heard a horse following; the rider was on the trot, but slackened pace when he came up with me. I had my parasol up, and never turned my head to look at him, but kept my face covered with my parasol whilst he was approaching. I was imagining it might be Mr. Grundy following me, to give me some information or other, and when for a minute he walked by my side, I peeped a little under my parasol, and saw the legs of a fine horse, and the accoutrements of a well saddled one, but raised my eyes or uncovered my face no further—how fortunate that I did not! for, when he had got a few yards before me, I ventured to look out, and—beheld Mr. Stock! dressed in a beautiful dark puce-coloured coat, and every thing else corresponding. He was either tipsy, or one of his nervous agitations had come upon him; he wriggled and twitched upon the horse most comically, pulling the horse to stop, and whipping to make it go. At length, the harrassed animal tried what a trot would do, and away they went, jogglety, jogglety, and were soon out of my sight. Mr. Stock never saw my face, and whether he knew me, I cannot say; I suspect he did.

It was very unlucky I should be overtaken so short a way from Parr Hall; had I been nearer Prescot, I should not have cared; he will suspect my errand, and the old woman at the cottage will be prevented admitting me again. I dare say he was at Parr Hall whilst I was at the cottage—it cannot be helped now!

It was Mary herself who told me, that her aunt Perkins last Christmas, when she was at Mr. Stock's house for a part of Mary's holidays, urged him every day to alter his present system as regarded his wife and child. I had not an opportunity of asking Mary more particularly what it was precisely that her aunt said to her father, but it raised my hopes so much, that 2 days after, I walked to Liverpool and called upon them.

April 6. Went by Sothern's caravan to Liverpool. The dust was almost intolerable; for the last fortnight, nay, 3 weeks or a month, we have had no rain, but beautiful, bright, sun-shining weather, such as I never remember in March, and so early in April before. It is as fine and warm as June, with the exception of frosty nights.

The roads laid on McAdam's plan, are better for carriages and easier for draught horses, but for human beings in dry weather, are almost beyond endurance; they are one continued cloud of dust, blinding to the eyes, filling the nostrils, going down the mouth and throat by quantities to suffocation, and completely ruinous to all decent cloathing. Houses by the road are inundated with dust, and all cleanliness destroyed and useless. The fields are so covered on each side, according as the wind blows, that they are of much less value an acre, than those more distant from it. If Mr. McAdam could lay the dust as *well* as the roads, he would be a clever fellow.[1]

To all present appearance, the dry weather will continue some weeks longer, and will perhaps be a forerunner of aweful thunderings and even earthquakes. Whether we in this part of England shall suffer from the latter effect, I cannot tell, but I should not be surprised if we did, and I am really expecting something of the kind in some part of the kingdom.

I spent a pleasant day in Liverpool, calling at Mrs. Roxburgh's; then, going to the Panorama in Tarleton St.; next, walking down to the Regent's Pier; the tide was up, and the water without a wave; 'twas beauteous! Return-

[1] 'Water-bound' macadam roads are still in use on lightly trafficked roads, and according to the 1931 Traffic census, observation posts were located on 2,686 'tarmacadam' stretches—roads surfaced on macadam principles with the addition of a modern tar binding.

ing, I proceeded to Miss Dalrymple's, and talked with her of an intended Tour into N. Wales. At 4 o'clock I set off home on foot, and but for McAdam's dust, should have had a pleasant walk home. I was up to the knees in dust; aye, and further.[1]

In all, about 11 miles.

*   *   *

To MRS. STOPFORD, Roby Mill. near Up-Holland.

Prescot Apr. 9 1825.

In acknowledging the receipt of the Quarter's annuity, due 25th. of March last, I address myself to you, my dear Mrs. Stopford, and through your medium, to express my thanks to Mr. Stopford for the attention he has ever paid to the transmitting the money to me so regularly.

I am glad to find, from Miss M. Braithwaite, that she believes you are all in good health. I was inquiring particularly after Mrs. Smith, and she informs me that she is very active and well, considering her years, which I was much pleased to hear; for I have always felt a great respect for her. When Mrs. Braithwaite was taken, I felt as if I had lost a mother; but there are three left, that have at one period or another, been as mothers to me—Mrs. Smith, Mrs. Hawarden, and Mrs. Marsden; they shewed

---

[1] Adam was made of borrow'd dust;
    So says the Bible; and 'tis plain,
    Macadam, to discharge the trust,
    To dust turns all *the ways of men.*
                    The Economist and General Adviser, 1824.

That the dust plague was universal, there is frequent evidence. About this time Miss Mitford, another sufferer by a very near relative, and, like Miss Weeton, a great walker, was voicing the public mind upon this vexed subject:

'Oh, dusty world! No foot could make three plunges into that abyss of pulverized gravel, which had the impudence to call itself a hard road, without being clothed with a coat a quarter of an inch thick. Woe to white gowns! Woe to black! Drab was your only wear.'
                    Miss Mitford: *Our Village.*

kindness to me when I was in affliction, and may Heaven be their reward.

I cannot but express my approbation at your kindness in giving an asylum to poor Mrs. Littler.[1] I feel deeply concerned for her. I had long suspected that she was a sufferer like myself; hers is a situation most miserable! none can have even a distant idea of it, but they who have suffered likewise. I hope she will have friends more willing to exert themselves for her than any I ever had, that she may not fall a sacrifice, as I have done, to brutality, depravity, hypocrisy, falsehood, and an unfeeling world.

Had I one real friend *even now*, I should not be deprived of my child as I am, and pining, friendless, and in solitude, a wanderer on the face of the earth, without a home, and no prospect of any thing better so long as I live. And what is painful to the last degree in situations like Mrs. Littler's and mine, when our husbands use us cruelly, the whole world are open-mouthed against us too, instead of pitying, soothing, and comforting us. A wife, though her conduct be as correct as mortal's can be, yet if her husband unnaturally drives her from his roof, from the ferocity of his own disposition, she is avoided as if she were infamous. This is cruelty to cruelty; yet so have I found it, and so I fear will poor Mrs. Littler. My heart bleeds for her; but if she have any determined friends, they may do much. Your family are tender-hearted, we can both say, and much comfort have you bestowed upon us.

A few months ago, I heard of an affair as regards Miss Stopford, which pleased me greatly—I mean, that she made her father and mother her confidants, as regarded Mr. Battersby; yet the company I heard it in, were all against Miss Stopford for having done so, and called her

---

[1] Wife of Dr. Thomas Caldwell Littler, to whose memory a tablet was erected in Upholland Church, recording his services as surgeon for 27 years in this district.

silly and foolish, and said she would know better another time than tell her papa and mamma. Tell her from me, as one of the sincerest friends she has, that she never can know better, and that I hope she will invariably act in the same way. Whoever advises her to keep any thing secret from her parents, are her decided enemies, and theirs too; they are only seeking their own interest, and if she had no prospect of any fortune, they would not give themselves the trouble so much as to speak to her.

[JOURNAL]

Sunday, Apr. 10. At one o'clock in the afternoon, I took a walk to St. Helen's to meet my little darling again; an unusual trepidation and anxiety seized me as I went, but exerting as much fortitude as possible, I endeavoured to divert my thoughts by the beauties of the scenery; for indeed, my indulgent Father had gilded the prospect by a glorious sun and a clear atmosphere. I proceeded to the farther part of St. Helen's, but had not met my child. My knees trembled so, that I went into one of a row of cottages where a fruit shop was kept, and requested leave to sit down. A very neat-looking young married woman was in, and was very civil indeed. As I sat waiting, I told her my situation as regarded my child, and she seemed to pity me much. I said I was afraid that when Mr. Grundy and Mr. Stock found that I made a practice of meeting her on the way to Chapel, they would prevent her going; but I had no other method left, and I considered it to be my duty to see her in any way I could. I was afraid that this might be the last time; and I added, 'Judge then what must be my feelings at this moment,'—for I was very faint.

Bye and bye Miss Jackson, the head teacher, came past, and the whole train of boarders; my anxiety confused my sight, and I could not recognize my Mary. I sat in a corner by the window, so that they could not see me; for I was afraid the young woman might suffer some unpleasant treatment on my account if they saw who afforded me shelter; for such is Mr. Stock's unceasing bitter and dreadful persecution against me, and I should be sorry that a single human being should lose so much as a penny on my account, or have one uneasy moment.

When the whole of the Parr Hall family had passed, I issued forth and hastened to overtake them, that I might be quite sure whether Mary was there. I asked Miss Hammond, one of the teachers who walked last, whether Mary was there; she replied she was at the front, with a very haughty, forbidding nod, which I cannot soon forget. Oh, my Father, have pity, have pity on thy suffering servant! Thou knowest that from my fellow creatures I deserve not this cruel treatment.

I hastened forward and saw my Mary next after Miss Jackson; the change from Winter habiliments to Summer ones, had been one means of preventing my knowing her. Miss Jackson spoke and looked kindly. Heaven bless her for it! but it is in her very nature. We were soon at Chapel, and I determined on entering, that I might enjoy the sight of my child another hour. Miss Jackson directed me to the Pew next Mary's. During service, Mary became very faint; poor child! I know thy feelings are harrassed. One of the young ladies, apparently about 14, looked at me with a peculiar degree of compassion. On coming out, Mr. Grundy and Wm. Woodward (Mr. Stock's brother-in-law) had got their heads together, talking in a low tone. Mr. Grundy perhaps was afraid that Wm. Woodward might tell Mr. Stock that he had seen me at Chapel in Mr. Grundy's pew, as if Mr. G. encouraged me, and so perhaps he was explaining.

I took leave of Mary at the Chapel door, timid and spiritless, afraid of going to too great lengths; yet Mary's indisposition would well have justified me in going part of the way homeward with her. I have repented ever since that I had not; but I have not the spirit of a mouse. I was just arrived at the outskirts of St. Helen's when two young women speaking to me by name, requested I would go with them home to tea. I hesitated a moment, not knowing them, but their looks were kindly, and I, expressing myself pleased with the friendliness of their manner, accompanied them. They led me near a mile, and I began to wonder where they were taking me to. At length, they made up to a gentleman's house and grounds. Will they lead me to the front door, thought I; but I inquired not. At last they entered a cottage in an out-building, where was an elderly, sickly-looking woman, laid on a sopha, and there I sat down.

They had heard of my situation, and offered me the calling there at any time when I wished to meet with Mary at Chapel, as it lay between St. Helens and Prescot, and in Summer is a very pleasant way through fields. The Almighty raises me Comforters among the poor, if I want friends among the rich. They appeared to be a pious family, and told me they rented the garden belonging to the late Col. Fraser, whose house it had been which I had just passed. I felt much pleased with the mother and daughters; there was a good deal of fine expression in their countenances.

I found from them that Wm. Woodward was much my enemy. Alas! he is poor and will turn to either side for money.

*　　　*　　　*

To MISS DENNETT,[1] Up-Holland.

Prescot Apr. 15 1825.

The very great kindness, my dear Miss Dennett, of your conduct towards me, and your long continued friendliness,

[1] Miss Margery Dannett, of Holland Grove, died in April 1846, aged 75, though she was not at that time residing at Holland Grove. Miss Weeton

and likewise that of Mrs. Ducker, induces me at this time to make a request, which if you comply with, may possibly be of essential service to me, and will, I hope, be no great trouble to you, although it must be some.

I will state what it is. A few months ago, it was suggested to me by one who well knew Mr. Stock's temper, that if I could get a petition to him, drawn up as a testimonial of the natural goodness of my temper, my patience, mildness, disinterestedness, integrity, piety, generosity, humanity, &c., and signed by those who have known me well, that it would be the most probable means to induce him to permit me the frequent and *unrestricted* liberty of seeing my child. My talents, my prudence, or my abstemiousness, he never called in question, I am told. These, therefore, are not so necessary to insert; yet it may be as well to include them.

When this was first mentioned to me, I knew not how to set about it; for I could not write it myself in my own praise; neither could I tell who to apply to; but my distress about my poor, delicate child, urges me to lay aside all nicety and diffidence, and to ask you—if you can conscientiously, and with that regard to truth so evident in all I have ever known of you, and which I desire you to adhere to now, assist me in forwarding such a business. I think Henry Latham, with your instructions, would be well able to draw it up, so as to be taken for signatures to all those in Holland and its neighbourhood who have long known me, and are willing to do so; for I would desire none to sign who cannot do it heartily.

For a little while I would have it kept very secret, until it is drawn up and I have seen it, lest any thing should require altering; for that reason, as my Cousin Latham is not very good at secret keeping, if you would be kind

indifferently varies the spelling of her name—sometimes Dannett, and alternatively Dennett.

enough to send for Henry to your house, I should be obliged.

The children I had at school, can testify how far from severe, or violent, I was with them, and how fond they were of me at all times, so that even in play hours they were not happy without me; it was quite an affectionate contest amongst them, which should be nearest to me, who should go to walk with me, or spend a Winter's evening at my house. My cousin Latham knows that I never charged her a farthing schoolwages for her two boys, yet at that time I was very poor. I had generally one of Mr. Billington's for nothing, and sometimes two; and many other children I taught gratis.

Miss Heyes, of Holland Moor, would I think, obtain some signatures. The Hootons of Orrel Post, and others.

When completed, if Mr. Stopford could be induced to present it to Mr. Stock, and could call in the aid of one or two respectable gentlemen besides, they might render me an essential service. As an act of benevolence, Mr. Stopford might be induced to prevail with Mr. Gaskell of Holland, and of Wigan too, to assist him. And, if, after all, there is no good done, it can do no harm; and you shall all have my lasting and sincere gratitude.

I should be glad if Miss Braithwaite and Mr. Bird would assist in promoting it. I have not yet mentioned it to Mrs. T. Jackson, but mean to do so.[1]

Every one I have lived with, I am sure, would sign it (out of Mr. Stock's family), and many of my servants.

If several gentlemen together, of wealth and influence, would call on Mr. Stock with it, I sincerely believe he would comply, particularly if Mr. Gaskell of Wigan would be one.

---

[1] Nicholas Heyes, the three local Gaskells, and Mr. Stopford are all listed in a contemporary Roll Book, as Surveyors of the Roads. The Rev. John Bird, B.A., succeeded the notorious Rev. T. Meyrick (1802–21) as incumbent of Upholland church.

To MISS HAWARDEN, Wigan.   Prescot April 16 1825.

As you promised to write again, I thought I would write no more till I had first heard from you; but having seen my Mary lately, by meeting her on the way to Chapel on a Sunday, and finding that Mr. Stock cultivates an intimacy on Mary's account with the Robys, it has occurred to me that Mrs. Roby, whom I know to be a feeling woman, might be prevailed on to exert herself with Mr. Stock to induce him to allow me to see Mary without *any restrictions*. Could you be prevailed upon to try your powers of persuasion with Mrs. Roby? and to induce her likewise to use her utmost influence with Mr. and Mrs. Alston; for I do think something might be done, if they would frequently speak to Mr. Stock upon the subject, saying a little at a time, and representing it to be his duty to shew kindness to me (for hitherto, I fear, they have encouraged him in his bitterness).

Mary's health requires a mother's care; there is not a girl in the whole school who looks so ill. Mr. Grundy always represents her as enjoying good health—with no better motive, I fear, than the emolument of her board; for I hear a very poor character of him, both in Prescot and St. Helen's, for meanness, avarice, and bad temper. Mrs. Grundy, it is said, never knew a moment's happiness after she married him. It is very necessary that Mary should, for a year or two, be unconfined in any school, or she will be thrown into a consumption; besides, it is astonishing to many, that Mr. G's school should flourish as it does, with a widower like him at the head of it, and a set of young unmarried women only, to manage it. I have a high opinion of Miss Jackson, but she cannot act against Mr. G's will in any thing; her situation depends upon pleasing him.

I do not wonder that Mr. Grundy should have taken

the pains he has, to prevent my coming to Parr Hall to see Mary, after what I hear; he is afraid I should discover deficiencies which cannot be observed in general by any but visitors at the house, owing to his retired situation. He has stood in his own light, I think; for I heard a few days ago that Mary was to leave the school, which I hope is true. Had Mr. Grundy been quiet, I could have gone to Parr Hall, and no one scarcely could have known it, it is so secluded; but now that I have been forced to resort to the method of seeing her on the way to Chapel, she will not remain long, I dare say. If she be taken away soon, she will probably be sent elsewhere; but if Mrs. Roby would lose no time, but get her husband likewise to second her, Mr. Alston's, or any others who have any influence with Mr. Stock, something may be done.

Mary has evidently, to many, worsened in her looks ever since she was taken from under my care. Mr. Price was noticing it when he saw her in Liverpool some months ago.

I went to Liverpool purposely about 3 weeks ago to see Mr. and Mrs. Perkins (Mr. Stock's sister) on the subject. Mr. Perkins only was at home; he promised his influence, but I fear Mrs. Perkins is against me as I never have heard more. I have since written to them very earnestly, but have received no answer.

To MISS STOCK, Parr Hall.   Prescot April 22 1825.

When you open the parcel, my dear love, you will find the print which I have procured for you; there are two patterns, a yard each. I hope it will be enough; if not, I will purchase as much more as you may want.[1]

I have some thoughts of taking a little excursion for a

---

[1] To procure this material for her daughter, Miss Weeton walked to Liverpool and back—'sadly fatigued—20 miles'.

few weeks this Summer, to the neighbourhood of Bangor
(which is in Wales). I would make the tour of Wales if I
had but money enough; but as I have very little, I am
obliged to be very careful, and if I go a journey anywhere,
I must live very sparingly for many weeks before I go, that
I may save enough to pay travelling expences and the rent
of lodgings; for, deprived as I am of your dear society, my
beloved Mary, I find change of scenery quite necessary
for my health and spirits. I should weep till I died for
the want of you, if I did not strive all I could to amuse
myself by going from home sometimes. I would travel
much if I had money enough, but as I am poor, I am
obliged to let it alone; for coach hire is too expensive, and
I have not strength enough to walk to every place I should
wish to go. If I stay at home, I become low spirited for
want of your entertaining company; for I cannot afford to
invite my acquaintances often. And besides, as I cannot
keep a servant, it is so much trouble to wait upon them
myself, that it prevents all the pleasure of their society,
and I do not choose to visit where it is inconvenient to
invite them again.

If I were rich enough to buy furniture, and to take a
house and keep a servant, I could have as much society—
highly respectable—as I could wish; for I have many
friends who invite me often, and treat me with great kindness, but I frequently decline their invitations, except at
Mr. T. Jackson's; but I avoid going to tea even there often,
for I am of opinion that it is mean to eat at another's
expence where I cannot conveniently bestow as much
again. I often go after tea and remain till bed-time, taking
no supper; for I seldom eat any. I consider supper eaten
at 8, 9, or 10 o'clock, as it generally is, as most extremely
pernicious to the health, and the cause of many diseases,
and increases many complaints that have arisen from
other causes, whether consumptive, bilious, scorbutic, or

apoplectic; for which reason, do you, my dear Mary, avoid eating anything after 6 or 7 o'clock in an evening.

Present my respects to Miss Jackson. Good bye, my dear girl.

*   *   *

[JOURNAL]

May 7th. Saturday. I went to Liverpool this morning, in the caravan, to make the necessary inquiries as to the facility of procuring lodgings in Bangor, lest if I set out and could not easily procure them after my arrival, I should be obliged to return again the following day by the Packet I went in. Mr. Dalrymple says I need not hesitate; for, so early in the season, I am sure to obtain lodgings any time after I get there.

8th. Sunday. Set out at 1 o'clock to meet my Mary again at Chapel; this is the 3d time that I have done so. Just arrived in time to see her and her schoolfellows enter the Chapel, and I followed in, seating myself in an opposite Pew. When service was over, I joined her and walked part of the way towards Parr Hall with her, and but for the rain, would have gone farther. We had a good deal of chatter. I thought she looked rather better. 8½ miles.

9th. I left home at 12 at noon, and walked to Holland (11 m.), for I found, from Miss Dannett's answer to my letter, that she had greatly mistaken my meaning, or else that she was become quite a different woman to what I had ever known her before; for indeed, her letter was so cool and unkind, that it required all my fortitude to bear it with composure, and I never saw any unkindness when I was with her, and I have always heard that she expressed the greatest esteem for me to others. She decidedly refused my request in her letter; but I found when I saw her, that she was still what I had ever seen her before, and complied without hesitation, and even with apparent pleasure, to serve me. How unaccountable are these

354

things! I took no notice of the unkindness of her letter, to her; some other time, I may.

On Tuesday, I sent a boy to fetch Henry Latham, who came that evening and put the business in such a train, that I can do without being obliged to the unwilling; for I have reason to think that a great number will cordially sign the testimonial to my disposition and character. There is nothing like bestirring one's self in one's own affairs. Miss Dannett thought that I wanted her to go about the country to get signatures. No such thing! but I knew she could easily *send* to various places, she knows so many people, many of whom, passing her door, would readily have done it and have forwarded it themselves without giving her the trouble of going beyond her own gate. Miss Braithwaite and Miss Heyes promised to sign.

13. Walked to Liverpool after dinner, to inquire the hour the Bangor Packet would sail on Thursday, the 19th., and to request Mrs. Roxburgh would permit me to sleep there the previous night. I intended to ride home in Southern's caravan, but had walked 2 miles towards Prescot before he overtook me. I then got in. (10 miles).

15 Sunday. Immediately after dinner, I set off to St. Helen's to see my Mary once more; as I was a little too soon for Chapel, I walked down the road from St. Helen's to meet her, about ½ a mile, and returned with her to Chapel, sitting in an opposite Pew. As soon as service was over, Miss Jackson, the head teacher, crossed over to me, and told me Mr. Grundy desired her to ask me if I knew the consequence of my repeated visits to St. Helen's. I knew well enough the purport of the question, but thought there might be something further. 'What consequences?' I inquired with a smile. 'Mary would certainly be removed,' she replied. 'If I don't see her at all, it matters not to me,' I said, 'where she is.' (I had like to have said, nobody will be the loser but Mr. Grundy, but caution prevented me). 'If I can see her here,' I continued, 'I shall wish her to stay; if not, I care not where she is.' 'But,' said Miss J., 'it will be such a loss to the child.' (Thinks I to myself, I can't see that; well done, Mr. Grundy's vanity, to think there is not such another school in England). 'The loss of a mother,' I replied, 'is the greatest loss she can sustain, and it shall not be my fault if she is without one.'

We then left the Chapel, and continued talking as we walked down the street; my little darling held my hand and we gave each other many an affectionate squeeze. Tears were in Mary's eyes; bless the tender-hearted child. Whilst Miss Jackson continued to represent to me the *dreadful* and *tremendous*, the *deplorable* and *terrible* consequences of my coming to see my Mary, I vindicated myself most strenuously. All of a sudden, Miss Jackson popped into Dr. Gaskell's shop without saying a word, and left Mary and me quite alone; this was an unexpected delight, so we walked on above a mile, and got a great deal said. I assured her most solemnly that I never would desert her. She asked me for a coloured miniature portrait of myself, and I requested some of her copy books and drawings, and a little of her needle work.

At last, Mr. Grundy overtook us. I took not the least notice of him; at length he opened his mouth, and he spoke, but only on indifferent subjects, to which I replied civilly. Not a word did he say upon the subject of his instructions to Miss Jackson—a mean fellow, to load a blunderbuss for her to fire, and dare not produce a pop-gun himself.[1]

At last, Miss Jackson came up, just as I had arrived at

---

[1] Johnson, of whom Miss Weeton was an admirer, has this to say of Bolingbroke—'Sir, he was a scoundrel and a coward: a scoundrel, for charging a blunderbuss against religion and morality; a coward, because he had not resolution to fire it off himself, but left half-a-crown to a beggarly Scotchman to draw the trigger after his death'.

the wooden bridge near Parr Hall gate, and I then took leave, an affectionate leave, of my Mary, possibly for the last time! When she found that I stood in the road looking after her, she continued turning her dear face to the last moment, as she walked on to the house. When the hedge intervened, she continued jumping up to look again at me, and again. At last, she quite disappeared. Oh, what hearts of stone those are that can separate mother and child. I got home, weary and depressed. 12 miles.

16 & 17th. Were passed in preparing for my journey.

WALES

MAY–JULY (?) 1825

WALES

18th. Rode to Liverpool in the Caravan, dined and drank tea with Mrs. Roxburgh, and slept at Miss Dalrymple's, with whom, and her brother, I breakfasted on
Thursday. 19th. They both treat me with great civility and kindness, and how can I make them any return? At 9 o'clock, I set off in a Car to the Llewellyn Steam Packet,[1] and was one of the first on board; to this, I had no objection, for the Mersey at Liverpool, on a fine Summer's morning, is a busy, interesting scene to me, whose general mode of life is so still. I sat more than an hour before we set off. The fare in the steerage was 5s., which, as it was the lowest, I chose, as I must be very managing. This frugal plan ill suits my inclinations, for as it throws me amongst the lowest classes, I am obliged to be constantly on my guard, and at the same time to keep up a certain degree of reserve to prevent familiarity; and to act and speak with so much openness as not to wound their feelings, but much rather to conciliate and win. I am ill-calculated to act in a studied and guarded manner. I love the whole world, and those whom I cannot esteem, I pity. I am of too open a temper to get well through this world, but—I should be no Christian if I were more reserved, and I despise those little, narrow, calculating, cautious ways that some think so wise; they may be the wisdom of men, but the wisdom of God is simplicity and sincerity; and Oh, my Father, thy ways are my delight.

---

[1] 'Steam Packets. Beaumaris and Bangor—*Prince Llewelyn* and *St. David*, (of 75 horse-power each) sail regularly from St. George's Dock pier head, for Beaumaris and Bangor, North Wales, average passage six hours.' Baines's *Lancs. Directory*, 1825.

As we were proceeding along, amidst the noise of steam, and steam-engine paddles, and double drum, clarionet, fiddle, and French-horn, I leaned over the side of the vessel, much interested with the gliding scenery, and considering whether I should any longer continue this Journal; for I always feel my own littleness in the world, and can assign no reason why I have continued it so long; but—the thought of my darling Mary shot into my mind —I will continue it for thy sake, my little one; those expressive eyes of thine will one day perhaps read a mother's thoughts with eagerness; thy warm and tender heart will enter into all a mother's feelings; and to delight my child, I will continue it. Bless thee, my love. Heaven Bless thee!

I knew not one creature on board, not one creature in the country I was going to, nor a word of Welsh, yet I ventured. Is not God with me? To Him I can always speak. He despises not a lonely woman, nor does He suffer me to be injured. I go about in confidence, none making me afraid.

On landing at Garth Ferry, I was sadly annoyed by the porters to carry my luggage; that point settled, I had next to find private lodgings, which was not so soon done. Some could speak no English, and many asked extravagant prices. At last I was conducted by a civil woman to a little huxter shop, and found an old man and his housekeeper, so respectable-looking, and the place so clean, that I engaged with them for one week at least, at 6s. for a bed room. It was about 5 o'clock in the afternoon when I got settled at Mr. Wm. Pritchard's; as soon as I had my tea I strolled out towards the Menai, and, espying the famous Bridge about 2 miles off,[1] I went to it, returning home between 8 and 9.

I am sadly puzzled with Mr. Pritchard and his servant,

---

[1] The Menai Suspension Bridge, in process of erection by Telford, was opened the following year. It was commenced upon in 1819.

for they can speak little English, and I can understand no Welsh; so, between us, there will be peace. At present it amuses me highly; we are like 3 dumb people, making noises and signs, and we all laugh at it. Mr. Pritchard contrived to ask my name. 'Mrs. Stock,' I replied. 'Oh, Stock, Stock, a goot Stock a very goot thing,' said he, laughing. He says he understands more than he can speak. I replied, I wish I knew enough of Welsh to be witty in it. I slept so comfortably in my bed, that I am convinced there was no dampness, bugs, or fleas.

20. I went down to the waterside and over the Ferry to visit Beaumaris: the road was very pleasant, although the day was hot. I rambled a good deal round about the town, and got home to a 3 o'clock dinner; took tea likewise at 5, that I might have time to mount the hill just above the town of Bangor. I was entertained to discover that every body's *back premises* were exposed to my view as I stood first upon one pinnacle, and then upon another.

When I returned, Mr. Pritchard sent for his daughter (who is in a respectable service near), to talk with me; she speaks English well. She is such a pretty, genteel, innocent-looking young woman, that I greatly admire her; intelligent and modest.

21. Walked in the morning to Aber and back; bought a penny loaf at a little shop in Aber, and ate it in the Church yard under the shade of a yew tree. A young foal and its mother (I should suppose, belonging to the parson)[1] were my only visiters. They came and looked at me; 'ye know, ye need not fear me,' said I, 'for I would not so much as frighten any living creature intentionally.' For the first time I saw the manner of decking a Welsh grave; many of these were trimmed with—what had been green and pretty, but were all now withered, like those interred

---

[1] The parson alone had pasturage and mowing rights of the churchyard in old English law.

underneath. I sat a long time at my dinner, on a nice smooth grave-stone of blue slate, refreshed by the coolness of the shade, and a fine view of Beaumaris bay and town before me. Father! thou never ceasest to be kind to me.

Everything was new to me. As I suppose I am not so wise as Solomon, I can take delight in these varied scenes. I go along, speaking to no one, visiting no gentleman's domain, or attempting to see anything that is not open to every one; for I am of too retiring a disposition to intrude myself upon any one's notice: the open road and the mountain path suffice me.

I was much tired out when I got home to a late repast of tea. Mr. Pritchard sent his daughter up at 6 o'clock to my bed room, to say he was going to Pentir, and wished to know if I would go with him. Tired as I was, I went; we could not talk, but I noticed that whoever he met, he had always something pleasant to say to them, for they all looked pleased and good-humoured. At last we got near to a public house at Pentir, where Mr. Pritchard seemed to be going. I took leave of him here, and returned leisurely home alone, pleased although tired. My morning's walk had been 11 miles, and this, 7 m.—18.

22d. Sunday morning, I arose quite refreshed. I wonder how it is, that at 48 years of age, I should have so much of the elasticity of youth, both in body and mind; for I am as playful as a child. I went to a congregational Chapel at ½ past 10. I was too soon; the place was filled with men and boys. I felt quite confused at being the only female, for they were employed in teaching and learning in Welsh. At 11, they every one went out, and for a few minutes I was left totally alone, expecting to be locked in if I had not my wits about me. Soon, an entirely different class entered, and a preacher, and the service was conducted in English.

At tea time this evening, Mr. Pritchard came up into

his room, which is only separated from mine by boards, and told me, as well as he could, that the water boiled.

The story of Pyramus and Thisbe struck me at the moment so ludicrously, speaking as we did through a wall, that I could not forbear laughing repeatedly at the idea of my old Pyramus, and his not very young Thisbe[1]— to the no small surprise of Mr. Pritchard, to whom I could not explain. Really, my situation is very droll, and many a singular incident occurs, owing to our ignorance of each other's language.

May 23d. Monday morning, after breakfast, I went to see the pillar erected in honour of the Marquis of Anglesea[2], beyond the new Bridge at Bangor Ferry. I crossed the ferry in company with 3 or 4 horses, and 2 as wild Welsh cows as ever were ferried over, besides a number of men and women. I had a very extensive prospect from the top of the rock on which the Pillar is erected. After dinner, I walked down to the shore at Garth Ferry, strolled over the Hill above it, and amused myself with my spying glass, remaining some hours.

24. Wrote to Miss Dalrymple this morning. She is the only person who has asked me to write during this journey, and I shall therefore, I think, write to no other.[3] Not a person in England knows at this moment where I am, or appears to care. How we are neglected when we are in adversity! What anxiety there would be about me, were I affluent! Oh, my Mary, if ever you read this, feel for your mother, and be grateful for those who shewed her kindness.

---

[1] Pyramus loved the beautiful Babylonian Thisbe, and, living in adjoining houses, they often secretly conversed with one another through a hole in the wall, despite parental opposition.

[2] The first stone of this pillar erected on the summit of Craig y Dinas was laid on the anniversary of the Battle of Waterloo, to commemorate 'the consummate skill and bravery' displayed by the Marquis at that battle.

[3] This letter was apparently rewritten on 6 June and sent off then. Miss Weeton adhered to her resolve not to write elsewhere.

There had been heavy rain in the night; a hard gale of wind succeeded; notwithstanding, I ventured over at Garth Ferry after dinner, to take a stroll round about Beaumaris. Few people ventured upon the water this day; but I am so fond of water, that a trifle does not prevent my sailing. I have the opportunity but seldom; only when I leave home. I am a sailor's daughter, and perhaps inherit a portion of his taste and spirit.

The sun shone clearly upon the mountains, except when a cloud glided between, and the water was blue as the sky; every place looked beautifully. I rambled round Baron Hill, and up many a road where I could go without asking leave; for I dislike to do that. I want to go no where, where man, putting up his sign board, says proudly—'thus far shalt thou go, and no farther!' Strolling towards the shore, I perceived a bathing house, where, finding two women, one of whom could speak English, lingering idly about like myself, I was glad to have a bit of chatter. The wind blew roughly, but setting our backs to a high wall that sheltered us from it, we conversed a long time; then, taking leave, I turned homeward. The ferry man at Garth is a singular looking mortal, very corpulent, and very short; he rolls about the boat like a hogshead; coarse features, and a rough voice, with plenty to say; but I find he can argue on two sides of the question[1]—so a fig for that man's sincerity whose ingenuity rises above it. Being

---

[1] This particular ferry receives mention in a MS. journal (in the possession of the editor) of an anonymous gentleman, who, on his way to Ireland in July of the year 1819, thus records *his* experience and opinion of it:
'We stopp'd & lunched at the Inn at Bangor ferry while the carriage was crossing; we then crossed ourselves, when the fellows had the modesty to charge, for the

carriage	.	.	.	.	10s. 0d.
for ourselves	.	.	.	.	4s. 0d.
for themselves	.	.	.	.	2s. 0d.
					16s. 0d.

We were obliged to grin & bear it. So much for a welch ferry.'

safely ferried over a 2d. time, I remained sitting on the hill 2 or 3 hours, amusing myself with my spying glass, and watching the approach of the Steam Packet.

25th. As I intend going to Carnarvon to stay a few weeks when I leave Bangor, I set off this morning to take lodgings. Mr. Price, of Seymour St., had given me a reference to a Mrs. Bridget Evans, wife to the Capt. of a trader, or her daughter. I soon inquired them out, and found the daughter a very nice woman, considering her station. She took me to many places to procure lodgings. At length, I fixed upon a snug place at 4s. a week. I wished a view of the Menai from my window, but on seeing more of the town, I found that was not practicable, on account of the walls. I was greatly pleased with the attention shewn to me by this young woman; she said she would put me in a way to get every thing at the cheapest.

I arrived at home again about 7 o'clock, very little fatigued after a walk of more than 18 miles. Snowdon was enveloped in the blackest clouds, and the neighbouring mountains but appearing very dimly. I had one heavy shower as I went, but I took shelter near an hour in a little farm house. On my return, it again began to rain when I had 5 miles to walk, but I never minded it. I had my umbrella, and got home very dry and comfortable. I quite enjoyed my day's walk, and never was in a happier frame of mind.

26. Thursday. An annual meeting was held this day at the Market Place in Bangor, by the Ministers of the Independent denomination. I attended morning and afternoon. There was something primitive in thus standing out of doors to hear preaching; it reminded me of many parts of the Acts of the Apostles, as well as of the preaching of Jesus. It is not at all uncommon with the Dissenters of the present day, but it was unusual to me. I felt concerned to see none of the wealthier part of the community attending; are they ashamed of it? Two ministers lodge here for the time, but they appear somewhat shy; they should follow the example of the great Apostle Paul, and be 'instant in season, and out of season;' but there are many who can preach better than converse, yet conversation is the most powerful means of conversion; preaching is but secondary to it; it was the first and only means by which an impression was made upon my mind, of the truths of religion and its comforts.

27. I did not go out in the morning, the weather was so piercing cold. After dinner took a walk to see the slate quarries near Ogwen Bank;[1] but when I had got within 200 yards, I dared approach no nearer. A lonely woman, going among so many men, required more courage than I possess; for of men I have an indescribable terror, they do so much injury to women, as my own experience can testify; and the Papers daily bring added instances. Oh, if men would ever become the protectors of women, and cease to be the brutal tyrants! the robbers! the seducers! the oppressors!

I turned off along the Capel Curig road; piercing as the air was, it was brilliantly clear, and had I known in time that I should have been so near some of the highest mountains, I would have ascended one or two of them instead of pursuing a fruitless road to the quarries; but the day was far advanced, and I had far to walk home again; so I proceeded beyond Ogwen Bank about a mile, and would have gone much more, the road was so interesting to me, had I had time and stength. Carnedd David, close on my right hand, appeared very easy of ascent, and Glydar Vawr before me, practicable; but I was obliged to think

---

[1] 'Every sensible observer admires the liberality and taste that distinguishes the estates of Lord Penryn here past; much is also expended throughout his vast slate quarries, which are prosperously working amidst the vast circle of mountains a few miles eastward.' *The Imperial Guide*, 1801.

The first Lord Penrhyn expended £120,000 on these quarries, which are now claimed to be the largest excavation of their kind in the world.

of returning, and amused myself with watching the progress of the noisy Ogwen, as it dashed along its rocky bed,
until the road separated from it, leaving it to foam on-
wards through the woods and grounds of Penrhyn Castle.
The Castle is at present undergoing alterations, and workmen are taking down the towers; this I saw with my spying glass, for I went none near them.[1]

As thin as I am, and as skinny and bony, yet my bones
cannot be dry bones, but must be 'full of marrow and fat-
ness,' or I could never be able to endure such long walks,
and be so little fatigued; my feet swell sometimes, but I
can skip like a lamb amongst the rocks, and enjoy the
sport, after a 10 or 12 miles walk. This day I rambled
about 16 miles.

28. There had been much rain in the night, and frequent showers continued most of the morning, with a good
deal of hail; the air was still piercing, and I sat at home
repairing stockings until afternoon, when I walked as far
as Plas Newyd, but did not attempt to go into the grounds.
I wanted to see the Cromlech, mentioned by Williams[2] as
close behind the house; but I suppose it must be inclosed in
the plantation, for I could perceive nothing of the kind
near the road, nor the adjoining fields. Anglesey appears
a barren, dreary-looking place, and I have looked almost
over the whole of it from the neighbouring rocks in Carnarvon, and from the high rock on which the Marquis of
Anglesey's column is raised.

I examined Menai Bridge to-day very minutely, yet
cannot discover how the passengers are to get on, or off,
at the Anglesey end; the other end will have a fine

---

[1] Perhaps a personal coincidence will be excused at this point; close upon
one hundred years after Miss Weeton viewed from the outside Wyatt's
pseudo-Norman castle, the editor found himself billeted in a wing of it; and
from one of its towers (he being young), penned letters of a length which
would have won the decided approval of Miss Weeton, even as their matter
was hopefully calculated to charm a certain collateral descendant of hers.

[2] Whose Guide, along with Bingley's, Miss Weeton made use of.

entrance, but this is as yet not discoverable. The sun shone brilliantly upon the mountains, all except Snowdon. I saw it with great distinctness in every part fronting towards Anglesey, but the sun seldom touched it, and blackness was its distinguishing vesture all afternoon. All the week it has been veiled with the blackest clouds, and 'thick darkness has covered it.' And why? it is very little higher than several mountains near to it, which have only had mists and rain upon them, but not near so aweful looking, nor so often invisible.

This day's walk was about 11 miles.

29 Sunday. I did not go out, except to Chapel in the morning, and took only a short walk in the evening. The sun shone very clearly, but the air was so piercing cold, that there was no comfort without a fire, and I sat chiefly by it. Yesterday morning, Jane, Mr. Pritchard's housekeeper and niece, appeared to be in great grief, and made many signs to me as if some great calamity had befallen some one in the mountains; but it was not until to-day, that I could obtain the exact information of what really had occurred, from Mr. P's daughter. An aunt of Jane's, a widow, has a farm, at which 2 or 3 years ago she had employed a husband-man; since then, the man has worked at a slate quarry. It is said he has lately been insane, but had not been confined. On Friday last, he went to the house of his late mistress, and, seizing a hatchet, broke both her arms, and otherwise dreadfully bruised her. On Saturday he was taken through Bangor to Carnarvon Castle. Jane had just seen him conveyed, and heard of the affair, when I saw her so agitated.

30. I crossed at Garth Ferry immediately after dinner, and walked to Bangor Ferry; a rout I had not before taken. The view from this side is the most beautiful of any I have seen in the vicinity of Bangor, and if I wished to reside in its neighbourhood, it would be here. Snowdon, as well as all the other mountains, was peculiarly clear and bright.

31st. At 9 o'clock this morning, I left home to walk to Conway (15 miles). I would have gone by a Stage coach, had there been any; but a Mail only travels there at 7 o'clock every evening through Bangor. I felt a little timid at the idea of accomplishing so long a walk, and to return on foot next day. I had never attempted such a task for near 15 years, when, at the Isle of Man near 15 years ago, I one day walked 36 m. This morning was extremely fine, and I enjoyed the beauty of the scenery greatly. Beaumaris bay was in full tide. The road under Penmaen Mawr is certainly aweful, and today it was, all the way, very lonely. I felt somewhat afraid, and as it proved, unnecessarily.

Before I reached Penmaen Mawr, I passed 2 men lying at one side of the road, basking in the sun. One had a bundle of printed papers, which I suppose he was going to cry through the streets of some town, detailing some wonderment for a half-penny each; the other, apparently an Irishman, had nothing with him which bore a semblance of any intended employment. These two were presently joined by a man coming from a gentleman's house, with a barrel organ at his back. They arose, and walked at his pace, which could not be very quick considering his burthen. I perceived this, and proceeded very nimbly, that I might get out of sight of them; but the road ascending as I approached the mountain, I could not outwalk them. I turned, and found the organist had left them, and they were close behind; I preferred having them before me, so I stood to look over the wall to the sea, and they passed quietly. It would have been easy in this part to have robbed, and thrown me into the sea, without discovery; but I perceived 2 or 3 passengers approaching at a distance, which determined me to stop a little here. I sat down, and ate the bread and butter which I had brought with me, and they went out of sight. 4 or 5 miles farther, I again came unexpectedly upon them, lying, as before, to rest. I passed as speedily as possible, and got safe into Conway. I dare say the men had no unlawful thoughts.

As I had loitered much upon the road, it was 3 o'clock when I got to Conway. I soon found the ferry and crossed it. The chain Bridge building here, is not nearly in so forward a state as that at Bangor Ferry.[1] It will be a beautiful object to some of the gentlemen's seats on the opposite shore. I rambled a good deal about, before I set out to look for a bed for the night; then, calling at a little shop, I inquired where I could have a private lodging, and was directed over the way, where I soon engaged. After tea, I took another walk, to view the walls outside; and finding myself less tired than I could have expected, I ascended the hill of Benniarth Wood, and walked all round it. It is nearly all oak, and I think one half lay prostrate, felled by the woodman's axe, which resounded on every side. Stacks of bark were piled here and there, the spoils of the slain, and naked oaks lay thickly all over the hill. It reminded me much of a field of battle. Were the trees mine, I should ill bear to hear the blows that felled them; it would grieve me to see the vacant place where they once had stood.

The vicinity of Conway is peculiarly romantic. I was glad I had walked so far to see it. I retired early to rest, much tired with an 18 miles walk.

June 1st. Wednesday. In the night, I heard the roaring of a storm—and the previous evening was so lovely! I arose at 8; the storm continued, but it was yet fair. I hastened to eat breakfast, that I might return. I dared not stay to see more of the place, which I had intended, for I saw the

[1] Commenced by Telford in 1822 and completed in 1826.

storm would increase, and I must return to-day, as I leave Bangor to-morrow entirely. I had a prospect of walking a few miles before much rain fell; so, giving the landlady a shilling, which was 3 times what she asked, (I found my own provisions), I took leave at 9. The wind blew furiously, and when I had gained about 7 miles, the rain fell heavily; the remaining 8 was winterly indeed! I was drenched thoroughly. I looked for each succeeding mile stone most anxiously. When at last I got home, between 1 and 2, every part of my dress was wet; the rain had run off my bonnet, down my neck, wetting me inside as much as out; for I had no umbrella or cloak. The wind had blown in my face all the way, furiously, and yet when I got dry cloaths on, I was very little fatigued with a 15 miles walk. Let me raise a thought of gratitude to Thee, Oh my Father, for this!

As soon as I got home, Jane informed me that her poor, mutilated, unfortunate aunt, was dead! Jane looks quite ill with grief.

2d. The storm still rages, and people pass by as if they were drunk, the wind is so strong. The blackness of Snowdon last week, it seems, was a forerunner of this. I find from the N. Wales gazette, that Jane's aunt was not a widow. The young man's name is John Roberts. Nothing is said of his insanity, but that in a violent rage, he went to the house, which was in the parish of Llanddeniolen, and called Fron Chwith, and perpetrated the deed with a bill-hook. Besides injuring her arms, he made a dreadful incision on her head. She died on Wednesday morning. He also cut the servant man and girl with the hook, for attempting to save the mistress. The difference in the accounts is occasioned by my not being able to understand Jane, nor she, my questions.

3d. As Thursday was so wet and stormy, I was obliged to defer my removal to Carnarvon to to-day (Friday), and had a very agreeable walk, the roads not dusty, and no more wind than was necessary to keep the air from being too hot.

✳   ✳   ✳

To MISS DALRYMPLE, Liverpool.

Carnarvon. June 6 1825.

I have just got myself comfortably settled at Carnarvon, after a fortnight's sojourning at Bangor, so now I hope I shall hear from you soon.

When I had been near a week at Bangor, I took a walk to Carnarvon, to take lodgings there, previous to removing thither; it is so very uncomfortable to go to any place, and have a place of abode to seek afterwards.

Mr. Price's reference was of great service to me. I soon found out Mrs. Evans's daughter, who assisted me, and took me to a Capt. Hughes's, where I have engaged a bed room for a month at 4*s*. per week, and the accommodations far superior to those I had at Bangor at 6*s*. I was imposed upon there, but I shan't fret about that; it was no ruinous concern; they took advantage of my immediate want of lodgings at a lower price than 10*s*. 6*d*. I could have had plenty, at that rent, for a sitting and bed-room. Mrs. Evans knew how to manage; she would have taken me herself, but I did not like the closeness of the situation. Here, I am opposite to the river and shipping, and have a fine view of the Castle, and a pretty green hill over the river, surrounded with wood. I have a side view into Castle Square; for you must know, Ma'am, I am in Love-Lane, and I really love the Lane very well. An animated view from my window is really necessary, where I am so much alone.

For 5 or 6 days after I got to Bangor, the weather was hot; it then became severely cold, but the air was peculiarly clear, and the sun shone with great brightness. Last

Tuesday, May 31, I walked to Conway. It was as if I had the whole world to myself; nothing living was visible but a couple of sea gulls. The first thing on my arrival was to visit the new chain Bridge. It is quite a miniature piece of work compared with Menai Bridge; it will be long before it is finished. Had the succeeding morning been as fine as the previous one, I would have seen more of the neighbourhood. I arrived in Bangor at 2 o'clock P.M., like some poor wretch just saved from drowning. However, when I had put dry cloaths on, I was not a jot the worse, and I am very glad I assumed resolution to go the journey. I should have been sorry to have missed seeing so singular and romantic looking a place.

The storm continued with unabating fury till next day at evening; the people reeling in the streets as if they were tipsy, the wind drove them about so rudely.

The family I have left, and the one I am come to, can neither of them speak English, except a *very* little, which causes some droll mistakes often, besides being mortifying to me; for I am *rather* fond of talking, which is somewhat *surprising* in a *woman*.[1] The market women try me first in Welsh, but when they find they can make nothing of me, they speak English rather than lose a bargain.

Since the English have visited them so much, they have most of them, in towns, been obliged to learn that language for interest sake; and probably in another century, the Welsh will have become almost extinct; for national schools are universal in the principality, and I think the children are taught in English.

I have as great a loss in religious services as any thing; for they are comparatively few, and very short, to what

[1] At any rate, Miss Weeton had not fallen into a 'state of languor and vacancy', the inevitable fate of one, according to Dr. Johnson, 'whose whole felicity is conversation', and who contemplated retiring into Wales, in despair of finding a community of knowledge. Quoted *Queeney Letters*, ed. Lansdowne, 1934.

we have them in England. I consider myself happy, however, in finding both families I have lodged with, professedly pious people.

If you have an opportunity, please to let me be remembered to Mr. Price's. Mr. P. is one who will leave no
stone unturned to serve a friend; he fears no trouble.

*   *   *

[JOURNAL]

June 8th. The storminess of the weather is still such as
wholly to prevent my going out, except a few errands; the
wind, as well as rain, is violent. I find from the papers, that
there was a tremendous thunderstorm at Manchester the
night that I was at Conway. It seems to have let loose an
amazing quantity of wind. For amusement, I have been
obliged to resort to a circulating library (Pool and Hard-
ing's). 'Brighton on the Steyne,' a satirical work, was the
first I got hold of. I would not have wasted my time with
it, had I known what kind of composition it was; a great
deal of profligate sentiment is elicited, and the vilest conduct towards women, particularly wives, treated with the
utmost levity, as a very trivial kind of offence; nay, even
as affording much amusement; and characters ranking
high as to title and warlike achievements, are little, if at
all, censured for the most diabolical conduct towards
women, when, if there be one crime of greatest magnitude, it is that!

If man injures man, the injured has a great portion of
power to defend himself, either from natural strength of
body, of resolution, of the countenance of many of his fellows,
or from the laws; but when man injures woman, how can
she defend herself? Her frame is weaker, her spirit timid;
and if she be a wife, there is scarce a man anywhere to be
found who will use the slightest exertion in her defence;
and her own sex cannot, having no powers. She has no

hope from law; for man, woman's enemy, exercises, as well as makes those laws. She cannot have a jury of her peers or equals, for men, every where prejudiced against the sex, are her jurors; man is her judge. Thus situated, thus oppressed, she lives miserably, and by inches sinks into the grave. This is the lot not merely of a few, but of one half, if not two thirds of the sex! That a man who will use a woman with cruelty, is a coward, a despicable villain, may be asserted by one of his own sex who has perhaps some share of probity. He is so. But then, according to that assertion, there is a prodigious number of cowards and of villains; I may justly say, seven eighths. I scarcely go into a house in which there is not a fornicator, a seducer, an adulterer, a tyrant. Even here—see a poor suffering creature in the person of Mrs. Hughes. She is consuming with a vile disorder, given to her by her wretch of a husband. She is in continual pain, and must die; she cannot be cured. To see such a sweet, innocent, mild-tempered woman, in such constant agony, rouses the utmost indignation against the fellow who could prove himself so like a fiend; yet this is not an uncommon case. My own experience of the world shews me many such. What numbers of men murder their wives; and that, by the most cruel of all means—slow torture.[1]

9 Thursday. Early after dinner, I walked to see Llanberris Lakes. The weather had cleared, but still the wind prevailed. After passing a bridge near two miles off, instead of turning to the left, which I ought to have done, I went right on, and soon arrived at a barren, dreary hill. I saw no way but of proceeding, for it was in vain to inquire the way; no one could understand me, neither could

---

[1] 'There is something unfeminine in independence. It is contrary to Nature, and therefore it offends. A really sensible woman feels her dependence; she does what she can, but she is conscious of her inferiority, and therefore grateful for support.' *Woman and her Social and Domestic Character*, by Mrs. J. Sandford, 1831.

I them. With much difficulty, I got to the top, over continued swamps, streams, and rocks; the late rains have
made the hills almost impassable. All on a sudden I
obtained a fine view of the lakes, which were of a bright
purple; the peculiar clearness of the air, I suppose, gave
them the hue, and the hollowness of their situation. The
sun shone brilliantly on the mountains. I sat on a rock a
long time, resting, and admiring. Snowdon, or rather
Withva,[1] was without a cloud, and I saw a way by which
I think I can easily ascend some day, ere long.

I had my spying glass with me, and distinguished many
objects mentioned in Williams's Tourist's Guide,[2] and on
my Map of N. Wales. Without these, I should be embarrassed indeed, for I cannot ask a single question; and
truly, I feel very desolate here; but—where am I not so?
Oh, my husband, you have much to answer for.

My walk today was between 11–12 miles.

10. The morning was so windy and gloomy, I did not
like to go out, except just to visit Coed Helen Summer
house, where I had not been before. In the afternoon, I
sate reading and sewing, and in the evening, had a very
pleasant walk along the Pwhllheli road, as far as a
romantic little village, a water mill, and a bridge, under
which flows a very rapid stream; and at present, a very
full one. This was the most picturesque spot I had yet
seen, and the most lovely; and the evening was as serene
as was ever Summer's Eve in June. 5 miles.

11. Intending to go to market this morning, I deferred
going any where else until after dinner. Even in the
market, the embarrassment pursues me as regards the
language. I applied to two or three butchers before I
could make a purchase, and then was indebted to a young
woman passing by, to become my interpreter. I am so

---

[1] Properly spelled Wyddva but pronounced as under [*orig. note*].
[2] *Tourist's Guide to the County of Carnarvon*, by P. B. Williams, 1802.

easily repulsed, so soon disheartened, that I am ill fitted
for this rude world; my mind is too delicate for a mingled
multitude. I often think of the poet Cowper, for I think I
am much like him in disposition and sentiment; I do not
mean in talent. This day I trembled as I walked through
the market, so many eyes were upon me, or I fancied so;
and, when refused by two butchers so small a cut as two
pounds off a neck of veal, I turned dejected out of the
market, and went home unprovided. All my life time, I
dreaded nothing more than going into a butcher's shop.
I cannot bully, and put on a face of assurance as I see
most other women do. I cannot barter and depreciate the
article I want to buy, as is customary. I went home, as I
said, dejected this day. I felt my unprotected, isolated
situation most painfully! When I arrived at home, I could
but smile—a melancholy smile—at my own weakness, at
thus being endangered the going without provision for
want of a little confidence. I forced myself to go again
immediately, and by the help of an accidental interpreter,
procured what I wanted.

I do certainly observe myself to be looked at here more
than I ever recollect before; for why, I cannot discover.
Perhaps because I am a stranger, and alone; then, I am
taller and thinner than most women, and very plain-
featured—yet, I think, not so ugly as to attract passers-by
—perhaps I am; few of us know how we appear in the
eyes of others. Many of the country people I meet on the
road, bow or courtesy to me, as if I were of some rank or
respectability of appearance; but the market people turn
almost one and all to look after me, and when I inquire
the price of any thing, ask exorbitantly. My dress is very
plain, that I may pass unnoticed; a dark print, no way
remarkable in the make of it, and a bonnet likewise plain.
Strangers, I should think, are so common here, that they
would excite little attention.

379

After dinner, I set out to take a long walk, half inclined to ascend Mynydd Mawr, or Moel Elio, whichever I found to be most practicable; but I found the heat so intense, and my head ached so acutely, that I did neither, but walked straight up the Beddgelert road as far as the foot of Cwellyn Lake. It was an unexpected sight, and I got upon a rock that commanded a full view of it, and sat resting a long time. It would have been exactly the day for an ascent upon some of the highest mountains; not too cold, and beautifully bright and clear; but—I had not strength. I had already walked 7 miles, and must 7 more, so I returned home, gratified with what I had seen.

I shall be obliged to go to Llanberris or Beddgelert for a night or two, if I must visit Snowdon; and I dread an Inn as much as a butcher's shop. 14 miles.

12. There was no English service at the Chapel to day until half past 3 o'clock, so I sate at home writing my journal (which was a week in arrears), all morning and evening.

13. The 2^d set of books from the library please me much more than the first; the first had certainly much wit, perhaps talent, but I can make no allowances for talent misapplied. These—'The Paris Spectator,' translated by W. Jerdan, are worth reading. There is a great deal of good sense; and the manner, style, and variety, render the work highly interesting.

I left home this morning to cross the Tal y Foel ferry at 9 o'clock. The conductor told me, when I arrived on the pier, that it would be a quarter of an hour before a boat would go. I thought this would allow me time to fetch some thing I had forgot. I hastened home, and returned within the time—and the boat was gone! and I had to wait 1½ hour for another. I remained on the terrace all the time, lest I should be again disappointed. When at last I got into a ferry boat, it was 11 o'clock. The weather this week has become intensely hot. Only 5 or 6 days ago, the air was so cold as to render a fire in my room quite desirable, and for 2 days I had one. Setting sail so late, I had to endure the whole heat of the day; whilst I was on the water, it was refreshingly cool, but when I landed, it was scorching. I trudged onward over a dusty, uninteresting road, through Newborough, and seeing a Church a little beyond, I went and seated myself on a low grave stone, on the most shaded side of the Church, and ate some bread and butter, the only dinner I had provided.

Newborough is a city of hovels; and the Church, like almost all I have yet seen in Wales, as comfortless and shabby within as an old barn. I often see Churches or Chapels marked on my map, which I cannot find when I reach the place; the only way I use, is to discover if possible some building without a chimney. Now and then I see one, with a rope hanging down outside the wall to jingle the bell with; and often in a place so lonely, that if any person were to hang themselves by it on a Monday morning, they might, to all appearance, dangle there till Sunday-Morning before they were discovered. I often laugh as I pass this appendage to a Welsh Chapel, it hangs so *invitingly*!—'not ready yet,' say I. Indeed, I think there would be fewer suicides committed, if materials were ready provided for the purpose by government in a building for the occasion; it would look so like a slaughter house, that the most melancholy would sigh as they passed by, and say—'not ready yet!; and even the ruined gamester, repulsed, would turn, and consider a little longer.

When I had rested and refreshed myself, I proceeded; I soon got amongst sand-hills, for my object was to get to the sea shore, to look at the shells, and then to go to Llanddwyn rocks, light-house, and perch. The view of the Carnarvonshire mountains was very grand to-day, and all that coast; for I could see from Penmaen Mawr, all the way to Braich y Pwll most distinctly. The view under my feet, and for a couple of miles or more before me, was dreary, blinding, and cheerless; sand, marsh, star, and bare rocks, composed the barren prospect. As I mounted sand-hill after sand-hill, I began to ask myself why I wearied myself so? What induced me voluntarily to undertake these profitless labours? what pleasure was there? For indeed, these succession of sands, for a much greater way than I had anticipated, the heat, the pain to my eyes, had almost been too much for me; yet the natural perseverance of my mind urged me on, and when at last I arrived at the water's edge, on the Malldraeth sands, about 2 miles above Llanddwyn, I felt as if my labour was repaid. I am passionately fond of water, and now it was the more delightful as the tide was just beginning to flow; the breeze was cooling, the sands firm, and covered with shells, the water a beautiful purple; it was now 3 o'clock, and the sun would soon abate of its fury, and the view southward over the bay was fine indeed. I stood admiring, or rambled about in a luxury of delight. I rejoiced I had come.

I should have been so glad to have bathed; modesty prevented me, for I must have taken off all my cloaths. Not a human being was to be seen, but some one *might* appear, when I should least be prepared to *receive company*; yet, as I approached the rocks, I saw many a snug aperture amongst them, which would have served for both bath and dressing room, and I cast many a wishful eye on the tide as it flowed in amongst them.[1]

At Llanddwyn point is a high rock, on which a lofty, circular building is erected, very like a light-house; on this rock I stood some time; the prospect was noble! Any one as fond of the beauties of creation as I am, will come

[1] Modesty, however, did not prove an insuperable barrier in the case of the gentleman of the MS. diary already quoted. At Conway, 'the sea coming in so beautifully, I could not withstand the temptation, so doff'd my cloathes & rolled myself in, & most delightful it was'. 17 July 1819.

as far on a clear day in June as I have done, to see it, and say as I did—I am glad I have come.

At last I turned homeward, and taking what I thought a nearer rout over a marsh, I met with a river, too wide to jump over, too deep to ford; for, had it only been knee deep, I would have plunged in; and to my vexation I had a whole mile to return, thus losing 2 miles before I got to the high road to the bridge. I had seen 2 or 3 women, of whom I would have enquired had there been any chance of obtaining an answer, but I am like one dumb, for I cannot make myself understood, so it is of no avail speaking; even at my lodgings, the servant understands no English, and Mrs. Hughes so little, that we cannot converse.

I had long been looking out for water, for I was parched with thirst, having drank nothing since breakfast; and to call at the cottages I passed, was of little use, the people would have been some time before they would have known what I wanted. I could see no wells, and the river water was only like ditch water; however, I took some up in a shell I had gathered, and drank a little. It did me good.

The prospect before me was so fine, that it beguiled the weariness I felt, and I arrived at Tal y Foel just in time for a boat, so I had not to be teased with waiting, which I could not so well have borne; for I had had little to eat since breakfast, and nothing to drink but a little turfy water. I had a delightful sail, and glad was I to sit down, for it was a luxury I had scarcely known the whole day. I arrived at home about ½ past 7 o'clock, after a walk of 15 miles, besides being on my feet 1½ hour at the terrace before I left in the morning. Tea, and a warm bath, and a good night's rest, enabled me to rise quite refreshed and well next morning. Should I not thank Thee, my Protector, and my Supporter, for all these mercies?

Tuesday, June 14. To-day I enjoyed the luxury of resting,

yet not wholly sitting still. I wished to see the baths that the Marquis of Anglesea has lately constructed; I was told they were quite elegant. I went this morning, and took a cold bath, which I liked so much, that were it not for the expence, I would go every day whilst I staid. When the place is considered, the retirement, convenience, and comfort, one shilling is cheap for a single bath; very cheap, and can never, I should think, pay interest for the money expended. It would be dear to me, merely on account of my circumscribed income. The baths are each lined with white china tiles; the floors of the bath landings, and dressing rooms, are purple tiles and red alternately (some say, of marble) in squares, and fitted up with every requisite.

I like to be alone when I dress and undress; many people have no scruples of delicacy in this respect. My excellent mother was strict in this part of our education; for my brother was taught to have as great a regard for personal modesty as I was, and never were we exposed to each other in washing and dressing, as I see most families of children are. From a child, I could never bear to suffer any one to be witness to my preparing for bed at night, or to quit my room in a morning, nor any exposure of person at any other time. I introduce this subject here, with the impression that my darling Mary may happen to peruse what I write. You have no mother to teach you, my love, as I had; and no other person will ever supply my place. You will not, most probably I fear, learn true modesty at a public school; and you are unhappily deprived of the precepts and of the example which your mother could have set you.

For the above reasons, I like to bathe alone, and a private bath is just to my taste. I have seldom bathed but at Southport, and there it is sadly exposing, as all who resort there well know, and the modest complain much, gentlemen's and ladies' machines standing promiscuously in the water! Besides, at spring tides, it is hardly possible to have a machine for only one person, such crowds resort there to bathe; and as there are no dressing rooms, time is positively not allowed for any one to dress in the machine before quitting it. Perpetual rappings at the door, and 'Oh, do come out,' 'Do make haste,' reiterated until we are thrown into a trepidation, so as not to be able to finish dressing; and probably, on issuing forth, 2 or 3 *gentlemen*, to your utter confusion, at the door, ready to jump in! The bustle, hurry, and confusion, are most extremely disagreeable; the only comfort is, that amongst such a crowd we may pass unnoticed perhaps.[1]

The afternoon I sat at home, repairing stockings, &c. To this, Mary, my mother ever required me to pay the strictest attention; and I have never since disobeyed her. I am not afraid to take off my shoe at any time, for I have no holes, or soil, to hide.

In the evening, I had a short, but pleasant walk to Llanbeblic Church, and turning to the right over some

---

[1] 'The ceremony of ladies bathing is accompanied with some peculiarities. . . . A painted board, placed in a conspicuous position in the rear of a score or upwards of bathing machines standing in a line, decrees that those of the gentlemen shall not advance nearer than one hundred yards to those of the ladies; and farther, that all pleasure-boats are prohibited from approaching to the ladies when bathing, within the distance of thirty yards, under the penalty, in case of contempt of the regulation, of five shillings.

'All the old bathing women at Southport (to make use of an Hibernicism) are young men, that is to say, stout lusty fellows under middle age. The guide, having taken his post in front of the door of the machine, in the usual manner, the young lady undresses within. Having disencumbered herself of her apparel, she puts on a dark blue bathing dress, (in which I perceived no other difference from those commonly used, than that it was invariably fastened with strings about the ancles) and in this *costume* makes her appearance . . . on the upper step of the sanctuary. Presenting both her hands, and supported by his grasp, she then falls backwards on the wave, receiving the embraces of old Neptune as young ladies usually do, with the accompaniments of squeaking, giggling, kicking, splashing, and wincing.'

So wrote Sir George Head, in his *Tour in the Manufacturing Districts*, published in the year 1835. Making all allowances for the novelty of the thing, surely we may take this as pure 'journalese'—can we imagine Miss Weeton, young or old, behaving so; or for that matter, hundreds only slightly less singular? Too much nonsense, then and now, has contributed to the making of the 'girl of the period'.

fields, rambled along the Seiont. All the children in Carnarvon, apparently, were here assembled together, sporting on its banks, or in its stream; here a group of boys, there of girls, for nearly half a mile.

From Llanbeblic Church down to the river, is a highly romantic walk; words can faintly describe so complete a landscape. Lofty mountains in every gradation of height, form, and distance; the river, woods, scattered dwellings, shipping, the town of Carnarvon with its beautiful ruin of a castle, the Menai, the isle of Anglesea, and the sea beyond!! what would you more?

I began to meditate an ascent of Snowdon; of course, alone, for I knew nobody. I therefore applied to the driver of the Mail through Beddgelert, to take me as far as Quellyn Lake (or Llyn Caewellyn) at the foot of one of the ways to its top. The man had only a kind of little mail cart; he proposed my going as far at Pont Aberglaslyn, to which I agreed for 3*s.*, and not quite determined whether to ascend Snowdon this time, leaving it to my own feelings of strength and inclination when I should be at the foot of it, after walking from P. Aberglaslyn.

June 15. Set off at 8 this morning on the mail to P. Aberglaslyn, with another passenger, a poor young woman, with a little girl of 2 years old. She was going to her parish![1] Her husband was a sailor, and for 2 years had deserted her; for the last 15 months she had heard nothing of him. How frequent are these instances of cruelty to wives! What hard hearts men have, and how little punishment they meet with for this description of profligacy. If they steal a sheep or a horse, they are pursued and hung; to desert a wife is a thousand times a greater crime; yet no police pursues him for this—is a wife no better than a sheep or a horse? is her misery to be nothing accounted of? The very parish

---

[1] Deserted wives, as soon as, or before, they became a charge upon the parish of their adoption, were passed back to their native place.

officers take no cognisance of a husband's desertion, whilst she asks for no money from them.

At Pont A. I left the mail; it was between 11 and 12 o'clock, for we had stopped above half an hour at Beddgelert,[1] to rest the horse, who, poor thing, had to accomplish the whole journey. During this pausing time, I sat under the shade of a tree in the Inn yard, quite at my ease. At P.A. I sat on the battlement of the Bridge, eating part of the bread and butter which I had brought from home, and then walked slowly to a spot I had noticed in passing, near Llyn Cawellyn, where I had to begin my ascent; and, feeling able and eager, I ventured.

I had got up about one third of the way, when, being thirsty, and a tempting rill just by, I took off my bonnet and bent my head to the water, drinking very comfortably. I had provision in a small bag, but a drinking vessel I had forgotten; the drink—the best of all liquids, I knew the Provider would furnish.[2] It was now near 2 o'clock, as I judged by my shadow; for my watch I had left at home for fear of accidents. Just as I raised my head from the water, I saw a gentleman descending with his guide, at a short distance. They espied me. I had already left the regular path a little, merely to quench my thirst; and now deviated a little more, purposely that they might not distinguish my dress or features, lest, seeing me at any other time, they should know where they had seen me; and I should dread the being pointed at in the road or the street as—'That is the lady I saw ascending Snowdon, alone!'[3]

[1] The first Lord Penrhyn was responsible for the establishing of a coach route between Bangor and Bettws-y-Coed in 1801, and, probably it was on one of these local coaches that Miss Weeton performed her journey, though the Irish Mail was now using this route.

[2] The Rev. W. Bingley, whose Guide she was using, afforded a tip (which should surely have jogged her memory)—'acting upon the advice of the clergyman who attended me in this and many other excursions, [I] always took a long pint of brandy, the whole of which we used to drink, without experiencing the slightest degree of intoxication'.

[3] Elizabeth Smith, the last of the blue-stockings, born in the same year as

The guide, seeing I was out of the path (only because he was in it, if he had but known), called out to me, but I was *quite* deaf. He continued shouting, and I was *forced* to hear; he was telling me to keep in the copper path, &c. I knew the way perfectly well, for my Map and my Guide had been well studied at home. I could find from what the gentleman said, that he imagined I had called for the guide at his dwelling, and finding him engaged upon the mountain, had gone so far to meet him; for he intreated the man to leave him. 'I can do perfectly well now,' he repeatedly said. I never turned my face towards them, but walked as fast as I could, hanging down my head; the Guide again giving me some directions—with the best intentions, I am sure, and partly, I think, as a little strata-gem to draw me nearer; but I had no fancy to be the heroine of a tale for him to amuse future employers with, and to describe me as young or old, handsome or plain, ladylike or otherwise; and if he could have drawn me near enough so as to have known me again, next thing, perhaps, I should have figured in some newspaper; or some tourists, glad to fill a page of their journal, would have crammed me there, as 'A singular female!'—I am not thus ambi-tious. No! No!

To the Guide's civility, I twice called out, 'Thank you!' But now my deafness had left me, I had got a stiff neck. When I had mounted a considerable height above them, I turned, and saw the gentleman standing looking up after me, with his hands on his sides as if in astonishment, and the Guide trudging downwards, vexed perhaps that it should be seen that any body could ascend without him,— and a woman, too! and alone! for the lift in his shoulders seemed to indicate as much.

Miss Weeton, and educated mainly by her mother (as was Miss Weeton), also climbed Snowdon—on a moonlight night, in order to see the dawn from the summit; she achieved yet another ambition, in the mastery of nine languages, self-taught, dying at the early age of 30.

It was my wish to ascend on the Bettws side, to cross over the summit if practicable, and descend at Llanberris.[1] I knew it would lengthen the journey greatly not to descend where I had commenced, but I did not like to do it. I wished to have an entire range and view down every side. I persevered, and reached the first height; I was now higher than ever I had been in the world before. I had often turned and sat down to rest and look at the prospect, but here I remained some time. I could count at one time, from 10 to 14 lakes, some of them mere pools certainly, and a sea of mountains rising in every direction, like wave beyond wave; not a cloud was to be seen, but a slight haze partly obscured the distance; nearer objects were quite distinct. Had I ascended either 1 or 2 days sooner, I should have had a brilliantly clear atmosphere, but timidity had prevented my bringing my resolution to the sticking place sooner. Even this morning, on rising, I felt irresolute. I had passed most of the night disturbed by distressing dreams (and dreams of any kind are very unusual to me), occasioned, I dare say, by the feeling of anxiety with which I had retired to rest; yet I knew that as I was not obliged to go, I could any moment return if I saw a prospect of danger. Here I stood, perched on a ridge like a crow on the point of a pinnacle; not a human creature could I see anywhere; for aught I knew, I had the whole mountain to myself. It was a grand elevation; an eastward precipice exceeding deep, I dared not look down, standing. I laid myself flat, and examined it; fatigue and a refreshing coolness, made me drowsy, and I had nearly sunk to sleep. I jumped up to shake it off, and proceeded.

[1] Bingley, apparently, disliked this route, for he says: 'The road was much more rocky and tiresome than that from Dolbadern. In one part I passed for near a quarter of a mile over immense masses of rocks, laying upon each other in almost every different direction, and entirely destitute of vegetation.' The old and modern routes can be consulted on pp. 285–91 of Carr and Lister's *The Mountains of Snowdonia*, published in 1925.

Not far before me, the path wound along a most aweful precipice. Now I *was* startled! for the first time. This was wholly unexpected. I could not recollect that I had read of such a road, either in Bingley or Williams. I thought when once I was at the top, the summit would be broad, and that I should not be obliged to encounter any rocky ridges like these before me. I hesitated some time; there was no crossing lower down. I must either return home as I had come, or climb the only way there was. I reflected, numbers of gentlemen and many ladies must have crossed before me; certainly then, I may. I had taken the precaution, on coming to Carnarvon, to write my address on a card, both to my lodgings there and my dwelling at Prescot, and wore it in my pocket, so that.if any accident should befal me, whoever found me would discover where to apply. I could not but be amused at thus wearing my direction *inside*. Some years ago,. at Up Holland, there lived an old woman of the name of Peggy Catterall, wife to the old William alluded to in one of the earlier of these Vols. in a Parody on 'When William at eve.'[1] This old couple had an only son, who, when arrived at man's estate, happened to marry, and went to reside about 12 miles distant. Occasionally they would send him presents, and as Peggy was wondrous managing, she undertook the packing of these parcels. One of these, being intrusted to some one not used to taking them, was returned; the man knew from whom he had received it, but had forgotten where it was to go. Peggy, in her usual coarse masculine

---

[1] This jingle occurs in a letter written to Mrs. Braithwaite in the year 1808. It concerns a lost cow, whose disappearance greatly concerned its old master, William, until his heart was gladdened by the location of it in a narrow back alley—thus celebrated in a final stanza, in Miss Weeton's raciest strain (calculated to the taste of the wife of the parson-schoolmaster):

> Just then the old songstress did put forth her snowt
> and William most joyfully cried,
> 'Egad! maister, see if hoo's [she's] not cumming eauwt [out],
> Eigh, eauwt of owd Ann Smith's backside!'

voice, exclaimed 'A greyt noddy! what did tou bring it back for?' 'There was no direction,' replied the man. 'No direction, yo greyt noddy! didn't I get James Smith to write one, and I put it myself safe enough ith *insoide*? but sum folk ar sich naitrils!'

Thus—I was directed *inside*, but I hoped to be brought safe back again. Strange feelings and ideas mingle! the next moment I raised a thought aloft to Him who is the Highest. Be my Protector still, I said. He heard—and on my way I sped.

Whilst crossing the ridge, perhaps 100 yds., perhaps 200, or even more, for I was too terrified to ascertain—the precipice on my right and left both, was too much for my head to bear; on my right, if I slipped ever so little, nothing could save me, and Oh! it looked like an eternity of falling; it seemed to my giddy head, half a mile down. I drew my bonnet close over my right cheek, to hoodwink me on that side. On the other side there was a low ridge of rocks to hold by, and I soon crossed. I breathed now, and again surveyed the dangerous road. Often have I read of such paths, but truly I suspected the authors of exaggeration. I beg their pardons now. I will be less incredulous in future.

When I attained the second summit, a boisterous wind blew upwards from the bottom; this was a phenomenon to me;[1] it was so rough as once to blow me down; but it was safe falling on this side. Had the wind blown the contrary way, it would have been madness to brave it on the edge of the precipice; for the whole circumference of the summit, East and North, appears to me for some miles to be perpendicular for almost half a mile down; it looked aweful and grand. I could see the various post roads, winding among the valleys like a white thread; but houses

---

[1] A phenomenon which was to be taken full advantage of by gliding enthusiasts a century later.

or cottages I could not see one. I could have wished to have remained some hours longer, but observing my shadow to have lengthened considerably (for, amongst other precautions, I had left my watch at home in my box, lest I should break it by some fall or other, or be robbed), I prepared to descend. In passing a little inclosure near the summit, where were some bags filled with copper ore,[1] and a quantity lying loose on the ground, I picked up 6 or 7 small bits as a memorial, at some future period, of the spot from whence I had gathered them. I was a little curious to see what difference there was in that in the bags, but as no owner was near, nor any other person, I would not so much as touch them.

I found descending more disagreeable than ascending; my shoes became so slippery that I often fell, but never got hurt. The heath was dry, and the rocks flinty and polished like slate, so that it was difficult to stand or walk. I had a very long walk before me, if I descended on the Llanberris side; it would have saved 2 or 3 miles or more had I gone down on the Bettws side; but then, I must have repassed that dreadful ridge, and I dared not without a real necessity. Snowdon, on the Llanberris side, has many subordinate summits, yet very lofty ones; sons and daughters, as it were. I peeped down between each of these, and as I looked down from several of the loftier openings, the bottom was so low, I could not distinguish either houses or any other buildings, distance so levelled them with the ground.

It was now about 6 o'clock, and I had at least 12 miles to walk; still, I could not help playing truant, and peeping between every succeeding opening. This lengthened my walk greatly, but I was very little fatigued, and I forgot to

[1] The output of copper ore in 1913 was 124 tons, and, according to R. D. Richards, in his chapter on 'The Industrial Activities of Snowdonia' contained in Carr and Lister's *Mountains of Snowdonia*, that ended the chapter of copper ore enterprise.

be frightened, I was so much pleased with the various views, and with the vale and lakes of Llanberris, as they became gradually more and more distinct, and no fogs or mists arose. At last, Dolbadern Castle appeared; a rivulet, a bridge, cottages—some upon brows, some on their sides, and others at the bottom—plantations, and gardens. What a romantic landscape! Looking upwards, how grand, how majestic; downwards, how lovely and heart cheering! for here, I, who had been for many hours, soaring Queen of the Mountains, had now arrived amongst my own species again, and on a level with my fellow creatures. I had but met with 2 men in my descent, any more than my ascent. They were cutting turf; they spoke not, looked quietly at me, but not rudely.

At 8 o'clock, I passed the Inn at Llanberris; I was then 8 miles from home. I now urged my utmost speed; for the last 5 hours I had eaten nothing, nor drank anything. Snowdon has few streams, and of these few, I could not drink for want of a cup. I tried to reach them laid down, but could not without wetting my cloaths; and I was too thirsty to eat. When I got into the open road, I passed many a tempting stream, in some of which I dipped a little bread, and it sufficed until I arrived at home at ½ past 10 o'clock, tired certainly, but highly gratified and delighted.

The servant girl was waiting for me, and made me tea; whilst it was preparing, which was scarcely more than 5 minutes, I drank plentifully of cold water, for I was not hot. The night was so serene and calm! and Oh!—that I may sincerely add, I was so grateful to Him who had conducted me safely home again, to a comfortable, a very comfortable habitation, after a walk of more than 25 miles.

June 16th. I arose at 8, refreshed and rested, and not the least footsore or stiff. After breakfast, I went down to the shore and bathed, and the remainder of the day I sat at home, writing my journal, until after tea, when I went to the top of a lofty rock behind the Uxbridge Arms, from whence there is a fine and extensive view.[1] I had not been here before; feeling that I could go any time, I had deferred from day to day, until I should have no other object in view.

17. Immediately after breakfast, I again went to the shore to bathe; I carried my own bathing dress, shoes, and towel, in a small basket, and went to a house about half a mile off, under the Bangor road, where, for 3d, ladies are accommodated with a room to dress and undress in. For 6d each, they may have bathing dress, &c., and an attendant into the water. I prefer bathing without assistance, and as here there is no machine, every one must walk in. I bathed snugly by myself, for the place is quite retired; no one was in view, and the water is as clear as spring water. I got home to dinner, and remained till after tea, when I walked to Coed Helen summer house, and sat some time, reading under the window. 3 miles.

18. Took a walk after bathing, down the shore of the Menai, below Coed Helen; the tide was still rising gently, and the air calm and refreshing. I did not proceed above 2 m., but I enjoyed it greatly. After tea, I set out, determined if possible to find the site, or the place of Segontium, and its remains; and likewise a fort, not far distant. I had twice before set out with this intention, but not understanding exactly from my 'Guide' what kind of appearance they made, I had both times failed in my object.[2] I do not like to permit any difficulty to baffle me; I therefore

[1] 'From the top of the rock, behind the hotel, I had an excellent bird's eye view of the town.' Bingley's *Tour Round North Wales*, 1800.

[2] Probably Bingley's, which thus vaguely directs the visitor to the spot: 'About half a mile south of Carnarvon are a few walls, the small remains of Segontium.' Actually those remains of a Roman station or city cover an area of seven acres, modern excavation having uncovered much that was hidden.

studied my book more accurately, and this evening, walking more deliberately than usual, I perceived the ruins of the Fort; a locked gate prevented my examining the field or fields where Segontium stood. I shall make another effort yet. From Llanbeblic Church yard, I crossed the road over some fields to the Seiont and stood, or sat, on its banks, amused with watching the children frolicking in the water as usual. 6 miles.

Sunday, June 19th. I feel a reluctance at going to a Church here. I cannot make Mrs. Hughes understand my questions as to where English service is performed, and when; and my natural diffidence has taken such strong hold upon me, that I stay at home, rather than go to find it out myself. I find I manage best in crowds, for in London, I was as much at home as if I had always lived there. It is the language that is such a teaze. Most of the people in Carnarvon who take in lodgers, can speak English. I am rather unfortunate.

At ½ past 3, I went to the service in English at a neighbouring Methodist Chapel; it only lasts an hour. I feel the loss greatly of the frequent opportunities we have in Lancashire. I lose ground sadly. I condemn myself, and say, religion is not an innate principle with me, but the force of continual examples and the perpetual repetition of precepts; or why am I not as constant and as fervent by myself in my own chamber, as when influenced by mingling among frequent crowds of worshippers? Every situation has its advantages and disadvantages; I admire Carnarvon greatly, but I shall be glad to get near to my old acquaintances again in England.

This morning I received a letter from Miss Dalrymple, which was very welcome.

20th. The weather has again taken a complete change; the wind is bitterly cold, dust rises in whirls, and heavy black clouds all portend a continued storm of at least some

395

days. I dared not venture to take any long walk, nor to cross the Ferry, which had previously been my plan for to-day, that I might spend some hours on the Anglesey shore among the sands, shells, and rocks during the flowing of the tide; and carrying my bathing dress in my basket, have enjoyed an invigorating bath in some secluded place. I went down at 10 o'clock to the shore, where I had bathed before at the bathing house; the water was so cold as to be quite benumbing. I was soon out again. Many slight showers continued falling at intervals.

After dinner, I took a walk along the Pwllheli road, as the rain seemed to put off, for about 3½ miles, but the atmosphere thickened so in many places, I dared proceed no farther; reading and sewing filled up the other intervals of the day. I have, for some years, entirely given up all kinds of needlework which has no real utility to recommend it. I do not say anything in condemnation of ornamental needlework, although I could say much, and I think, justly. If it amuse others, I let them employ their time as pleases them, expecting the same privilege. It does not amuse me. When I sew, it is to make necessary clothing, and to keep it in repair; and as my Mary may read what I now write, for her information I shall be more minute in many of my observations than I should be had I no daughter; and Mary, I keep my apparel in the exactest repair; and when I lived at Wigan and had a house and family to attend to, I kept the whole quite neat. It is so little of an amusement to me, that were I rich enough, I should employ others to do it, for I think it a duty in the affluent female to let others live. I do not look upon it as a merit for any young person to make her own dresses, bonnets, shoes, or lace, if she be rich; I do consider it a merit that she should be *able* to make them; for no one so affluent but may suffer a reverse, and every female should know how to earn a living.

I consider it as so disgraceful to wear rags, or any part of my apparel with ever so small a hole in it, that I daily find at least a *little* employment for my needle; for I am too poor to buy new, frequently. My cloaths, if examined, would be found to have fewer holes and more patches and darnings, than those of almost any other person; yet, I think I am as respectably dressed, and as neat in my *every day apparel*, as any of my acquaintances; they many of them exceed me in visiting dresses.

Books are my amusement, books my employment; but not novels or any light reading. I have long been sick of them. I seek instruction, but I have always been sadly lost for want of the means. Music has high wrought charms for me—but—my poverty has ever been in the way. I could never purchase an instrument, except a flageolet, nor afford the price of instruction even on that; yet it sweetens many a solitary hour! With care and saving, I could now procure an organ; for that should be my instrument; but I am too old. Yet, old as I am, I am strongly tempted to purchase one, as I know a person who would sell me a small finger organ for less than 20£—a very good one. I can, self taught, amuse myself with my Flageolet; I could do so with an Organ. I have an Harmonicon, on which I could soon play tolerably, but it is too trifling an instrument to afford me any amusement.[1]

---

[1] Though the imagination positively boggles at the notion of Miss Weeton's playing upon the mouth-organ, it is pleasing to find the sentiments expressed in the preceding dissertation heartily endorsed by the contemporary *Young Woman's Companion, or Female Instructor, being a Guide to all the Accomplishments which Adorn the Female Character*. 'Ladies, who are fond of needle-work, generally chuse to consider that as a principal part of housewifery; in a middling rank, and with a moderate fortune, it is a necessary part of a woman's duty, and a considerable particle of expence is saved by it. Many young ladies make almost every thing they wear; by which means they can make a genteel figure at a small expence'—after which sound advice, the 'young ladies' might settle down to the section subtitled CHRONO-LOGY, with the following comforting preface—'as there is no history, except that in the Bible, of any thing before the flood, we may set out from that event. . . .'

The solitary life I lead, is not from choice; I see no way of avoiding it. In lodgings, I have hitherto found it unavoidable; and I have found no family to board with, who would take me on such terms as I can afford—such a family, I mean, as I could wish to reside with; for I could not be comfortable to mingle continually with people of coarse manners, vulgar, and illiterate. I appear to be condemned to solitude for life. I am naturally of a lively, social turn, and to be often in the company of such as possess highly gifted and highly cultivated minds, would be a gratification to me, superior even to books. . . . But! God has said 'Set your affections on things above, and not on things on the earth.'—and therefore appears to have specially deprived me of all those things on which I could have set my affections. Thy will be done! I see Thy mercies and Thy Graciousness in this, and am thankful.

And on this beautiful but tragic note the manuscript comes to an end. The rest must be told in other words than hers. The probation had been a long and stormy one; but now the work was done; the pen could be laid aside; she could enter forthwith into the world of the Braithwaites, the Aunt Bartons, the Pedders, the Mrs. Tom Weetons—on equal terms at last.

EPILOGUE
by
EDWARD HALL
Revised, May 1968

AN interesting, if somewhat unfortunately belated, repercussion of the publication of Miss Weeton *in the course of the 1930s was the revelation of fresh material bearing directly upon her forbears; this was currently in the possession of a collateral descendant of her brother* Tom, Willoughby Scott Darlington, MA, *who kindly accorded permission to make use of extracts therefrom should the occasion arise. We are now in a position to take advantage of the ingrained snobbery of* T.R.W., *primarily in a correction and expansion of the footnote directly concerning him which occurred on page 49 of Volume I (at a point midway in paragraph two), amended to conclude thus: '. . . She (Mrs. Bevan) recovered sufficiently to expose malversation of funds on his part, also forgery. He wriggled in yet another long pamphlet, but he was a beaten man, and obviously finished locally; to quote from his pamphlet entitled: "Mrs. Bevan's Will",—"I am injured in my income, and what is worse, in honourable character; no longer Clerk to the Magistrates, and thereby losing sanction and emolument." ' He appears to have retired in the year 1837, doubtless in high dudgeon, either to a house of his own, or more probably to the home of his son-in-law and daughter in the village of Adlington (Worthington), near Standish; and there he died on 5 March 1845—but more of that later.*

Mr. Darlington obliged with relevant extracts both from T.R.W.'s *monumental* Genealogy, *and from the personal diary maintained by his own father, John Darlington, the son-in-law in question—he who at the age of eighteen became the husband of Jane Weeton, T.R.W.'s second daughter and third child—a distinctly advantageous connection, viewed either financially or socially; and in addition, Jane herself was an heiress of sorts, benefiting by acquisition of the Greenhalgh-Willoughby estate (Rigby House, situated at Adlington), through the decease of her mother. Alas, she failed of her heritage, for there were no sons of the marriage, and the estate passed to John's brother Ralph, and subsequently by reversion to Col Sir Henry Clayton Darlington (son of Henry Darlington of Wigan, and born 1877). But to return to T.R.W.* *and the manuscript and printed remains, so complimentary to his industry and method where his own interest was concerned; and first and foremost, that imposing production in a large folio volume entitled* Stemmata Parentalia Collecteanea, *bound in half calf, with green paper-covered boards, and graced with an armorial book-plate inside its cover, bearing quartered, in the 1st and 4th quarters, the arms—the disputed but indubitable arms—of T.R.W.* *and his somewhat minor branch of the ancient Weetons. In fact he was, or rather his branch of the family was, fifth in order of the pedigree; to wit, the somewhat reduced Weetons, late of Scale Hall, as already indicated by his sister in the course of her own pedigree-hunting and slant.*

As briefly then as possible, here are the established facts, ignoring the tedious detail and involvement of earlier generations of the Weetons:

John, son of Thomas Weeton and Mary (Gibson) Weeton, of Scale Hall, was baptised 27th Dec. 1719; married 24 Dec. 1741, to Agnes, one of the three daughters of Edmund Chippendale, of Bolton Sandside, near Lancaster; he sold Scale, and removed to Sunderland (not far away) and was drowned crossing the Wyre; their son Thomas married Agnes Chippendale, of Sunderland, at Preston, and subsequently lived at Lancaster; and in due course, arrived Thomas, the naval Captain and father-to-be of T.R.W. *and his sister Nelly (as baptised); he was baptised 3 February 1744, at Overton Church; married at Preston, on the 7th of August 1744, to Mary, one of the three daughters and co-heiresses of Richard Rawlinson, of Preston. Lived at Lancaster, and was killed at*

sea by a cannon shot, 11 Sept. 1782, aged thirty-eight.
And *T.R.W. provides his own gloss to the account given by his sister of the heroic death of their male parent.*

I had heard, however, my Father always spoken of with pleasure and with praise. All spoke highly of him as a brave, high-spirited, honoured man. I heard that his first battle was in a small vessel carrying twelve guns, with which he fought and captured a French one of eighteen guns, of heavier metal. I heard also of the Indiaman he had taken, and the various other prizes, and of his gallant death in the fight. Captain Jackson told me that in one engagement, Captain Weeton had lost many men, so that he was obliged to serve the guns himself, determined to sink rather than be taken; and tho' too enfeebled to capture [his opponent], he succeeded in beating his enemy off [in margin—'circa 1780'] . . . My Mother lost a fortune in the death of my father. He had placed all his money, his hardly-earned prizes, in the hands of my grandfather, Abraham Rawlinson, who would never own to my Mother that he had any money in his hands of my father's; nor could Mr. Colton prevail upon him to account. With a broken spirit she retired to Upholland, and died when I was turned fourteen. Of course I learned but little from her; she never mentioned my Father without flooding tears . . .

All very touching and filial; but somehow one thrills rather to the parallel account given by his sister; and one would have been grateful for something a little more to his credit as a brother than the bare record accorded his sister: 'NELLY, *born at Lancaster, 25th Dec. 1776; baptised 25 January 1777, at St. John's Chapel, Lancaster; married [blank in manuscript] Sept. 1814, as second wife to Aaron Stock (b. 24 Jan. 1776), Wigan, cotton merchant. Separated, January 1832.' And that was* that—*from he who must have known, or should have known, whether she was still alive or dead when he penned the reference, and we are left to assume from other vague sources of information that she died presumably in the year 1844; for in that year her daughter is*

401   D d

singly recorded as resident in the Standishgate house of her (? late) mother. As for Mary Stock. the daughter in question, her uncle just contrived to indicate her current existence, nothing more. However, and to compensate for the unsatisfactory record where his sister and niece were concerned, we do have the following where he himself was concerned:

THOMAS RICHARD [alas, the Rawlinson was a figment, it is to be feared, of his sister's imagination], of Leigh, solicitor and magistrate's clerk, born at Lancaster, 24 January 1781; baptised 8 Feb. 1781, at the Parish Church, Lancaster; married at Wigan, 3 Oct. 1803, to Jane Scott, youngest of the four daughters (and co-heirs ex parte maternal) of Thomas Scott, of Wigan [see Scott pedigree on pp 4–5 of the Stemmata], and Catherine his wife, who was daughter and sole Heiress of Thomas Greenhalgh, of Adlington (near Worthington, Wigan), Lancashire, and great-grand-daughter of Lord Willoughby of Parham, vide Collins and Banks 'Peerage.'

No wonder Nelly Weeton, spinster, proved such a thorn in the side of such a well-bred and endowed sister-in-law!

Upon page 10 of the Genealogy, T.R.W. relates just how in the course of the year 1818, he came to take a positive interest in his family history and genealogy, revealing incidentally just how his vanity could not resist the blandishments of a perceptive Liverpool book-dealer. Seals were engraved, and book-plates ditto; and the bill for engraving the family crest upon twenty-three separate pieces of silver plate, amounting to the sum of £2 3s od, was duly pasted into the record—his sister meanwhile dining, when she did dine that is, upon common earthenware, in the enforced seclusion of a back room of her own—or rather her husband's—establishment. Of course T.R.W.'s claims did not pass either unregarded or unchallenged by the current Heralds, and T.R.W. has painfully to record his astonishment at the assertion of Sir Thomas Heard himself that no Weeton of Weeton, Lancashire, had arms registration; but, 'I need not copy any more references from my minutes and collections to show that Heralds at all times, particularly in more early ones, have been erroneous, inconsistent, delusive, and presumptuous . . .' And then, on p 47, he joyfully places on record his own discovery, so long and so unavailingly sought after and almost abandoned as hopeless, of the positive arms of Weeton of Weeton! And at this point, this particular aspect of his researches may be abandoned, in favour of something less remotely concerning himself, and revealing him in a somewhat more favourable light; indeed, making all allowances for the bias of the diarist, it provides a corrective to what has gone before relative to the character of T.R.W., who must have been his own enemy, all things considered: 'Mr. Weeton, a dear delightful old man, genial, literary, and brilliant. Taken of pleurisy, I think I see him for the last time, going upstairs with arms full of books, none of which he opened. Dr. Rigby bled him next morning, and again in the evening, when he fell into a swoon, and died!—the last of the male Weetons.'

T.R.W.'s marriage resulted in one son, Thomas, and two surviving daughters (four others died in infancy). No information apart from that quoted above is available with regard to Mrs T.R.W. herself, but her presence at the bed and board of her husband at Adlington must have been calculated to add some zest to the domesticities, if the decided opinion of her sister-in-law is anything to judge by, however prejudiced. However, he had at least in her one true if tried friend still left, presuming a record in the Upholland Poll Books can be adduced as serving to establish the regard till death of his injured sister; for he certainly came into possession of her cottage property, situated in that parish, in the year 1844: conclusive evidence perhaps of her actually being dead and buried—but where? Exhaustive search in likely parish registers in both Lancashire and Cheshire revealed nothing. Perhaps she died whilst seeking relief from some illness or upon some distant visit, and the expense of returning the remains to her native place proved beyond the means of her executors—and likewise of brother Tom. But to return to T.R.W., or rather his offspring, and in particular

Thomas junr, earlier hopes of whom were apparently never realised; he was educated at Manchester Grammar School, practised subsequently as a solicitor at Preston, and then seems to have emigrated to America, where he married, but the evidence is not conclusive. His death occurred in the year 1834, without local comment. His sister Jane did of course rather better for herself, as already and sufficiently indicated, marrying hopefully but dying prematurely, on 17 January 1846, without producing a son and heir, and she lies buried at Horwich—no nameless grave for her.

And now, to take up again the story of the currently rather less important Nelly Weeton! Owing to her comparative obscurity, and the paucity of local records covering the period involved, but few particulars emerge calculated to throw light upon the latter portion of her life. It has been possible to ascertain (principally by reference to the MS History of Hope Chapel, Wigan, *beforementioned) that her fortunes took a decided turn for the better, and that her wandering, homeless days were ended shortly after her return from the Welsh Tour. Just how long she continued to endure the mockery of that sort of a 'holiday', a stranger in a strange land, it is not possible to determine; presumably she returned to Lancashire shortly after the termination of the adventures she related in the last of the series of Letter Books available, either of her own volition or expedited by pressure upon a sadly depleted purse. Once again she resumed occupation of her lodgings in dull Prescot, where doubtless she continued to agitate, and to seize upon every opportunity of any amelioration of the lots respectively of herself and her daughter Mary. It is apparent that at long last some of the less pertinacious of her enemies were indicating a desire to change a state of affairs so obviously injurious to Mary's moral and physical well-being. And the first direct record is a sufficiently significant one, providing evidence that at least the iniquitous residential ban had been lifted; it was penned (doubtless with much satisfaction) by her old friend and adviser, the Rev Wm Marshall. 'At a Meeting held on Thursday Evening, July 22nd.,*

1827, Mrs. Stock, who had been admitted a Member of the Independent Church in Prescot, requested to be allowed to fill a place in our Church, having become resident in Wigan. No objections being offered, her name was ordered to be enrolled.'

That 'no objections' rings unpleasantly enough; still, the itemised unanimity of the chapel folk must have brought a measure of satisfaction to the quondam Sunday School teacher, and local outcast. A couple of years later the mother's heart must have been further rejoiced, for: *'Mary Stock was proposed, and Ed. Alston appointed to have conversation with her upon the subject. June 7th., 1829.'*—followed by: *'Mary Stock was this evening received into the Church by the general consent of the members present. July 2nd., 1829.'* And four years later, the young initiate was further advanced into full church membership: *'This evening Mary Stock was admitted a Member, Mr. Marshall's account of her experience and views being held satisfactory. July 30th., 1833.'* The enrolment of Mary affords an interesting particular in the sequel. It was apparently the custom, following upon cessation of attendance of a church member duly accredited, to signify the reason against either his or her name; and Mary Stock was duly recorded as having 'resigned' in the year *1844*—significantly the identical year in which her mother's name ceases to be registered as a resident rate-payer. Unfortunately, in the latter's case, there is the tantalizingly bald entry 'dead'.

The MS History of Hope Chapel *provides further evidence of the active interest in the chapel activities taken by both mother and daughter; for instance in the year 1832 we learn that there was established one of those typically patronising nineteenth-century evidences of 'good works'—'A Society for the Aid of the Sick Poor belonging to the Congregation', which within its stated limitations, we are informed, 'has been the means of much temporal good'. Inserted loosely too in the Chapel Register is a printed slip entitled 'The First Annual Report of Hope Chapel Benevolent Fund, instituted January, 1832', with the name of one contributor, 'Mrs Stock', figuring in the list of Committee and*

Visitors. Thus was Miss Weeton officially rehabilitated and vindicated, on an unimpeachable plane, for all locally to witness and wonder at—including doubtless her own bemused self.

The local directories of the period also establish the pertinent fact that, as Mrs Stock re-entered Wigan with banners flying, so her husband Aaron Stock bowed himself out—enough was enough, where he was concerned, apparently. Abandoning cotton-spinning (could it be that he had, with malice intent, thrown the factory in Chapel Lane back upon the hands of Tom Weeton's irate mother-in-law?) he now commenced to take an active interest in a coal-mining venture. On his removal from the recently-purchased house in Standish, he moved into the Ashton-in-Mackerfield district, where already resided a near relative of his, one Samuel Stock; and in Slater's Directory of the Year 1844, *Aaron Stock duly figures in his new capacity as coal-owner, with a house situated at Seneley Green. Again in 1848, Messrs Eccles & Stock, of Stanley Colliery, are listed; and it was this particular colliery which was destined to figure unpleasantly enough when a more than usually dreadful colliery disaster added its complement to the local graveyard. As for Aaron himself, he lies buried in the churchyard of Ashton-in-Mackerfield; and the memorial tablet in his favour, erected initially in the old church situated at Seneley Green, was eventually transferred to its successor at Ashton-in-Mackerfield. As for his late residence in Standishgate, that became the property of his daughter Mary, according to the records in the local Rate Books. A contemporary illustration of Standishgate itself includes the Stocks' house, situated on the extreme right-hand side. It was subsequently taken over for the offices of the Wigan Education Committee, but has since been absorbed into the premises of a modern store. Miss Weeton (or rather Mrs Stock) was still in occupation as late as the year 1844, as a county directory testifies—given a year more or less of marginal reliability where individual tenancy was concerned. And in that year the house was apparently sold, and the proceeds invested in other local house property. Unfortunately*

406

no local newspaper was in circulation at this time, and a careful check upon the British Museum files of the Wigan Times *from the date of its inception in the year 1849 to the year 1851 revealed no trace of an obituary notice; nor, perhaps to more purpose, anything remotely attributable to Miss Weeton's ready pen. Accordingly it is to be assumed that obscurely as she lived, so obscurely she died; but not before having ensured the safe-custody of her life's history for the benefit of posterity—and not necessarily her own. There they rest, those neatly written, close-packed volumes— not on 'somebody's musty Shelf', but in an honoured position upon the shelves of a splendid local Public Library, in that place late of 'mental barrenness', Wigan; the Wigan she could now be proud of, even as it has every reason to be proud of her—and indeed is.*

Finally, what of brother Tom—rejected by Leigh, just as his sister had been by Wigan, though with rather less justification? That a reconciliation of some sort was still the latter's aim in life, is shown by a copy of one of her letters to him, not hitherto available, which owed its preservation to brother Tom's compilation of his precious Genealogical Memoirs. *Doubtless Tom's sister was well aware of the existence of this sumptuous volume and of its significance in his life—and also in hers, if she went about it in the right way; nor could she have failed to observe the signet ring gracing Tom's index finger, and bearing the family crest. Here undoubtedly was the chink in his armour which might prove vulnerable in her favour. Some place might be found amongst those illustrative data, the numerous prints, the portraits, the loose documents which grangerised the work itself, for her modest contribution of fact—or was it fancy? And thus it came about that out of the scores of letters which* T.R.W. *had received in the past from the proudest Weeton of them all—his sister—one of them, and one only, was destined for preservation by him, in virtue of its directly bearing upon the subject so dear to his heart.*

But the heart had gone out of its writer. Written in 1837

407

and addressed formally enough (not, as customary, to 'My Dearest Tom' but to 'Dear Brother', though signed as ever 'Your affectionate Sister'), it is a sadly rambling, unsatisfactory sort of affair, devoted entirely to an account of an 'apparition' which was anxious to reveal the existence of certain vital 'writings', reputedly hidden under the flooring of a room in the old family mansion, Scale Hall—'then an old, neglected, dilapidated and almost tenant-less building; reported to be haunted, an old man and woman only occupying one of these apartments . . .' And to these latter a certain persistent Miss Stubbs made application for permission to investigate on her own account, suffering no impertinent obstruction from the ancient couple, as she pursued her local researches. And of course, Miss Weeton simply had to follow up the trail: 'The 16th being very fine, I went by the railway (to Warrington) at nine o'clock in the morning . . .', only to find it a wasted journey; and alas, all we get upon the subject of the hidden documents is this highly improbable story of a disembodied ghost, and no clue as to what happened as a result of Miss Stubbs's activities. Incidentally, this particular lettre was written whilst she was still in occupation of the relegated house in Standishgate, not more than three miles away from that of her brother then residing in Standish—she who had traversed ten times that number of miles in the course of a single day; she who would doubtless, and willingly enough, have undertaken to repeat the feat of endurance, were it destined to terminate in a loving embrace, that gesture which still, in her heart of hearts, was the only object in life dear to her; a life dedicated, on and off, to the one person she had only really and passionately loved—her unworthy and vindictive brother Tom.

JOURNAL AND LETTERS

INDEX